Diplomatic Counterinsurgency

War does not stop when the armed conflict ends. This compelling eyewitness account of a key political crisis in Bosnia and Herzegovina in 2007 demonstrates how interventions from foreign powers to end armed conflict can create new forms of conflict that are not only determined and resilient, but can lead groups to challenge the power of fragile states through political and legal means. Countering such challenges is an integral but often ignored part of peace processes. How do these nonviolent wars evolve? How can the power of fragile states be challenged through nonviolent means in the aftermath of armed conflict? And what is the role of diplomacy in countering such challenges? This book offers key insights for policy makers dealing with fragile states who seek answers to such questions.

Philippe Leroux-Martin is a Canadian lawyer who worked for the Office of the High Representative in Bosnia and Herzegovina as a member of a team of legal advisors who oversaw the legal aspects of the Dayton peace agreement implementation. Mr. Leroux-Martin also acted as chief legal advisor to the Police Restructuring Commission of Bosnia and Herzegovina chaired by former Belgian Prime Minister Wilfried Martens. Following his work in Sarajevo, he headed the legal department of the International Civilian Office, an organization established to supervise and coordinate Kosovo's accession to independence in 2008–9. He is currently a Fellow with the Future of Diplomacy Project of the Belfer Center for Science and International Affairs at the Harvard Kennedy School.

To those affected by war

Diplomatic Counterinsurgency

Lessons from Bosnia and Herzegovina

Philippe Leroux-Martin

Future of Diplomacy Project
Harvard Kennedy School of Government

CAMBRIDGE
UNIVERSITY PRESS

CAMBRIDGE
UNIVERSITY PRESS

32 Avenue of the Americas, New York NY 10013-2473, USA

Cambridge University Press is part of the University of Cambridge.

It furthers the University's mission by disseminating knowledge in the pursuit of education, learning and research at the highest international levels of excellence.

www.cambridge.org
Information on this title: www.cambridge.org/9781107546264

© Philippe Leroux-Martin 2014

This publication is in copyright. Subject to statutory exception and to the provisions of relevant collective licensing agreements, no reproduction of any part may take place without the written permission of Cambridge University Press.

First published 2014
First paperback edition 2015

A catalogue record for this publication is available from the British Library

Library of Congress Cataloguing in Publication data
Leroux-Martin, Philippe, 1973–
Diplomatic counterinsurgency : lessons from Bosnia and Herzegovina / Philippe Leroux-Martin, Harvard University, Kennedy School of Government.
   pages cm
Includes bibliographical references and index.
ISBN 978-1-107-02003-0 (hardback)
1. Yugoslav War, 1991–1995 – Peace.   2. Kosovo War, 1998–1999 – Peace.   3. Peacebuilding – Bosnia and Hercegovina.   4. Peace-building – Kosovo (Republic)   5. Postwar reconstruction – Bosnia and Hercegovina.   6. Postwar reconstruction – Kosovo (Republic)   7. Mediation, International.   8. Dayton Peace Accords (1995)   I. Title.
DR1313.7.P43L47   2013
949.703–dc23   2013022248

ISBN 978-1-107-02003-0 Hardback
ISBN 978-1-107-54626-4 Paperback

Cambridge University Press has no responsibility for the persistence or accuracy of URLs for external or third-party internet websites referred to in this publication, and does not guarantee that any content on such websites is, or will remain, accurate or appropriate.

Contents

Foreword by Nicholas Burns . . . . *page* vii
Acknowledgments xi

Introduction 1

Part I   The Battle

Prologue 7

1 We Fired First 9

2 They Fire Back 26

3 The Battle 44

4 The Defeat 65

Part II   Reflections on the Battle

5 Nonviolent Wars 85

6 Nonviolent Insurgency 122

7 Diplomatic Counterinsurgency 150

8 The Avalanche 171

9 Looking Forward 198

Epilogue 225

Notes   233
Bibliography   293
Index   315

Foreword

The violent breakup of Yugoslavia and resulting wars in Bosnia and Kosovo were among the most difficult international crises of the 1990s. One of the most dramatic moments came during the summer and autumn of 1995. From the Srebrenica massacre in July to the decision by the United States and NATO to intervene militarily in September to the Dayton peace agreement in November, the end of the war in Bosnia and Herzegovina was a dramatic and pivotal event. That story has been chronicled by many, including most notably the late Richard C. Holbrooke, who deserves eternal credit for having stopped the fighting, in the riveting account of his bulldozer diplomacy, *To End a War*.

The story not yet told, however, is the stolid, difficult, complex, and vital work done in the eighteen years since the Dayton Accords by an army of international civil servants, diplomats, and lawyers to save Dayton's peace and build it brick by brick in a sometimes hostile and unforgiving landscape. In the years following Dayton, more than a few skeptics charged that Dayton delivered a weak and seemingly ungovernable state where power was shared uneasily among the former warring factions – the Muslim, Croat, and Serb residents of Bosnia. There were many occasions when the unstable state threatened to collapse amid the political infighting and power struggles of these three competing groups.

The work to preserve Dayton and build a new state was led by the UN-appointed High Representative and his staff. The great majority of these people were not high-profile generals or diplomats but mainly young, often idealistic, and dedicated international civil servants and government officials from Europe, Canada, and the United

States like Philippe Leroux-Martin. Their job was to implement the Dayton Accords by convincing the people of the country to live and work together, to compromise, and to share power grudgingly if not always peacefully. More often than not, the local political factions representing Serb, Croat, and Muslim interests appeared as political insurgents in a fight to preserve the past or, at least, the interests of one group above the other. The High Representative and his staff can be seen as practitioners of counterinsurgency to maintain the peace. And, thus the title of this interesting and important book – *Diplomatic Counterinsurgency*.

"War does not stop with the end of armed conflict," writes Leroux-Martin in his own Introduction to this book. Political battles continued over some of the very issues that caused war in the first place. The story he has written thus fills in the blank pages of the war in Bosnia and its aftermath. It tells the story of how peace was preserved and violent conflict did not recur as many had predicted following Dayton's hesitant and unstable beginning. The lessons of this time are well worth learning for all of us who believe that the challenge of building and preserving peace is the core work of the United Nations in an often unstable world.

In a much larger sense, Leroux-Martin's book is a tribute to diplomacy – the sometimes forgotten art of preserving peace and stability among the more than 195 states in the world today. Diplomacy is often misunderstood and unappreciated because it is the antithesis of war – slow, begrudging, painstaking, difficult, and sometimes inconclusive. But diplomacy's great promise is that we humans can find a way to resolve or regulate our differences and find a better way forward than by fighting each other.

Philippe Leroux-Martin is the right person to tell this story. Like hundreds of others, he worked for peace in a country torn apart by war. A young attorney from Montreal, he spent years in the Balkans, first in Bosnia and then in Kosovo, to help the people of the region to recover from the bitter and bloody conflicts of the 1990s and find their way to stability and then an uncertain peace. He tells the story of the twists and turns, pressures and compromises of the daily work of peace from the perspective of an insider.

Foreword

Philippe is a Fellow in a program I direct at the Harvard Kennedy School, the Future of Diplomacy Project, under whose auspices he wrote this book.

This is an important book with a vital message. Peace in places like Bosnia can only be built by the tireless work of people who understand that a return to violent conflict is unacceptable. Although he is too humble to say it, Leroux-Martin's book is a tribute to both him and the many others who had the courage, dedication, and tenacity to work for a better future in the Balkans and in the world.

Nicholas Burns
Professor of the Practice of Diplomacy and International Politics
Kennedy School of Government
Harvard University

Acknowledgments

This book would not have been possible without the help and support of many people. I want, first and foremost, to thank my family and my parents, André and Régine, for their continuing love and support through the years.

I also want to thank Nicholas Burns and Cathryn Clüver at the Future of Diplomacy Project, Belfer Center for Science and International Affairs at the Harvard Kennedy School of Government, for hosting me and supporting me throughout this project. I am also profoundly indebted to Greg Harris for convincing me to write this book, and for his continuous support and advice during the entire project. His kindness, generosity, and advice have allowed me to persevere. I am also particularly grateful to Amy Clipp, Jamie Purdon, Michael Haltzel, Bruce Hitchner, Justice Richard Goldstone, and Andrew Radin for their willingness to review early drafts and provide feedback. Special thanks must also go to Antoine Artiganave, Tanja Bilbija, Borut Del Fabro, Bernard Duhaime, Kris Clerkin, Annika Goldman, Claude-André Guillotte, Chris Lawrence-Pietroni, Anna Lawrence-Pietroni, Meredith Shiner, David Tier, Karen Zarindast, and the anonymous reviewers at Cambridge University Press for their valuable input. I am also grateful to Kristin C. McConnell for her help with the book's references. The content of this book is based on my personal notes, documents, and research. Any error or inaccuracy contained herein is consequently attributable to me, and me alone.

I had the great fortune to meet and live alongside exceptional people during my time in Bosnia and Kosovo. I would like to thank each of them for their friendship and support during these years. I want to thank especially John Farquarhson, Branka Pešić, Majda Idrizbegović, Edouard d'Aoust, Michael Doyle, Mirna Jančić, Alexis Hupin, and Daniel Bronkhorst.

I have also been fortunate to work with exceptional colleagues at the Office of the High Representative in Sarajevo. I am particularly grateful for having had the privilege to work with Azira Šepić, whose friendship, professionalism, and dedication made working there a rewarding experience for many of us. She left this world too soon, and my thoughts have often been with her as I researched this book. I also want to give special thanks to Slaviša Vračar, Mudzahid Hasanbegović, Andreja Šporer, Biljana Potparić, Damir Gnjidić, Michael Haner, Jelena Sesar, Dijana Satara, Senad Zlatar, Catherine Fearon, Matthew Lawson, Ian Patrick, Daniel Korski, Ric Bainter, Amna Kajtaz, Archie Tuta, and Boris Ruge. I am also extremely grateful for the privilege of having worked with many dedicated people at the International Civilian Office in Pristina. I am particularly indebted to Steven Hill, Lynn Sheehan, Nexhmi Rexhepi, Adriana Çeta, Aferdita Smajli, Sabine Erkens, Suzana Gashi, Megan Kossiakoff, Sameer Saran, Marianne Fennema, Henry Kelley, Louis Crishock, Andy McGuffie, Ben Crampton, Andy Michels, Maria Fihl, Johanna Stromquist, David Slinn, Christophe Pradier, Raphael Naegli, Pedro Ataide, Rudi Lotz, Severin Strohal, Labinot Hoxha, Kai Müller, Alison Weston, Jonas Jonsson, Peter Grassman, Fletcher Burton, and Pieter Feith.

I want to thank John Berger at Cambridge University Press for believing in this book, and for his patience and advice throughout. I am also indebted to the staff at the Widener Library at Harvard University and the European reading room of the Library of Congress for their help throughout my writing.

Finally, I want to thank my wife, Julie Stitzel, whose love, understanding, and contagious positive outlook on life have allowed me to finish this book while raising a young family. I am forever indebted to her.

Introduction

In November 2008, while my colleagues and I were working late at the International Civilian Office in Kosovo, a bomb exploded under our office. The low-intensity explosion shattered the front part of our building. Stunned but unhurt, we evacuated outside the organization's compound amid alarm bells, smoke, confusion, and panic. A group called the Army of the Republic of Kosovo claimed responsibility for the explosion. The persons responsible for the bombing were never apprehended.[1] Given that our organization had been established to support and supervise Kosovo's accession to statehood, many of us could hardly understand why we had been bombed.

The explosion had shattered more than windows and doors. It had shaken a certain sense of certainty conveyed by the acronyms, timetables, media briefs, and coordination meetings that filled our days. Kosovo was not in the midst of armed conflict. The cafes, restaurants, schools, museums, and shops of its capital were bustling with activity. Stability and security had returned to Kosovo. The former province had just declared its independence a few months earlier – a process our organization was mandated to support. Many billboards displayed messages thanking countries who had recognized Kosovo's independence, including my own. Who could, or would want to, bomb us in Pristina almost a decade after the end of armed conflict in Kosovo?

The blast deepened a sense of doubt about delineations between war, violence, peace, and conflict in my mind. These doubts had started to occupy my thoughts a few years before, during my work in the Legal Department of the Office of the High Representative in Bosnia and Herzegovina (OHR), the international civilian enforcement mechanism of the Dayton peace agreement. As a young lawyer from Canada, I had arrived in Bosnia and Herzegovina with well-delineated conceptions of war and peace. But in 2007, an intense political crisis rocked the country and directly challenged the foundations of such conceptions. Republika Srpska, the majority Bosnian Serb Entity of Bosnia and Herzegovina, had been resisting international efforts to knit Bosnia back together since the end of the war in 1995. In an attempt to strengthen the efficiency of the country's parliamentary and governmental institutions, our office enacted measures that triggered an intense confrontation with the leadership of Republika Srpska and that had crucial consequences for the fragile state of Bosnia and Herzegovina.

★ ★ ★

This book opens by telling the story of this political crisis. Its first part captures the personalities, the politics, and the mistakes that shaped this confrontation. It provides an account of the pressure, the surprises, the panic, and the loss of perspective that characterized the work of those involved in the crisis. Although the 2007 crisis lasted for only six weeks, its strategic significance was important. Its outcome emboldened the pursuit of wartime objectives amongst the divided political factions of Bosnia and reduced the capacity of the international community to manage conflict. Underneath the immediate crisis, tectonic plates were shifting quickly. Studying their movements provides us with unique insights.

Reflecting on these events, the second part of the book proposes three main points.

First, it suggests that, in places such as Bosnia and Kosovo, war does not stop with the end of armed conflict. Clausewitz wrote that "war is merely the continuation of policy by other means."[2] This book suggests that, in societies emerging from armed struggle, politics is often the continuation of wars by other means. As foreign powers intervene in war-torn environments, they do not merely implement peace processes. They push armed conflict to morph into intense nonviolent confrontations where parties continue to pursue war objectives through nonviolent means. They intervene in the nonviolent extension of war. They intervene in *nonviolent wars*.

Second, the experience with the peace process in Bosnia suggests that it is perfectly possible for parties engaged in intense nonviolent confrontations to undermine or overthrow the power of states – and that of foreign actors supporting them – through nonviolent means. Insurgency and counterinsurgency are not exclusively military concepts. The experience in Bosnia and Herzegovina illustrates how countering legal, administrative, and political challenges against fragile state structures may form an integral part of peace processes – a process for which this book suggests the name *diplomatic counterinsurgency*.

Last, the book argues that the capacity for intervention to manage nonviolent wars is limited. Rather than engaging in protracted confrontations, intervention ought to consider approaching conflict more strategically. Those shaping intervention strategy ought to consider applying power more densely against critical points in conflict systems, and use remaining sources of power to steer conflict away from its violent potential.

★ ★ ★

The reflections and suggestions in this book stem from my practical experience working on the legal aspects of the peace processes in Bosnia and Kosovo for almost a decade. They are therefore linked, and influenced, by these particular contexts. Understanding the dynamics of international intervention in such contexts provides valuable insight for policy makers grappling with similar forms of intervention elsewhere.

This book is not directly concerned with the extensive debates and discussions pertaining to whether, when, and under what conditions it may be justifiable for outsiders to intervene in a state's internal affairs to protect populations in need. Rather, it offers insights about concrete problems and questions that emerge once such interventions are under way.

Nor does this book outline a model purporting to accurately predict conflict mutations. After many years of direct involvement in this field, I do not believe that such a model can exist. Plans and models are essential to manage intervention. But they can create a false sense of certainty and become misleading. This book proposes, rather, a number of considerations and insights to help frame the thinking of those directly intervening in conflict systems. Those immersed in the unique and complex realities of a given conflict are in a much better position to predict and manage its potential mutations and dynamics. I am aware that some of the propositions of this book may challenge a number of assumptions about peace processes and spark disagreement. I humbly submit them in the hope they will stimulate discussions and debate in this field.

★ ★ ★

Tolstoy wrote in *War and Peace* that young persons coming back from war had a tendency to describe war not as it had happened but as they wished it had happened. But aren't those of us involved in peace operations suffering from similar tendencies? Don't we harbor idealized notions of peace as we intervene? Don't we idealize the peace outcomes we think we can create? The lines between war and peace are not as clear as we may wish. Our quest for certitude, predictability, and certainty prevents us from seizing more fully the complex and unpredictable world in which we intervene. While illusions of certainty may provide us with comfort, they expose us to surprises. These surprises can be costly. This is what many of us in the Office of the High Representative were about to discover in 2007. A crisis to which this book now turns.

Part I The Battle

Prologue

On no other morning since I started working as a legal advisor at the Office of the High Representative for Bosnia and Herzegovina had I felt such dread crossing the Vrbanja bridge over the Miljacka river in Sarajevo. As I walked toward the monolithic white building where our office was located, I could feel thoughts pulsing through my brain. I knew it was exhaustion. The crisis had been going on for six weeks. How much more could I take?

Located on a street named after Emerik Blum, a famous Sarajevo engineer born at the turn of the twentieth century who had founded one of Yugoslavia's biggest engineering firms, the office looked like a giant seamless block built by aliens as a symbol of their presence. Flanked by a flower shop, a gas station, and a small cafe bar, it stood across the central parliamentary and governmental institutions of Bosnia and Herzegovina and acted as a foreign magnet in the political landscape of Sarajevo. Vehicles of embassies and international missions came and went through its gates. Journalists and demonstrators would often gather in front of the building. I showed my ID to the security guard at the gate and pressed my way through the metal doors, as I had every working day of the past four years. I made my way to the Legal Department and, before going to my office, stopped by the office of its head, my boss. Every morning, we would discuss the main points that had emerged from the daily morning briefing with the High Representative. Each day came with a new problem. Could we block attempts from Bosnian Muslim politicians to rename the Sarajevo Airport after one of their wartime heroes, inevitably perceived as a villain by the other sides? Did a resigning minister have an obligation to attend sessions of the government until replaced? What level of government owned the military barracks of the former Yugoslav army under Bosnia's new constitution? These were the kind of questions that dominated our daily thoughts.

Through the years, my boss's skills and hard work had transformed his office into one of those informal hubs that one finds in many organizations. Groups of advisors from different departments would gather there spontaneously and discuss the latest developments in Bosnia's affairs until late at night. Sitting in the sofa or at the small circular conference table in his office, advisors would discuss freely. My boss excelled in this environment. Widely respected in the organization, he had a unique understanding of the country and the region and had served under several High Representatives. He had an affinity for complex federal structures of multinational states and could quickly see through the legal and political ramifications of any problem. He had come to Bosnia and Herzegovina shortly after the end of the conflict to work on electoral reform and rose quickly within the ranks of international organizations. We liked each other from the first day we met and had worked closely together for the past four years.

I found him sitting silently behind his desk. He was playing with his pen and did not look up.

"Lajčák has decided to strike a deal," he said.

"What? Are you serious?"

"Yes, I think this is the end."

We had not slept much since the crisis had started. Miroslav Lajčák, the High Representative for Bosnia and Herzegovina, was meant to announce his decision at the morning meeting. He was going to make crucial concessions – something we had strenuously advised against.

On my way to Lajčák's office to attend the daily morning meeting, my hands were shaking. An external force seemed to be propelling me through the corridors as my mind struggled to understand what was happening.

I knew we had been defeated.

1 We Fired First

Many years ago, Harry (the Hat) Walker spoke for many of us when he opposed changes in the rules of baseball: "I think it is dangerous to fool around with fundamentals because they can have a chain effect on other parts. Every move in that direction should be taken with extreme caution because the consequences could be disastrous."[1]

Six weeks before, my boss had come to my office to give me an update on the outcome of negotiations on police reform:
"Dodik killed Lajčák's proposed deal on police reform. Lajčák is apparently very upset," he said.
"And what are we going to do now?"
"The Political Department has called a meeting to discuss the way forward."
As I walked through the corridors leading to the secure room where the meeting had been scheduled, I had no idea that we were on the eve of what would develop into the most serious crisis in Bosnia since the end of armed conflict in 1995.

★ ★ ★

Throughout history, the Balkans have often been associated with ethnic tensions, intrigues, and problems. The word *balkanization* is used to describe a process by which an entity disintegrates into mutually hostile units. Although such clichés have little connection to the nuanced reality of life in the region, they have certainly been revived by the wars that swept through the region during the violent collapse of Yugoslavia in the 1990s. Bosnia and Herzegovina, the most multiethnic republic of the former Yugoslavia, has often been portrayed as a territory haunted by old, intractable ethnic tensions. The complexity of its politics, history, and structures tends to baffle most observers, including those of us who have worked there. They are worth a quick review.

Until 1991, Bosnia and Herzegovina was not a country. It was one of the six republics that composed the Socialist Federal Republic of Yugoslavia. Marshal Tito, the leader of the Partisans (the communist resistance group that regained Yugoslavia from Nazi Germany) ruled over Yugoslavia until his death in 1980. His regime kept Yugoslavia together and controlled ethnic nationalism through a policy known as *brotherhood and unity*. In Bosnia, Bosniaks (Bosnian Muslims), Croats, and Serbs, the main ethnic groups, had lived together peacefully as part of Tito's communist Yugoslavia. His death and the fall of the communist one-party system created a political vacuum that led to the rise of nationalist parties throughout Yugoslavia. Slobodan Milošević's embrace of nationalism in one of the federal republics, Serbia, ignited a fire that caused Yugoslavia to burn.

Through a number of complex maneuvers, Milošević disrupted the delicate political balance of the Yugoslav federal system. Tito's regime had been mindful of the need to prevent one single republic from being able to impose its will on others. Tito achieved this objective by counterbalancing the votes of the Serbian government with those of two autonomous regions in Serbia: Vojvodina and Kosovo. After his rise to power, Milošević abolished the autonomous status of Vojvodina and Kosovo, significantly strengthening Serbia's position in the Yugoslav system.[2]

Refusing to remain part of a federation dominated by Serbia, the republics of Slovenia and Croatia declared their independence in 1991.[3] The secessions of Slovenia and Croatia made the prospect of evolving within a Serb-dominated Yugoslavia an acute concern for many in Bosnia. This fear would contribute to Bosnia's descent into war. Bosnia and Herzegovina's declaration of independence followed shortly after those of Slovenia and Croatia. But Bosnia's path to statehood would be tragic. In a disintegration process marked by ethnic nationalism, the most multiethnic republic of all former Yugoslav republics would prove particularly vulnerable to attempts by neighboring republics Serbia and Croatia to annex parts of its territory inhabited by Bosnian Serbs or Bosnian Croats.

Three main nationalist parties had emerged from the December 1990 elections in Bosnia, each claiming to express the views of Bosnia's three main national groups. Founded in 1990 by Alija Izetbegović, a Bosniak and former political dissident under Tito's Yugoslavia, the Party for Democratic Action (SDA) was the main Bosniak political party. The Serbian Democratic Party (SDS), founded by Radovan Karadžić – the wartime Bosnian Serb leader facing trial before the International Criminal Tribunal for the Former Yugoslavia (ICTY) on charges of genocide and crimes committed against civilians – was acting as the main Bosnian Serb party. Finally, the Croatian Democratic Union (HDZ), an offshoot of a party bearing the same name founded in neighboring Croatia, was the main representative of Croats in Bosnia.[4] Leading the party with the highest number of seats, Alija Izetbegović formed a government of national unity that included members of the SDA, the SDS, and the HDZ.

Several Bosniaks and Bosnian Croats in the Izetbegović government saw Bosnia's secession from Yugoslavia either as an appropriate defense mechanism or as an opportunity to push forward with their own secessionist objectives. The leadership of the SDS, favorable to maintaining ties with a Yugoslavia in which they would form the majority, saw things differently. These competing interests unleashed a rapid succession of events. On October 14 and 15, 1991, SDA and HDZ representatives voted in favor of Bosnia's sovereignty during a session of Bosnia's Parliamentary Assembly. The representatives of the SDS walked out of the session and established a Serb National Assembly a few days later. During the winter of 1991–2, Bosnian Serbs positioned heavy artillery across Bosnia's territory. On December 20, 1991, the members of the Bosnian presidency voted in favor of Bosnia's independence. The Serb representatives voted against the decision. A referendum on Bosnia's independence took place on February 29 and March 1, 1992. Sixty-four percent of the electorate voted in favor of a sovereign and independent Bosnia and Herzegovina while the SDS called on all Bosnian Serbs to boycott the referendum. In reaction to the Bosnian authorities' intent to secede from Yugoslavia, the SDS had initially declared parts of the Bosnian territory to be autonomous Serbian regions and requested the protection of the Yugoslav National Army (JNA). The JNA, by then an instrument increasingly dominated by Milošević's regime in Serbia, deployed accordingly. The SDS would later declare the establishment of an independent "Serb Republic" in the territory of Bosnia and Herzegovina.

The SDS was not the only actor willing to run away with part of Bosnia's territory. The Bosnian Croat alliance with the Bosniaks against the JNA would soon break apart. On May 9, Bosnian Croat forces attacked the Bosnian government forces in Mostar and commenced a siege of the eastern part of the city mainly inhabited by Bosniaks. Supported by Franjo Tuđman's government in neighboring Croatia, the HDZ declared the establishment of a "Croat Community of Herzeg-Bosnia" in the western part of the country in July 1992.[5]

With their eyes set on the end of the Soviet era, Western states appeared nervous about the mounting instability in Yugoslavia. They turned a blind eye to Milošević's actions in the hope that his behavior could quickly stabilize developments in the country. Their inaction signaled to Milošević that he could push forward with his power grab.[6] The United States hid behind Europe.[7] Europe hid behind the diverging foreign policies of its member states.[8]

Confused and ineffective, the international community was unable to stop mass atrocities in Bosnia, including genocide in Srebrenica, a small Bosnian town that had been designated as a United Nations (UN) "safe area" at an earlier stage in the conflict. In July 1995, Bosnian Serb forces led by Ratko Mladić (currently facing trial before the ICTY) entered the town of Srebrenica and massacred several thousand Bosnian Muslim men under the eyes of a Dutch contingent of the United Nations meant to protect the area. The occurrence of genocide in Europe several decades after the end of World War II shamed an international community already discredited by its incapacity to end the armed conflict in Bosnia. Previously reluctant to intervene, the Clinton administration finally decided to assume a more proactive role in 1995. Pursuing a strategy that combined military force and diplomacy, U.S. diplomat Richard Holbrooke dragged the belligerent parties into intense peace negotiations at the Wright-Patterson Air Force Base in Dayton, Ohio, a process that culminated in a comprehensive peace agreement known as the Dayton Accords.

Peace came at a cost, though, in the form of a complex constitutional arrangement. Bosnia and Herzegovina would emerge from the war as a federation composed of a central level of government with limited responsibilities and two entities. One of the two entities, the Federation of Bosnia and Herzegovina, would itself be a federation composed of ten cantons (smaller federal units) each inhabited by a Bosniak or Bosnian Croat majority. The other federated entity, Republika Srpska, would be a single entity inhabited by a Bosnian Serb majority. The entire convoluted arrangement would be as if the state of California had declared itself independent, gone through war, and had emerged as an internationally recognized state with two federal units, one of them, the "Federation of San Francisco," a federation composed of ten counties.

The Dayton agreement provided for an international military presence with authority to maintain peace and stability in Bosnia. It also provided for a civilian presence to ensure the implementation of civilian aspects of the agreement. Our office, the Office of the High Representative (OHR), was the international civilian enforcement mechanism provided for by the Dayton peace agreement. The High Representative enjoyed sweeping powers, such as the power to enact legislation or remove public officials to ensure implementation of the peace agreement. After the ratification of the Dayton Accords, the international community considered strengthening Bosnia's central structures a key objective. Doing so would cement the country back together and neutralize internal secessionist aspirations. We called this process "state building." Those who had resisted the establishment of a unitary system of government in Bosnia and Herzegovina before the war were now resisting state-building efforts.

The person who came to epitomize this battle most was a man called Paddy Ashdown, the energetic former leader of the Liberal Democrats in the United Kingdom who acted as High Representative between 2002 and 2006. A former British military commando and a charismatic politician, Ashdown's style resembled that of an unstoppable tornado, one that was at odds with the mild-mannered approach of Sarajevo diplomats. New state institutions in the field of defense, intelligence, indirect taxation, and judicial appointments mushroomed under his mandate. Using the media to put pressure on local politicians, cajoling them in private on the ski slopes, making sure that ambassadors united behind a single message, his style combined a unique blend

of tactical intelligence, energy, and charm. I remember accompanying him to a meeting with local police officers who had been dismissed following a certification process conducted by the United Nations. They argued that the process contained irregularities, and wanted the High Representative to reverse it. While offering to intervene on their behalf before the UN, Ashdown made clear that he had no legal authority to reverse the process. While doing so, he kept repeating that he was bound to protect "world law." I glanced several times at the interpreter, hoping that his unorthodox legal terminology would be translated as "international obligations" or "UN Security Council resolutions." He well understood the legal mechanics behind the problem and knew that while terms such as "world legislator" and "world law" may have hardly made any sense for a lawyer, they conveyed the substance of his point effectively. After the meeting, he looked at me like a mischievous child who knew he had done well and said, smiling:
"You must admit I was right, Philippe?"
"Well, sort of," I replied, amused.
Several High Representatives had preceded Ashdown. Bosnia's first High Representative was Carl Bildt, a former Swedish prime minister who had served as a European Union (EU) special representative to the former Yugoslavia during the war. He also participated in the peace negotiations at Dayton.[9] Carlos Westendorp, Spain's former ambassador to the United Nations and minister of foreign affairs, replaced Bildt. Wolfgang Petritsch, an Austrian diplomat, followed Westendorp. A former Austrian ambassador to the Federal Republic of Yugoslavia, Petritsch had acted as an EU special envoy for Kosovo in 1998–9 and was the EU chief negotiator at the Rambouillet peace conference for Kosovo in 1999. Petritsch's tenure marked the beginning of a more assertive use of the powers of the High Representative – an assertiveness that Ashdown pushed to new levels under his mandate.

International forcefulness would, however, be significantly reduced by the policies of Ashdown's successor: Christian Schwarz-Schilling. A retired German minister, Schwarz-Schilling came to Bosnia with the strong belief that the forceful approach of the international community had been counterproductive. In 1992, Schwarz-Schilling had resigned from his position in the German government to protest against the German and European inability to end the armed conflict in Yugoslavia. By the end of the conflict, he had started working as a mediator to help solve local disputes in Bosnia. As he assumed his functions as High Representative in 2006, he believed that the role of the High Representative should be limited to overseeing and supporting processes allowing Bosnians to solve issues on their own. His mandate was characterized by a significant reduction in the use of the High Representative's powers.

This was the context under which Miroslav Lajčák, a young and energetic Slovak diplomat, was appointed as the new High Representative in the summer of 2007. A career diplomat, he had previously served as Slovakia's ambassador to Japan, and Serbia and Montenegro. He had been appointed as the personal envoy of Javier Solana, the European Union high representative for common foreign and security policy, to oversee the Montenegro independence referendum process in 2006. Having managed the process effectively, he was coming to Bosnia and Herzegovina with an excellent reputation. Speaking Bosnian, Croatian, and Serbian fluently, he conducted all his meetings and his press conferences without any interpreter. He spoke intelligently and calmly at meetings, with a style that combined youthfulness and elegance. Some members of our staff joked about the number of flattering comments their mothers would make when they saw him on television. Just like Bosnia, his country, Slovakia, had once been part of a larger East European communist country. Lajčák intended to focus on such similarities as well as Slovakia's recent integration to the European Union to build bridges with Bosnian politicians. He firmly believed in the power of prospective European Union membership for Bosnia to stimulate consensus among its divided political class. There was something in Lajčák's confidence and energy that was reminiscent of Ashdown. Armed with ambitious goals, he did not seem to fear battle. However, Lajčák had come to Bosnia at a very different time and faced a particularly difficult landscape – both internationally and domestically.

Before his appointment, key international players had indicated their wish to see him restore the credibility of the OHR and had given him the assurance of their full support. But the international community was divided on the exact role of the OHR. While willing to restore its credibility in the short term, many European capitals wanted to replace the heavy-handed OHR with a more discreet European presence in the longer run. The United States, which acted as a powerful driving force for many years in Bosnia, was supportive of a more assertive role for the OHR, but its focus and resources had shifted away from Bosnia given its involvement in Iraq and Afghanistan after the September 11 attacks. By 2007, Bosnia and Herzegovina was perceived as a relative success. Security and stability had been restored, and freedom of movement reestablished. More than one million persons displaced during the war had exercised their right to return to their homes of origin as guaranteed by the Dayton peace agreement.[10] With a GDP that grew consistently for several years and new central institutions, Bosnia was considered by many in the international community to be ready to transition from peace implementation to European integration.

Domestically, the fragile and difficult relationship between the country's political factions began to worsen after the Parliamentary Assembly failed to adopt a package of constitutional amendments aiming at strengthening the country's common institutions in 2006. Despite the support of Bosnia's main political parties, the amendments – negotiated under a U.S.-led process – failed to secure the required majority in the Parliamentary Assembly by two votes. The Croatian Democratic Union 1990 (HDZ 1990), a small nationalist Bosnian Croat party, and the Party for Bosnia and Herzegovina (SBIH), led by Bosniak nationalist politician Haris Silajdžić, had succeeded in their efforts to block the package's parliamentary adoption.

The rejection of constitutional reform marked the return of Silajdžić to Bosnian politics. Silajdžić had served as foreign minister and prime minister of Bosnia and Herzegovina during the war and had participated in the Dayton negotiations. He returned to the Bosnian political scene by taking control of the SBIH in May 2006. A charismatic politician, he appealed to a particularly nationalistic segment of the Bosniak population by aggressively promoting the idea of a unitary Bosnia and Herzegovina. His objections to constitutional reform were linked to his unitarist views. Considering Republika Srpska an illegitimate entity founded on genocide and ethnic cleansing, he made no secret of his wishes to see it abolished. He campaigned against constitutional reform. He claimed that Bosniak representatives should refrain from adopting the proposed amendments to the constitution agreed at Dayton (which recognized the existence of Republika Srpska) because, by doing so, they would implicitly recognize the legitimacy of Republika Srpska.

Silajdžić's rhetoric had antagonized another important political actor in Bosnia with whom Lajčák would also have to contend: Milorad Dodik. Recently elected prime minister of Republika Srpska, Dodik was the equivalent of a wild grizzly that had been unleashed in the Bosnian political arena. A charismatic political figure, he was known for stopping in local restaurants to sing folk songs at weddings while on the campaign trail. Born in a small Bosnian municipality called Laktaši, he had studied political science in Belgrade and had been a member of the Bosnian parliament before the war. Nevertheless, his limited ties with the officials of the self-proclaimed Bosnian Serb Republic during the war helped him to nurture an image of someone with clean hands. Intuitive, realistic, and intelligent, he spoke with disarming clarity and frankness at meetings. Known for his rough play, he did not hesitate to insult journalists on television, sometimes even alluding to the reputation of their mothers. He could also switch the charm on within seconds. I remember seeing him hugging a colleague after a tense meeting in our office. Slightly embarrassed, the poor girl looked like she was just about to suffocate in his embrace while everyone else was laughing. Many in the international community saw him as a good alternative to the SDS. He already had been elected prime minister of Republika Srpska in 1997. His election had been the product of an intense power struggle. A few months after the end of the war, Karadžić's indictment by the ICTY had forced him to relinquish the presidency of Republika Srpska. Biljana Plavšić, a former biology professor at the University of Sarajevo who had served as vice president under Karadžić during the war, replaced him in 1996. Plavšić was an ultranationalist who would later be sentenced to prison by the ICTY for crimes against humanity. She had decided to fight against Karadžić's corrupt network as soon as she replaced him. In 1997, she called for elections to counteract attempts by Karadžić's people to remove her from office.[11] It is within this context that Dodik was initially appointed prime minister of Republika Srpska.

Dodik had been one of Yugoslavia's youngest mayors before the war. His town, Laktaši, had a reputation for being efficiently managed under his tenure as mayor. Partly enriching himself during the war, Dodik was at the center of many commercial interests in Laktaši after the war. He owned a factory that produced furniture for IKEA. His love for basketball had also led him to acquire IGOKEA, a basketball team named after his son Igor and his client IKEA.

Dodik had coordinated his second rise to power in 2007 very well. His party, the Alliance of Independent Social Democrats (SNSD), beat the SDS in a landslide victory. By 2007, he enjoyed broad support not only within Republika Srpska, but also within the international community. Dodik had supported the U.S.-led efforts to reform Bosnia's constitution in 2006. Soon after he retook power in 2007, his government had implemented a number of reforms to stimulate economic growth in Republika Srpska. His policies had contributed to his reputation as a positive alternative to the SDS within the international community generally and within the U.S. embassy in Sarajevo more particularly.

Dodik was irritated by Silajdžić's reference to war crimes and genocide to undermine the legitimacy of Republika Srpska. Dodik had refused to be associated with war crimes during the conflict and reportedly helped protect people across the ethnic divide throughout the war. Silajdžić's campaign gave Dodik a golden opportunity to appeal to the more nationalistic segments of Republika Srpska. Its electorate, already very nationalistic, was reluctant to see a stronger and more united Bosnia and Herzegovina. Its more extreme factions still thrived on hopes of seceding from Bosnia – an objective that had contributed to throwing the country into war in the 1990s. During the 2007 elections, Dodik sent shock waves throughout the region by openly referring to the potential secession of Republika Srpska in the event its existence came under threat from Bosniak nationalists. Dodik's embrace of secessionist rhetoric led several members of the international community to worry. Secession has indeed been a taboo subject in Bosnian postwar political discourse. Anyone involved with the former Yugoslavia in the 1990s knew very well what had thrown Yugoslavia into the abyss. With such memories fresh in their minds, Western officials had reason to worry about a galvanized Dodik riding a wave of nationalist sentiment in 2007.

This is the political situation in which Lajčák found himself as he arrived in Bosnia. The difficulty of his position was compounded by the fact that he was not only mandated to restore the credibility of the High Representative, but had to do so while also tackling an ambitious state-building reform: police reform. At the eve of the crisis in 2007, Ashdown was gone, but his mark on Bosnia and Herzegovina was still strong. State-building forcefulness was displayed at its greatest through police reform, a process Ashdown had started in 2004 by establishing a commission chaired by former Belgian Prime Minister Wilfried Martens. The Martens Commission had recommended that all constitutional responsibilities for police matters be transferred from Bosnia's entities to its central level of government. The European Union had further conditioned the signature of a Stabilization and Association Agreement (SAA) with Bosnia (a preliminary step toward EU membership) to sufficient progress on police reform. Police reform was the most important battle of the day in 2007. Pooling police forces represented an enormous loss of political capital for individual leaders of Bosnia's multiple levels of government. Also, the reform struck at the very heart of Bosnian Serb resistance to a more integrated Bosnia and Herzegovina. The particular intensity of Bosnian Serb nationalism combined with the tight relationship maintained between political power and the law enforcement apparatus – a common characteristic in many former socialist countries – partly explained why Republika Srpska had been so fiercely opposed to police reform since 2004. More important, Silajdžić's call to abolish Republika Srpska had polarized positions and made many Bosnian Serbs fear that police reform was the first step of a broader plan to dismantle their entity. From their perspective, agreeing to police reform would have been tantamount to giving back part of the effective control gained through war.

Police reform remained Bosnia's main obstacle on the road to European integration and Lajčák knew that Dodik was the biggest political force behind that obstacle. Lajčák assessed that, to succeed with Dodik, he needed to reestablish the authority of the High Representative soon in his mandate. Members of his cabinet were divided on the effectiveness of his powers. Some believed they could be reactivated. Others thought that Schwarz-Schilling's policy of non-intervention had undermined them beyond repair. Lajčák opted for a strategy that sought to reassert their effectiveness through an incremental approach.

He would first focus on enacting a number of measures pertaining to ICTY cooperation, an issue considered low risk, and for which Dodik had little room to maneuver. Before the measures were enacted, a member of his cabinet flew to Dodik's ranch by helicopter to warn him of the decision to come. Dodik was not happy with Lajčák's decision, but indicated that he would not oppose it. In July 2007, Lajčák went ahead and adopted the measures, unopposed.[12] Lajčák and his cabinet felt the strategy had worked. He had demonstrated that the powers of the High Representative were still effective and that he intended to use them more assertively than had his predecessor.

Shortly after, Lajčák tried to solve police reform. He offered several key concessions to Republika Srpska, hoping to get Dodik to move. Some in the office had tried to persuade him otherwise, warning against the danger of offering a large carrot to someone who had never shown any willingness to agree to police reform. Lajčák persisted; he wanted a relationship of trust with Dodik. Problems with this strategy emerged when Dodik rejected Lajčák's new model. Local media had interpreted Dodik's reaction as a slap in Lajčák's face. He now wanted to turn to the stick and use his powers as High Representative to force Dodik to come to an agreement on the issue. The meeting of the Political Department to which I was hurrying aimed to explore ways Lajčák could do just that.

★ ★ ★

The secure room was an institution in itself in our office. It was a small room made up of thick glass with a system of ventilation that one needed to activate before coming in. We were told that it protected us from outside attempts to spy on our meetings. I questioned the room's usefulness, as people would often continue their discussions on their way out of the secure room. Although I liked to publicly pretend that the whole construction was useless, I secretly felt happy to take part in meetings held there. Heads of international missions and ambassadors received their weekly briefings in this room. An issue seemed somehow to become more important and more structured once exposed in the secure room. We used it that day to conduct the meeting called by the Political Department. The meeting was punctuated by long discussions between several advisors.

"Lajčák has no solid ground to use his mandate as High Representative to punish parties for a failure to agree on a EU reform. It's EU integration stuff and it has nothing to do with Dayton. The EU will never support this!"

"That's exactly why we need to go down the Dayton road! Lajčák could come out and say that there are still a number of unresolved Dayton issues that need to be addressed. By throwing new measures related to Dayton at Dodik, we will gain enough leverage to force them to agree on police reform."

"So you suggest that we tell Dodik the following: either they agree to police reform, or we will make their life more difficult by imposing measures based on the Dayton agreement?"

"Exactly."

"And what are we going to do if the Serbs decide to boycott the central institutions?"

A long silence followed. The question had raised an issue that most of us were happy to ignore. The constitutional architecture of Bosnia was replete with mechanisms designed to ensure that none of Bosnia's main ethnic groups would be able to impose its will on the others. By simply staying at home, a number of their representatives could bring the executive and legislative branches of Bosnia's central institutions to a standstill. After long discussions, we agreed to propose a number of Dayton-related measures for Lajčák to enact to increase pressure on parties. Such measures would include amendments designed to reduce the capacity of representatives to block the legislative and executive branches of government by boycotts. They would need to be enacted first. This was, in itself, a significant step to increase the efficiency of the central level of government – an objective that all members of the international community could support.

★ ★ ★

It came down to our team in the Legal Department to prepare the amendments. Because blockages by absenteeism could occur on the basis of rules regulating quorum[13] or decision making[14] within both the executive and legislative branches of government, we had to work on two distinct sets of amendments: one pertaining to legislation regulating the Council of Ministers and another one amending the rules of procedures of the Parliamentary Assembly. Tackling all these variables at once would be complicated but necessary if we wanted to effectively streamline decision making in Bosnia's central institutions.

I was heading the public law unit at the time, and took the lead in preparing the first draft. The unit was composed of a small number of legal advisors who specialized in Bosnian constitutional and administrative law matters. In an organization so heavily involved in state building, the public law unit played a strategic role. Its members transformed state-building policy into legislation. I worked with a close colleague of mine, a young Sarajevo lawyer who possessed a solid understanding of governmental and parliamentary structures at all levels of government in Bosnia. During breaks at work, he told me stories about his youth during the siege in Sarajevo, and how Sarajevans became experts at urban sniper avoidance. They had erected a system of protective walls at several points around the city to minimize their exposure to snipers posted on the hills surrounding the city. "The real challenge was to run from one protected area to the other," he told me.

Our department's head translator helped us translate all the amendments from English to Bosnian, Croatian, and Serbian. His was a crucial skill, because what was once considered a single language in the former Yugoslavia had been split into three allegedly different languages in postwar Bosnia and Herzegovina. Nationalism had penetrated the sphere of linguistics with "experts" on all sides busily trying to identify minor variations and differences in the languages so that they could assert their entitlement to a separate language. The OHR published its documents in all three languages, which imposed a heavy burden on our translators.

He was our most experienced translator and I insisted that he work with us throughout this process. He had a solid command of English, a good understanding of legal terminology, and a very thorough mind. He would often call me to ask for clarifications: "In our languages, this could mean that the votes *must* include or *could* include members from this group. Can you clarify what you mean in the English version?" We got along very well. He never skipped an opportunity to talk about jazz. One day, he confessed to me he had written a personal letter to Miles Davis in his teenage years: "We were isolated in Yugoslavia and had little access to some of the music in the West. I wanted him to send me a few of his albums. Instead, I received a generic postcard with an encouraging note probably written by a random person in an office in the U.S.!" We talked a lot about Canada. He had an image of Canada as the best country on earth. I tried, with limited success, to promote a more realistic perspective on the issue by pointing to our own constitutional problems. As a Québécois who had witnessed the 1995 referendum campaign organized by a government keen to gain its independence from Canada, I thought I could dismantle some of his romantic perspectives. He remained skeptical. He had worked for Canadian soldiers during the war. "They were great. They were real professionals and interacted with us as equals," he said.

We worked for several days on the amendments. We had thought that the exercise would be straightforward. According to our initial assessment, we only had to draft a few amendments to the law on the Council of Ministers and the Rules of Procedures of the Parliamentary Assembly. But as we started looking into the matter more closely, it became apparent that we were dealing with a much more complex task. Eliminating obstacles in the parliamentary and governmental systems required many more amendments than we had foreseen.

For example, decisions in the Council of Ministers required different voting thresholds depending on whether they addressed final issues or issues that needed to be sent to another institution for further consideration (i.e., a draft law to be adopted by the Parliamentary Assembly). Moreover, an act had to pass through various parliamentary committees before reaching one of the houses in the Parliamentary Assembly. The decision-making process in each of these committees was also constrained by similar blocking mechanisms. Amending the formal decision-making procedure in the houses of the Parliamentary Assembly would be futile if a committee at an earlier parliamentary stage could simply block the same issue. We decided to tackle the system as a whole and remove obstacles at every point of potential blockage. When looking at our illustrated byzantine charts mapping the parliamentary process, we made fun of ourselves: "This is what our 'simple amendments' need to address."

We managed to deliver on time. We felt confident that our proposed amendments struck the right balance. They preserved all the constitutional vetoes but reduced the capacity of members of the

Parliamentary Assembly and the Council of Ministers to block central institutions by staying at home. To make sure that we were on solid ground, we had communicated with an American lawyer who had helped draft the constitution of Bosnia and Herzegovina at Dayton.[15] We were very confident that the Dayton agreement had never intended to put in place a system of blockage by absenteeism.

★ ★ ★

We presented our proposal to Lajčák in the secure room. Listening carefully to our explanations, he understood the substance of our proposal. He was surprised to see how easily these blocking mechanisms could be activated and felt that making the central institutions more efficient was the right thing to do. As we talked, I began to worry that we were, in some way, missing the forest for the trees and that our discussions were revolving too much around the technical nature of the proposal rather than its political impact. By revisiting the application of the very constitutional mechanisms that had convinced parties to end the conflict in 1995, our amendments were clearly addressing sensitive political issues. While the substance of these mechanisms would remain unchanged, it would no longer be possible to trigger them simply by staying at home. I knew that these distinctions would be lost quickly in any public debate to come and thought it was important to assess the political consequences of pushing through with our amendments. Experience had taught many of us that Bosnian politicians would focus immediately on the big symbols, such as fears of ethnic domination. I made the point that we were sitting on a potential political bomb.

Many jumped in to downplay these "alarmist" statements. Some advisors even argued that Nikola Špirić, the chairman of the Council of Ministers, would welcome our amendments given his past complaints to Lajčák that the Council of Ministers was always blocked. I thought this was a ludicrous argument. Anyone who knew Bosnian politics was aware that these measures would touch on very delicate issues, and that Špirić's position would be identical to that of Dodik. Dodik was the prime minister of Republika Srpska, and had designated Špirić, a member of his own party, to act as chairman of Bosnia's central government. Špirić was not going to call the shots in any political battle that would follow. Dodik would. All the more so if he felt that Lajčák's measures were going after his interests more than those of other political parties.

In the end, Lajčák decided to go ahead with our proposal as a first step. He would enact amendments to the law on the Council of Ministers, and instruct the presidency of the Parliamentary Assembly to amend parliamentary rules of procedures to eliminate the sources of blockage we had identified.

As for me, I left the meeting slightly puzzled. I felt that some in the office were underplaying the importance of the potential storm ahead of us. I was not against the decision to impose these amendments. On the contrary, I was convinced that we should go forward and even thought we should have done so many years ago. But I questioned our preparedness for the battle to come. My boss also looked perplexed.
"I don't think they fully realize what's ahead," he mumbled after the briefing.
"I assume they know what they are doing," I replied.
"We'll see."

★ ★ ★

On Friday, October 19, 2007, Miroslav Lajčák signed the decision imposing amendments to the law on the Council of Ministers and instructed the presidency of the Parliamentary Assembly to amend parliamentary rules of procedures in accordance with the proposals we had prepared.

The first shot had been fired, and we had fired first.

2 They Fire Back

"Did you see Dodik's reaction yesterday?" my boss asked.

"No, I didn't have a chance to look at the media reports," I replied.

It was Monday morning. The reactions from the Bosnian Serb politicians had been swift and bold. Dodik had come out during the weekend claiming that the High Representative's decision was unconstitutional. He argued that it was contrary to the very peace agreement Lajčák was mandated to protect. Dodik undoubtedly felt attacked, and he was going to react strongly. By contrast, we had the Bosniak media on our side. They praised Lajčák's decision. We now knew where this was going. The Bosniak political parties would give their entire support to our measures and use the opportunity to paint Dodik as someone who had no interest in a stronger and more efficient Bosnia and Herzegovina. Dodik, on the other hand, would try to portray this as yet another attack on the Bosnian Serbs and a clear attempt to punish them for having had the courage to protect their own police and institutions against assimilation.

A sense of nervousness was setting in. Several of us were surprised to learn that Lajčák had immediately gone to Banja Luka, the capital of Republika Srpska, to meet with Dodik. There was a danger that politicians in Republika Srpska would interpret his visit as a sign of weakness. After his meeting, Lajčák stated that his decision had been misinterpreted. He would not amend it but offered to issue an explanatory note to clarify any potential misunderstanding. On my way back to my apartment that evening, my cab driver, glued to the news reports as many in Bosnia were when ethnic tensions were rising, questioned Lajčák's visit:

"Why did he go there? Dodik should have come to Sarajevo to meet with Lajčák and not the other way around."

I smiled, paid him, and went home.

★ ★ ★

At that time, I lived in an apartment in a part of Sarajevo called Ciglane. I liked my apartment and was rather sad when I had to let it go. It was part of a large complex of massive, monolithic buildings built on the flank of a small hill in Sarajevo that once hosted a brick factory. An old Roma settlement sat on top of the hill just behind my apartment. A colleague working at the United Nations High Commissioner for Refugees (UNHCR) office had told me that Roma families had been living on this hill for more than a century. Following the war, the city had considered authorizing the construction of more apartments on their plot of land. The families had managed, with the support of a collection of nongovernmental organizations (NGOs), to force the city of Sarajevo to abandon such plans. The city finally allowed the construction of houses for the families, to be financed by the NGOs. On the other side, the apartment offered a stunning view of Sarajevo. During the summer, you could hear the several calls to prayers emanating from the various mosques in the valley.

The building, just like many other residential buildings built under the socialist regime, surely would have done poorly in an architectural contest. Its heavy shape, linear angles, and disproportionate size made sure it would never seduce any person passing by. Its external awkwardness was, however, compensated for by spaciousness inside. It was well heated during winter and loads of daylight penetrated each room. I came across several such buildings in the region. Every time, I was struck by how their relative outdoor ugliness could morph into nice and pleasant interior spaces. I often wondered whether this was not the reflection of choices made by socialist architects keen to build solid, comfortable, and practical apartments for all workers. Between esthetic and practical comfort, they had opted for the latter.

I took pleasure in immersing myself in this new architectural environment. As I traveled throughout the former Yugoslavia, I always made an effort to stay in or visit hotels built under the socialist regime. For a Westerner, they felt like museums. The dark wooden interior, the large mirrors, the keys with a heavy room number attached to them, the yellow lights, the archaic phone and tape recorder in rooms had all been preserved. The Hotel Bellevue in Split, the Hotel Slavija in Belgrade, or the Hotel Bristol in Skopje ranked on the top of my list. Most provided the lowest levels of comfort for the highest possible price, but they offered something unique: access to history. While in them, I imagined scenes from the Cold War; party officials spied on, foreign journalists and diplomats lying on their beds and pondering ways to escape restrictions imposed by the regime. It connected me to the past. What was life like in the former Yugoslavia? What was the atmosphere like in Belgrade when Tito decided to stand up to Stalin in 1948? That had been a defining moment. Milovan Đilas, a former vice president of Yugoslavia, wrote a fascinating account of the Soviet-Yugoslav discussions that led to the historical split in 1948. In *Conversations with Stalin*, Đilas chronicled the growing divergence between the two regimes.[1] While initially impressed by Stalin, Đilas grew increasingly disillusioned as their meetings proceeded. In one passage of the book, he illustrated the stifling effect of Stalin's authority:

> Stalin broke in with the observation that customs unions are generally unrealistic. Since the discussion had again subsided somewhat, Kardelj observed that some customs unions had shown themselves not to be so bad in practice.
>
> "For example?" Stalin asked.
>
> "Well, for example, Benelux," Kardelj said cautiously.
>
> "Here Belgium, Holland, and Luxembourg joined together."
>
> STALIN: "No, Holland didn't. Only Belgium and Luxembourg. That's nothing, insignificant."
> KARDELJ: "No, Holland is included too."
> STALIN, STUBBORNLY: "No, Holland is not."
>
> Stalin looked at Molotov, at Zorin, at the rest. I had the desire to explain to him that the syllable *ne* in the name Benelux came from the Netherlands, that is, the original designation for Holland, but since everyone kept still, I did too, and so it remained that Holland was not in Benelux.[2]

Expelled from the Communist Central Committee in 1954, Đilas was arrested and imprisoned by Tito's regime following his criticism of the regime in interviews, articles, and books he had written. Đilas wrote continuously while in prison. Many of his books were published outside Yugoslavia. He wrote a biography on Tito in which he praised him for having freed Yugoslavia from Nazi occupation but condemned the impact of his insatiable thirst for power on Yugoslavia. According to Đilas, Tito valued himself to such a degree that he made certain to have no successor. Đilas believed this decision to place personal interests before Yugoslavia would cost the country tremendously. While criticizing Tito's decision to enact a constitutional change to ensure that he would be succeeded by a collective leadership, Đilas noted: "In making his role impossible to duplicate, Tito sought to project himself into history."[3] "Tito made certain that he, and everything that had to do with him, could not be equaled or surpassed."[4] "His collective leadership will consist of Titoist Communists who, like Tito, have a non collective concept of power.... The stability of Tito's Yugoslavia derived from the stability and absoluteness of Tito's personality. There is no comparable figure in Yugoslavia today. The structure of power is based on equality, on the equal participation of the republics in that power. By his autocratic superiority and authority, Tito insured [sic] harmony. The slightest disagreement now could provoke a great disturbance."[5] With hindsight, his writing seemed particularly premonitory. Many years after Tito's death and a tragic war, had Bosnian officials not extended similar mechanisms of governance during their 1995 negotiations at Dayton by ensuring that all constituent peoples shared power equally in many of the country's common institutions?

★ ★ ★

Here we were, in 2007, trying to mitigate the consequences of our tinkering with such mechanisms in Bosnia. We spent a few days drafting the explanatory note that Lajčák had offered to issue. While we were aware that this issue could be interpreted as a political attack against Bosnian Serbs, we felt that the measures had been first and foremost designed to strengthen the efficiency of Bosnia's central institutions, and many in the office agreed that we should counter attack at the technical level.

The explanatory note needed to make a number of points. First, we emphasized that Lajčák's measures were in accordance with the constitution. Dodik and other Republika Srpska officials had claimed that the measures were unconstitutional but had failed to indicate any specific violation. Second, our explanatory note argued that all measures applied equally to all members of the Council of Ministers. Republika Srpska representatives were trying to frame the measures as an attack on the rights of the Bosnian Serb representatives as a constituent people. They were wrong. Our measures applied equally to all constituent peoples. Moreover, none of the members belonging to the other constituent peoples of Bosnia (Bosnian Muslims and Bosnian Croats) had raised any issue in relation to the measures. Our final point pertained to the fact that our amendments did not abolish any protection mechanisms of the governmental or parliamentary decision-making process. The amendments only required that representatives be present to activate them.[6] From a purely technical point of view, I felt we were on solid ground. Our team in the Legal Department had worked well. The political battle to come, however, would have little to do with technical elements.

On Wednesday, October 24, 2007, Ivan Busniak, the deputy High Representative and head of the OHR Banja Luka field office, delivered our explanatory note to Republika Srpska officials. He made a public statement in which he stressed that Republika Srpska politicians had failed to indicate "a single fact that would show how the High Representative's Decision violates the Dayton Peace Accords, the BiH Constitution or the interests of entities or constituent peoples."[7]

★ ★ ★

The following day, we saw the quickly spreading fire our measures had ignited. Vojislav Kostunica, the prime minister of neighboring Serbia, issued a statement that reverberated throughout the region. Speaking from Belgrade, he indicated that Lajčák's measures violated the basic interests of the Serb nation. The measures, he argued, were linked to an international proposal by which Kosovo would declare its independence from Serbia.[8]

Kosovo was now included in the picture. We should have seen this coming. Of all our blind spots, this was one of the largest. Kostunica was the opposition candidate who had defeated Slobodan Milošević in the Yugoslav presidential elections in October 2000. A constitutional lawyer by training, he had replaced Milošević as president of the then Federal

Republic of Yugoslavia and had since been prime minister of Serbia. He was known for his nationalistic positions – and was now clearly trying to rile Serbian national sentiment by linking Lajčák's measures in Bosnia with the final determination status process of Kosovo – one of the most active points of nationalist dispute in the former Yugoslavia.

He was linking them in service to other political goals. To understand why – and why the blind spot was so large on our part – Serbia and the international community's recent history with Kosovo needs to be understood.

The international proposal to which Kostunica had alluded was related to a different conflict that had occurred in Bosnia's neighbor, Serbia. In March 2007, Martti Ahtisaari, the special envoy of the UN secretary-general, had submitted a comprehensive proposal to settle the status of Kosovo, a former autonomous province of Serbia with a majority Albanian population.[9] Ahtisaari, a former president of Finland and a 2008 Nobel Peace laureate, had been appointed in November 2005 to preside over talks between Belgrade and Pristina regarding the future final status of Kosovo.[10] Between 1998 and 1999, Slobodan Milošević's regime had conducted military operations against the Kosovo Liberation Army (KLA), an Albanian guerilla movement fighting for the independence of Kosovo. With the horrors of the Bosnian conflict still fresh, Western governments brought parties to the negotiating table in February 1999 in Rambouillet, outside Paris, to discuss the elements of a peace agreement. While the Kosovar Albanian delegation reluctantly agreed to the terms of the agreement, Milošević refused to sign and continued his military campaign in Kosovo. Faced with his refusal, Western governments authorized NATO military strikes in Serbia to force Milošević's regime to accept the provisions of Rambouillet. NATO's bombing campaign lasted for seventy-seven days and ended on June 10, 1999 when Milošević's military started withdrawing from Kosovo. On the same day, the UN Security Council adopted a resolution that authorized the establishment of an interim international civil administration in Kosovo and that called for a political process to settle its final status.[11] Marti Ahtisaari had been appointed to lead this very process six years later.

Despite several months of negotiations under his leadership, Belgrade and Pristina had not been able to come to an agreement.

Pristina insisted on independence, while Belgrade refused to let go of Kosovo. Recognizing that no agreement could be reached, Ahtisaari submitted a final proposal in March 2007 that recommended that Kosovo be recognized as an independent state under international supervision. The Serbian government rejected Ahtisaari's proposal and continued to claim that Kosovo would remain part of Serbia. Pristina, on the other hand, was planning to declare its independence in early 2008 in accordance with Ahtisaari's proposal.

To us, it seemed like nonsense to link the Kosovo final status process to our measures in Bosnia. These processes were addressing distinct issues in two different countries and there had been no connection between them during their respective inceptions. Kostunica was indirectly asking Western governments to explain why they insisted on respecting Bosnia's territorial integrity when simultaneously supporting a process calling for Kosovo's independence. The reason was simple. The Milošević regime had killed several thousand Albanian Kosovars and pushed hundreds of thousands more away from their homes during the Kosovo conflict. It had previously supported similar actions by Bosnian Serb secessionists in Bosnia. Kostunica's attempt to equate the situation of Kosovo to that of Republika Srpska in Bosnia was therefore not only cynical, but a reflection of a broader failure to acknowledge the extent to which these events had shaped the perspectives of Western governments. Aware that the brutal actions of Milošević's regime had made Kosovar Albanians unwilling to accept any reassertion of control by Serbia over Kosovo,[12] Western states argued that recognizing Kosovo as an independent state provided stronger guarantees of stability in the region.

Whether or not the facts merited such a connection, Western governments had no interest in seeing a second front opening in Bosnia at a time when their efforts were focused on minimizing the potential consequences of Kosovo's final status process. This is why Kostunica's statement made many people nervous. Kostunica's remarks also led to another set of problems for us in Bosnia. Many politicians had reacted strongly to his remarks. Sulejman Tihić, the leader of the SDA, and Zlatko Lagumdžija, the leader of the socialist SDP party, were quoted in the media as accusing Kostunica of interfering in Bosnia's internal affairs and linking his statement to the prewar policies of Slobodan

Milošević. The harshest statement came from Željko Komšić, the Croat member of Bosnia's tripartite presidency, who warned Kostunica to keep his hands away from Bosnia and Herzegovina or he would get his fingers and his nose hurt.[13]

Almost twelve years after the end of the Bosnian conflict, I was disturbed to see how quickly our measures had reignited old and dangerous patterns. The rapid emergence of dormant synergies was an indicator that the political situation was still volatile. In less than a week, the enactment of our amendments had triggered a political storm that reached beyond Bosnia. To make things worse, the media was now reporting that Dodik had convened a special session of the Republika Srpska National Assembly the following Monday to discuss Lajčák's measures. Demonstrations were slated to take place throughout Republika Srpska on the same day. There was little doubt that the explanatory note had failed to appease Dodik. Backed by politicians in Belgrade, he was opting for escalation.

★ ★ ★

On October 27, we drove to Banja Luka to meet with Republika Srpska representatives. We were scheduled to discuss the provisions of Lajčák's amendments to the law on the Council of Ministers. Located in the northwestern part of Bosnia, Banja Luka is a relatively pretty city. The city's old buildings, as well as its streets, flanked by long lines of trees, project a relative sense of elegance. The second largest city in Bosnia and Herzegovina, it had replaced Pale – the wartime capital of the self-declared Serb republic in Bosnia – as the capital of Republika Srpska.

Before the 1992–5 war, it had been one of Bosnia's numerous multiethnic cities. Bosnian Croats, Bosnian Serbs, and Bosniaks lived there in relative harmony. It had Orthodox and Catholic churches and numerous mosques. Things were now different. Many refugees of Serbian origin had fled neighboring Croatia to find refuge in Banja Luka. At the same time, most of the city's Bosniak and Bosnian Croat population had left the city. In an ugly display of ethnic hatred, numerous mosques had been destroyed. The war had transformed Banja Luka into a "Serb town." My first exposure to Banja Luka was through Bosnian television. Only a few days after my arrival in the country in 2001, I watched footage of crowds of Bosnian Serb nationalists beating people during a ceremony meant to commemorate the reconstruction of the city's main mosque. Breaking through the police security cordon, the crowd had disrupted the event and had forced officials in attendance to take refuge in the Islamic center before finally evacuating.[14] The place had calmed down since then. Several of the city's mosques had been rebuilt and some Bosnian Croats and Muslims had returned.[15]

We met the representatives of Republika Srpska in the government building. The atmosphere inside was tense. Walking in silence, government staffers accompanied us through security and showed us to our meeting room. We hardly exchanged a word. We were taken to the room where the Republika Srpska government held its sessions. The room had a large table in its center and wooden walls covered with Serbian symbols that made it feel like a baroque space.[16] Our delegation was rather small. My boss and I were accompanied by a young lawyer who acted as a liaison between the Legal Department and Lajčák during the crisis. He had come to the OHR as part of Lajčák's cabinet. He wore small glasses, had a sophisticated demeanor, and had a sharp eye for details. Educated in France, he spoke impeccable French, which allowed us to communicate in my native tongue throughout the crisis. Our head translator completed our delegation. His great skills were crucial in a debate that would be fought constantly through words, paragraphs, and commas.

Their delegation finally came in. They outnumbered us by a ratio of almost three to one. They made sure to sit our smaller delegation at one end of the table so as to encircle us. Rajko Kuzmanović headed their delegation. A professor of constitutional law in Banja Luka and the president of the Academy of Arts and Science of Republika Srpska, he had been chosen to become the next president of Republika Srpska because of his close ties with Dodik's SNSD. He wore thick, large glasses. Zoran Lipovac, the minister of administration and local self-government, and Džerard Selman, the minister of justice, were in attendance. Miroslav Mikeš, a Republika Srpska-based lawyer who presided over a caucus of a parliamentary committee in Republika Srpska, was also present. Quietly scanning the room, looking at each participant, my boss turned to me: "Slavko Mitrović is here. He is the main advisor to Dodik's SNSD on legal affairs. He is very sharp." I had never met him before. He was quietly looking through his papers while the others were chatting.

Kuzmanović took the floor first. He made a long speech that alluded to broad principles of constitutional law. Expressing his firm belief that we could come to a solution, suggesting that we look at areas of consensus, he tried to position himself as the moderate, older figure who was above the dispute. We took the floor, explaining that we were willing to provide any explanation to dissipate any misunderstanding. An intense exchange of arguments followed. Each participant took turns and attacked Lajčák's decision: the decision was unconstitutional; it violated a fundamental aspect of the Dayton agreement; it disturbed the delicate balance achieved under the previous law; the Dayton peace agreement did not allow for one constituent people to be outvoted. They gave us an earful. Their tone was aggressive and at times contemptuous. Then Slavko Mitrović took the floor. He had been silent since the beginning of the meeting. His intervention confirmed our initial assumptions. Of all the interventions, his was the most focused. He sought to demonstrate, step by step, how the replacement mechanism of absent ministers we had enacted opened the door to abuse and outvoting. Initially taken aback, we regrouped and managed to demonstrate that his scenario could not occur under our amendments. With our own fair share of contempt, we sought to reject his arguments one by one. We were clearly at odds. After a long and exhausting session that had clearly polarized each side even further, we decided to end the meeting. We agreed to meet again in a few days. Both delegations went their own way without exchanging more than standard polite wishes.

A few things were clearer for us. As expected, this was not going to be an easy discussion. Any hope that anyone in Sarajevo may have entertained about the possibility of quickly solving the crisis through technical discussions was going to be crushed. This was going to be a difficult process. No one from Republika Srpska was there to be finessed through explanations. One lawyer seemed keen on being constructive. Miroslav Mikeš came to see us after the meeting. He was calm and reassuring. "I am sure we can find a way out. I have a few ideas."

★ ★ ★

On Monday, October 29, demonstrations were held in many municipalities in Republika Srpska. Protesters carried signs attacking Lajčák's measures and showing pictures of Vladimir Putin – a reference to historical ties between Serbs and Russians. Dodik used the occasion to reiterate his message against our measures. Addressing a crowd of ten thousand protestors in Banja Luka, he framed the demonstrations as a natural reaction to Lajčák's actions. Despite the pressure put on him, he could not accept the measures. In a well-coordinated series of events, the Republika Srpska National Assembly convened on the same day. The following day, its members planned to issue a formal declaration, which would coincide with a meeting of the Steering Board of the Peace Implementation Council (PIC), the body responsible for giving political guidance to the High Representative.[17] As feared, Dodik had also threatened a Bosnian Serb boycott of all central institutions.

On Tuesday, October 30, the governments of France, Germany, Italy, the United Kingdom, and the United States delivered a joint message to the government of Serbia in Belgrade by way of an official *démarche*. They informed the Serbian government that they expected Serbia to act in accordance with its obligations as a signatory of the Dayton peace agreement. They further expected Serbia to refrain from linking the events in Bosnia and Herzegovina to the process of determining Kosovo's final status. They hoped that this would tame Belgrade's support for Dodik and lower the political temperature in Bosnia. Later in the evening, the Steering Board of the PIC met in Sarajevo. The party leaders of Bosnia's governing coalition attended the meeting. Dodik's words would be carefully analyzed to get a sense of the intentions of the Bosnian Serb leadership.

The PIC Steering Board meeting took place in the building of the Parliamentary Assembly in Sarajevo. The buildings were a sad sight, still rife with bullet holes and other marks of war. The main tower had been left unrepaired for almost a decade. Located on "Sniper Alley" in front of the Holiday Inn hotel where most foreign journalists had stayed during the conflict, the parliamentary buildings had been in the background of numerous international media reports from Sarajevo during the war. It was in these buildings where Radovan Karadžić, the wartime leader of the self-proclaimed Serb Republic in Bosnia and Herzegovina, had alluded to the extermination of the Bosnian Muslims during parliamentary debates in 1992.[18] Between fifty thousand and one hundred thousand Bosnians of all origins had gathered in front of the parliamentary building on April 5, 1992 to protest against violence. Snipers fired at the crowd, killing demonstrators. Nowadays, the state of the parliamentary buildings epitomized the postconflict struggle for Bosnia and Herzegovina. The building's repair had been going slowly, its state of destruction a physical reminder of the unwillingness of many to strengthen common institutions. Just like the idea of a united Bosnia and Herzegovina, furthermore, the building had many detractors.

The Assembly was flanked by another historical sight: the Vrbanja bridge. It is on this bridge that the story of a young couple who became known as the Romeo and Juliet of Sarajevo came to a tragic end. Told in a documentary produced by PBS's *Frontline* and the Canadian Broadcasting Corporation (CBC),[19] their story moved many around the world. Boško Berkić and Admira Ismić met when they were sixteen at a New Year celebration in 1984, the year Sarajevo held the Winter Olympic games. He was a Bosnian Serb; she was a Bosnian Muslim – mixed couples were a common fact of life in the former Yugoslavia. Boško and Admira were each other's first and only loves. During the war, they walked several kilometers across Sarajevo, avoiding snipers all the while, to visit each other at their parents' homes. Boško, like many Bosnian Serbs who decided to stay in Sarajevo under the siege, did not want to fight. He survived by selling petrol and diesel on the black market with an associate. After his associate had secretly fled Sarajevo with military codes belonging to the Bosnian forces defending the city, Boško's neighborhood started to suspect him of being a Serb collaborator, and he was soon summoned to appear at a police station. Fearing for Boško's life, the couple decided to leave Sarajevo and planned to escape as part of a prisoner exchange arrangement on the Vrbanja bridge – a no man's land during the siege. As they crossed the bridge, snipers opened fire and Boško was killed immediately. Injured, Admira crawled back to Boško and hugged him. They died in each other's arms on the bridge. In an all too familiar display of the cruel irrationality of war, their bodies lay there for a week as opposing sides accused each other of breaking the terms of the exchange. They were finally moved to the Bosnian Serb–controlled area and buried next to each other. Admira had sent letters to Boško during his military service many years before in which she had promised that nothing could separate them. She kept her word on the Vrbanja bridge.

Bosnia and Herzegovina is replete with such stories, each of them hiding behind streets, shops, bridges, schools, and rivers.

More than fifteen years later, a few meters away from the Vrbanja bridge, the country's opposing factions were still arguing. This time, they were arguing over Lajčák's measures in their own Parliamentary Assembly at the invitation of the international community – a community very used to cyclical variations in political tensions, but alarmed now to a greater degree than usual. There was a sense that the recent developments were different.

Inside the building, the atmosphere was tense. From my chair in the back row, I watched the preoccupied faces on Bosnian politicians while each representative of the PIC countries took turns addressing them. I usually felt embarrassed for the Bosnian officials who had to listen to ambassadors constantly lecturing them during these meetings. This time, however, I secretly hoped that PIC members would send strong messages to the Republika Srpska politicians. I felt it was particularly important for the international community to appear united behind Lajčák at this moment.

Most ambassadors did, in fact, use strong language and insist on the need to comply with decisions enacted by the High Representative. This part of the session was long and seemed particularly painful for Dodik, who had to listen to criticism each time a country took the floor. Finally, it was Dodik's turn to address the members of the PIC Steering Board. As he turned his microphone on, members of the various delegations reached for their headphones and waited for the translation. Dodik had no inclination to be lectured by international officials. He directly challenged the legitimacy of Lajčák's measures and stressed that it was unacceptable for an international official to impose legislation in Bosnia in 2007. He argued that there were no reasons for Lajčák to do so and that his measures were invalid. Rather than imposing norms, Dodik argued, the international community ought to encourage local leaders to solve issues through their own democratic processes.

The head of our political department turned to me after the meeting: "The PIC better issue a very strong declaration tomorrow."

★ ★ ★

The next day the Republika Srpska National Assembly issued a formal declaration restating Dodik's earlier position that our measures were unconstitutional. The resolution also called on the members of the PIC to put an end to the powers of the High Representative. Republika Srpska officials had used their Assembly several times to increase political pressure in the past. They had done it again.

The delegations of the PIC Steering Board met with the members of the Council of Ministers. All eyes were turned toward Špirić that morning. Given his formal position as chair of Bosnia's Council of Ministers, Špirić would play an important role during the meeting. While officially representing Bosnia and Herzegovina, he would use this forum to advance Republika Srpska's position. Those were the realities of Bosnia's complex system of governance. Špirić was an important political actor in Bosnia. A team player and a smart tactician who was used to dealing with opponents in Sarajevo's parliamentary corridors, he was an ideal asset for Dodik. He had been credited with gaining the support of many of the more nationalist members of Republika Srpska's electorate during the last elections. The Bosnian Serb leadership would use him well during the crisis to come. While in a perfect position to constrain governmental action internally, he also could travel abroad and use such opportunities to publicly oppose Lajčák's measures. In many ways, Špirić's role was similar to that of former Russian President Medvedev. Dodik assumed a more discreet role as prime minister of Republika Srpska, but, just as Putin did in Russia, he remained firmly in control.

Špirić did not wait long to show his cards. Just like Dodik, he launched a full-fledged attack against Lajčák's measures. He accused him of creating a crisis and disturbing the stability of Bosnia and Herzegovina. His body language was tense and he was clearly emotional. He asked the members of the Steering Board to allow Bosnians to manage their country or to manage the country themselves. They had a clear choice: either they supported Lajčák or him, the elected representative of the people of Bosnia and Herzegovina. Should they decide to support Lajčák, an unelected official with the power to impose laws, there would be no need for him to pretend that he had any legitimacy to chair the Council of Ministers, and he would be forced to resign. If Špirić were to do so, he would, according to the law, bring down the whole Council of Ministers with him. Špirić was acting under Dodik's instructions and it became clear that Dodik and the Bosnian Serb leadership in Banja Luka had used these meetings to draw their line and send their warning. Their signal could not have been clearer to the members of the PIC Steering Board: they were ready to escalate the crisis.

The delegations then proceeded to discuss the content of the Steering Board's declaration. As they sat down to review the draft declaration, they raised few objections. Then they reached the paragraph pertaining to Lajčák's measures – and the Russian ambassador asked for the floor. There was a pause in the room.

"Here we go!" said a colleague sitting next to me.

Russia's involvement in the international efforts to end the war in Bosnia and Herzegovina had been a diplomatic success for the Clinton administration. With the Cold War just behind them, the Russians had not only supported U.S.-led diplomatic efforts but had also agreed to participate in an international military presence in Bosnia with Western countries, including the United States. After decades of Cold War dynamics, Russian and American forces worked together on the implementation of the military aspects of the Dayton peace agreement. They had common missions, common rules of engagement, a single air traffic control system, and even intelligence exchanges.[20] As members of the Steering Board of the PIC, both countries also worked together on the implementation of the civilian aspects of the peace agreement. This was no small achievement and served the international community very well during the peace implementation process in Bosnia. Having the Russians on board allowed the international community to speak with credibility when delivering messages to Bosnian Serb political leaders as Russians shared several ties with the Serbs. Both Serbia and Russia have majority populations of Christian Orthodox faith and Russia had also been Serbia's ally during the First World War – an alliance that still resonates.

In 2007, however, the U.S.-Russian relationship had become more difficult. Former members of the Soviet military establishment had not digested NATO's military intervention in Kosovo in 1999. In their view, the Soviet Union had agreed at the end of the Cold War to withdraw its troops from Germany under the understanding that NATO was not an aggressive expansionary military alliance. NATO's subsequent expansion to other countries and its 1999 military campaign in Serbia (a non-NATO country with a majority Slav population) was seen by several

They Fire Back

of them as a breach of trust.[21] Russia had opposed the U.S.-led intervention in Iraq and had more recently objected to the Bush administration's plan to build missile defense systems in Eastern Europe. It also had signaled its opposition to U.S. intentions to recognize Kosovo as an independent state. Some were speculating that the Russians would now try to use Bosnia and Herzegovina as an additional source of friction.

The Russian ambassador proposed an amendment that looked innocuous on the surface. As I read it more closely, though, I realized that the proposed amendment would significantly tie the hands of the High Representative. It referred to the need for the High Representative to consult with political parties in Bosnia and Herzegovina before enacting any future decision and stipulated that he should only enact such decisions in cases where domestic consensus had been reached. I walked to my boss who was sitting just behind Lajčák.

"Have you seen this?"

"Yes, they are trying to push through a Serb veto over the High Rep's powers," he said.

"This is crazy. We cannot let this go. I am sure they negotiated this with Dodik himself last night!"

We passed a written note to Lajčák at the main table. After a side conversation with us, Lajčák indicated to the PIC members that he could not accept the Russian amendment. He explained that it would make any future use of his powers practically impossible. He proposed new wording to defuse the impact of the proposed amendment, which forced the Russian ambassador to ask for the floor again. With a serious tone, he indicated that he could not change the wording of his amendment, as it came directly from Moscow. I thought this was pure bluff. There was no way anyone in Moscow was paying such close attention to a place like Bosnia twelve years after the end of the war. My boss jokingly observed to me that the ambassador was reading his "Moscow amendment" from a napkin. What was clear, however, was that the Russian ambassador in Sarajevo felt comfortable enough to dissociate himself from Western governments and side with the Bosnian Serbs. Lajčák asked for a break and proposed that a smaller delegation negotiate the wording of the Russian amendment in a separate room. A smaller group that included the U.S. and Russian ambassadors accompanied Lajčák.

The group came back after thirty minutes, apparently having reached an agreement. The Russians had refused to support the paragraph in the draft declaration and insisted on having a footnote in the declaration to express their "special opinion." They had agreed, however, to dilute the wording of their initial amendment. The relevant paragraph of the PIC declaration issued on October 31, 2007 noted that Lajčák's decisions and proposed actions were "fully in line with his mandate and the Constitution of BiH." It also noted that certain political leaders had "overreacted to such measures in order to create a political crisis" by challenging "the legitimacy and the authority of the High Representative and the Peace Implementation Council" and called upon Republika Srpska leaders "to abide by their obligations."

The Russian footnote indicated, on the other hand, that the Russian Federation wished to express its "deepest concern by the consequences of the measures taken by the High Representative." Taking into account "the lack of agreement on these measures among the BiH leaders," the Russian text indicated that "the elaboration of the measures in a more stable environment would have been more productive."[22] Dodik had managed to divide the PIC. Many around Lajčák were visibly disturbed.

In his press conference after the meeting, Lajčák said that he was "disappointed" by Špirić's speech and by his threat to resign. "It was over-emotional, irresponsible and insufficiently rational," he pointed out. Noting that Špirić had often complained to him about the dysfunctions in the Council of Ministers, he stated that it was his "prerogative to resign, however it would be completely irresponsible and inappropriate for him to do so."[23]

Without many illusions, we crossed our fingers in the hope that the PIC declaration and the *démarche* in Belgrade would send a strong enough message to the Bosnian Serb leadership and prevent any further escalation.

★ ★ ★

The following day, Nikola Špirić handed in his resignation as chairman of the Council of Ministers of Bosnia and Herzegovina.

They Fire Back 43

In a statement that would be reported in the international media, he said:

> Bosnia and Herzegovina is absurd. If the international community always supports the High Representative and not the institutions of Bosnia and Herzegovina, then it doesn't matter if I am the head of that state, or Bart Simpson.[24]

They had fired back.

3 The Battle

> When we arrive, around 3 AM maybe, everything is dark, with the exception of a small room that is only half lit. Commandant Navereau softly repeats the information he receives over the phone. The others stay silent. Général Roton, the *chef* of the *État-Major*, is slouched in an armchair. The atmosphere resembles that of a family keeping watch over the body of a dead family member. Georges stands up and stands in front of Doumenc. He is extremely pale: "Our front gave way at Sedan. There have been several breakdowns."[1]
>
> –Général Beaufre, describing the French État-Major's reaction when learning that German forces were attacking around the Maginot Line through Sedan in May 1940.

During the days that followed Špirić's resignation, the atmosphere in the OHR changed. Advisors in the office walked silently through corridors, looking down, absorbed in their thoughts. We were conscious of facing an outcome we could no longer entirely predict. The crisis had become our black hole. It absorbed our time, perceptions, and thoughts.

As the crisis became the center of our world, its contours became clearer. It all started to make sense. By linking his resignation to the PIC's support for the High Representative, Špirić exacerbated tensions within the PIC membership and was therefore destabilizing the system of diplomatic support behind Lajčák. He had forced the members of the PIC Steering Board to support either Lajčák – an unelected foreign representative – or the elected chair of Bosnia's central government. This maneuver put them in an uncomfortable position. While committed to the implementation of the Dayton Accords, PIC members were primarily committed to helping Bosnia become a sustainable country governed by its citizens. Were they not recognizing their own failures by supporting strong action by the High Representative twelve years after the end of the conflict? This discomfort was compounded by the desire of many EU member states, such as France, Germany, and Italy, to close down the OHR and replace it with a more discreet European Union presence in Bosnia. They were surely not too enthusiastic about supporting Lajčák's measures. As for Russia, it had made its position clear: it was willing to publically distance itself from the PIC in order to support the Bosnian Serbs.

Weakening international support for Lajčák was not the only objective that Dodik and his party were pursuing. During our initial meetings with their legal experts, it became clear that one of their main objectives was to force Lajčák to amend his decision. This became even clearer when, only a few days after having tendered his resignation, Špirić declared that he was willing to reconsider his decision in the event that Lajčák changed the amendments he had imposed. The boldness of this declaration made clear that the Bosnian Serb leadership was no longer interested in simply challenging *what* the High Representative had enacted; they were now questioning *whether* he had the authority to do so. The *rapport de force*, which had defined the relationship between the High Representative and Bosnia since the end of the conflict, was under direct challenge. The crisis came down to one simple question: Who had authority over whom in Bosnia?

Republika Srpska's strategy was motivated by several factors. First, its representatives genuinely feared the prospect of being outvoted in Bosnia's central structure of government – a fear we had seriously underestimated. Equally important was the particular antagonism that the role of the High Representative had engendered in Republika Srpska. In many ways, the Dayton peace agreement had reversed some of the gains that Republika Srpska had made during the war; persons were entitled to return to their home of origin and central state structures had to be rebuilt. Some in Republika Srpska were therefore inevitably going to perceive the international authority responsible to implement the agreement as a threat to their own exercise of power in Bosnia. Finally, an increasing number of Bosnians was growing tired of the OHR. After twelve years of international supervision, they understandably wanted to conduct their own affairs through their own democratically elected representatives and had become increasingly impatient with international officials telling them what to do. This discontent was now being channeled toward one man: Miroslav Lajčák.

This battle for amendments would be fought on a legal battleground. While demonstrations, declarations, speeches, accusations, and attacks were all taking place in the political arena, these tactics ultimately were aimed at forcing changes to paragraphs, sentences, words, and punctuation in legal texts we had prepared. Because Lajčák's changes concerned two distinct pieces of legislation – the law on the Council of Ministers and parliamentary rules of procedures – the battle for amendments would follow two tracks. The first pertained to the law on the Council of Ministers. The initial meetings we had with our counterparts from Republika Srpska had evolved into an autonomous process – which the media was now referring to as the "legal expert" process. Lajčák wanted us in the Legal Department to keep the process alive by continuing our consultations with Republika Srpska's legal experts.[2] The second track – which would unfold later – was linked to the parliamentary rules of procedures that Lajčák had instructed the Parliamentary Assembly to amend. We were to meet with parliamentarians to discuss such amendments at a later stage.

Our objective was simple: protect Lajčák's authority. According to our calculations, this could only be achieved by avoiding an amendment to his decision. The Bosnian Constitutional Court had reviewed the constitutionality of legislation enacted by the High Representative before – a review to which the High Representative had consistently consented for many years. But never had the High Representative changed the content of his decision post facto on the basis of political pressure by one party. It was important to maintain that position. One may counter that this crisis could have been easily averted if we had taken a more flexible position. But flexibility was hardly an option. Lajčák's powers were close to those of a referee during a football game. Allowing one player to overturn a referee's interpretation of the rules would have endangered the very structure of the game itself in our opinion. Given Lajčák's mandate as the final authority for interpreting the civilian aspects of the Dayton peace agreement, it was difficult to conceive how such authority could have effectively survived once overturned. To many observers, the amendments that Dodik was trying to force on Lajčák may have seemed a quick fix for a small problem. But these perceptions were misleading. Dodik was, in reality, attacking one of the pillars on which the system of international supervision in Bosnia had been established.

We were already on the defensive. By agreeing to participate in discussions on Dodik's amendments, the High Representative was, for the first time, discussing the content of his decision with parties post facto. There had been numerous instances in the past when his decisions had been enacted on the basis of consultations or recommendations by domestic commissions and working groups. But such consultations had taken place before the issuance of a decision, not after. It was therefore important for us to portray these discussions as mere consultations rather than negotiations. By doing so, we could at least pretend that these post facto consultations were justified by the particular sensitivity of the matters at hand and that, acting in good faith and realizing the particular sensitivities of the subject matter, the High Representative had decided to issue an authentic interpretation of his decision and wanted to consult parties before doing so.

As the dust from Špirić's *coup d'éclat* settled, it became clear that the outcome of the crisis depended on one major factor: Would Lajčák maintain or amend his own decision?

★ ★ ★

On November 5, we met with our counterparts from Republika Srpska. We had briefly met again in Sarajevo on October 31. Our discussions had revolved around concerns that the chair of the Council of Ministers could be permanently replaced by one of his or her deputies in case of absenteeism. We had argued that our measures did not provide for such a possibility and had agreed to meet again at the OHR field office in Banja Luka on November 5 to discuss the issue further.

The drive to Banja Luka felt particularly long that morning. Stuck in a minivan that had left Sarajevo at dawn, we reviewed the text of the authentic interpretation and made final adjustments to our strategy for the meeting. Long moments of silence followed, as everyone returned to his individual thoughts. I tried to catch some sleep. I had not been sleeping well recently. Not only was I working until late but I also was foolishly playing out scenarios in my head, trying to resolve the problem at night. Half asleep, I looked at the peaceful Bosnian landscape. It seemed particularly idyllic from the window of our minivan that morning.

My daydreaming ended as we entered Banja Luka. The OHR Banja Luka field office was somewhat bizarrely located in a residential neighborhood of the city. The several journalists standing in front of the office made it seem even stranger. Their appearance suggested that we had to present ourselves as confident and purposeful. As our van stopped in front of the office, we clumsily extracted ourselves from the vehicle. Rushing toward the office, we did our best to look busy and unstoppable. Once inside, we found ourselves in an empty conference room and realized that our meeting wasn't going to start for another thirty minutes. Looking at each other, we laughed:

"That felt particularly ridiculous!"

"Yes, and now we are stuck here!"

Such meetings amongst legal advisors rarely would attract the attention of the local media. But what had started as mere technical discussions had grown into a process covered by the media – a sign that we were not only dealing with simple amendments. There was something broader, more important at play. We knew it. So did they.

Our counterparts arrived on time. The composition of their delegation had changed. Mile Dmičić, professor at the law school of the University of Banja Luka, had joined their group. He had a gigantic red tie around his neck (which made us refer to him as "Red Tie" in many of our ensuing conversations). Snežana Savić, a former judge at the Bosnian Constitutional Court and professor at the law school of the University of Banja Luka, had joined as well. She immediately walked toward us and introduced herself with a firm handshake. Bosnian colleagues in the office respected her. Her confident attitude made me wonder if she knew something we didn't. Had they found a loophole? Is that why they were bringing new people into the process? Those were the kinds of thoughts that crossed my mind at the sight of each new participant in our discussions. We knew that, every day, many people were scrutinizing our amendments, hoping to identify flaws, and that one major deficiency meant we were in serious trouble.

The Battle

We started the meeting by explaining the changes to our draft authentic interpretation. Taking their time, they proceeded methodically and tried to demonstrate how, under the new law, Bosnian Muslim and Bosnian Croat representatives could convene a session of the Council by surprise to outvote Bosnian Serb representatives. What if they convened a session while Serb representatives were celebrating an official holiday? What if Serb representatives could not attend because of bad weather? According to them, all such scenarios were clear signs that we had opened up many possibilities for outvoting Serbs in the Council of Ministers.[3] We argued that this was not possible under the new law, but offered to address their concerns in the authentic interpretation if this would provide them with additional reassurances. They disagreed with our explanation and – to no one's surprise – insisted that the law be changed. We maintained our position and made clear that we were not mandated to discuss any amendment to Lajčák's decision. In our view, the law offered ample protection against the scenarios they had presented. With both sides again refusing to budge from their position, we ended the meeting by agreeing to meet again.

As I was stuffing things back into my briefcase, Mile Dmičić – "Red Tie" – approached me. We had been less than impressed by his interventions during the meeting. Unlike other participants, most of his comments had either been beside the point or stated purely political positions.

We exchanged a few polite words. Lowering his voice, looking around, Dmičić showed me a document. My Serbian was not good enough to continue one-on-one with him, so I had to rely on translation for the rest of the exchange:

"What is he showing us?" I asked our translator.

"It's a copy of Alija Izetbegović's *Islamic Declaration*. Do you want me to continue translating?" he replied.

He had asked the question as he knew very well where Dmičić was trying to go with this.

"No. Just tell him we are in a hurry to get back to Sarajevo before tonight," I replied.

I was stunned by this bizarre incident. The document Dmičić had shown us was a copy of the *Islamic Declaration*, a manifesto written in 1970 by Alija Izetbegović, the leading Bosnian Muslim figure behind the push for Bosnia's secession from Yugoslavia in 1992.[4] Willing to frame the Bosnian conflict as a battle between Christendom and Islamic fundamentalism, Serb propaganda had tried to portray his declaration as a blueprint to transform Bosnia into a fundamentalist Islamic state during the war. The manifesto did not call for the establishment of an Islamic state in Bosnia, in fact the document did not mention Bosnia once.[5] It was as if Dmičić had shown me a copy of a book written in the 1970s by a Bosnian politician that referred to Karl Marx's *Das Kapital* as evidence of a secret plan to transform Bosnia into a Stalinist state.

Neither was Izetbegović a fundamentalist Islamist. He had founded the Party for Democratic Action (SDA) – one of Bosnia's main political parties supported by the more nationalist segments of the Bosnian Muslim electorate. Given his position as Bosnia's wartime president, he had been its main representative during the Dayton peace process. Shortly after the Second World War, Tito's partisans arrested Izetbegović for his association with a nationalist group called Young Muslims. He was imprisoned for three years and would remain under constant police surveillance for the following decades.[6] The publication of his manifesto had led to his second imprisonment by the communist regime in the 1980s and had transformed him into one of Yugoslavia's best-known political dissidents.

While in prison, Izetbegović continued writing notes about politics and religion, using codes to replace words such as "religion," "Islam," "freedom," "authority," and "democracy." His notes – which he later published[7] – contained thoughts that could hardly qualify as the work of a fundamentalist. He wrote, for example, "Europe is strange. It considered itself the cradle and teacher of democracy and has simultaneously shown an extraordinary 'ability' for dictatorships and totalitarian ideas."[8] "When it has weapons and power, stupidity does not appear that stupid. Then we see it as strictness and danger. When it loses that power, stupidity becomes what it has been – stupidity."[9]

In his account of his efforts to end the war in Bosnia, Richard Holbrooke wrote of Izetbegović that he "had kept the 'idea' of Bosnia alive for years under the most difficult circumstances. It was an extraordinary achievement, a tribute to his courage and determination. At the age of seventy, after surviving eight years in Tito's jails and four years of Serb attacks, he saw politics as a perpetual struggle. He had probably never thought seriously about what it might mean to run a real country in peacetime. Even minor gestures of reconciliation to Serbs who were ready to re-establish some form of multiethnic community were not easy for Izetbegović. His eyes had a cold and distant gaze; after so much suffering, they seemed dead to anyone else's pain. He was a devout Muslim, although not the Bosnian ayatollah that his enemies portrayed. Yet though he paid lip service to the principle of a multiethnic state, he was not the democrat that some supporters in the West saw. He reminded me a bit of Mao Zedong and other radical Chinese communist leaders – good at revolution, poor at governance. But without him Bosnia would never have survived."[10]

Anyone who has spent enough time in Bosnia knows that the country's Muslims are among the most secularized Muslim populations in the world and would frown at attempts to link Izetbegović's declaration to the existence of a fundamentalist Islamic threat in Bosnia.[11] My reaction was no different that day as I tried to decipher the motives behind Dmičić's actions. Was he trying to convince us that our amendments were part of a secret plan to turn Bosnia into an Islamic state? Was he not aware that I had been directly involved in drafting the amendments? None of us had had any contact with Bosnian Muslim representatives during the process. Moreover, could he not see that our amendments also held sway over the interests of Bosnian Muslim representatives who had also blocked decisions by boycotts in the past? The real question in my mind was why someone like Dmičić had been included in these talks. While I disagreed with the perspective of other members of their delegation, they were competent and professional in their interactions with us. I concluded that he must have been an outlier who, by some bizarre turn of events, had managed to insert himself into the process.

On our way back to Sarajevo, we wondered about their tactics. They had still not managed to identify any serious technical deficiency with the amendments. Were they trying to buy more time and let the political pressure increase? We had survived another round of discussions, but what was their next move going to be?

★ ★ ★

The same evening, Dodik gave a long interview on a public affairs program broadcast on RTRS, Republika Srpska's public network. In his typical style, he bulldozed his way through the interview. Accusing, challenging, and attacking, he was on the offensive again. He continued to argue that Lajčák's measures were unconstitutional and contrary to the Dayton peace agreement. According to him, the measures had disturbed the balance between Bosnia's constituent peoples in a way that served the interests of the Bosnian Muslims representatives keen to build a more unified Bosnia – an indirect reference to a unitary Islamic state. There was no need for Republika Srpska representatives to participate in central institutions in which they could be outvoted. He threatened to withdraw Republika Srpska representatives from such institutions – one by one – if no solution was reached. Framing Bosnia and Herzegovina as an international protectorate, he accused the OHR of following an unacceptable logic of force, pressure, and threats. If there were no Republika Srpska, there would be no Bosnia and Herzegovina. He then announced that he had a proposal to solve the situation.

Going through the full transcript of his interview in my office the following morning, I wondered which proposal he was referring to. We had just met representatives of Republika Srpska, and none of them had shared any proposal with us. I was also struck by Dodik's reference to the interests of Bosnian Muslims to build a more unified Bosnia. Such references were tapping into fears amongst Bosnian Serbs that the majority Bosnian Muslim population's main interest was to build an Islamic state. Maybe Dmičić's views were more widespread than I would have liked to imagine. I doubted that Dodik truly believed this, but he was clearly surfing a wave of fear to strengthen his position within his constituency. Dodik's fear politics were feeding themselves from a select series of symbols and facts – a type of à la carte view of Bosnia's complex reality. This was by no means a Bosnian Serb specialty. Fear was a common political commodity in Bosnia and was promoted by Bosnian Muslim and Bosnian Croat nationalist politicians as well. I just happened to be staring at the ones spread by Dodik that morning.

Back in the secure room, we assessed the different potential courses the crisis could take. According to the assessment of our Political Department, in the weeks to come, Republika Srpska probably would continue to reject Lajčák's measures while gradually withdrawing its representatives from Bosnia's central political institutions. We also examined other potential scenarios, such as a Republika Srpska referendum on its future status or a withdrawal from newly created central administrative institutions. Our discussions then focused on Dodik. In a recent interview given to *The Economist*, Lajčák had been asked whether he would use his legal power to remove Dodik if things got worse. Lajčák had replied "with a firm 'Yes.'"[12] But could we afford to remove Dodik? Just as he had done with our recent measures, he would most probably refuse to comply with a decision that removed him from office, and we would then be dragged into a quagmire while trying to enforce our decision. Did we have the support of the PIC to go that far? Would EUFOR – the international military presence – be willing to back us up? Given the impact on regional stability of a potential declaration of independence by Kosovo next door, could the international military forces stationed in the region afford to simultaneously deal with instability in Bosnia and Kosovo? Primarily concerned about Kosovo, Western governments would be unlikely to support any increased military engagement in Bosnia.

"Well, this assumes that their mandate will be renewed in the first place."

"What do you mean?"

"In just a few weeks, the UN Security Council is supposed to renew the mandate of the international military force in Bosnia. What if Russia starts conditioning its vote?"

A sense of nervousness crept into the core organs of the OHR as we realized that we had missed another major blind spot. How could we have ended up in this mess? We could not "go all the way" if things got worse. We realized how the *rapport de force* had suddenly shifted. We were vulnerable. If Dodik had not realized this already, he soon would.

We therefore decided that it was important to refrain from any action that would turn Dodik into a political martyr. Our strategy should focus on neutralizing his impact instead. Dodik's strategy sought to illustrate that Bosnia and Herzegovina could not function without Republika Srpska. By doing so, he could claim that it was better for Bosnia to have Republika Srpska on board – under its own conditions – rather than outside. This strategy was not without risk.

By showing how it could so easily block Bosnia's central institutions, Banja Luka was exposing some of the very systemic problems that our measures were trying to redress. Some of us thought that their strategy could backfire and be turned to our advantage. The more they persisted in blocking Bosnia's central institutions, the more our measures would appear justified. In the meantime, we needed to constrain their capacity to fuel the crisis through measures that fell short of removing Dodik from power. We needed to signal to them that their intransigence prevented the international community from perceiving them as partners. Such signals could be sent by temporarily weakening the links between the international community and the Banja Luka leadership. This, we assessed, could be done through a number of actions taken gradually, such as a temporary suspension of diplomatic contacts with Dodik, the withdrawal of key diplomatic presences from Banja Luka, and visa travel bans targeting key members of its leadership to be imposed by PIC countries.

I wondered how much traction such suggestions would get within Lajčák's cabinet. A subtle boundary had started to appear between the technical departments of the OHR on one hand and Lajčák's cabinet on the other. Members of his cabinet had become more silent, less willing to argue with counterparts during meetings. The information flow had been disrupted. We started hearing complaints about poor communication from people who learned about meetings and actions after the fact. We also heard about Lajčák's growing tendency to be secretive. Considering that staff members had miscalculated the potential impact of the measures he had enacted, he had decided to take his distance from certain parts of the organization. His reaction was compounded by the fact that the OHR was not an entirely safe space. The organization was, by its very construct, a point of convergence of several states and interests. Several of the OHR staff members were seconded to the organization by various states and were expected to report back to their embassies in Sarajevo. As the crisis evolved, Lajčák would feel increasingly isolated within an organization he perceived as porous.

None of this affected us. The communication between Lajčák and our department was still very good. As far as our work with legal experts was concerned, it was clear that Lajčák wanted this process to continue. My boss and I had recently debriefed him. Sitting in the sofa in his office, he listened carefully to our explanations. Noting that their main objective was still to force an amendment to his decision, he reiterated his bottom line: there would be no change to his decision.

★ ★ ★

On November 6, Lajčák and Dodik met on Mount Jahorina, a Bosnian skiing center that had hosted competitions during the Sarajevo Winter Olympics. The mountain had been the scene of political discussions before. It was at the Heavenly Valley Hotel on Mount Jahorina that the Bosnian Serb representatives had rejected the Vance-Owen Plan in 1993.[13] The plan, named after Cyrus Vance, former U.S. Secretary of State and a UN special envoy to Bosnia, and Lord David Owen, former U.K. Foreign Secretary and an EU representative, had been one of many that sought to solve the Bosnian conflict.[14] It had proposed to divide Bosnia into ten provinces defined along ethnic lines. While maintaining Bosnia as a state, it sought to establish a weak central government while devolving substantial powers to the provinces.[15] The Bosnian government initially rejected the plan but, following immense international pressure, had finally decided to back its content. The Bosnian Serbs had rejected the plan, for it denied them one single contiguous territory. In Belgrade, Milošević – feeling the pressure of fresh UN sanctions – had decided otherwise. After initial hesitations, he became determined to force Bosnian Serbs to adopt it.[16] During a summit in Athens, conveyed with the specific aim of pressing Bosnian Serb representatives into accepting the plan, Karadžić had finally signed it.[17] But his signature had been conditioned on the approval of the Bosnian Serb self-proclaimed "parliament." Days later, Slobodan Milošević, Greek Prime Minister Konstantin Mitsotakis, and Montenegro President Momir Bulatović all traveled to Mount Jahorina to convince Bosnian Serb representatives to accept the deal. Their answer was clear: they would never accept it.[18] Neither the interests of greater Serbia nor Milošević's pressure managed to make Bosnian Serb representatives yield that day.

Dodik and Lajčák did not agree on a way out of the crisis on Mount Jahorina. After their meeting, Dodik stated that he was confident that the process between Republika Srpska and OHR legal experts would lead to a solution to the crisis. Just as he had done during his interview on RTRS the day before, Dodik alluded to a new proposal. Because no one had yet seen this proposal, we wondered what he was playing at. Was he looking for an elegant way out? Maybe he had run out of arguments and wanted to settle this issue.

Our questions were soon answered. On November 8, Minister Selman sent us a proposal regarding the law on the Council of Ministers. Colleagues in our press department were getting calls from journalists informing us that RS representatives had reportedly linked this proposal to Špirić's resignation. Their tactic was becoming clearer. They wanted to use Špirić's resignation as one last opportunity to force a change to Lajčák's decision. In order for Špirić's resignation to be effective, Bosnia's tripartite presidency needed to formally accept it. Banja Luka was sending us signals that Špirić could revoke his resignation before its formal consideration by the presidency should we accept their proposal. In Brussels to brief NATO and EU officials, Lajčák was eager to get our feedback. Our Political Department was also on our back, as it wanted to prepare its briefings for PIC ambassadors.

"Yes, we just got the changes. Give us a few minutes," we kept repeating over the phone.

As we scrutinized the proposal, our hopes of discovering an olive branch deflated quickly. Dodik's proposal was simple: it suggested two changes, which, while innocuous at first sight, struck at the very heart of Lajčák's amendments. Not only was their proposal seeking to reintroduce blockages by absenteeism, but it also tried to clog quorum and decision making in the Council of Ministers with conditions that went far beyond those that existed before our amendments.[19] Our assessment was clear: Dodik's proposal required an amendment to Lajčák's decision – which was off the table – and would render decision making in Bosnia's government more difficult than before. Once informed of our assessment, Lajčák asked the political department to inform embassies that he could not accept the proposal.

The next day, the OHR issued a press statement that indicated that the proposal "did not constitute a basis for further discussions."[20] The statement further noted that "instead of streamlining and improving the decision-making process in the Council of Ministers" the RS proposal introduced "new possibilities of blockage that did not even exist

The Battle

before the High Representative's Decision of 19 October." It noted further that the "decision of the High Representative" was "in force" and "not negotiable" but recalled that the OHR "remained open to a constructive dialogue" and stood ready to "provide an 'authentic interpretation' of the High Representative's Decision."[21]

The following Monday, the presidency accepted Špirić's resignation. We had resisted the latest push.

★ ★ ★

People from Sarajevo knew how unreliable appearances were. Most of them thought that the war would never reach Sarajevo in 1992 – a city too tolerant, too multiethnic, and too civilized to be ravaged by ethnic hatred. Yet war had finally reached the city, spreading quickly and destroying neighborhoods, streets, shops, libraries, schools, families, and friendships on its way.

It was probably such memories that fueled a certain sense of unease in Bosnia at that time. While such discomfort was not yet generalized, doubts had started to appear in some people's minds. There was a growing sense that a larger confrontation was at play beyond the outward calm. There were rumors of people stocking oil, flour, and sugar. Bosnian friends told me how they regretted teasing their grandparents who had stocked such products on the eve of conflict in 1992. This nervousness permeated our office. I remember a colleague telling me after a meeting: "One day, we may be asked to explain to a TV camera how a bunch of young international officials helped mess things up in Bosnia twelve years after the war."

None of us had gone through this war. Yet the system of international supervision in Bosnia gave the High Representative the capacity to enact measures that could potentially throw the country back into violence. A full resumption of war seemed unlikely given the international military force stationed in Bosnia. But what if our actions had triggered events that we could not fully control? Foreigners in a country we were meant to help stabilize, were we not always going to be partially disconnected from its reality despite our best intentions? Doubts started to creep into my mind.

This was compounded by the fact that the international media, which only sporadically referred to Bosnia nowadays, had recently been covering the developments in the country more closely. In just a few days, *The Economist*, *The Financial Times*, and *Le Monde* had all covered Špirić's resignation and the rise in tension in the country.[22] While their coverage still occupied a relatively minor place compared to stories from Iraq or Afghanistan, this coverage was an indicator that things were going in the wrong direction.

It was also around that period that the European Stability Initiative (ESI) published a highly critical report. The ESI was a Brussels-based think tank that had become influential in circles responsible for EU enlargement policy in the Balkans. Founded by former members of the OHR, the ESI had published several reports over the years that had been very critical of the OHR and the international community's policies in Bosnia, including a much-publicized article comparing the High Representative to a European Raj.[23] Its most recent piece argued that Bosnia's prospects for European integration were being hurt by the international "protectorate" in Bosnia.[24] Unlike Serbia, which had just recently signed a Stabilization and Association Agreement with the EU, Bosnia was prevented from making similar progress because of its failure to agree to police reform, the report underlined. It further questioned the need for Bosnia to reform its police structures and criticized Lajčák for having enacted amendments to force parties to come to an agreement. It concluded that Lajčák had "inherited a problem from the past" that he was "unlikely to be able to resolve using coercion" and that he should be seeking a way forward "through serious dialogue." According to the report's conclusion, "Bosnia, Europe and the new High Representative" deserved "to be associated with a more sophisticated and ultimately successful policy" than the one that had guided his actions so far.[25]

With momentum on his side, Špirić, acting under a caretaker mandate since his resignation, addressed the Parliamentary Assembly of Bosnia on November 13. During his address, he resumed his attacks on Lajčák's decision and framed his own resignation as an act of protest against a system that allowed foreigners to run Bosnia. Echoing the emerging sense of unease in Bosnia, Zlatko Lagumdžija, the leader of the Social Democratic Party (SDP), said during the same session that people in Bosnia were afraid to go back to 1992 and that the Assembly had a responsibility to tell them that there would be no war and no partition of the country. Lagumdžija had been part of the Bosnian government during the armed conflict. His insider awareness of the events that led to conflict in 1992 gave credibility to those claiming that Bosnia was on the verge of falling back into a spiral of violence.

On the same day, we sent a new draft of the authentic interpretation to Selman, addressing points we had discussed at our last meeting in Banja Luka. We offered to meet in Sarajevo the following week to review our changes to the interpretation.

On November 15, Lajčák was in New York to address members of the UN Security Council. According to his mandate, the High Representative submitted regular reports to the secretary-general of the UN, which he then presented to the UN Security Council.[26] However, it was not Lajčák's briefing to the UN that would reverberate back in Bosnia that day, but Špirić's sudden appearance at the Security Council. Despite his resignation, Špirić had, in another characteristic tactical maneuver, flown to New York to attend the session of the Security Council.[27]

Špirić's attendance was greeted with some disbelief in Sarajevo given that foreign policy was a competence of Bosnia's tripartite presidency under the constitution. It was unusual for the chair of the Council of Ministers – let alone one who had just resigned – to be in attendance at the Security Council. Since tendering his resignation, Špirić had not convened any session of the Council of Ministers – thus blocking Bosnia's central level of government from adopting a budget. Yet there he was, sitting in New York, attacking Lajčák's measures before the Security Council.

Back in Sarajevo, Željko Komšić, the chairman of the tripartite presidency, immediately issued a press release characterizing Špirić's actions as an attempt to undermine the presidency. Komšić also complained that his office had yet to receive any information as to who had invited Špirić to attend the Council's session, and on which grounds. This was one of many chapters of a recurrent story. Members of Bosnia's tripartite presidency regularly accused each other of misusing international forums to make statements that favored the positions of only one of Bosnia's three constituent peoples. Špirić had raised the dysfunctions to a new level; trampling on the presidency's competencies even as a nonmember.

The session of the Security Council was marked by similar dynamics to those that had permeated the PIC Steering Board session a few weeks earlier. Preliminary reports from the session in New York indicated that Russia had accused Lajčák of destabilizing the situation in Bosnia through unilateral actions. The United States, the United Kingdom, and other European members on the Council supported Lajčák's measures.

★ ★ ★

While Špirić was active on the international scene, Dodik continued his attacks on our measures back in Bosnia. He published a long op-ed in *Nezavisne Novine* and *Dnevni Avaz*, two of the country's most important dailies. His piece heavily criticized Lajčák and the OHR. Its publication in *Nezavisne Novine*, a Banja Luka daily generally supportive of Dodik's government, was hardly surprising. The same could not be said, however, about its publication in *Dnevni Avaz*, a Sarajevo-based paper with a particularly strong readership within the majority Bosnian Muslim population. Dodik, it seemed, had decided to stop talking exclusively to his own constituency and was now reaching across Bosnia's ethnic boundaries by tapping into the daily frustrations engendered by the High Representative. He argued that, because the High Representative had legislative, executive, and judicial powers, there was no need for elections, parliaments, governments, or citizens in Bosnia.[28] He wrote that the High Representative and his staff in the OHR were "universal surrogates" in Bosnia while "the citizens of BiH were simply extras in an eternal film entitled: 'I am your OHR and you shall have no other gods before me.'"[29]

Since the beginning of the crisis, we had been defending our measures as a necessary means to improve the efficiency of Bosnia's central governmental structures. Dodik constantly tried to reframe the debate as a conflict between self-determination and foreign supervision in order to broaden his support base. It was difficult to assess the extent to which he would generate any support amongst Bosnia's other constituent peoples. My guess was that he would only make marginal gains. Deeply suspicious of seeing a politician who had recently alluded to Republika Srpska's secession from Bosnia suddenly embrace Bosnian self-determination, Bosnian Muslims and Bosnian Croats were unlikely to move en masse to his side. What was clear was that

The Battle

Banja Luka was on the offensive. Willing to change its tactics, taking the initiative and looking for allies to encircle us, it kept putting the OHR on the defensive.[30]

I was immediately asked to work on potential counterarguments to each of the points Dodik had raised in his op-ed. Lajčák wanted to use them in his dealings with the media. Convinced that we were right on substance, we were losing the broader perspective. The marginal benefits of throwing more technical arguments into the public debate were low, and yet our communication strategy seemed to revolve around pouring more technical explanations onto the troubled waters of public opinion. We were merely pouring oil on water. The more technical our messages became, the more we looked merely slick.

Dodik had managed to muddy the water since day one of his opposition to our measures. Regardless of their merits, his arguments consolidated his political position. Very few people paid close attention to the technical aspects of the debate between Republika Srpska and OHR. Those who did were likely to conclude that things were not so clear; that at the center of this crisis was a difference of opinion between two sides. This, in itself, was a tactical victory for Banja Luka. In the courtroom of public opinion, it did not really matter whether we were right on substance. Banja Luka pressed its case, and no third party had any authority to solve this dispute. Yet we kept arguing that we were right.

On November 19, we met our counterparts from Republika Srpska once more in Sarajevo. Sitting in the large conference room in the OHR, we reviewed the latest version of the draft of the authentic interpretation.

With its numerous provisions hanging like bobbles and its text filled with red and green segments inserted in tracked changes, the draft started to look like a Christmas tree. While dealing with legal matters, it was hardly a purely legal document. The document had been a political instrument from the outset – a tool that gave us the necessary space and flexibility to avoid amending Lajčák's decision while keeping discussions alive. We entered the meeting wondering what additional reassurances we would add to reassure their side.

Only Selman and Lipovac had come this time. We had gone through this process together from the start. Even though we were representing diverging interests, a number of bonds had been established between us. There were smiles, longer handshakes, more candid introductory remarks. A form of mutual respect had started to take shape. We were most likely not going to see much of each other after the crisis, but until its resolution, we were destined to spend more time together.

After we explained our latest changes to the authentic interpretation, Lipovac said he was worried about the turn events had taken. Alluding to the atmosphere that prevailed before the war in 1992, he called for more understanding. Although his comments came across as genuine, I thought they were destined to increase the pressure. I was frustrated. Replaying the crisis in my mind, staring silently at Lipovac across the table, I could not help thinking: "Wait a minute! *You* guys have been fueling the crisis; *you* brought down the central government; *you* blocked the central Parliamentary Assembly; *you* support massive demonstrations throughout Republika Srpska and now you would like *us* to agree to your proposal because you are concerned about instability?"

They maintained once more that our amendments were unconstitutional as they opened the possibility of Republika Srpska representatives being outvoted in the Council of Ministers – a point we had consistently disagreed with. Again, they pushed for amendments to Lajčák's decision that would impose more stringent requirements for a quorum. Finally, they presented us with a written opinion that outlined the aspects of Lajčák's decision they found problematic. We agreed to examine it, send our response in writing, and meet again in Banja Luka the following Tuesday.

After the meeting, there was a growing sense that we were soon going to reach the limits of this process. Our meetings with the Republika Srpska legal experts had been convenient for both sides: it bought time for all of us. However, we had now discussed the amendments to the law on the Council of Ministers from almost all possible angles. There was little more we could add to address their concerns. The broader battle was still raging, and neither side had given in. They still wanted Lajčák to amend his decision. We had managed to avoid such an outcome. How long could this go on?

★ ★ ★

"Philippe, can you pass by my office?"

The Battle

It was Jozef Pandur, Lajčák's senior advisor on the phone. A Hungarian former ambassador to Serbia and Montenegro, he had been advising Lajčák during his work on the independence referendum process in Montenegro. Pandur was Lajčák's closest advisor. Both diplomats from Eastern European countries, they were of similar age. He had a round face with shocks of unruly white hair. His big glasses and his thick Eastern European accent made him look like a character out of a spy novel by John le Carré. He rarely intervened during meetings. Sitting in silence, he listened to other participants and took notes.

Only a few weeks into his mandate, it was he whom Lajčák had asked to solve the complex police reform deadlock. Thrown into this process with little advance preparation, he had displayed a pragmatic and focused approach. Conducting a series of meetings with the parties, he had tried to identify possible common ground. During internal discussions about whether the new proposal should refer to the new state police force as "Police of Bosnia and Herzegovina," "Bosnia and Herzegovina Police," "BiH Police," or "State Police," and conscious that we were trying to placate Bosnian Serb opposition to any symbol alluding to the centralization of their police – Pandur said calmly: "Let's just call it "Police."

Pandur's efforts had culminated in Dodik's refusal to endorse police reform. It was this very refusal that had convinced Lajčák to take tough measures intended to force Dodik to back an agreement. This lack of success had not diminished Pandur's influence. Police reform was the toughest nut to crack. Many people had failed to secure agreement on police reform. My relations with him were good. He and Lajčák had occasionally invited me to play doubles against them at one of Sarajevo's tennis centers. Pandur never missed an opportunity to tease me when the score was in his favor.

I made my way up to his office immediately after I hung up the phone. His office was located on the fifth floor of our building, close to Lajčák's. I found him sitting on his sofa. Next to him was a young man who introduced himself as a diplomat from the Hungarian embassy in Sarajevo. As I sat, Jozef explained that they had been thinking about ways to solve the disagreement over the law on the Council of Ministers. Slightly puzzled, I listened to the Hungarian diplomat, who had started explaining his solution. He suggested conditioning the decision-making rules in the Council of Ministers to the votes of its chair and two deputy chairs. According to their suggestion, final decisions of the Council would need to be supported by a majority of its members, which in turn needed to include the votes of the chair and deputy chairs. I was stunned. Just as in Dodik's earlier proposal, this proposal would make decision-making in the Council even more difficult than it was under the very law we had amended. We had been trying to remove several conditions to decision making in the Council, but their suggestion brought the conditions back with a vengeance.[31] More important, their proposal would have required Lajčák to amend his decision – something he had instructed us to avoid at all cost. I interrupted the man from the Hungarian embassy: "I don't think we can do that. First, this is worse than what we had before. Second, it requires an amendment to Lajčák's decision. This would have huge consequences, and the Peace Implementation Council would need to be consulted before we ever do this!"

"Understood. We are simply trying to be helpful," Jozef replied calmly.

The conversation stopped there. I left Jozef's office puzzled and rushed back to work.

Bumping into my boss later in the day, I told him about the meeting: "I was called to Jozef's office to meet a guy from the Hungarian embassy who proposed that we condition the Council's decision-making rules to the votes of the chair and the two deputy chairs as a way out."

"This would require an amendment."

"That's what I told them."

"Why is Jozef suddenly included in this? I thought we were the leads on this?"

"You tell me," I replied.

It was difficult to interpret the significance of this meeting with Jozef. Was there a second channel of discussions above ours? Why was someone from the Hungarian embassy suddenly involved in discussions on a potential solution to the crisis? Hungary was not even a member of the PIC Steering Board. Little did I know that all these questions would be answered within the next few days.

4   The Defeat

> You have, as leaders of your country, proven the "Cassandras" wrong – those who predicted an eternal political crisis or even worse. Instead, Bosnia and Herzegovina has been able to break the political stalemate and take a major step on its road towards European integration. Bosnia and Herzegovina should and will become master of its own destiny in the framework of the European Union and European integration.
> –Olli Rehn, EU Commissioner for Enlargement, Sarajevo, December 4, 2007[1]

As we moved deeper into the crisis, the sense of division between Lajčák's cabinet and the rest of the organization sharpened. Trust was eroding. Sitting in the secure room to discuss potential avenues to resolve the crisis, a member of the cabinet distributed a document to heads of departments and advisors. I remember the long looks exchanged when he explained how slight variations in language had been inserted in each copy in order to trace back potential leaks.

The pressure was building on Lajčák. He had arrived in Bosnia hoping to quickly stabilize the country by reigniting its EU integration process. Several months later, the country was stuck in a deep political confrontation with little prospect of satisfying European demands that it reach agreement on police reform. The relatively small size of Slovakia meant that Lajčák was not as inoculated from domestic pressure as his predecessors who came from larger European states. These dynamics were highlighted as reports reached our office of a meeting between Špirić and Slovakia's prime minister scheduled to take place on November 22. "Why is the prime minister of Slovakia meeting with Špirić? He is actively undermining Lajčák in Bosnia," I thought. Just as he had used his position to attend the meeting of the UN Security Council in New York, Špirić was now using his position to court a close source of support to Lajčák: the government of his own country. On November 22, Špirić was welcomed to Bratislava on an official visit.

On the same day, back in Bosnia, Lajčák met with the party leaders of the country's governing coalition. He hoped he could convince them to reach an agreement on police reform and agree to the measures he had enacted. In a press release issued the day before, Lajčák said: "EU requirements will not go away, and party leaders must finally meet their commitments and deliver results."[2] An agreement did emerge from the meeting, but our hopes were, once again, short-lived. The agreement fell short of meeting the conditions the European Union had set for an acceptable deal on police reform.[3] The agreement's text provided for the establishment of several coordinating bodies and postponed the elaboration of a police structure in line with EU conditionality to a future constitutional reform process.[4] It was as if members of the U.S. Congress had agreed to reform the United States tax code, but only as part of a future reform of the United States constitution. The agreement fell far below the conditions maintained by the European Commission.

Meanwhile, the crisis continued to generate international interest. On November 25, Richard Holbrooke expressed his concern over the situation in Bosnia and Kosovo in a column published in the *Washington Post*. Troubled by the rising tensions between the United States and Russia over the future of Kosovo, Holbrooke noted: "Exactly 12 years after the Dayton peace agreement ended the war in Bosnia, Serb politicians, egged on by Moscow and Belgrade, are threatening that if Kosovo declares its independence from Serbia, then the Serb portion of Bosnia will declare its independence. Such unilateral secession, strictly forbidden under Dayton, would endanger the more than 150,000 Muslims who have returned there."[5] He continued: "Using some of his petrodollars, Putin turned its mildly pro-Western leader, Milorad Dodik, into a nasty nationalist who began threatening secession. The vaunted Atlantic alliance has yet to address this problem at a serious policy level." Fearing further destabilization in the region,

The Defeat

Holbrooke called on the Bush administration to temporarily deploy additional troops in the region to prevent a return to violence.

The following day, *The Guardian* printed a piece highly critical of the OHR strategy: "By changing the way the ethnically-based quorum is calculated, Lajčák's decision removes the requirement of consensus amongst Bosnia and Herzegovina's three constituent nations – Bosniaks, Bosnian Croats and Bosnian Serbs – potentially allowing for one of the constituent nations to be outvoted by the other two. By insisting that he will impose the reforms if they are not adopted by December 1, Lajčák has further stifled the development of representative elected bodies and a democratic culture. Issues of this importance and magnitude need to be dealt with through full and frank discussion amongst Bosnia and Herzegovina's political elites and citizens, not through stated technical-bureaucratic initiatives. As the departed Špirić observed, Bosnia and Herzegovina 'is unfortunately not a sovereign state.'"[6]

The pieces in the *Washington Post* and *The Guardian* reflected the broader tension between the two main perspectives on the role of the international community that had plagued Lajčák's mandate from day one. Two groups of states were asking him to pursue different trajectories. On one hand, the United States and the United Kingdom favored a more assertive use of the High Representative's authorities and had been particularly supportive of Lajčák's measures during the crisis. On the other hand, officials from the EU institutions in Brussels as well as EU members states such as France, Germany, Italy, Sweden, and Greece thought he had gone too far already and that his actions were slowing down Bosnia's progress toward EU membership. Given that most Bosnians aspired to join the European Union, there were, according to their perspective, sufficient systemic incentives to foster agreements amongst Bosnia's divided groups.

The dynamics of Lajčák's cabinet had imported this broader tension. Some members thought that the powers of the High Representative were, despite attempts to revive them, no longer effective. Others believed that Lajčák had enough support to use them assertively. This tension, which had permeated discussions in Lajčák's cabinet from the start of his mandate, were now shaping debates on how to solve the crisis. Looking ahead, strategic options gradually coalesced around two main avenues: remaining firm until the Republika Srpska leadership complied with the measures enacted or accepting a number of compromises to get out of the crisis. Lajčák had remained firm since the beginning of the crisis and had consistently refused any change to his decision. His directives to us remained intact: no change to his decision.

It is within this framework that we continued participating in discussions regarding his measures. The governing coalition's meeting of November 22 had reenergized discussions on the amendments to parliamentary rules of procedure Lajčák had proposed on October 19. He had made it clear that, should the Parliamentary Assembly fail to remove blockages by absenteeism from its decision-making process by December 1, he would enact these amendments himself. The Republika Srpska leadership had instructed Republika Srpska representatives to boycott the Parliamentary Assembly in the event Lajčák enacted such changes.

With only a few days left before the expiration of the December 1 deadline, discussions in the Parliamentary Assembly intensified. The chair and vice chairs of the House of Representatives and the House of Peoples had requested that we be present during their discussions scheduled for November 28 to answer a number of points regarding the amendments that Lajčák had proposed.

We spent most of the day on November 27 preparing for the meeting. We examined a number of points raised in previous parliamentary discussions. Members from Republika Srpska had argued that Lajčák's proposed changes would, if enacted, allow the Parliamentary Assembly to adopt constitutional amendments without the vote of any representative from Republika Srpska. Neither Lajčák's proposed amendments nor the constitution allowed for such an outcome.[7] Although false, the suggestion played on powerful fears. We decided to counter it during our parliamentary discussions. I worked on a note outlining our position, which we intended to share with members of the Parliamentary Assembly during our meeting.

On the same day, Lajčák met in Brussels with EU Commissioner for Enlargement Olli Rehn. According to the account of their meeting, Lajčák told Rehn that the international community no longer enjoyed the power to enforce decisions in Bosnia – something Milorad Dodik was now aware of. For Lajčák, progress on EU integration was the only way to get Bosnia out of the crisis. Lajčák suggested to Rehn that although the latest agreement reached on November 22 fell short of complying with European conditionality, the EC ought, nevertheless, to consider it acceptable in order to open the way for a Stabilization and Association Agreement (SAA) with Bosnia. He would then be in a position to use the prospects of an SAA as leverage with Bosnian leaders to find a way out of the crisis. By delaying agreement to police reform until a later stage, the EC would not be seen as publically backing down from its own conditions. Rehn expressed concerns that such a course of action could be interpreted as a form of reward for Dodik's obstruction. Unable to commit to his proposal immediately, Rehn nevertheless called Lajčák later to confirm that he would go ahead with his suggested approach.

This information dropped like a bomb on those of us directly involved with the crisis at the OHR. I thought that Lajčák's proposed approach would seriously undermine the credibility of the EU in Bosnia, and by extension, that of the broader international community. The EU had been maintaining publicly for several years that any agreement on police reform needed to comply with its three basic conditions. Only a few months prior, while addressing the members of Bosnia and Herzegovina's Parliamentary Assembly, Olli Rehn had been explicit about this issue: "We need concrete results on police reform to improve the security and law enforcement in the country. It is important that the state and entity authorities, together with the political parties, finally agree on the reform in line with the Police Directorate's proposal and the three EU principles. I am concerned and disappointed for the lack of agreement on the police reform. Without an agreement there will be no SAA," he had told the assembly.[8] While the EC would try to argue that it had simply agreed to postpone the need for an agreement on police reform, it would nevertheless be clear that it had effectively agreed to dilute its own conditions. By postponing a solution to police reform until constitutional reform (an even more difficult and contentious process), the EC had effectively buried police reform. There was no doubt that its decision rewarded Republika Srpska's resistance.

Looking back, these developments should have been sufficient signals warning us of what was coming. But at the time, I thought that EU credibility was a matter for the EU to assess and that Rehn's decision was based on longer-term considerations that escaped us in Sarajevo. I did not subscribe to the dichotomies drawn between a hard and soft approach. These approaches were not mutually exclusive. Bosnia's capacity to progress toward the EU was not contingent upon disarming the High Representative. The use of the High Representative authorities would – as it had for many years now – continue to gradually decrease as Bosnia's progressed on this path. The powers of the High Representative were part of a transition toward European integration. They acted as an insurance policy. No one could predict future events in Bosnia with absolute accuracy. What if things unraveled? What if European integration on its own proved unable to prevent Bosnia from spiraling downward? The powers of the High Representative were a matter for the PIC to decide, not Brussels.

More important, the authorities of the High Representative and those of the European Union were closely intertwined. The High Representative acted as the European Union special representative in Bosnia. The police reform process had been instigated by the Office of the High Representative, but the EU had made it an explicit milestone for Bosnia to enter into a Stabilization and Association Agreement. Sacrificing the powers of the High Representative was bound to affect the legitimacy and credibility of the EU's own capacity to effect outcomes in the future – something that some in Brussels seemed to be either overlooking or underplaying. We had fought for weeks to prevent changes to Lajčák's measures in order to protect the integrity of these powers. It was with these considerations in mind that we continued to do so in the days that followed despite reports of the November 27 meeting in Brussels.

★ ★ ★

The following day, our team headed to the Parliamentary Assembly to meet with the chairman and vice chairmen – a triumvirate called *Collegium* – of the House of Representatives and the House of Peoples. Given that changes to parliamentary rules of procedure had to be adopted by both houses, discussions were held in a joint session – a format called *extended Collegium*. Beriz Belkić from the Party for Bosnia and Herzegovina (SBIH), Niko Lozančić of the Croatian Democratic Union (HDZ), and Milorad Živković of the Alliance for Independent

The Defeat

Social Democrats (SNSD) formed the Collegium of the House of Representatives while Ilija Filipović from the Croatian Democratic Union (HDZ), Mladen Ivanić from the Party of Democratic Progress (PDP), and Sulejman Tihić of the Party of Democratic Action (SDA) formed that of the House of Peoples.

Sitting opposite the members of the extended Collegium, we answered questions for several hours. We made clear that Lajčák's proposed changes did not allow for any constitutional amendment to be adopted without representatives of Republika Srpska being present. Mladen Ivanić, an experienced politician from Republika Srpska, relentlessly asked us questions about previous opinions issued by the OHR that, according to him, directly contradicted the basis of Lajčák's proposed changes. We countered that there was no such contradiction and that, in any case, it would be difficult to see how Lajčák would be bound by positions expressed by a subdivision of the OHR several years before. Some of the extended Collegium's deliberations focused on a proposal by which sessions of both houses could be suspended in cases where representatives of an entity were absent. In our opinion, the proposed suspension provided additional reassurances without reintroducing the possibility to block decisions by absenteeism, and were consequently an avenue worth exploring. By the end of its session, the extended Collegium failed to reach agreement. Its members decided to reconvene the following day and invited us to join their discussions.

Back in the office, we debriefed about our meeting and prepared for the following day. I stayed in the office late that evening, reviewing the text of an op-ed the lead legal advisor at Dayton had offered to submit to the local Bosnian media. His piece supported our measures and argued that the parties at Dayton had not intended to design entity protection mechanisms in ways that allowed representatives of one entity to block decisions in the House of Representatives through boycotts. This was good news. I hoped the op-ed would get published quickly, as it directly contradicted claims made by Republika Srpska officials to the effect that our measures were unconstitutional and anti-Dayton.

On November 29, the extended Collegium resumed its discussions and proved, once more, unable to reach agreement. Frustration increased as accusations and counteraccusations dominated the deliberations. Judging by the rigidity of positions defended, it appeared as if some members had already concluded that the solution would not be reached within this forum. We also were becoming more entrenched in our position. After having spent many weeks defending our own measures, our perspectives were more polarized. We repeated that Lajčák's measures were in line with the constitution and with the Dayton peace agreement.

A member of the extended Collegium then suggested to simply copy the relevant provisions of the constitution to replace the most contentious proposed amendment to the rules of procedure. We intervened and explained why this apparent solution was, in our opinion, inadequate. Blockages through boycotts were consequences of a misinterpretation of the constitution that needed to be corrected. Merely recopying the text of the constitution would consequently not solve anything. Some members suggested that Lajčák should attend their next session in person. We declined to comment, cognizant that involving Lajčák in a deeply divided forum with no prospect of any agreement was a recipe for disaster. We emerged, once more, from several hours of discussions with no agreement in sight.

Analyzing the dynamics of the meeting on our way back to the office, we had a sense that we were isolated. We knew that representatives from Republika Srpska would do everything to prevent an agreement on Lajčák's proposed changes. But there was hardly any pushback against their resistance. The Bosnian Croat and the Bosniak representatives, generally supportive of measures strengthening the central state structures, were far from forming a common front. Niko Lozančić, the Bosnian Croat representative from HDZ, had proposed amendments that would have either reintroduced blockages by absenteeism in the work of the assembly or left the problems unresolved. Belkić, the other Bosniak representative, had only rallied lately behind Lajčák's measures and appeared relatively quiet during the proceedings. Only Tihić from the SDA seemed to energetically support the substance of Lajčák's measures.

On the same day, we learned that Lajčák had gone to Banja Luka to meet with Dodik. We had not been asked to submit any talking points or provide any update on where we stood in the technical discussions. The sense of frustration about the secretive manner in which Lajčák's cabinet was proceeding had now reached our team. Things were not

The Defeat 73

moving in the right direction. We had been asked to lead technical negotiations from day one and felt that we, just like other parts of the organization, were now being kept in the dark. What was going on exactly, and why were we not informed?

★ ★ ★

I learned about Lajčák's intentions the following morning as I showed up in my boss's office.
"Lajčák has decided to strike a deal," he said.
"What? Are you serious?" I replied.
"Yes, I think this is the end."
I made my way to the daily morning briefing where Lajčák planned to announce his decision.

★ ★ ★

The atmosphere in Lajčák's office was tense. Advisers, department heads, and liaison officers silently sat around the large conference table as I entered. I was one of the last people to make it to the meeting. Someone pulled up a chair for me. I sat directly across from Lajčák at the other end of the table.

Speaking quickly, he announced that he had found a solution to the crisis. He explained the modalities of his solution. First, he would provide additional guarantees against outvoting in the Council of Ministers by requiring that any decision needed to include the vote of the chair and deputy chairs of the Council of Ministers. These additional guarantees were, according to him, acceptable to Republika Srpska. I was confused. "But ... these are the arrangements Pandur and the representative of the Hungarian embassy proposed to me the week before! It requires a change to his decision," I thought. Lajčák moved on quickly to preempt any questions, insisting that this solution did not require any change to his decision.

He then explained how the problem with the rules of procedures in the assembly would be resolved. From the explanations given, I understood that the extended Collegium would simply copy the relevant provisions of the constitution in the most contentious provision of the rules of procedure. Lajčák would personally attend the session today and give his blessing to this solution. These were the very changes that we had rejected the day before for leaving the most crucial component of the problem unaddressed.

Finally, the Council of Ministers would adopt the action plan on police reform agreed upon by the coalition party leaders on November 22. The European Commission was now willing to consider the agreement as sufficient to initial the SAA with Bosnia. Commissioner Rehn and EU High Representative Javier Solana had agreed to be in Sarajevo on December 4 for the SAA initialing. Lajčák would use their visit and the prospect of an SAA as leverage to ensure that parties agreed to the solution he had outlined. The room was silent. Many of us around the table were in a state of confusion and disbelief. He adjourned the meeting swiftly and asked that all departments immediately start working on the implementation of the solution.

It all made sense now. I was able to connect the visit to Brussels to the broader political crisis. Lajčák's meeting in Brussels was not only about police reform. It was about the entire crisis. Lajčák had tried to restore the authorities of the High Representative. But, as he had tried to do so, he had faced profound divisions within the international community which, in his opinion, had prevented him from restoring such authorities. Under immense pressure, he had decided to rely on the European integration pull factor to extract the country from its current quagmire. An able and intelligent diplomat, Lajčák took a controversial decision – one that other diplomats would certainly have taken in his position given the tremendous pressure he faced.

I, however, disagreed with his decision. While certainly preferable, full consensus in the international community had never been a requirement to move forward until then. A great number of actions undertaken by previous High Representatives had failed to achieve full consensus in the Peace Implementation Council, but were nevertheless implemented. While it was true that the powers of the High Representative had been eroded by his predecessor, the powers were not dead. They were being challenged. With the support of the United States and the United Kingdom, Lajčák was in a good position to remain firm. Many options, short of removing Dodik, remained available to him such as diplomatic isolation, travel bans, asset freezes, and suspension of aid programs to Republika Srpska. The price paid to extract the country from the crisis was too high in my mind. Rather

The Defeat

than using EU integration to overcome resistance to police reform and functional state institutions, we would be using it to convince everyone else to accept the conditions set by those who had obstructed these processes. As I walked back to my office, a colleague told me: "This is a garage sale. Dodik got everything he wanted for 1/10 of the price. We caved in on police reform, the Council of Ministers and the parliamentary rules of procedure."

As I analyzed further the modalities of Lajčák's solution to the law on Council of Ministers, it became clear that we had consented to a change in the substance of the decision. There would be no amendment to the law. But Lajčák wanted the additional guarantees included in the authentic interpretation on which we had been working for weeks. From a legal point of view, it hardly made any sense. The interpretation would be adding conditions that were not foreseen by the law. Moreover, the guarantees secured by Lajčák made decision making in the Council of Ministers even more difficult than it was before we enacted changes on October 19.[9] The solution to the parliamentary rules of procedure was hardly better. Recopying the integral text of the constitution failed to clarify the most crucial point at the center of the debate over the parliamentary decision-making procedure.[10] While many changes enacted in October 2007 would remain in force, they were mostly secondary and accessory in nature. Standing on their own, they did not remedy the problem we had tried initially to solve. Blockages by absenteeism would be removed from the decision-making processes of parliamentary committees, but would remain available for the final vote in the House of Representatives.

I had to draft the provisions outlining the additional guarantees in the authentic interpretation. It all came down to this. Weeks of discussions and negotiations were now going to be condensed into a few lines inserted in a legal interpretation. It was one of the most painful passages I have ever had to write. I opposed this solution. I had fought to prevent this outcome. I now had to write it down myself. Defeats need to be recorded. Someone, somewhere officially registers defeat, records its occurrence. Someone must draft the agreement to put an end to a given battle. Those who do so are often third parties or belong to the victorious side. In our case, we had to draft the terms of our own defeat, and that task had administratively trickled down to me.

The office functioned as usual on that day. Looking from my window, I could see diplomats in their official cars coming and leaving. They were now briefed on the solution of the crisis. Nuances and technical details would be downplayed; they would be relieved initially that the crisis was over. But a tectonic plate had shifted. I was registering its movement on my computer without knowing exactly whether or how my immediate environment would be affected.

★ ★ ★

On December 4, Olli Rehn flew to Sarajevo to initial the Stabilization and Association Agreement. EU High Representative Javier Solana was unable to make it because of bad weather. During the initialing ceremony, Rehn said: "I want to congratulate the leaders of Bosnia and Herzegovina, in particular, for acting in a true European spirit of compromise and paving the way for a normalisation of the political situation and for the implementation of police reform. You have, as leaders of your country, proven the 'Cassandras' wrong – those who predicted an eternal political crisis or even worse. Instead, Bosnia and Herzegovina has been able to able to break the political stalemate and take a major step on its road towards European integration. Bosnia and Herzegovina should and will become master of its own destiny in the framework of the European Union and European integration. I want to thank EU Special Representative Miroslav Lajčák as well for his substantial contribution to this watershed of a political development in Bosnia and Herzegovina."[11]

I had dinner with friends from the diplomatic corps in Sarajevo that day. I offered my version of events and how I thought they would negatively affect the authority of the international community. I explained at length that the amendments enacted masked a broader defeat. "Those that were finally enacted are only accessory measures that we developed to implement the main ones," I insisted. They looked at me with polite smiles. Fearing to be seen as someone refusing to let go, I stopped talking. My perceptions had been blurred by the last few weeks. I had lost the broader picture. Maybe my personal involvement prevented me from analyzing this more calmly and objectively so soon after the facts. Maybe this was not as serious as I thought. I surely had exaggerated the importance of these events and gotten caught up in my own disconnected narrative. "Maybe I have

The Defeat

been wrong all along," I wondered in the taxi taking me back home that night.

★ ★ ★

On December 5, going through our media reports, I noticed that Džerard Selman, the minister of justice from Republika Srpska and one of our counterparts during the discussions on the law on the Council of Ministers, had given an interview to *Nezavisne Novine*. "The Expert legal team of the Republika Srpska government has proved that the decisions of the High Representative can be changed, because we, with our legal arguments, we have managed to have a norm changed through the authentic interpretation, which had never happened in the past, but they simply had no other option," he said.[12] While many people were still trying to see more clearly through the fog of the crisis, a few people in Republika Srpska knew exactly what had happened. Dodik, who had resisted EU demands to reform the police for years and who had just refused to comply with decisions of the High Representative, came out of this crisis with the firm belief that the international community was neither able nor willing to implement its will in Bosnia like it once did.

★ ★ ★

In February 2008, I tended my resignation from the OHR. I had been invited to head the legal department of the International Civilian Office (ICO) in Kosovo. Kosovo was meant to declare its independence soon, and the ICO was responsible to supervise and support Kosovo's accession to statehood. I had gone back and forth about the resignation, but ultimately the sense that we had failed to live up to our responsibilities was so strong that I was unable to continue working with the same level of motivation as before. I entered the office of the head of administration at OHR. A tall, athletic man with piercing eyes, he looked calmly at my letter before saying:
"This must be the shortest letter of resignation I have ever seen."
"There is little else to say, really."

★ ★ ★

Lajčák resigned from his position as High Representative on January 22, 2009 to become Slovakia's minister for foreign affairs. "I don't want to be the rider on a dead horse," he noted after his resignation.[13] Valentin Inzko, an Austrian diplomat, replaced Lajčák as High Representative.

Lajčák would reengage with Bosnia and Herzegovina in 2011 in the midst of another political crisis. The initialing of the Stabilization and Association Agreement in 2007 had failed to stabilize the situation in the country. Bosnia and Herzegovina had spiraled down into a state of generalized dysfunction. New elections in 2010 had strengthened the hand of Zlatko Lagumdžija, the leader of Bosnia's socialist party (SDP). Milorad Dodik's party (SNSD) also had done relatively well. Dodik had left his functions as prime minister of Republika Srpska to become its president.

The political crisis that rocked Bosnia in 2011 began in the Federation of Bosnia and Herzegovina, one of Bosnia's two entities. Lagumdžija's party sought to form a government in the federation without the support of HDZ and HDZ 1990 – the two main Bosnian Croat parties. This maneuvering triggered waves that extended beyond the entity. While a government in the federation could be formed without the HDZ and HDZ 1990, their support was nevertheless required to form a government at the central state level. Lagumdžija's maneuvering in the federation had angered HDZ and HDZ 1990. Both parties had decided to block his attempt to form a government at the central state level. It would take more than a year for a coalition to reach an agreement on the formation of the country's central government.[14]

The SDP's attempt to marginalize Bosnian Croat nationalists from government led to the establishment of a self-proclaimed "Croat National Assembly" in Mostar in April 2011, a body allegedly responsible for coordinating policy in municipalities and cantons with Bosnian Croat majorities.[15] These actions – reminiscent of past Bosnian Croat nationalist maneuvering either at the earlier stage of the 1992–5 armed conflict or during the peace implementation process in 2001 – were not the only worrisome developments.[16] The exclusion of the Bosnian Croat nationalists in the federation had created political opportunities for Republika Srpska's leadership to further undermine Bosnia's central state structures. In April 2011, the National Assembly of Republika Srpska adopted conclusions that considered the authorities in the federation illegitimate.[17] The move consolidated dangerous centrifugal synergies between the Bosnian Croat and Bosnian Serb nationalists.

The measures examined by the Republika National Assembly that day did not only address the legitimacy of federation authorities. They also directly attacked central state institutions.[18] The assembly's conclusions argued that a number of central state institutions had been established pursuant to unconstitutional and illegal transfers of competencies – a position that finds no support in Bosnian constitutional law.[19] But more important, the assembly had decided to call for a referendum seeking to ask the population of Republika Srpska whether it supported laws imposed by the High Representative in Bosnia, in particular the laws that had established Bosnia's state court and prosecutor's office. Having successfully blocked international efforts to rebuild and strengthen state institutions in 2007, Republika Srpska was now embarking on a campaign to challenge the legitimacy of the state institutions. The question of the referendum read as follows:

> Do you support the laws imposed by the High Representative of the International Community in Bosnia and Herzegovina, particularly those pertaining to the Court of Bosnia and Herzegovina and the Prosecutor's Office of Bosnia and Herzegovina, and their unconstitutional verification in the Parliamentary Assembly of Bosnia and Herzegovina?[20]

The tone of Milorad Dodik's speech before the assembly that day illustrated the extent to which he had further radicalized his positions since 2007. The face of nationalism was now fully in front of its mask, unrestrained. Dodik, the very man who had kept his distance from the Bosnian Serb nationalists during the war and who had agreed to constitutional amendments to reinforce state institutions in 2006, was now framing international efforts to rebuild the country's state institutions as part of a wider plot to help Bosniaks establish a centralized Islamic state against the will of Bosnian Serbs and Bosnian Croats. Dodik's remarks made no mention of the numerous Peace Implementation Council declarations that have reaffirmed continuously the existence of Republika Srpska under Dayton. Although international strategy has surely focused on rebuilding and strengthening state institutions in the aftermath of the war, the idea that this process had been carried out to abolish Republika Srpska was absurd. Not once during the many years I had worked at the OHR had I encountered an international official who even contemplated such an idea. On the contrary, many of us spent numerous hours seeking to ensure that the responsibilities of Bosnia's entities were respected as we implemented the peace agreement. Colleagues made fun of the vigor with which I defended the spheres of competencies of entities and jokingly drew parallels between my Québécois origins and my propensity to defend Republika Srpska's constitutional position during internal debates.

These realities had no place in Dodik's speech that day. Trying to depict Bosnian Muslims as vectors of a broader Islamization project, he said: "If in the civil war in which nations fought against each other, and Bosniaks even mutually as well, there were about 100.000 victims, of whom nearly 30.000 Serbs, the question is then who killed them often after gruesome tortures. When that was not enough, then they cut their heads to serve as monstrous trophies, for the purpose of new recruitments of Mujahideens around the world. In this, for Muslims, holy war, the jihad against the infidels non-Muslims in BiH, the future Islamic terrorists were trained to kill innocent people around the world."[21]

It is within this context that Lajčák intervened in Bosnia and Herzegovina in 2011. EU High Representative Catherine Ashton had appointed Lajčák as managing director in the European Union External Action Service after his tenure as Slovak foreign minister. His new position threw him, once again, into a political crisis in Bosnia. Lajčák and Ashton convinced the Republika Srpska leadership to abandon its plans to hold a referendum. In exchange, a "structure dialogue" with Bosnia and Herzegovina and the European Commission on judicial matters would be launched. This process, which had been used in neighboring Croatia as part of the EU integration process, managed to convince Dodik to abandon his referendum plans. But many international officials in Bosnia were highly critical of what they saw as another quick fix. Chief amongst those voices was that of Paddy Ashdown who, in an interview with *The Telegraph*, criticized Lajčák and Ashton's deal. "I think it was bought at a price which we shouldn't have paid," he said.[22] "The EU has always preferred the path of the short term, anything to avoid a crisis rather than facing up to the issues....

The Defeat

I think the effect has been to enhance the status of the person, Dodik, who is leading the process of breaking up Bosnia and diminishing the standing of the EU and its foreign minister," he added.[23]

After the defeat inflicted on the OHR in 2007, the international community had been unable to prevent Bosnia's downward spiral. The European integration gamble of 2007 started to show worrisome cracks. The OHR authorities could now only partially contain Republika Srpska's campaign to dismantle state institutions. While the authority of the OHR was still enforced in part of the country, that no longer was the case in Republika Srpska. The European Union's decision to reinforce its presence in Bosnia had not changed the course of events. A report published by the International Crisis Group published in May 2011 noted: "Virtually all international institutions in Bosnia have lost authority; many, including the Office of the High Representative (OHR), are seen as favouring one side or party. Local leaders demand support from OHR and state institutions alike and ignore rulings that go against them. There is no broadly respected authority in the country, only regional or partisan champions."[24]

Part II Reflections on the Battle

5 Nonviolent Wars

> [T]he ultimate outcome of a war is not always to be regarded as final. The defeated state often considers the outcome merely as a transitory evil, for which a remedy may still be found in political conditions at a later date.
>
> —Carl von Clausewitz[1]

In 1961, the Swedish Academy awarded the Nobel Prize for literature to Ivo Andrić. Born in the northern town of Travnik in Bosnia at the end of the nineteenth century, Andrić was one of those exceptional characters who seem to take part in every major historical event of their time. As a young student, he was arrested on suspicion of revolutionary activity against the Austro-Hungarian regime, which then ruled over parts of what was to become Yugoslavia. Soon after his release from prison, he joined the newly established Yugoslav diplomatic service. Deployed to Germany at the eve of the Second World War, he directly witnessed Europe's descent into war. A few years later, Nazi Germany occupied Yugoslavia and put him under house arrest in Belgrade. It is during this period that Andrić wrote what is commonly referred to as his *Bosnian Trilogy*.

In *Bosnian Chronicle*, a book that forms part of his trilogy, Andrić depicts the various battles of influence between the Ottoman, French, and Austrian empires in Bosnia during the Napoleonic Wars. At the beginning of the novel, rumors are circulating in the town of Travnik – then part of the Ottoman Empire – that Napoléon has requested permission from Istanbul to establish a French consulate. An early scene in the novel shows a group of Bosnian men discussing the rumors. The oldest and most respected man in the group speaks in a slow and clear voice: "As for these consuls, who knows what's what? Maybe they'll come, maybe they won't. And even if they come, the Lashva won't turn around and flow backwards – it will run the same as now. We're here on our own ground, anyone else who may come will be on strange ground and he won't tarry long. Armies have gone through here before and they never could hold out for long. Many have come here to stay, but so far we've always managed to see the back of them, just as we will see the back of these consuls too, even supposing they come."[2]

As I arrived in Bosnia in 2001, I assumed that the country would ultimately conform to the objectives of its modern consuls. With a large international military force in control of Bosnia's territory and a civilian authority with powers to intervene in the country's legal system, the foreign presence struck me as the stronger variable in the equation. How could we fail?

When I left the country seven years later, the international authority had sustained a serious defeat. For the first time ever, the High Representative's authorities had been successfully challenged. No one in the office had predicted such an outcome. It felt as if Bosnia had quietly tolerated the actions of its modern foreign consuls before abruptly reclaiming control. A discreet character sitting on stage during the entire play, it had suddenly taken the lead role to tell the audience: "This is how this play is going to end."

Defeats tend to engender humility. I will never fully understand what happened during the fall of 2007 in Bosnia, nor will I ever be able to fully explain it to someone else. This is one of the lessons I take from this defeat. Models devised by the human brain can never fully encapsulate the complexity of a given reality, especially when such models pertain to an entire country. Moreover, the very elements that such models leave out are often those that will likely prevail in the end – while planners are looking the other way. Author Friedrich Dürrenmatt once wrote: "The more human beings proceed by plan, the more effectively they may be hit by accident."[3] Chance did hit us hard in the fall of 2007, and the story told in the first part of this book chronicles the end of many plans and models.

In the midst of action, one loses perspective. The lack of sleep, the time constraints, the constant need to quickly react to events triggered by others all contribute to this phenomenon. This is partly why, by the end of the crisis, many of us felt as if we had been hit by a tornado that came from nowhere. It had actually come from a very specific place: a place where we were not looking. So what was this crisis all about? What was the source of this tornado?

Looking back at this period, it is tempting to analyze events through tactical considerations and focus on the impact of personalities, short-term calculations, and maneuvers. When scrutinizing events through this lens, there is no doubt that we committed several tactical errors during the crisis. Starting with me. Had I not failed to see the broader context in which we were operating? Throughout the entire crisis, I firmly believed that the points raised by the officials in Republika Srpska could all have been solved through further negotiations on rules of procedures and by-laws. With the benefit of hindsight, it should have been clear to me that many Bosnian Serbs genuinely feared the prospect of Bosniak politicians imposing their will on them. Their resistance to our measures stemmed from deep fears and mistrust. How realistic was it to amend laws regulating governmental and parliamentary decision making in a postwar country marked by so much distrust, and expect parties to calmly work out their differences by enacting by-laws? Such perceptions were a clear sign of my own disconnect with Bosnia's realities.

Lajčák and his cabinet also committed serious mistakes. The failure to consult with their international partners before imposing changes to governmental and parliamentary decision-making rules had serious consequences. Had Lajčák coordinated with the United States, the United Kingdom, France, Germany, and the EU before jumping into this battle, he would have most likely been told – at the very least – to wait until the situation in Kosovo had been settled before enacting his changes. Such consultations may have allowed him to proceed at a better time, with better coordination, and with much stronger support from the international community. By convincing the European Commission to dilute its conditions on police reform and by yielding to local political pressure to change the October 2007 measures, his actions undermined the credibility of the international community in Bosnia and Herzegovina and created many more problems down the road.

But as interesting as they may be, tactical considerations alone only take us so far. The most valuable lessons lie elsewhere. Better coordination would have allowed the Office of the High Representative to survive this particular crisis. I seriously doubt, however, that it would have allowed it to survive similar challenges in the future. Examining this crisis exclusively through tactical considerations prevents more productive reflections. Many of the developments during the crisis were the manifestation of broader systemic forces. It is by analyzing them that we will extract the most meaningful lessons.

In trying to examine the events of fall 2007 at a more systemic level, one may be tempted to look at them as part of a broader confrontation between the High Representative and the Bosnian Serb leadership over the role and authorities of the High Representative. This perspective is certainly valid and supported by the facts. Immediately after the initial public statements from Republika Srpska's officials challenging Lajčák's measures, the Peace Implementation Council tried to bring Banja Luka back within its box. On October 31, 2007, the Council issued a formal declaration warning that by challenging the legitimacy and authority of the High Representative, Republika Srpska leaders were breaching their obligations under the Dayton Peace Agreement.[4] The Bosnian Serb leadership maneuvered around this straightjacket by pressing ahead with its challenge. Špirić immediately resigned as the chair of the Council of Ministers. Later during the crisis, Dodik consistently portrayed the High Representative and his staff in the OHR as "universal surrogates." By the end of November 2007, the opposition of Republika Srpska leaders to the High Representative had reached the level of a direct and open confrontation.

Although valid, a perspective centered on the political conflict would only partially capture the essence of the broader story unfolding during the October 2007 crisis. I believe that understanding these events requires us to interpret them within an even larger framework, one that recognizes the existence of a protracted conflict over power in Bosnia and that positions international intervention within this conflict. The story told in the first part of this book is indeed much more than the account of a confrontation between an international official and the prime minister of a federal unit in a postwar country. It is the most recent chapter of an old conflict – a conflict with its own history and its own dynamic. Just like the Lashva River described in Andrić's story, this conflict has survived centuries of consuls and foreign armies passing through but not having the last word.

I argue in this chapter that we were not merely implementing a peace process after the end of armed conflict in Bosnia and Herzegovina. We were actually involved in an ongoing conflict fought through nonviolent means. We were involved in a *nonviolent war*. This nonviolent war is linked to the manner in which the international community intervened militarily to end the armed conflict in Bosnia. Using limited means to achieve limited objectives, international military intervention had indeed established a space for diplomacy to manage the nonviolent continuation of war. Akin to culture wars, nonviolent wars are intense forms of conflict fought over power. Although waged through nonviolent means, they maintain a particularly close relationship with violence insofar as their developments can disrupt fragile peace processes. Understanding their nature and evolution is key to international efforts to restore and maintain peace.

An Old Conflict Morphs into a Nonviolent War

Yugoslavia's disintegration in the 1990s did not create a new conflict in Bosnia and Herzegovina. It triggered, instead, the violent resurgence of an old conflict within Bosnia; one in which Bosniak, Bosnian Serb, and Bosnian Croat nationalist leaders simultaneously tried to establish their power over the entire Bosnian territory or part of it. Political in nature for several decades, this conflict morphed into an armed confrontation between 1992 and 1995. Partial and tentative at first, international efforts to end the violent phase of the conflict finally culminated with the signature of the Dayton Accords in 1995. But while these efforts had finally stopped the armed phase of the conflict, they had not solved the wider clash of wills at its source.

Far from disappearing, the conflict merely adapted itself to a new environment – one in which war was no longer waged through armies but instead through parliaments, ministries, laws, and newspapers. No longer able or willing to resort to physical force – mainly because of the large international military force deployed after 1995 – Bosnia's opposing factions tried to achieve their objectives through other means. This is what we were facing in 2007: we were addressing a nonviolent war through diplomacy.

There is a profound link between war and diplomacy. Military force and diplomacy are different means to achieve an end. The manner in which military force is applied as foreign actors intervene to end armed conflict will inevitably have an impact on diplomacy. The experience of the international community in implementing peace after the end of the armed conflict in Bosnia in 1995 offers a window for exploring the nature of this impact. As this next section illustrates, diplomatic management of nonviolent wars is linked to the evolution of warfare.

War

Carl von Clausewitz, perhaps the most cited Western military thinker, defined war as "an act of force to compel our enemy to do our will."[5] For Clausewitz, one of the easiest ways to conceptualize war is to think of two wrestlers. Both are trying to impose their will on their opponent. They do so through physical force, and victory is achieved when one renders his or her opponent powerless.

But war, like many other things, is in constant evolution. The wars we fought a few centuries ago bear little resemblance to those in which large powers tend to be involved today. While Clausewitz's definition of war remains relevant – despite going back almost two centuries – war has evolved significantly since then. There is a rich literature that analyses this evolution. Military analysts have coined expressions such as *old wars, new wars, total wars, modern wars, or interstate wars* to conceptualize the various shifts. In many ways, the evolution of war follows the means that a party is able and willing to use to impose its will on its opponent. There are theoretically no logical limits to the application of physical force at war. In their respective quest to render each other powerless, each side can potentially compel the other to embark upon a series of actions that can lead, in theory, to extremes.[6] The two world wars of the twentieth century are concrete manifestations of such dynamics. But there are other dynamics as well. These can be viewed through the lens of the means employed and the importance of the objective that one tries to achieve through war.

Interstate Industrial Wars

When we think about war, we tend to think of large armies, tanks, and planes colliding in a large battle to achieve a decisive victory. While still part of our collective memory – mainly because of the two world wars of the twentieth century – these images have little to do with the nature of modern international military interventions such as those that took place in Bosnia, Kosovo, or, more recently, Libya. These images are the reflections of an old war paradigm. General Sir Rupert Smith, a British general who commanded UNPROFOR during the conflict in Bosnia and who later acted as NATO's deputy supreme allied commander in Europe during the alliance's intervention in Kosovo, traces this conception of war back to the old paradigm of *interstate industrial war*, a war paradigm forged by Napoléon and Clausewitz at the beginning of the nineteenth century.[7]

The paradigm of interstate industrial war is based on the premise that, in war, a belligerent ought to dare all to win all. This becomes clearer as one looks at the theoretical framework Clausewitz developed. According to his conception, to defeat an opponent, one must first identify the focal point around which all the power of one's opponent revolves. Once identified, all efforts and energies should be directed at destroying this center of power to achieve complete victory.[8] This conception of war as an act of force in which one dares all to achieve a decisive victory lies at the very heart of the war paradigm of interstate industrial war.

Clausewitz's thinking had been very much influenced by the success of Napoléon's Grande Armée – which he had witnessed firsthand as a soldier. Napoléon's military successes in Europe were due, in large part, to his decision to conceive military force within a new strategic model, one that provided him with a strategic advantage over his opponents.[9] By examining the impact of the French Revolution on warfare, one can better understand some of the elements at the center of Napoléon's new strategic model.

Before the French Revolution, European armies were composed of persons recruited to fight for a monarch – something the French Revolution would drastically change.[10] Soon after the abolition of the system of absolute monarchy headed by Louis XVI, France would be attacked by European powers claiming to restore the French monarchy. In September 1792, in Valmy, armies led by Prussia decided to retreat after a large French army of young citizens fighting for the nation inflicted serious damage to them. The Prussian armies, together with other European powers, came back the following year and invaded France. Attacked from all sides, the revolutionary government decided to raise an army of six hundred thousand men to defend the newly established republic in 1793. The mass army had just been created.[11] Clausewitz would note many years later: "[P]eople at first expected to have to deal only with a seriously weakened French army; but in 1793, a force appeared that beggared all imagination. Suddenly war again became the business of the people – a people of thirty millions, all of whom considered themselves to be citizens."[12] An entire people, bound by a common citizenship, now participated in war to defend the nation.

Building on the opportunities created by the French Revolution, Napoléon assembled a large army of citizens who were all fighting for their country.[13] While unprecedented masses of soldiers had emerged from the French Revolution, no French general had yet managed to move such masses efficiently. Fearing for the republic's fragile stability, the new revolutionary authorities had been reluctant to concentrate too many men in the hands of one general. When Napoléon established his authority over France, he elaborated systems that allowed him to move large armed forces with efficiency and flexibility.[14] Moreover, by codifying conscriptions – which he based on a legal duty to defend the state and buttressed with the ideas of *liberté*, *égalité*, and *fraternité* – Napoléon also managed to regularize his supply of manpower and consolidate his military strength.[15] Able to continuously replenish his army through numerous *levées en masse*, he gained a sustained strategic advantage over his opponents; an advantage he would exploit to its fullest.[16]

Traditional military limits and constraints disappeared under Napoléon. The resources mobilized to support the war effort seemed endless. A new strategic model had been devised; a model in which one sought to defeat an opponent by mobilizing ever more men, horses, and firepower. By declaring war on his opponents, Napoléon dragged them into a process during which he would ultimately destroy their will to fight. Napoléon used his military might to completely destroy his enemy's force.[17] He gave military force a new utility: to achieve a political objective by a decisive military act.[18] This objective lies at the heart of the paradigm of interstate industrial war.[19]

Things had been different before Napoléon. Rather than mobilizing government, industry, and nation behind a decisive war effort, states used war as a limited instrument; one that sought to support diplomacy. Decisions to go to war were made on the basis of means available to a given monarch at a given point in time. The greater a monarch's financial means, the greater the army a monarch could raise. The Spanish crown's capacity to raise large armies on the basis of its increased supply of gold from its American territories illustrates this dynamic. Before Napoléon, means were not *determined by* war objectives. Rather, means themselves *determined* war objectives. Because the means available were limited and known by all, war was therefore deprived from its most devastating dynamic – its tendency toward seemingly endless escalation.[20]

Before Napoléon, states were neither able nor willing to risk losing an entire army. If their military force was annihilated, they did not have the resources to immediately throw another army at their opponent. Military commanders were thus compelled to use their armies with caution. "Even a royal commander had to use his army with a minimum of risk. If the army was pulverized, he could not raise another, and behind the army there was nothing. That enjoined the greatest prudence in all operations," observed Clausewitz.[21]

The conduct of war was thus part of a continuous game where everyone's power had to be preserved – with each belligerent trying to improve its relative position.[22] Military force was used *together with diplomacy* to achieve objectives. War was then "a somewhat stronger form of diplomacy, a more forceful method of negotiation, in which battles and sieges were the principal notes exchanged. Even the most ambitious ruler had no greater aims than to gain a number of advantages that could be exploited at the peace conference."[23]

By leading a continuously replenished Grande Armée into decisive battles against enemy forces that were unable and unwilling to dare all to win all, Napoléon relentlessly exploited a systemic advantage. He refuted the premise according to which rulers and states had to be preserved despite the various exchanges of land and provinces achieved by war. His precise aim was to overthrow rulers and absorb states within his empire.[24]

By the mid-nineteenth century, Napoléon and Clausewitz had forged a war paradigm that would shape military thinking for years to come.[25] Industrialization, new modes of transportation, and technological developments would help transform war into an increasingly devastating affair. With states relying more and more on their population and industry to fuel their capacity to wage war, cities and industrial infrastructure became military targets.[26]

The American Civil War was a manifestation of this trend – a war in which the North sought to destroy the South's infrastructure, farms, and workplaces to neutralize its capacity to wage war. James M. McPherson, an American historian, noted about the American Civil War: "The kind of conflict that the Civil War had become merits the label of *total war*. To be sure, Union soldiers did not set out to kill Southern civilians. Sherman's bummers destroyed property; Allied bombers in World War II destroyed hundreds of thousands of lives as well. But the strategic purpose of both were the same: to eliminate the resources and break the will of the people to sustain war. White people in large parts of the Confederacy were indeed left with 'nothing but their eyes to weep with.'"[27]

Consolidating the thinking of the military leaderships in Europe, the American Civil War would be followed by increasingly destructive wars on the European continent – a trend that ultimately resulted in the two world wars of the twentieth century. Just a few hours before Churchill was summoned to Buckingham Palace on May 10, 1940 to replace Chamberlain as prime minister, Hitler's armies had stormed across the frontiers of Belgium, Holland, and Luxembourg.[28] His address to the House of Commons on May 13, 1940, is often cited in relation to his claim that he only had "blood, toil, tears, and sweat" to offer the people of Great Britain. Looking further into his address, there is little doubt Churchill fully understood the nature and dynamic of the war effort ahead of him:

> We have before us an ordeal of the most grievous kind. We have before us many, many long months of struggle and of suffering. You ask, what is our policy? I will say: It is to wage war, by sea, land and air, with all our might and with all the strength that God can give us; to wage war against a monstrous tyranny, never surpassed in the dark, lamentable catalogue of human crime. That is our policy. You ask, what is our aim? I can answer in one word: Victory – victory at all costs, victory in spite of all terror, victory, however long and hard the road may be; for without victory, there is no survival.[29]

Wars of Management

As significant as their impact may have been on our perceptions of war, the large epic military campaigns of Churchill, Stalin, Hitler, and Roosevelt have ceased to exist today. While large powers maintain significant military capacities, the manner in which they use military force changed significantly during the latter part of the twentieth century. The discovery of the atomic bomb, its use at Hiroshima and Nagasaki, and the subsequent dynamics of *mutually assured destruction* that came to define the military confrontation of the Cold War relegated the interstate industrial war paradigm to the past.

Since the end of the Second World War, large industrial powers have stopped relying on war as a means to resolve conflict amongst themselves. Some explain this by pointing to the fact that democratic regimes rarely, if ever, declare war against each other;[30] that interstate industrial war has ceased to be a practical option since the invention of the atomic bomb,[31] or that the need to resort to war has been neutralized by the unprecedented levels of economic and political interdependence of today.[32] Whether this state of affairs is a permanent or a temporary fixture of the modern system of international relations remains to be seen, but war seems – at least for the time being – to have been abandoned as a means to solve conflict among large industrial states.

But war has not disappeared. Armed conflicts have indeed been raging in the former Soviet Republics, the former Yugoslavia, Angola, Somalia, Sudan, Congo Liberia, Ivory Coast, Indonesia, and Libya in the past few decades. War's geographical distribution has, however, shifted. War now tends to be fought regionally, in the non-Western world[33] in the form of intrastate conflicts fought amongst citizens of the states in question.[34] Instead of waging wars amongst each other, Western powers seem to often *manage wars* fought elsewhere.[35] They tend to fight *management wars*.

The important point to retain for our purpose is that management wars differ significantly from the large interstate industrial wars of previous centuries. One main difference pertains to the relationship between war and society as a whole. Under the previous paradigm, war mobilized entire societies. During the two world wars, the government of the United States appealed to the civilian population to grow gardens on farms, in towns, and at schools to help with the war effort. Posters with notes such as "Plant a Garden for Victory" or "War Gardens for Victory" were common features. The U.S. government ran "victory gardens" campaigns to stimulate food production to win the war. "Food production is war production" noted a publication by the U.S. Department of Agriculture and the U.S Office of War Information in 1943.[36]

But interstate industrial war not only mobilized entire societies; it also targeted them. In its coverage of the Allied air campaign in Dresden in February 1945, the *New York Times* reported, for example, that the city had "been turned into a heap of ruins," that irreplaceable art treasures had "been transformed into smoking, pulverized rubble" with "huge oceans of fire" still raging after the attacks. It added that "never before during this war has any town been turned into such ruins as Dresden within twenty-four hours." Dresden, according to the *New York Times*'s account, had "ceased to be the capital of Saxony"; between twenty thousand and thirty-five thousand of its people "had been killed ... during the first twenty four hours of the Allied air assaults against the city," while "200,000 residents had fled in panic."[37]

Cities are still eradicated by warfare nowadays. When entering the Syrian city of Homs in March 2012, the United Nations under-secretary-general for humanitarian affairs and the United Nations emergency relief coordinator noted that the city – which had been under constant attack from Syrian government forces for several weeks – was "completely devastated" and seemed "completely closed down."[38] While enjoying similarities with some of the military operations conducted during the Second World War, the military attacks on Homs were not launched by an international coalition involved in a large interstate war. Instead, these attacks were part of an internal conflict; one in which armed forces under the control of the Syrian regime used military force against a segment of its own population.

Recent international military interventions in Bosnia, Kosovo, and Libya have affected many lives and required significant resources. They differ, however, from the kinds of war that ravaged the world during the first half of the twentieth century. By way of illustration, during World War II, U.S. armed forces consisted of more than 16 million people. Its force today is estimated at 1.4 million active personnel.[39] A recent survey from the Pew Research Center indicated that the percentage of the population in the U.S. armed forces reached approximately 0.5 percent between 2001 and 2011.[40]

While interstate industrial wars dominated society by suspending normal economic and political life, management wars, on the other hand, tend to be subordinated to the normal administration of economic and political affairs.[41] Rather than dominating entire societies, contemporary military interventions such as those in Bosnia, Kosovo, and Libya must comply with existing political, economic, or military requirements established at home. While they may capture the full attention of the public and leaders for a brief period of time, they do not dominate entire societies and governments the way interstate industrial wars used to.[42]

This is not to suggest that previous interstate industrial wars were devoid of any political calculations. The distinction between both types of war pertains more to the intensity of the interests at the source of military intervention. In contemporary management wars, states will not usually intervene on the basis of a core interest, such as defending their very existence, their sovereignty, or territorial integrity. They tend, instead, to intervene on the basis of interests perceived as secondary or tertiary.[43] While political leaders would encounter little resistance in justifying military actions aimed at defending the existence of the state against an imminent threat, intervening in a foreign conflict is, on the other hand, a much more complex political undertaking. It will usually be based on a delicate political calculation – one that takes into account the electoral impact of a given intervention.

This political calculation will seek to ensure that the military intervention is legitimate both at home and internationally. This quest for legitimacy will have an important consequence on the manner in which states intervene in management wars. First, they will have a tendency to intervene in coalitions.[44] Second, the need to create or maintain coalitions will force states to negotiate the modalities of their military actions. While some of these modalities may have already been negotiated in advance – UN member states have consented to resort to the use of force only in cases of self-defense or if authorized to do so by a decision of the UN Security Council, for example[45] – some modalities will be determined by further negotiations.

This process alone will inevitably erode the nature and amplitude of military interventions. Far from mustering all necessary means to decisively win the clash of wills at the source of a conflict, multilateral interventions will tend to deploy limited means to fulfill limited objectives.[46] The cases of the recent international military interventions in Bosnia, Kosovo, Afghanistan, and Libya can all serve as illustrations of this fact.

Constraints on Intervention in Bosnia

When armed conflict emerged in Bosnia in 1992, many factors stood in the way of an effective international intervention. Many governments focused on managing the consequences of the fall of the Berlin Wall. Soon after assuming his duties as president of the United States, Bill Clinton was confronted with the loss of several American soldiers following an attack launched by U.S. soldiers against members of the clan of warlord Mohamed Farrah Aidid in Mogadishu, Somalia, an event that significantly fueled skepticism regarding intervention. On the other side of the Atlantic, European leaders had, from the outset, signaled their willingness to take the lead vis-à-vis Yugoslavia, but were struggling to find common objectives and positions.

This difficult political landscape did not completely prevent the international community from reacting. In the earlier phases of the war in Bosnia, the UN Security Council authorized the use of military force to protect Bosnia's civilian population. Acting under Chapter VII of the UN Charter, the Security Council authorized an international military force (UNPROFOR) to use force to ensure the safety of UN and other personnel engaged in delivering humanitarian assistance to the civilian population.[47] It banned military flights in the airspace of Bosnia and Herzegovina,[48] established safe areas for the civilian population,[49] and authorized UNPROFOR "acting in self defense, to take the necessary measures, including the use of force, in reply to bombardments against the safe areas by any of the parties or to an armed incursion into them."[50]

But while such measures were important steps, they illustrated the tendency of governments to use limited military means to achieve limited ends in such contexts.[51] Despite the presence of foreign troops, entire villages were ravaged amidst intense ethnic cleansing campaigns. The cities of Sarajevo and Mostar remained under siege. Camps filled with undernourished detainees multiplied throughout the country. Even worse, in July 1995, nearly three years after the beginning of the conflict, Bosnian Serb forces under the command of Ratko Mladić entered the UN "safe area" in Srebrenica – supposedly protected by UN armed forces – and slaughtered several thousand Bosnian Muslim men.

While the continuing atrocities finally led to a shift in strategy by the summer of 1995, military force was still only partially applied. After the tragedy of Srebrenica, it was decided that NATO forces would intervene to finally end the armed conflict. But despite being the largest military action in NATO's history until that time, NATO's use of force itself remained limited. NATO's military force was used to support diplomatic efforts to end armed conflict rather than to achieve decisive military victory on the ground. By way of illustration, on the day the bombing started, U.S. diplomat Richard Holbrooke told Slobodan Milošević he would consider recommending the suspension of the bombing if Milošević could guarantee an end to the siege of Sarajevo.[52] NATO suspended military actions shortly afterward to allow for the negotiation of such arrangements with the Bosnian Serb military leadership.[53]

Second, NATO's use of force was also curtailed by constant diplomatic monitoring from member states. On September 10, 1995, following the Bosnian Serb military leadership's refusal to end the siege of Sarajevo, NATO resumed its air strikes and fired thirteen Tomahawk cruise missiles at vital military targets near Banja Luka – a town then under the effective control of Bosnian Serbs.[54] France, Spain, Canada, and Greece immediately criticized the attacks, qualifying them as an unauthorized escalation.[55]

Intervening in Kosovo

Similar dynamics within NATO would reemerge several years later as the alliance debated whether to intervene militarily to force Milošević's hand in Kosovo. Only a few years after the conflict in Bosnia, many governments feared that Milošević's military operations against the Kosovo Liberation Army (KLA) in Kosovo during 1998 and 1999 would lead to another bloodbath in the former Yugoslavia. After having failed to convince Milošević to agree to a peace agreement to settle the conflict in Kosovo, member states decided to rely on military force to stop the armed conflict. But once the decision to resort to force had been made, NATO's use of force would, once again, be constrained by negotiations over the nature and extent of the armed intervention.[56]

In his account of the NATO military intervention during the Kosovo conflict, Supreme Allied Commander Europe (SACEUR) at NATO General Wesley Clark wrote at length about the complex web of domestic and international variables that he confronted as he supervised and planned the execution of NATO's campaign. Focused on implementing a U.S.-approved military strategy that prioritized the Persian Gulf and Northeast Asia, the military leadership in Washington, DC was indeed very reluctant to commit resources for a military action in Kosovo, which was seen as a less vital region.[57]

Divisions within NATO about *whether* to intervene subsequently extended to the question of *how* to intervene. Clark was aware that while airpower could inflict serious damage on Milošević's force and infrastructure, there was no assurance that NATO could force his troops out of Kosovo and stop the violence without a ground force.[58] In a private meeting with Prime Minister Tony Blair, during which Blair asked him whether NATO could win without ground troops, Clark replied: "I'll do everything possible to make it happen, but I cannot guarantee it with air power alone."[59]

Pressure from Congress, the Clinton administration, and other NATO allies had, however, ruled out ground troops for the initial phase of the campaign.[60] When Clark approached Javier Solana, NATO's secretary-general, to discuss the possibility of raising the issue of ground troops in NATO's Council, Solana declined. According to Clark: "Solana saw no chance of maintaining NATO cohesion if the divisive issue of ground intervention was introduced at this point. In fact, Secretary Cohen and influential German leaders had been speaking in conferences ruling out a ground threat."[61]

But such limitations went beyond the strategic choice between resorting to air power or ground troops. NATO military commanders had to face many more constraints as they proceeded with the air campaign. After having been informed of Clark's preliminary plan for a potential intervention in July 1998, NATO diplomats in Brussels had signaled to him that they wanted something more limited.[62] Later during the operations, Clark had to seek the approval of NATO countries – in particular France, the United Kingdom, and the United States – as he identified targets.[63] For days, Clark asked for the authorization to target a Serb air base close to Podgorica in Montenegro – an authorization initially withheld over fears that the strikes could undermine the Montenegrin president's political position.[64] Later, when Washington wanted the air campaign to target Serbia's electrical system, the French were reluctant to approve such strikes. Clark recounted using the opportunity of his encounter with President Chirac and the French chief of defense during NATO's fiftieth anniversary summit in April 1999 to ask: "So, do I get approval for the electricity system targets, or not?"[65] French approval for the strikes came several days later.[66]

The military interventions in Bosnia and Kosovo offered a preview of the military constraints that would come into play in Afghanistan several years later.

War in Afghanistan

Shortly after the attacks of September 11, the United States invoked its right to self-defense to carry out military actions in Afghanistan with the declared objective of preventing and deterring further attacks on the United States.[67] Despite being referred to as the longest war in American history, the military campaign in Afghanistan was shaped by U.S. domestic politics. The Bush administration's decision to intervene in Iraq in 2003 shifted resources away from Afghanistan. Seeking to put the focus back on Afghanistan, the Obama administration decided to increase military resources in Afghanistan in 2009. But even as the administration moved to augment the number of American troops on the ground, war fatigue and the country's economic difficulties constrained the administration's decision. After announcing his decision to send an additional thirty thousand U.S. troops in December 2009, President Obama was, for example, careful to stress that "after 18 months, our troops will begin to come home" and that "having just experienced the worst economic crisis since the Great Depression, the American people are understandably focused on rebuilding our economy and putting people to work here at home."[68]

NATO intervened alongside the United States – albeit under a different mandate.[69] Similar factors affected the capacity of NATO governments to use military force in Afghanistan. NATO's intervention in Afghanistan was the alliance's first ground war.[70] The risks of casualties being higher, domestic political pressure incited many member states to restrict their participation through numerous caveats. NATO's mandate to maintain security in Afghanistan was initially limited to "Kabul and its surrounding areas."[71] It took an additional authorization by the UN Security Council to extend NATO's operations to other parts of the Afghan territory.[72] As a military alliance based on consensus, NATO, once again, inevitably conducted its military operations on the basis of its "political room to maneuver."[73]

This was a major tactical problem for commanders on the ground and led to increasing frustration on the battlefield as caveats, restrictions, and troop limits directly affected the alliance's capacity to shift troops and address focal points of resistance. "I'd like the NATO allies and their non-NATO partners in this alliance to properly resource this force ... and absent that, that they adopt the patience and will for a slower pace of progress," said the commander of the International Security Assistance Force in March 2008.[74]

The frustration on the battlefield extended to the diplomatic arena, where NATO members publically disagreed over strategy, troop levels, and rules of engagement. Countries such as Canada, the Netherlands, the United Kingdom, and the United States felt they were bearing the brunt of the effort. In 2008, Canadian Prime Minister Stephen Harper publically threatened to pull Canadian troops out of Afghanistan in the event NATO refused to deploy more troops and resources in the southern part of the country. "Canada has done what it said it would do and more. We now say we need help. I think if NATO can't come through with that help, then I think – frankly – NATO's own reputation and future will be in grave jeopardy," Harper told a news conference in January 2008.[75]

Forcing Qaddafi's Hand in Libya

The international military intervention in Libya in 2011 shared several of the characteristics of the previous engagements in Bosnia, Kosovo, and Afghanistan. The initial protests against the Libyan regime had, by March 2011, morphed into an armed insurrection with rebel forces controlling several of Libya's cities. Qaddafi's forces fought back and, by March 17, 2011, were about to close in on the rebel stronghold in the city of Benghazi. After Qaddafi's regime had vowed to show "no mercy" to its opponents, the world's attention turned to the UN Security Council.[76] While certain states were reluctant to support armed intervention, others pushed hard to intervene to avoid another Rwanda or Srebrenica. Having secured the support of the Arab League, the UN Security Council finally authorized the use of force in Libya and imposed a no-fly zone over the country on March 17, 2011, setting the ground for a NATO-led air campaign in Libya. While the Council's authorization for member states "to take all necessary measures ... to protect civilians and civilian populated areas under threat of attack in the Libyan Arab Jamahiriya"[77] seemed broad, it still imposed a number of constraints.[78]

More important, domestic politics shaped, once more, the conditions under which states would intervene. The debate that came to divide the political class in the United States regarding Libya serves to illustrate this point. On March 28, 2011, President Obama confirmed the decision of his administration to intervene in Libya in remarks delivered at the National Defense University in Washington, DC. During his speech, he justified the intervention as follows:

> Mindful of the risks and costs of military action, we are naturally reluctant to use force to solve the world's many challenges. But when our interests and values are at stake, we have a responsibility to act. That's what happened in Libya over the course of these last six weeks.[79]

He was however quick to add:

> Moreover, we've accomplished these objectives consistent with the pledge that I made to the American people at the outset of our military operations. I said that America's role would be limited; that we would not put ground troops into Libya; that we would focus our unique capabilities on the front end of the operation and that we would transfer responsibility to our allies and partners. Tonight, we are fulfilling that pledge.[80]

A fierce political battle with members of the House of Representatives ensued. Their political attack on the White House's decision to intervene in Libya would revolve around the provisions of the War Powers Resolution – a resolution adopted by Congress in the aftermath of the Vietnam War in an attempt to constrain the president's constitutional prerogative to involve armed forces abroad.[81] According to its provisions, the president is allowed to engage U.S. forces in hostilities without prior authorization from Congress. However, after a period of sixty days, the president must terminate the use of U.S. armed forces unless otherwise authorized by Congress.[82]

As the expiration date of the deadline approached, the Republican leadership in the House of Representatives went on the offensive. On June 3, the House adopted a resolution declaring, among other things, that the administration had neither sought nor received congressional authorization for military involvement in Libya. The resolution gave fourteen days to President Obama to provide specific information in relation to U.S. military actions in Libya.[83] On June 14, Speaker of the

House of Representatives John Boehner escalated the confrontation by sending a letter to President Obama in which he wrote: "Given the mission you have ordered to the U.S. Armed Forces with respect to Libya and the text of the War Powers Resolution, the House is left to conclude that you have made one of two determinations: either you have concluded the War Powers Resolution does not apply to the mission in Libya, or you have determined the War Powers Resolution is contrary to the Constitution. The House, and the American people whom we represent, deserve to know the determination you have made."[84]

A legal battle ensued within the administration. The Pentagon general counsel and the acting head of the Justice Department's Office of Legal Counsel indicated to the White House that the U.S. military's activities in Libya amounted to "hostilities" under the War Powers Resolution and that it was consequently required to either end or scale back its operations within the deadlines prescribed in the resolution. Other senior members of the president's legal team opined otherwise, considering that the U.S. military involvement in Libya fell short of qualifying as "hostilities" under the resolution. President Obama decided to side with the latter view, and on June 15, the White House finally argued it was not in violation of the War Powers Resolution.[85] Pointing to the fact that the U.S. involvement in Libya was confined to supporting other NATO member states, the administration stressed that U.S. actions did not qualify as "hostilities" under the resolution.[86] It had decided to throw the ball back into the House of Representatives' court.

On June 23, the House of Representatives announced its intention to vote on a proposal to cut funds for U.S. involvement in hostilities in Libya.[87] Under increasing pressure, Secretary of State Hillary Clinton met with House representatives to urge them not to support the proposal, warning that such an outcome would be disastrous for American interests.[88] The next day, the House escalated the confrontation by rejecting a resolution that sought to authorize the U.S. mission in Libya.[89] The battle effectively came to an end only when, a few days later, the Senate Foreign Relations Committee adopted a resolution authorizing limited use of force by the United States in Libya.[90]

Things were hardly easier for other NATO members. In the midst of these international and economic problems, NATO governments had to deal with skeptical public opinions. In late June, Italian Prime Minister Berlusconi came under heavy pressure from his coalition partners to fix an end date to the country's military involvement in Libya.[91]

These are the contexts in which wars of management are designed. They are the product of long, complex, political battles in which politicians, advisors, and lawyers sitting in Washington, DC, London, or Paris determine operational options on the basis of political compromises.[92] These determinations affect the manner in which military force is applied on the ground. Reporting on NATO's operations in Libya from Benghazi in April 2011, Nicolas Pelham, a reporter for *The Economist* and *The New York Review of Books*, noted:

> The demonstrations of gratitude in early April have turned to protests of accusation, after NATO took the reins of the allies effort from the US and ceased offensive bombing. Sorties increased, but the potency of the attacks sharply diminished as member states flinched from the prospect of collateral damage. NATO's efforts to overcome its internal fractures, between the gung-ho such as Britain and France and the force resistant such as Turkey and Germany, ensured that for most the lowest denominator prevailed.[93]

Wars of limited means seem here to stay. An increasing number of military operations are now conducted through unmanned drones. U.S. drone strikes in Pakistan and Afghanistan are now commonplace. The U.S. government reportedly authorized 146 drone strikes in Libya between April and October 2011.[94] As technology removes the human factor further away from war, it expands the political space within which officials can authorize such operations. Drone strikes have so far been hardly discussed before the U.S. Congress.[95] Technology, as such, may be pushing management wars toward even more limited means.[96]

This brief overview illustrates a simple point about the nature and intensity of wars of management. When contrasted with Churchill's promise to the British House of Commons in May 1940 "to wage war, by sea, land and air, with all our might and with all the strength that God can give us,"[97] recent management wars can be characterized as wars of limited means.

Wars of Limited Objectives

But there is another crucial difference between wars of management and the twentieth century's interstate industrial wars. Churchill's address to the House of Commons in 1940 made clear that Britain was willing and able to use all means at its disposal. Churchill also stated that such means would be used to achieve "victory at all costs, victory in spite of all terror, victory, however long and hard the road may be."[98] While interstate industrial wars sought to achieve victory at all costs, *management wars,* on the other hand, pursue more qualified objectives.

The international military interventions in Bosnia and Kosovo did not seek the complete annihilation of a given belligerent's force. They sought, instead, to create a space for negotiations.[99] There lies a crucial difference between interstate industrial wars and the type of management wars waged in Bosnia and Kosovo in the 1990s. In many ways, the contemporary prevalence of management wars marks a return to the kinds of wars that preceded Napoléon and Clausewitz – wars in which military force was used to strengthen one's position at the negotiating table. States involved in management wars will indeed rarely rely on force alone in their foreign interventions. They will pursue political objectives through a combination of force and diplomacy. In places such as Bosnia and Kosovo, war has, for example, been used to back diplomacy – a combination often described as *diplomacy backed by force*[100] or *coercive diplomacy.*[101] This contrasts with the large interstate industrial wars of the early twentieth century during which states pursued objectives through a combination that relied primarily on military force. The large interstate industrial wars of the last century may thus have been a temporary digression from a more common form of war.

This shift in war paradigms is interesting not so much because of its ability to illustrate recurrent historical patterns, but because of the impact it has on recent conflicts. While it is true that by participating in management wars, states have largely been successful in stopping armed confrontations, they have not been necessarily able to fully erase the conflict at the source of these armed confrontations. One explanation for this is related to the fluid nature of conflict.

The Fluidity of Conflicts

Conflicts are often associated with violence, and, of course, human history is replete with violent conflicts. Signs of human warfare have been traced back as far as forty thousand years ago.[102] But while conflict and violence are closely linked, the notion of conflict is broader than that of violence. Conflict can indeed take a multitude of forms. At a higher level of abstraction, its potential amongst humans exists whenever individuals or groups pursue goals that they perceive as incompatible.[103] Human conflict is ubiquitous; it shapes the dynamics of our daily social interactions and affects most aspects of human activity.[104]

The important point is that the mere fact that parties have agreed to end the violent phase of a conflict does not mean that the conflict itself will disappear.[105] This is even more the case with conflicts waged on the basis of ethnic identities, where post–armed conflict cooperation is more difficult to achieve.[106] It is perfectly possible for a conflict to last decades – or even centuries – and move from one episode of latency to another marked by violence.[107] The World Bank's 2011 World Development Report noted, for example, that "every civil war that began since 2003 was a resumption of a previous civil war" and that "90 percent of conflicts initiated in the 21st century were in countries that had already had a civil war."[108]

This is the case partly because parties can rely on a wide variety of means to engage in conflict, ranging from violent to nonviolent. Violent conflict often survives military victory achieved through conventional military power. One only needs to think of the recent insurgency wars in Iraq and Afghanistan that emerged soon after the initial success of military intervention. Overwhelmed by the superiority of the U.S.-led coalition in conventional warfare, factions on the ground changed their tactics to that of insurgency warfare. They opted to pursue conflict through violent means.

But even in cases where parties are neither willing nor able to use violence, they may still decide to pursue conflict by engaging their opponents through other means. Instead of embarking upon armed insurgency, a party may opt for a strategy that relies primarily on using politics, media, laws, regulations, and institutions to achieve its objective. Clausewitz's famous contention that "war is merely the continuation of policy by other means"[109] implicitly recognizes that other nonviolent conflictual means are used in the pursuit of a political objective. War is only one such means.[110]

Nonviolent Wars

This is not to suggest that interstate industrial wars were capable of completely eradicating the source of a conflict and that by moving away from this paradigm states have deprived themselves of the means of effectively managing conflicts. Such a contention would be problematic in several regards. Despite having been defeated in the First World War, Germany's subsequent remilitarization pushed the world into World War II only a few decades later.

It is important to focus on the degree to which a specific military intervention will effectively reduce the likelihood of seeing armed conflict change into a disruptive nonviolent conflict. By primarily seeking to break the will of an opponent though the decisive annihilation of its force by using all means available, the use of military force in interstate industrial wars did not necessarily end a conflict per se, but it significantly reduced the means available to a party wishing to pursue conflict.

On the other hand, by using lesser means and seeking lesser objectives, management wars may not only leave conflictual objectives alive; they may also leave intact many means by which these objectives can be pursued. These means can allow certain factions to maintain popular support for the objective at the center of a given conflict. Political leaderships, financial capacities, electoral networks, and bureaucracies may indeed easily survive management wars. Given that these are the instruments by which conflict continues to be waged after the end of armed confrontations, it is easy to conceive how disruptive nonviolent conflicts can survive management wars.[111]

Several examples can illustrate this point. After the signature of the Dayton Accords in Bosnia, Radovan Karadžić's political party, the SDS, continued to exist. It continued to harbor secessionist objectives while participating in the country's various levels of government. Further east, the Taliban, though weakened by the military campaigns in Afghanistan, is likely to remain an actor after the end of armed conflict in Afghanistan.

What are the dynamics of these nonviolent confrontations? How do they operate? These are the questions I now turn to.

The Dynamics of Nonviolent Wars

An article published in the *New Yorker* in 2011 chronicled the intense political battle fought over Planned Parenthood, an organization that provides health care, including prescription of birth control pills to approximately seventeen thousand women each year in the United States.[112] Women who go to one of the organization's affiliated clinics across the United States may, in addition to the other services provided by the organization, seek abortions.[113]

In 2011, Planned Parenthood found itself at the center of the wider conflict over abortion in the United States – a conflict fought by opposing activist coalitions. Each of these coalitions relies on a myriad of strategists, including political, legal, and communication experts. Emily's List, a coalition of women founded in 1985, raises money to support the election of prochoice candidates. Its antiabortion equivalent, the Susan B. Anthony List, invited Republican presidential nominees for the 2012 presidential elections to sign a pledge promising to defund Planned Parenthood if elected president.[114]

In February 2011, Michael Pence, a Republican representative from Indiana, introduced a measure in the House of Representatives that sought to eliminate all forms of federal funding for Planned Parenthood. The measure passed the House of Representatives, but later failed in the Senate.[115] Only a few days only before the Pence measure was introduced before the House of Representatives, a group called Live Action broadcast a video on the Internet. Shot through a hidden camera, the video showed a man disguised as a pimp accompanying a woman disguised as a prostitute to Planned Parenthood–affiliated clinics. They asked employees working at clinics whether young female teenagers who did not speak English could seek abortions there.[116] They broadcast videos on the Internet that included footage of a clinic manager suggesting under-aged girls lie to avoid age detection. During the same period, other antiabortion activists, who were in favor of more aggressive tactics, supported the introduction of "personhood" amendments in several state legislatures across the United States. Designed to strengthen future legal challenges to abortion, the amendments sought to ensure that the legal definition of a person included every human from the moment of fertilization.[117]

Actors involved in this conflict often invoke war terminology. In response to the Pence Amendment before the House of Representatives, Louise Slaughter, a Democratic member of the House, framed the proposed cuts as "the opening salvo in an all-out war on women's health."[118] In a statement supporting the more aggressive legal strategies pursued by antiabortion coalitions in different states, Julie Doehner, president of a county chapter of a group called Right to Life, said, "We've had 39 years of talk and regulation, it's time to win this war and actually protect babies with beating hearts."[119]

James Davison Hunter, an American sociologist, famously defined modern political conflicts fought over issues such as abortion, the place of religion in society, or gay marriage in the United States as "culture wars."[120] These confrontations, according to Hunter, originate from different systems of moral understanding and are particularly passionate. Because they are fought over principles and beliefs that "provide a source of identity, purpose and togetherness for those who live by them,"[121] culture wars are ultimately aimed at achieving and maintaining "the power to define reality."[122] Culture wars are waged on a variety of fronts, from the intimacy of families to the societal level of schools, popular media, and electoral politics.[123] In the legal field, the battle is waged before courts and extends to the judicial appointment process. By influencing the selection of judges, groups seek to ensure that judicial decisions will be aligned to their beliefs. In these highly competitive battles, coalitions raise money or send thousands of postcards to senators responsible for confirming presidential judicial nominations.[124] Though this example is very far removed from activities in a post–armed conflict setting, the approach is the same; culture wars mirror other nonviolent conflicts in their aims and methods. Although their violent potential is hardly comparable to the nonviolent wars of Bosnia and Herzegovina and Kosovo, culture wars also include a certain degree of violence. The bombing of abortion clinics in the United

States or the threat of violence against those providing abortion is a reminder of their potential for violence.

Just like culture wars, the type of nonviolent wars into which the international community was drawn in Bosnia and Kosovo are passionate conflicts over power fought through nonviolent means. As international intervention succeeds in pushing parties to end violence, and as belligerent armed forces are constrained by international military presences,[125] groups decide to pursue intense conflicts through governments, parliaments, and courts. Opponents rely on political parties, constituencies, media, schools, and administrative organizations under their control to achieve their objectives. While the means and resources available in a post–armed conflict environment may differ from those employed by those engaged in culture wars in a country like the United States, the tactics employed enjoy many similarities.

Nonviolent Wars of the Former Yugoslavia

The nonviolent wars of Bosnia or Kosovo of the early twenty-first century have been intensely fought. This is due, in part, to the ethnic nature of the violent conflicts that ravaged the former Yugoslavia. Ethnic conflicts are absolutist affairs. Ethnic belonging provides a powerful sense of identity and purpose for individuals.[126] Parties engaged in ethnic conflict build narratives around the notions of "us" and "them." Domination and subjugation by others is feared and opposing sides compete for power, as power is perceived as an antidote against domination and subjugation by others. Power is sought to confirm a group's sense of worth and to protect it against threat from others.[127] According to a common narrative, by holding power, not only are "we" more worthy than "they," "we" are protected from "them." Power is also sought on exclusive terms. Sharing it keeps the threat of subjugation by others alive. According to this logic, territories must be cleansed from the undesirable presence of others. The ethnic cleansing campaigns and the acts of genocide committed in Bosnia during the 1992–5 war are illustrations of this phenomenon.[128]

Deeply rooted feelings of pride and fear and belonging make ethnic conflicts resilient, violent, and unpredictable. The feelings aroused in ethnic confrontations are neither rational nor objective. Highly educated scientists participated in the savage killing campaigns of the recent conflicts in Africa, the former Yugoslavia, and the former Soviet Union. Narratives thriving on fear and domination seek to justify mass killing and ethnic cleansing. In a piece published in the *Globe and Mail* in 2011, a journalist recalled a dinner he had with Ratko Mladić in 1993. During dinner, Mladić, the very man who would order the execution of more than eight thousand Muslim men in Srebrenica less than two years later, was reportedly on the verge of tears several times. "In the village nearest to my birthplace they killed 42 Serbs. They cut an unborn baby from the belly of a pregnant woman and skewered it on a knife.... They killed everyone except an old man and a two-month-old girl, but they cut off the little girl's hand," Maldić said. "The Islamic world does not have the atomic bomb, but it has the demographic bomb.... The whole of Europe will be swamped by Albanians and Muslims," he added.[129]

There is a tendency amongst certain scholars to examine decisions to wage conflict on the basis of a rational calculation between costs and benefits. Such an approach is reminiscent of many models proposed by economists to explain various forms of human behaviors. The problem with such a suggestion lies in its premise, which assumes that human beings always act in a way to rationally maximize benefits. Not only does such an approach ignore the fact that actors in conflict act with incomplete information, it ignores the inherent "irrationality" of conflict. It fails to recognize that conflict dynamics are anchored in human emotions.[130]

Rational frameworks cannot explain an important feature of nonviolent wars, namely why people still choose, in times of peace, to prioritize symbolic political battles over those pertaining to more common economic and social issues.[131] Donald Horowitz, the author of a seminal work on ethnic conflict, notes: "Broad matters of group status regularly have equal or superior standing to the narrow allocative decisions often taken to be the uniform stuff of everyday politics. Fundamental issues such as citizenships, electoral systems, designation of official languages and religions, the rights of groups to a 'special position' in the polity, rather than merely setting the framework for politics, become the recurring subjects of politics. Conflicts over needs and interests are subordinated to conflicts over group status and over the rules to govern conflict."[132]

Ethnic conflict has an extraordinary capacity to transcend time and space. Writing in the *New York Times* about his experience while visiting a Yugoslavia-themed restaurant in New York, a young man of Bosnian origin noted: "Slowly, the bar began to Balkanize. Bosnians, Croatians, Montenegrins and Serbians sat in separate corners. One night, while the D.J. played Serbian turbo-folk songs, the $9 stuffed cabbage I ordered came with bacon. Then the D.J. played 'Last Supper' by the Serbian pop singer Ceca, whom I had hated ever since she'd praised her late husband, Arkan, an international war criminal. During the conflict, he ran 'Arkan's Tigers,' a paramilitary unit that robbed and murdered Muslims. I felt like a minority, alienated again on my own turf. We went back only once more. During another Ceca song, I saw a man waving the three-finger salute – to me, the equivalent of 'Heil Hitler' – and a switch went off in my brain. I flashed to the time my family was stopped at a checkpoint and a paramilitary cocked his gun at my back. The soldiers laughed, proud to demoralize a 12-year-old boy. I wished I could wake up the next day at age 18, to take revenge as a soldier."[133]

In 2003, Croatia's minister of foreign affairs cancelled a trip to Belgrade to protest against attacks on the Croatian embassy by demonstrators celebrating Serbia and Montenegro's victory over Croatia at the European Water Polo Championship. Disgruntled Croatian fans had beaten journalists, damaged the sports venue, and fought with police in the aftermath of the match in Slovenia. Demonstrators in Belgrade celebrated the country's victory by breaking windows of the Croatian embassy and replacing Croatia's flag with a Serbian one.[134] In 2009, Australians of Bosnian and Serbian origin threw chairs and bottles at each other after the conclusion of a tennis match between a Serbian player and an American player of Bosnian origin at the Australian Open.[135]

Cost-benefit models cannot explain the fluidity of tensions that lead people to identify with a specific ethnic group, fight, and destroy property at a tennis venue in Australia many years after the end of an armed conflict on the European continent. It is by looking at conflict as an emotional, resilient, and intense phenomena that we can start explaining why war may persist in times of peace. Analyzing these dynamics helps to explain why, almost two decades after the war, prosecutors in Serbia are still issuing extradition requests in Austria and the United Kingdom against former politicians, military officers, or labor union leaders from Bosnia and Kosovo deemed to have fought on the wrong side of the ethnic divide. It helps to explain why Haris Silajdžić, a Bosniak nationalist politician, was still trying to convince members of the international community in 2007 that they had an international obligation not to recognize the existence of Republika Srpska in Bosnia.

Just like culture wars, these "irrational" battles monopolize much of the public discourse and attention during times of peace. During 2007, the main political parties in Bosnia were all promoting objectives similar to those that led to the armed conflict in 1992. Haris Silajdžić was calling for the establishment of a unitary Bosnia and for the abolition of Republika Srpska. Milorad Dodik was publicly caressing the idea of Republika Srpska's secession from Bosnia and Herzegovina while the Croat nationalist parties were calling for the establishment of a third entity designed along Croat ethnic lines. Not only were such objectives in direct contradiction with one another, they were all residing outside the constitutional parameters agreed to at Dayton and had little to do with the country's European integration aspirations.

The dynamics of conflict in Kosovo reveal many similarities. Those of us who worked for the International Civilian Office (ICO) in Kosovo – an organization mandated to supervise and support Kosovo's accession to independence – witnessed the developments of Kosovo nonviolent war firsthand. The armed conflict in Kosovo had ended almost a decade earlier following the NATO air campaign. A NATO-led military force – KFOR – had been stationed in Kosovo to ensure a peaceful and stable environment ever since. But the conflict over Kosovo's status was still raging as of February 2008 and, given the mandate of the ICO, we were going to be part of it. With the international military force now assuming the role of a peacekeeper in the background, this conflict would be addressed primarily through diplomatic means in Kosovo's parliament, ministries, and courts.

Conflict over power between the Kosovar Albanians and Serbs in Kosovo goes back centuries. Even Tito's regime, often credited with the relative ethnic stability engendered by its brotherhood and unity policy, had to deal with social unrest in Kosovo. In 1981, crowds of angry Albanians had, for example, called for greater autonomy using slogans such "Kosovo-Republic" or "We are Albanians, not Yugoslavs!"[136] Such moves had prompted the Yugoslav authorities to declare a state of emergency and quash demonstrations by sending special police and tanks into Kosovo.[137]

Almost a decade later, Slobodan Milošević took power in Serbia by promoting a tougher line on Kosovo. Milošević's oppressive policies against the majority Kosovar Albanian population reignited a latent conflict. While the Kosovar Albanian response initially took the form of peaceful resistance – under the leadership of Ibrahim Rugova – it subsequently morphed into an armed resistance movement led by the Kosovo Liberation Army (KLA). The violent actions of the KLA quickly engendered a cycle of attacks and counterattacks with the Serbian security forces and, by the end of the summer of 1998, Milošević's armed forces had become actively involved in campaigns to expel Kosovar Albanians from entire villages.[138]

Following intense international pressure, representatives from Pristina and Belgrade attended a peace conference in Rambouillet in February 1999, from which a proposal for an Interim Agreement for Peace and Self-Government in Kosovo emerged. The text of the proposal called for a ceasefire and provided that Kosovo would govern itself democratically. However, the proposal postponed resolution of the conflict's central issue: Kosovo's status.[139]

Despite concerns that the arrangement would not be fully supported at home, the Kosovar Albanian delegation reluctantly agreed, under heavy American pressure, to ratify the text. Milošević, on the other hand, refused to agree to its terms.[140] Using force to back their diplomatic efforts, NATO member states launched a military campaign to coerce Milošević to accept the terms they had tabled in Rambouillet. NATO's air strikes ended on June 10, as Milošević finally agreed to withdraw his forces from Kosovo.[141] The UN Security Council adopted Resolution 1244 (1999),[142] which, while reaffirming the commitment of the international community to the sovereignty and territorial integrity of Serbia (then the Federal Republic of Yugoslavia), stripped control of Kosovo from Serbia and placed the territory under the authority of a United Nations interim administration mission in Kosovo (UNMIK).[143] Despite all such measures, the question at the heart of the conflict – Kosovo's status – had still not been solved. The clearest illustration of this fact could be found in the text of UNSC Resolution 1244 (1999). The resolution explicitly postponed a solution by calling for a political process to determine Kosovo's future status at a later stage.[144]

Diplomats, advisors, and lawyers sent to Kosovo to ensure the implementation of UNSC Resolution 1244 (1999) were soon confronted with Kosovar Albanians' and Kosovo Serbs' attempts to fulfill their respective objectives through nonviolent means. The Kosovar Albanians exercised constant pressure on UNMIK to devolve more power to domestic authorities and start the process of settling Kosovo's status, a process that in their view had to lead to independence.[145] Belgrade, on the other hand, did everything in its power to prevent Kosovo Serb participation in the provisional governing institutions of Kosovo established by UNMIK.[146] It actively undermined the legitimacy of such institutions by maintaining parallel administrative structures, paying salaries to Kosovo Serb civil servants, and supporting separate elections for Serbs in Kosovo. Moreover, Serbia adopted a new constitution that declared Kosovo to be an integral part of its territory.

Frustrated with the lack of progress concerning Kosovo independence, many Kosovar Albanians took to the street in March 2004. Stories of Kosovar Albanian youngsters who had drowned in a river because of the actions of Kosovo Serb youths triggered massive demonstrations and riots throughout Kosovo. The wave of violence destroyed homes, public buildings, churches, and monasteries and displaced some forty-five hundred Kosovo Serbs.[147] Shaken, the international community decided that the time had come to determine Kosovo's final political status. Martti Ahtisaari, former president of Finland and subsequent Nobel Peace Prize laureate, was appointed to lead this process.

The conflict returned, once more, to the negotiating table, with each side pursuing the same basic objectives as before. Kosovar Albanians made independence a condition sine qua non to any solution, while Serbia refused to endorse any solution granting statehood to Kosovo.

After months of discussions, Ahtisaari concluded that no agreement could be reached between the parties and submitted a proposal to the UN. His proposal recommended recognizing Kosovo as an independent state under the condition that the new government enacted a comprehensive system of guarantees for its minorities.[148]

On Sunday, February 17, 2008, Kosovo declared itself an independent and sovereign state committed to implementing all the provisions of Ahtisaari's comprehensive proposal. Far from putting an end to the conflict with Belgrade, these events unleashed new offensives from both sides. Seeking the highest level of international recognition, the new government in Pristina focused its energies on implementing the provisions of the Ahtisaari Plan while lobbying states to recognize it as a state. It adopted a constitution that complied with the provisions of Ahtisaari's comprehensive proposal. The new government also adopted more than fifty laws that implemented specific provisions of the Ahtisaari plan.[149]

Serbia, backed by Russia and other nonrecognizing states, retaliated. It firmly opposed Kosovo's declaration of independence; framing it as an illegal act of secession. It immediately embarked on a comprehensive diplomatic campaign to block further international recognition and to prevent Kosovo's entry into international organizations. It continued to support parallel structures in Kosovo and prevented Kosovo Serbs from participating in new political institutions established by Kosovo. In an attempt to undermine Kosovo's newly declared sovereignty on its territory, Serbia exercised constant pressure on the United Nations to maintain the authorities of UNMIK in Kosovo. It used its relationships with EU member states that had refused to recognize Kosovo's independence to dilute the European Union's collective positions and actions in Kosovo. It also erected administrative obstacles to contain Kosovo's claim to sovereignty by sporadically blocking, for example, the movement of persons and goods from Kosovo.

The conflict heated up once more when, on October 8, 2008, Serbia convinced the UN General Assembly to request an advisory opinion from the International Court of Justice (ICJ) to assess whether Kosovo's declaration of independence was in accordance with international law. The UN General Assembly finally approved Serbia's proposal. A question pertaining to the legality of Kosovo's declaration of independence would be referred to the ICJ. Belgrade had managed to win a round. Back in Pristina, the ICO and embassies of countries that had recognized Kosovo's independence were busy advising the government how best to react to these developments. The conflict had expanded to the ICJ.

It would take the ICJ almost two years to deliver its advisory opinion. In July 2010, it concluded that Kosovo's declaration of independence did not violate international law. On September 9, 2010 the UN General Assembly adopted a resolution that encouraged the European Union's willingness to facilitate dialogue between Serbia and Kosovo over Kosovo's declaration of independence. In 2013, EU diplomacy brokered a historic agreement by which both parties agreed to normalize their relations. After decades of confrontation, there is still no formal agreement between Belgrade and Pristina on Kosovo's status, but the recent success of EU diplomacy suggests that it may well be able to incrementally push conflict away from its most disruptive avenues through the European integration process.

These events illustrate well the dynamics of nonviolent wars. Both Milošević's regime and the KLA leadership were still in place in the aftermath of NATO's military intervention in 1999. Both were able to rely on their respective networks and resources to continue to fight over Kosovo's status. Although Milošević's rule came to an end, the subsequent governments in Belgrade nevertheless actively tried to keep Kosovo within Serbia. Conflicts do not disappear with the signature of a peace agreement, the issuance of a UN Security Council resolution, or the deployment of an international military force to stabilize a territory. Instead, conflicts adapt to new circumstances.

Framing Nonviolent Confrontation as War

Reflecting on the broad systemic forces that pushed the OHR to its defeat in 2007, this chapter has suggested that we were not simply implementing a peace agreement in Bosnia and Herzegovina in 2007. We were actually intervening in a conflict fought through nonviolent means. Using limited means to achieve limited objectives, NATO's military intervention in 1995 had established a space for diplomacy to manage the nonviolent continuation of war. Like culture wars, nonviolent wars are intense conflicts fought over power.

Had we been more conscious of these considerations in 2007, we could have better foreseen the intensity of the Republika Srpska's leadership reaction to the changes we considered enacting, the resilience of their challenge, the fears and the fury our amendments would unleash. By unilaterally amending rules that had temporarily stabilized a long conflict amongst communities in Bosnia, had we not just put our finger on Bosnia's most sensitive point of tension? Had we not – for a brief moment of time – fully been absorbed by Bosnia's conflictual vortex, while in a position of relative weakness? We were all conscious of the existence of conflict. But had we not severely underestimated the depth and power of its current?

Understanding that conflicts adapt themselves to new environments is important from a practitioner's perspective. This fact tends to be lost in the practical realities of international intervention. While a decision from a local actor to shift tactics from conventional to insurgency warfare may happen within days, the speed at which an international presence responds to this tactical shift will almost inevitably be much slower. Who can claim that the U.S. military immediately changed its strategy after the emergence of guerilla warfare in Iraq? The gap in its response probably occurred because of conflicting views within one department of the same government. One can only imagine the time required for different departments in a government to coordinate similar adjustments, let alone different parts within several governments trying to coordinate their action in a foreign theater. The same applies to nonviolent wars. Realizing that military interventions may convert armed struggle into nonviolent conflicts allows for a better practical acknowledgment of the respective roles of military force and diplomacy in addressing a common challenge, and may increase the effectiveness of foreign intervention in managing conflict. Winning the peace is, in certain circumstances, a function of our ability to manage nonviolent wars left behind by military interventions.

It is because they can potentially throw societies back into violence that nonviolent wars matter. For violence not only immediately affects life and property, but also has a long-lasting impact on economic development. According to the World Bank's 2011 World Development

Nonviolent Wars

Report, when compared to countries that were not affected by violence throughout the 1980s, countries affected by violence throughout the same period lagged in poverty reduction by eight percentage points. Furthermore, countries that "had experienced major violence throughout the 1980s and 1990s lagged by 16 percentage points" according to the report's findings. On average, the report noted, "a country experiencing major violence over the entire period (1981–2005) had a poverty rate 21 percentage points higher than a country that saw no violence."[150]

Some may object to qualifying nonviolent confrontations as "war." They will point to the fact that physical force is at the center of war's definition, and that war can therefore not exist without violence. But although waged through nonviolent means, the types of political and legal conflicts that immediately emerge after armed conflict entertain a particularly strong relationship with violence. Leaders involved in these confrontations are often those who were in charge during the armed conflict. The objectives they pursue are often those that pushed the conflict to become violent. Therefore, although waged through nonviolent means, such conflicts are still very much linked to violence.

But nonviolent wars do not correspond to any form of nonviolent conflict either. They represent a specific form of nonviolent conflict; one waged in the aftermath of armed confrontation by wartime elites and constituencies to achieve wartime objectives.

The recent experience in Bosnia and Herzegovina and Kosovo allows us not only to understand how conflict can morph from violence to nonviolence. It also provides crucial insight as to how foreign intervention affects nonviolent wars. As the next chapter argues, intervening in nonviolent wars will almost inevitably generate resistance. In environments where violence has been neutralized, peace operations that are deployed to manage conflict may face a particularly intense form of nonviolent resistance; one that I propose to call *nonviolent insurgency*.

★ ★ ★

6 Nonviolent Insurgency

> Mass action, even if it is intended by its promoters to be nonviolent, is nothing but the application of force under another form, and, when it has as its avowed objective the making of Government impossible, a Government is bound either to resist or abdicate.
>
> —Lord Darwin, Vice Roy of India, addressing both Houses of the Indian Parliament on July 9, 1931[1]

Despite their declared objectives and intentions, foreign interventions disturb ongoing conflicts and trigger resistance. Resistance to intervention may, under certain circumstances, be waged primarily through nonviolent means. Insurgency and counterinsurgency are therefore not necessarily violent phenomena. Contrary to certain assumptions, insurgency and counterinsurgency are not exclusive military concepts. The events in Bosnia demonstrate how complex peace operations deployed to manage war-torn societies may be forced to manage direct challenges against their power and those of state authorities they support – a type of resistance this chapter terms *nonviolent insurgency*. Before examining this particular form of resistance, we will briefly examine the recent evolution of international intervention to better contextualize the type of intervention in which the international community was involved in Bosnia. Placing the Bosnian intervention within its broader context is key to understanding the dynamics of resistance that foreign interveners encountered there.

Intervention

The people of Yugoslavia witnessed firsthand attempts by foreign powers to intervene in the country's internal affairs shortly after the end of the Second World War. On March 27, 1948, Stalin and his foreign minister, Molotov, sent a letter to the leadership of Yugoslavia accusing its members of maintaining anti-Soviet and anti–Marxist-Leninist positions. Tensions between Stalin and Tito had been rising for several months over Yugoslavia's assertive foreign policy toward Albania, Bulgaria, and Greece.[2] Yugoslavia had indeed clashed with Stalin over the potential inclusion of Albania and Bulgaria in the Yugoslav federation. Tito's support of the communist forces in Greece had become an additional irritant for Stalin who had been reluctant to confront the West over Greece.[3] The March letter accused some of Tito's closest advisors of being "dubious Marxists." It also condemned the lack of democracy in the Yugoslav Communist Party, and charged its leadership with harboring a British spy within its ranks.[4]

Having witnessed the purges of the Stalinist regime in the Soviet Union in the 1930s, Tito knew that confessing to Stalin's accusations would amount to submission, which would, at the very least, mark the end of his political career. In a bold move, Tito stood up to Stalin and rejected Moscow's accusations.[5] In a responding letter, he stressed that the Yugoslav experience had many unique features and that its leadership was indeed building socialism in a different form.[6] Irritated, Stalin increased the pressure even more. He sent a copy of his March 27 letter to all of the Eastern European leaders of the Soviet bloc. On May 4, 1948, Stalin and Molotov sent a new letter to the Yugoslav leadership affirming the right of the Soviet Union to interfere in the internal affairs of Eastern European states.[7] Stalin then invited the Yugoslav Communist Party to attend a special meeting of the Cominform – the Moscow-dominated group of communist parties – to solve their differences. Conscious that Stalin was trying to drag him into an arena directly coordinated by Moscow, Tito declined to attend.

In June 1948, the representatives of the Cominform met in Bucharest, without Yugoslavia's representatives.[8] It formally and publically expelled the Yugoslav Communist Party from its ranks. In a resolution adopted unanimously, its members indicated that the leadership of the Yugoslav Communist Party had "recently been carrying out, on the basic questions of foreign and home policy an incorrect line" that constituted "a departure from Marxism-Leninism."[9] Tito's regime, according to the resolution, was consequently "pursuing a policy unfriendly towards the Soviet Union."[10] According to its terms, the Yugoslav Communist Party had put itself and the party "outside the family of fraternal Communist Parties, outside the united Communist front, and consequently, outside the Information Bureau."[11] But the resolution did not stop with the expulsion of Yugoslavia's Communist Party. It called on Tito's regime to choose between conforming to Moscow's demands or running the risk of being overthrown. The Cominform called on the "healthy elements" in Yugoslavia to "compel their present leaders to admit their errors" and to "remove them" should they prove incapable of doing so.[12] Moscow and Belgrade had officially split.

The 1948 split engendered fears of a Soviet-sponsored military intervention within the Yugoslav leadership. These fears increased as the Soviet Union, together with its Eastern European allies, imposed a military blockade on Yugoslavia and massed troops along the Yugoslav frontiers that provoked numerous border incidents with Yugoslavia. In August 1949, the Soviet Union warned Yugoslavia that it would not tolerate the arrests of minority Russians and threatened to resort to more effective means should the arrests continue.[13] The Yugoslav regime actively planned for war against the Soviet Union.[14] It launched a campaign against thousands of Yugoslav communists suspected to be "Stalinists" or "Cominformists." Some of them were jailed, exiled, or killed.[15]

By the end of 1949, President Truman had publicly indicated that the United States would regard a Soviet attack on Yugoslavia as an act of aggression. The U.S. administration had decided that it was in its interest for Titoism to continue to exist as an erosive force in the Soviet bloc.[16] Fearing the broader consequences that its actions could trigger, the Soviet Union would finally refrain from intervening militarily in Yugoslavia.[17] Stalin focused on isolating Tito rather than toppling his regime.[18] The events of 1948 had nevertheless allowed Stalin to set the stage for future interventions in the Soviet sphere of influence. Leaders from satellite countries advocating policies diverging from those favored by Moscow were labeled "Titoists." Traicho Kostov, a founder of the Bulgarian Communist Party and former president of Bulgaria's Council of Ministers, was accused of Titoism and executed in 1949 after criticizing an economic agreement between Bulgaria and the Soviet Union. Lázló Rajk, Hungary's interior minister, was executed on identical charges the same year. In Hungary alone, the hunt for Titoists led to the execution of two thousand officials of the Communist Party while approximately one hundred fifty thousand of them were imprisoned.[19] Similar arrests and trials occurred in Poland and Czechoslovakia.[20]

The Soviet Union eventually intervened militarily in Hungary in 1956, in Czechoslovakia in 1968, and in Afghanistan in 1979. The United States would intervene militarily in Vietnam and Grenada and support counterinsurgency campaigns in many countries that fell within its sphere of influence. Such were the dynamics of the Cold War. Because of the interconnections within each bloc, both dominant countries feared that developments in the internal affairs of a smaller state would quickly spread throughout the bloc.[21] This perspective recognized an implicit entitlement for superpowers to intervene when broader interests were at play. The United States assumed communist governments in smaller countries were instruments of the Kremlin.[22] U.S. Secretary of State Dean Acheson stressed during a lecture delivered at the National War College on December 16, 1947: "I remember when it was accepted doctrine to say in the United States, 'We don't care if another country wants to be communist, that is all right, that is an internal matter, that is a matter for them to decide.' ... It was only as we had more and more experience with communism that we learned it was not a doctrine which people picked up and looked over and either adopted or rejected.... They were being coerced either by an internal organization financed by other countries, or by external pressure to adopt a system of government which had the inescapable consequence of inclusion in the system of the Russian power."[23]

Modern Interventions

Foreign interventions were not exclusive to the Cold War period. Interventions into another state's internal affairs have been a common feature of international affairs. The interventions of Corcyra and Corinth in the domestic struggles of the city of Epidamnus are said to have triggered the Peloponnesian War (431–404 BC) between Sparta and Athens.[24] While interventions in another state's internal affairs did not vanish with the end of the Cold War, the nature and the conditions under which they occurred did change. Instead of being driven by the desire to improve one's strategic position in a global contest for ideological supremacy, post–Cold War interventions are – although still primarily driven by national interests – mostly articulated in support of a declared intent to protect civilian populations. The 2011 intervention in Libya is the latest illustration of this trend.[25]

The end of the Cold War signaled a shift from a bipolar world to one temporarily characterized by U.S. unipolarity. This shift had an impact on international interventions as Western states were increasingly able to seize international mechanisms to intervene in the affairs of other countries. While the United Nations Charter prohibits the threat or use of force against the territorial integrity or political independence of a state, it nevertheless allows states to use force when acting in self-defense or when authorized to do so by the United Nations Security Council.[26] As the end of the Cold War removed the threat of quasi-automatic vetoes within the Security Council, it opened the way for an increasing number of interventions.[27]

The Security Council authorized military actions to restore international peace and security after Iraq's invasion of Kuwait in 1990.[28] The authorization to use force against Iraq fell within the paradigm of classic state conflicts the drafters of the UN Charter had in mind in 1945. But it also marked the beginning of a new era, one during which the Security Council would link actions to restore international peace and stability to the protection of civilians. During the Iraq war, the Security Council had condemned the repression of the Iraqi civilian population in Iraq and had explicitly linked the protection of the civilian population to international peace and security.[29]

Efforts to protect human rights had spread since the adoption of the UN Charter. Eager to prevent a repetition of the atrocities of the Second World War, states had gradually agreed to constrain their sovereignty by consenting to international instruments seeking to protect the rights of persons.[30] Several of these agreements recognized the authority of international bodies to monitor compliance with human rights norms or adjudicate cases brought against states.[31] France and Germany, which had been at the very center of both world wars, have since ratified the European Convention on Human Rights and have consented to the authority of a supranational body, the European Court for Human Rights, to adjudicate cases brought against them. Persons in France can, under certain conditions, bring a case against France before the European Court for Human Rights if they feel their rights under the European Convention have been violated. Concerns over the protection of human rights eroded rigid conceptions of state sovereignty previously held by most states.

The internationalization of human rights also provided a framework within which states could conceive and justify new forms of interventions. By obligating themselves to abide by human rights norms, states have, in a way, provided legal and political opportunities for other states to intervene in their domestic affairs.[32] Framed on the basis of ideological considerations during the Cold War, interventions would increasingly be framed and justified on the basis of human rights considerations after the fall of the Berlin Wall.

But despite the change in rhetoric, modern intervention remains very much linked to national interests. States' concerns over refugee exodus or regional stability are primary driving forces behind interventions. The dissonance between national interests and human rights rhetoric was apparent at the very outset of modern interventions. Saddam Hussein's regime was able to brutally crush civilian uprisings in Iraq immediately after a U.S.-led intervention liberated Kuwait. International action dramatically failed to prevent and respond to the occurrence of genocide, ethnic cleansing, and systemic murder and rape in Rwanda and the former Yugoslavia during the 1990s.

These failures have led some to argue for a redefinition of the conditions under which the international community could and should intervene. Reflecting on the broader tension between legality and legitimacy that permeated debates over NATO's military intervention in Kosovo, the Independent International Commission on Kosovo proposed a framework for principled humanitarian intervention in 2000.[33] Its work was followed by that of the International Commission on Intervention and State Sovereignty in 2001. The commission, composed of experts working with the support of the Canadian government, issued a report that considered the notion of sovereignty as one that implied a *responsibility* to intervene to protect people.[34] In cases where a population is suffering serious harm as a result of war, repression, insurgencies, or state failure and the state is unwilling or unable to halt or avert such harm, the principle of nonintervention in a state's internal affairs must, the report argued, yield to an international "responsibility to protect."[35]

While the responsibility to protect was enshrined, albeit with significant qualifications, by the General Assembly of the United Nations in September 2005, its application remains contested and inconsistent.[36] Some argue that the standard sets the bar too low for intervention.[37] Stronger states are, in practice, immune from intervention. There were no interventions in Russia during the wars in Chechnya. Stronger states are moreover likely to block interventions in another state to protect their interests. China's interests in Sudan prevented any decisive intervention in Darfur during the civil war in Sudan.

The various attitudes of states during the Arab Spring also illustrate the inconsistency with which states decide to intervene. As the rebel armed forces were closing in on Qaddafi's regime in August 2011, the regime in Syria was violently repressing opposition forces in its territory. While NATO forces – acting under the provisions of a UN Security Council resolution adopted pursuant to Chapter VII – intervened to protect the civilian population in Libya, they were nowhere to be seen in Syria.

Western powers imposed sanctions against Syria instead. On August 18, 2011, the leaders of France, Germany, and the United Kingdom issued a joint statement in which they expressed their "utter condemnation" of the "bloody repression of peaceful and courageous demonstrators."[38] The three countries called on the regime to stop the violence and "allow free access to the United Nations for an independent assessment of the situation."[39] Canadian Prime Minister Stephen Harper called on Syria's leader to vacate his position and relinquish power immediately, stressing that Canada had taken "decisive action" by imposing sanctions targeting members of the Syrian regime and its supporters.[40] U.S. President Barack Obama condemned the brutality of the Syrian repression and noted that the "violations of the universal rights of the Syrian people have revealed to Syria, the region, and the world the Assad Government's flagrant disrespect for the dignity of the Syrian people."[41] He called on President Assad to step aside and ordered sanctions such as freezing assets and prohibiting imports of Syrian petrol.[42] A few weeks later, French Minister of Foreign Affairs Alain Juppé accused the Syrian government of carrying out "crimes against humanity."[43]

Intervening in Syria risked disturbing the regional competition between Iran and Saudi Arabia. Syria exported most of its oil to the European Union. Russia maintained a naval base in the country. The size of Syria, its influence on wider interests, and the threat of Russian and Chinese vetoes in the Security Council all made military intervention more difficult to conceive in comparison to Libya – a fact the Obama administration publicly recognized early in 2012.[44]

The people of Yugoslavia directly witnessed the evolution of foreign interventions. In 1948, their regime feared military intervention from Stalin. More than forty years later, foreign countries intervened militarily in the successor states of Yugoslavia. This time, their interventions had little to do with superpowers engaged in global ideological confrontations. Violent conflicts had erupted in the Yugoslav republics and foreign states were trying, without much success, to do something about it. The UN Security Council deployed a protection force in Croatia, Bosnia, and the Former Yugoslav Republic of Macedonia as early as 1992 to mitigate the impact of conflict on civilians.[45] Several years later, NATO carried out air strikes in Bosnia to force peace negotiations in Dayton. In 1999, it launched a seventy-seven-day air campaign against Milošević's armed forces to stop violence in Kosovo.

This brief overview allows us to better understand the type of intervention in which the international community was involved after NATO's 1995 military campaign in Bosnia. The actions of the international community in Bosnia were part of a protracted intervention seeking to restore and maintain peace and security. The peace operations deployed to Bosnia belong to a particular brand of peacekeeping, one where peace operations are vested with comprehensive authorities. The Office of the High Representative – as well as UNMIK in Kosovo – had, for example, powers to enact and amend legislation. Practitioners tend to refer to such operations as "international administrations" or missions with "executive mandates." Scholarly work tends, on the other hand, to refer to them as "complex peacekeeping" or "multidimensional peacekeeping" operations.[46] The next section explains how complex peace operations disturb conflict systems and how they may engender particularly intense forms of resistance within such systems.

Intervention and Resistance

When they erupt, violent conflicts may seem like discrete and isolated incidents, but they are part of a broader interconnected web. When intervening in a conflict, a foreign actor will inevitably have an impact on conflict systems. The actions of actors within this system will adapt accordingly. Going back to the image of the two wrestlers used by Clausewitz, there is little doubt that intervention by a third party in an ongoing wrestling match will have an impact on the actions of each wrestler. Regardless of the form it takes, intervention modifies conflict and the relative position of parties vis-à-vis each other.

Even the lightest presence will have an impact. Rami Jarah, a young exiled Syrian citizen journalist who used his phone to live stream footage of protests against the Assad regime in Syria in 2011 said during an interview: "live streaming was very effective because while we were live streaming, the government would be aware of the fact that it was being live streamed and they would not attack the demonstrations, but once, for example, if the battery ran out, and the live stream went offline, within minutes, security forces and many plain clothes sent by the government would attack the demonstration and usually end up opening fire."[47]

Intervention can often lead to undesired and unpredicted outcomes. Trying to reduce the intensity of conflict in former Yugoslavia, the international community imposed an arms embargo in September 1991.[48] Instead of reducing violence in Bosnia and Croatia, the embargo consolidated the military advantage of Serb-controlled areas supported by the well-equipped Yugoslav National Army controlled by Belgrade. Many of the attempts to negotiate peace in Bosnia backfired. By offering to create cantons designed along ethnic lines to stop the war in Bosnia, the Vance-Owen Peace Plan of 1992–3 ignited competition over territory amongst Croats and Muslims in central Bosnia, for example. Ethnic cleansing campaigns intensified as each side sought to grab as much land as possible.[49]

By intervening in a system, a foreign actor will not only disturb it. It will become part of it. Parties to a conflict will adapt to the foreign intervener's presence. This happens even if the proclaimed objective of the intervening actor is to be "neutral." During the 1992–5 armed conflict in Bosnia, the office of the United Nations High Commissioner for Refugees (UNHCR) was mandated to deliver humanitarian assistance to populations in need. Access to these populations had to be negotiated with the armed forces that exercised effective control over the area where these populations were located. The price for access often had to be paid with wood, coal, and food which were, among other things, diverted to replenish the very armed forces that besieged populations in need.[50]

Foreign intrusion into conflict triggers reactions. Belligerent groups that perceive the intervening actor as a force capable of furthering their interests will attempt to harness its power to their advantage. On the other hand, parties that perceive the impact of an intervener as detrimental to their interests will seek to undermine its power. Resistance may take a multitude of forms and is a function of the intensity of a specific intervention. To better understand the main suggestion of this chapter – that complex peace operations deployed to manage war-torn societies may be forced to manage nonviolent insurgencies – we must differentiate between different types of interventions as insurgency is a reaction to a particular intense form of intervention. To better illustrate this point, we can categorize foreign interventions into three broad categories: *minimal, reinforced*, and *comprehensive* interventions.

Minimal interventions regroup interventions based on standard foreign policy instruments such as public diplomacy and the management of political, military, and economic ties. The actions of foreign governments during the popular protests against Tunisian President Ben Ali in 2011 fall within this category. Foreign states issued public statements supporting democratic and peaceful demonstrations and condemning violence. Some states also facilitated arrangements allowing President Ben Ali to flee Tunisia.

Reinforced interventions comprise those interventions that resort – in addition to standard means – to measures such as economic sanctions, suspension of membership in international organizations, or the deployment of observers to a given conflict. The Arab League's decision to impose economic sanctions against Syria in 2011 or its decision to deploy civilian and military observers to the country fall within this category.

Comprehensive interventions include actions by which a foreign actor establishes effective control over part of the environment in which it intervenes. This control can result from direct military intervention and/or the establishment of complex peace operations through negotiations or treaty-based mechanisms. The complex peace operations deployed to Bosnia, Kosovo, and East Timor in the 1990s fall within this category.

All types of intervention trigger reactions. In case of *minimal interventions*, resistance will often consist of countermeasures such as public condemnations, arrests, and deportations. In January 2011, President Ben Ali portrayed demonstrations against his regime as terrorist acts orchestrated by foreign forces trying to damage Tunisia.[51] The following year, while facing mounting opposition in Syria, President Assad referred to protestors as traitors taking part in a foreign-backed movement.[52] In February 2012, in the midst of the power transition process that followed the ousting of the Mubarak regime in Egypt, governmental authorities arrested nineteen Americans whom they accused of illegally training groups in election monitoring. "The government will not hesitate to expose foreign schemes that threaten the stability of the homeland," said an Egyptian official responsible for foreign aid.[53]

Reinforced interventions engender resistance as well. The Syrian government retaliated as soon as the Arab League imposed sanctions on Syria in 2011. It stated that the Arab League had declared "economic war" against Syria and immediately threatened to block access to its airspace and to prevent commercial traffic between the Persian Gulf and Turkey from passing through its roads.[54]

This leads us to an important point, one that pertains to resistance engendered by *comprehensive interventions*. As recent experiences in Afghanistan and Iraq illustrate, belligerent groups on the ground may decide to resist attempts by foreign interveners to exercise effective control – or their attempts to support the exercise of such control by a domestic actor – by directly challenging their power and authority. As such, there is a relationship between comprehensive intervention and *insurgency*. Insurgency – usually understood as a struggle to overthrow an existing order – can, under certain conditions, be conceived as an intense form of resistance to a particularly intense form of intervention.

Violent Insurgency

Insurgencies may be primarily violent. Facing military intervention from a foreign actor, a party may decide to resist an intervention through conventional military means. For example, the Iraqi army fought against the U.S.-led military coalition at the outset of both the 1990 and 2003 interventions in Iraq. In cases where the intervening actor has an overwhelming advantage in conventional warfare, a party may decide to resist the intervening force through other violent means. The U.S.-led invasion in Afghanistan in 2001 and in Iraq in 2003 pushed parties to move away from conventional warfare and to engage the intervening force through insurgency warfare. Parties on the ground have a tactical interest in switching to insurgency warfare.

David Galula, a former French officer who was active in the French counterinsurgency operations in Algeria, wrote a seminal book on this subject while at Harvard in the 1960s. Galula considered insurgency as a way – distinct from revolutions and plots – to seize power by force. He defined it as "a *protracted struggle* conducted methodically, step by step, in order to attain specific intermediate objectives leading finally to the overthrow of the existing order."[55] The *U.S. Army – Marine Corps Counterinsurgency Field Manual* defines *insurgency* as "an organized movement aimed at the overthrow of a constituted government through the use of subversion and armed conflict."[56] An insurgency is "an organized, protracted politico-military struggle designed to weaken the control and legitimacy of an established government, occupying power, or other political authority."[57] Armed insurgency is neither new nor an isolated phenomenon. It has been the most common form of warfare throughout history and remains so today.[58] The term *guerilla*, often used to describe armed insurgencies, was coined to describe the "small war" fought against Napoléon's two hundred fifty thousand occupying troops in Spain in 1808.[59] Insurgencies have been fought in France and Yugoslavia under Nazi occupation. They have also been fought in China, Vietnam, Algeria, most of Latin America during the Cold War, and more recently in Iraq and Afghanistan.

Counterinsurgency – also commonly referred to by its acronym "COIN" – is a corollary term used to describe the means by which one fights an insurgency. David Kilcullen, former senior counterinsurgency advisor to U.S. General Petraeus in Iraq, defines counterinsurgency as "an umbrella term that describes the complete range of measures that governments take to defeat insurgencies."[60] Such measures "can be political, administrative, military, economic, psychological, and are almost always used in combination."[61] The *U.S. Army – Marine Corps Counterinsurgency Field Manual* defines counterinsurgency as "military, paramilitary, political, economic, psychological, and civic actions taken by a government to defeat insurgency."[62]

Armed insurgency and counterinsurgency campaigns compete for the hearts and minds of the civilian population. The reason for this is linked to the nature of armed insurgency. Instead of directly attacking a conventional force, armed insurgents seek to hide behind the civilian population to attack an occupying force. They use the population to transfer arms and ammunitions; insurgents also take refuge among civilians before and after an attack. Mao famously argued that the guerilla fish needed to navigate in the people's sea to be effective. The civilian population is the oxygen of insurgencies. Unlike mechanized armies composed of soldiers in uniforms stationed in barrack camps or posts, insurgents are fluid and difficult to detect. To attack their opponents, insurgents will therefore need the support of the civilian population. The local population's tacit agreement or feigned ignorance about the source of an attack is an important asset for the insurgents. Eroding this connectivity and isolating the insurgents from the population is thus a key strategic objective of counterinsurgency campaigns.[63] An occupying force will attempt to do this by trying to win the allegiance and support of the local population. No longer able to hide behind the civilian population, the insurgents can become a more easily identifiable target. Once separated from the civilian population, the insurgency can, according to military doctrine, be pinned down and destroyed.[64]

The current nature of the U.S.-led military intervention in Afghanistan illustrates well such dynamics. After realizing that the civilian casualties inflicted by its air campaigns in Afghanistan were galvanizing resentment and playing into the hands of the Taliban, the International Security Assistance Force (ISAF) changed tactics. The new guidance issued by the ISAF acknowledged the nature of the struggle in which it was involved. Its 2009 *Counterinsurgency Guidance* states: "ISAF's mission is to help the Republic of Afghanistan ... defeat the insurgency threatening their country. Protecting the Afghan people is the mission. The Afghan people will decide who wins this fight and we ... are in a struggle for their support."[65] The guidance further notes: "We need to think and act very differently to be successful. The will of the people is the Objective. An effective 'offensive' operation in counterinsurgency, therefore, is one that takes from the insurgent what he cannot afford to lose – control of the population. We must think of offensive operations not simply as those that target militants, but ones that earn the trust and support of the people while denying influence and access to the insurgent."[66]

Winning the support of the population is an incredibly difficult task. Foreign presences are inevitably placed at a systemic disadvantage. Insurgents benefit from a "longevity advantage." From the point of view of a domestic actor, the foreign presence is an unreliable ally.[67] This plays into daily decisions for the local population. While allegiance may be presented as a broad strategic objective in the strategic guidance of foreigners, it is often a matter of life or death for the local civilian population. In the village of Deh Rawood in Afghanistan, a sixty-year-old woman and her seven-year-old grandson were pulled out of a bus by fighters in December 2007. They were reportedly accused of spying and summarily executed after the fighters found a U.S. dollar bill in the young boy's pocket.[68] In June 2010, a seven-year-old boy was found dead in the village of Heratiyan, Afghanistan. The boy had been hanged after his family had reportedly refused to cooperate with the Taliban. Members of the family had been denounced as NATO or U.S. spies.[69]

In the aftermath of the U.S-led military interventions in Iraq and Afghanistan, insurgencies have been framed primarily through a military lens. But are insurgency and counterinsurgency exclusively military concepts? Can they only be waged primarily through violence? Given that both resort to a wide spectrum of actions, ranging from violent to nonviolent ones, is it not consequently possible that both can be carried out primarily through nonviolent means?[70]

Nonviolent Insurgency

Nonviolent challenges to power are possible. They are actually neither rare nor new. One of the earliest records of nonviolent resistance has been traced back to 494 BC, when Plebeians extracted concessions from the Roman ruling class by withdrawing to a hill outside of Rome, thus refusing to join a military campaign.[71] Following the Second World War, Marxist-Leninist theories, combined with the active support of the Soviet Union to guerilla movements, fueled numerous armed insurrections around the globe. But by the end of the 1970s, the relative importance of armed insurrections started to decline.[72] Scholarly work has identified the occurrence of no fewer than thirty-one cases of major unarmed insurrections in lesser-developed countries between 1978 and 2001.[73]

Despite facing a large state security and military apparatus, Iranians toppled the Shah's regime by resorting to strikes, boycotts, and other forms of noncooperation in 1979.[74] No longer able to exercise power in a country paralyzed by protest, the Shah was forced into exile. The Iranian revolution marked the beginning of an extensive series of unarmed insurrections that spread to countries such as Bolivia, Poland, South Africa, Czechoslovakia, Hungary, Georgia, and the Ukraine. Slobodan Milošević, the very man whose actions triggered the fall of Yugoslavia, was removed from power following widespread civilian resistance campaigns in 2000. More recently, unarmed insurrections have forced presidents to resign in Tunisia and Egypt.

A recent study of 323 violent and nonviolent resistance campaigns conducted between 1900 and 2006 argues that nonviolent resistance is more effective than violent resistance.[75] According to this study, nonviolent campaigns are almost twice as likely as violent ones to achieve complete or partial success.[76] The higher rates of success of nonviolent campaigns can be explained by the higher levels of participation they tend to engender.[77] Given that barriers to participation in nonviolent campaigns are lower, they attract more participation. Participants are not required to present specific physical attributes or train to handle weapons, for example.[78] Greater participation engenders more resilience, more innovation, and higher levels of disruption from those who resist. This, in turn, increases the costs of maintaining the status quo and makes nonviolent campaigns more likely to succeed.[79] It is therefore perfectly possible for a ruling authority to be overthrown or undermined primarily through nonviolent means.

Dynamics of Nonviolent Insurgency

But how is power challenged through nonviolent means? To answer this question, we need to take a closer look at the nature and dynamics of power. In the words of Joseph Nye, power is like the weather. "Everyone depends on it and talks about it, but few understand it."[80] Recent literature on power has engendered an extensive vocabulary comprising expressions such as *soft power, hard power, smart power,* or other qualifications such as military or economic power. Such expressions are useful for better understanding a specific analytical perspective on power by describing either types of power or specific means by which it can be applied but drives us away from its essence. Power should be understood as a capacity, namely the *capacity to effect outcomes*.[81]

It is a common reflex to look at power as being concentrated in a single and fixed point. Nonviolent action strategists refute this proposition.[82] Gene Sharp, one of the most influential scholars of nonviolent action, argues that power is not a fixed quantity intrinsic to a ruler. Power is better conceived, according to Sharp, as fluid and distributed in a given society. To exercise power, a ruling authority must harness sources of power that are extrinsic.[83]

What are these sources of power? Sharp argues that there are six different sources of power. These sources are *authority* (the capacity to direct and be obeyed by others), *human resources* (civil servants, police, and military who implement a ruler's policies), the *skills and knowledge* of people implementing a regime's policies, *intangible factors* (a given society's attitudes toward power), control over *material resources* (financial resources, communication, and transportation), and the capacity to impose *sanctions*.[84] A ruler will rarely have access to all these sources of power at once. A given distribution of power is therefore never permanent and can change rapidly.

The Roman philosopher Cicero is believed to have coined the expression *Cum potestas in populo, auctoritas in senatu sit* (power lies with the people, authority rests in the Senate). His maxim captures the idea that, to maintain access to power, a regime needs the cooperation and obedience of the population. If power lies in the population, then the power of a ruler consequently depends on the degree to which society grants power to the ruler.[85] A ruler depends on the obedience and cooperation of persons, groups, associations, and members of the administration to enforce his policies.[86] Once persons, civil servants, the police, and the military refuse to carry out the policies of a ruling authority, little is left of a ruler's power. Obedience is therefore at the heart of political power.[87] This leads us to an important point about nonviolent insurgency: *consent is never fixed and can be withdrawn*.[88]

If power is neither permanent nor concentrated in the hands of a ruling authority, it logically flows that a core strategic objective of nonviolent resistance is to move a ruling authority away from its sources of power and its pillars of support. If marshaled and directed effectively by another actor, power is ultimately too great for any established ruling authority to resist.[89] Nonviolent insurgency, just like violent insurgency, is thus a competition to win the hearts and minds of a critical number of persons in a given population. The main difference lies in the nature of means employed.

Sharp has identified 198 methods of nonviolent actions that include, for example, mass media communication,[90] assemblies of protest and support,[91] boycott of legislative assemblies and government,[92] generalized administrative noncooperation,[93] and the establishment of parallel governing structures.[94]

A ruling authority whose power is challenged through nonviolent means can react by *ignoring* the challenge, trying to *conciliate* opponents (declaring new elections or establishing a commission), making concessions through *reform*, or *repressing* the challenge.[95] When repressing a given nonviolent challenge, a regime may resort to force. Nonviolent action often generates violent responses. The United Nations High Commissioner for Human Rights estimated at nineteen hundred the number of civilians killed during the primarily nonviolent phase of the anti-Assad movement in Syria between March and September 2011.[96] A regime may also decide to indirectly repress unarmed challenges through third parties.[97] For example, on February 2, 2011, supporters of Mubarak on horses and camels raided crowds of protesters on Tahrir Square. The Egyptian army did little to stop the clash during which three people died and more than six hundred were reportedly injured.[98]

Sanctions are a way for a ruling authority to enforce obedience.[99] Sanctions therefore require the participation and assistance of some segment of the population in order to be enforced. A regime needs bureaucrats, soldiers, and police officers to enforce sanctions.[100] While studies point to various forms of relationships between repression and social mobilization, it is generally assumed that repression or sanctions will inhibit mobilization.[101] It is also assumed that targeted repression is more effective than indiscriminate repression as the latter tends to affect the legitimacy of the ruling authority in the long term.[102]

But sanction and repression alone cannot ensure full compliance. Persons or groups may continue to tolerate the consequences of disobedience. In December 1981, Adam Michnik was arrested in Poland together with the leadership of the Solidarity movement. While held in prison, he wrote about his refusal to sign a "loyalty declaration," which the authorities had offered as a condition to release him from prison. "These declarations are supposed to make us into lowly and servile people, who will not rise up to fight for freedom and dignity. So by refusing to talk with the policeman, by refusing to collaborate, by rejection of the status of informer, and by choosing to be a political prisoner you are defending hope. Not just hope within yourself and for yourself but also in others and for others. You are casting your declaration of hope out of your prison cell into the world, like a sealed bottle into the ocean. If even one single person finds it, you will have scored a victory."[103] "But you know, as you stand alone, handcuffed, with your eyes filled with tear gas, in front of policemen who are shaking their guns at you – you can see it clearly in the dark and starless night ... that the course of the avalanche depends on the stones over which it rolls.... And you want to be the stone that will reverse the course of events."[104]

Nonviolent challenges can lead to a reversal of events. Repression can backfire against a regime and undermine its legitimacy and authority. Excessive repression may fragment a society's elite and may offer opportunities for challengers. In democracies, certain segments of a governing coalition may withdraw their support and align themselves with challengers. In nondemocratic regimes, divisions may start appearing between civilian and military segments of the regime, between "hard-liners" and "moderates."[105] In such cases, opponents to the regime may be able to turn a regime's power against itself.[106] Those who assist the regime may refuse to cooperate and instead choose to defect. Soldiers and police forces may disobey orders to shoot at civilians. External backers may withdraw their support. Regimes fighting for their survival are particularly conscious of this. In May 2011, Syrian armed forces were sent to the city of Ar Rastan in response to protests against the Assad regime. Marching through the streets in groups, soldiers were reportedly shooting indiscriminately at people and looting homes. Behind each military unit, groups of armed men were walking, ready to shoot any soldier refusing to obey orders.[107]

To be successful, nonviolent insurgency must first mobilize and then ensure that mobilization leads to effective changes.[108] Syria and Bahrain came up against significant obstacles in their attempts to mobilize against their respective regimes in 2011. While successful in mobilizing, it is still unclear to what extent protesters in Tunisia and Egypt managed to effect deep changes in their national constitutional architecture. The movements were successful in removing persons from office; both President Mubarak and Ben Ali were forced to resign as a consequence of the movements. But the extent to which such campaigns will affect the fundamental structures of power remains unclear. When successful, nonviolent resistance may force a regime to convert to its demands or accommodate some of them. This level of success may, at times, also lead to situations where the regime remains formally in place but is unable to exercise power. Such a situation can ultimately lead to the regime's disintegration.[109]

Nonviolent resistance covers a wide spectrum of means and objectives. It is common to encounter expressions such as "unarmed insurrection," "passive resistance," "civilian resistance," or "civil disobedience" in the literature exploring nonviolent action.[110] *Civil resistance* has been recently defined as a "type of political action that relies on the use of non-violent methods" and that "involves a range of widespread and sustained activities that challenge a particular power, force, policy, or regime." Civil resistance has been "used in many types of struggle in modern times," such as struggles "against colonialism, foreign occupations, military *coups d'état*, dictatorial regimes, electoral malpractice, corruption, and racial, religious, and gender discrimination." Civil resistance has been used "not only against tyrannical rule, but also against democratically elected governments, over such issues as maintenance of key elements of the constitutional order, preservation of regional autonomy within a country, defence of minority rights, environmental protection, and opposition to involvement in certain military interventions and wars."[111]

Civil resistance is a means to achieve an end. It can pursue different objectives. It has been used to regain power or to counter movements seeking to seize power. It prevented the attempt by German armed forces to install Wolfgang Kapp as Germany's chancellor in 1920. Kapp was reportedly unable to find secretaries willing to type his proclamations. Civil servants refused to obey his orders. Widespread disobedience led the putsch to collapse and Kapp quickly fled to Sweden.[112] Civil resistance was also used to counter the attempt of French generals in Algeria to challenge the power of President Charles de Gaulle in 1961.[113] Dissatisfied with de Gaulle's support for the decolonization of Algeria, a number of French generals seized control of the city of Algiers in April 1961. With the possibility of the putsch extending to the territory of France looming, de Gaulle addressed the people of France in a nationwide broadcast on April 23, 1961. "I order that all means, I say all means, be employed everywhere to block the way to these men.... I forbid every Frenchman, and all soldiers, to carry out any of their orders."[114] His concluding words left little doubt as to his understanding of where his power was ultimately lying. "People of France, help me!" de Gaulle concluded.[115] Faced with widespread disobedience, the leaders of the putsch were ultimately forced to pull out of Algiers on April 26, 1961.[116]

Peace Operations and Nonviolent Insurgency

So, how do complex peace operations come to face nonviolent insurgencies? Two main reasons help explain this. First, foreign interveners involved in complex peace operations are not merely implementing peace processes. They are, like other interveners, disturbing conflict systems and triggering intense forms of resistance within such systems. Second, nonviolent insurgency makes tactical sense for parties in conflict who seek to neutralize the impact of foreign interveners implementing peace processes.

Peace Operations are not Merely Implementing Peace Processes

Conflicts in which the international community intervenes are, at their highest level of abstraction, fought over power. Power is what is deployed and fought over, feared, and sought by groups in conflict. Power is what foreign interveners apply. It is what they disturb amongst belligerents. It is what foreign actors seek to reestablish in states that are unable or unwilling to protect those within their reach. It is what is being attacked as they try to do so.

Armed conflict within a state is a consequence of a power failure. As the state's Weberian monopoly over violence collapses, society quickly retrocedes into a Hobbesian state of nature. No central authority enjoys exclusive power and various groups maintain opposing claims to everything in the environment. As foreign actors seek to reestablish or strengthen a state's capacity to project power, they inevitably disturb positions and interests of parties engaged in conflict.

In cases where international intervention stops violent conflict before effective control has been decisively established on the battlefield, competition over power remains fiercely alive. Interveners are never merely rebuilding parliaments, courts, and police forces in their efforts to implement peace. Establishing new police forces, customs services, or courts in that context affects conflict. If too many constitutional competencies, taxation authorities, and judges fall under the control of one side, one's relative power will be diminished. Secessionist objectives become more difficult to achieve against an opponent who suddenly controls most of the army and police forces rebuilt by foreigners. Therefore, far from being a neutral process, international efforts to build or restore institutions become a fundamental part of the conflict. Peace processes are therefore highly destabilizing forms of intervention for parties in conflict. Opposing groups will adapt by either harnessing the power of interveners or by resisting its impact on an opponent's relative position. This resistance may be directed against the power of the domestic institutions the peace operation seeks to establish and/or against the peace operation's own power.

This resistance is waged on an institutional and legal battleground. Some authors exclude institutional political actions from the realm of civil resistance.[117] They consider that electoral processes, voting, and legislating would not fall within the scope of nonviolent action.[118] Even if one were to agree with this contention, there are nevertheless contexts in which contentious action can be taken through institutions and where outcomes are not prescribed. These include situations in which actors waging these battles take risks and accept to face negative consequences.

Events in Bosnia and Kosovo illustrate how parties can challenge the power of a foreign actor through their own institutions. Courts can refuse to apply legislation adopted by the foreign presence. Parties may refuse to subject their laws to the sanctioning power of a foreign representative. This is exactly how Kosovo authorities challenged the power of UNMIK in February 2008. It is through their executive and parliamentary institutions that Kosovars adopted, executed, or interpreted laws in a way that effectively denied the power of the United Nations special representative of the UN secretary-general on the ground. The UN secretary-general explicitly recognized this fact in his report to the Security Council on November 24, 2008: "As a consequence of the deeply diverging paths taken by Belgrade and the Kosovo authorities following Kosovo's declaration of independence, the space in which UNMIK can operate has changed. As is evident from the developments on the ground, my Special Representative is facing increasing difficulties in exercising his mandate owing to the conflict between resolution 1244 (1999) and the Kosovo Constitution, which does not take UNMIK into account. The Kosovo authorities frequently question the authority of UNMIK in a Kosovo now being governed under the new Constitution. While my Special Representative is still formally vested with executive authority under resolution 1244 (1999), he is unable to enforce this authority. In reality, such authority can be exercised only if and when it is accepted as the basis for decisions by my Special Representative. Therefore, very few executive decisions have been issued by my Special Representative since 15 June."[119]

Acting through domestic institutions, parties can challenge the legal and institutional framework that foreign actors are trying to enforce.[120]

Nonviolent Insurgency Makes Tactical Sense

Challenging a foreign intervening power through nonviolence is not only possible; it may make tactical sense. First, one of the core rules of an insurgency is to avoid confronting a superior opponent on its own terms.[121] Instead of channeling efforts where an opponent enjoys superiority, an insurgent force tries to bring its opponent into an environment where it has the advantage. These calculations are those that incite a party to switch from conventional to guerilla warfare. It may also incite a party to push the conflict into a nonviolent space by agreeing to peace. By doing so, the local actor drags an external power into an arena shaped by unfamiliar rules, institutions, and conventions – an arena that helps the local actor regain a systemic advantage.

Further, attacking the power of an external entity through nonviolent means does not require expensive resources, equipment, or training. Demonstrating, striking, and political outmaneuvering can be carried out by most members of the local population.

Finally, by shifting a conflict to a nonviolent arena, an insurgent force not only drags its foreign opponent into unknown territory; it brings the opponent into an environment in which it *ultimately enjoys the power to influence the rules according to which conflict is waged*. By switching to nonviolence, an insurgent brings the conflict into its parliamentary, judicial, and administrative institutions. By doing so, the insurgency gains control over the environment in which conflict occurs, and gains new opportunities to undermine and attack the power of the foreign presence.

The environment in which the Office of the High Representative found itself in Bosnia is a good illustration of such dynamics. The High Representative enjoyed the authority to enact legislation in Bosnia to ensure the implementation of the Dayton Accords. While comprehensive at first glance, the effectiveness of such powers ultimately depended on the willingness of domestic actors to cooperate with the High Representative. A local party willing to resist legislation imposed by the High Representative could ultimately amend the legislation in parliament. It could also challenge the law before its courts, or administratively block the legislation by refraining from publishing it in the *Official Gazette*, for example.

Factions resisting foreign intervention have an interest in dragging the foreign actor from one context to another, each time moving it away from its strongest position or from the position in which it is gaining strength. Peace is not necessarily imposed upon a party. A party's decision to end armed conflict may be partially taken on the basis of tactical considerations. Whether this is done consciously or intuitively, *agreeing to peace may nevertheless offer new opportunities to continue war.*

Qualifications and Definitions

If we are to accept that complex peace operations may be faced with nonviolent insurgencies, a number of qualifications then need to be made. There is a certain sense of unease with the term *insurgency*; a term that is both pejorative and relative. In an international context where peace operations are mostly agreed upon by a core of powerful states in order to manage conflict at their peripheries, there is a danger for the term *nonviolent insurgency* to be used to categorize any type of opposition against norms and models promoted by these powerful states. It would be difficult to see how political opposition to the privatization of states' assets in a postconflict setting could be equated to insurgent actions, for example. The expression ought therefore to be used conservatively, and calls for a number of important qualifications.

First, not all nonviolent resistance can – or should – be equated to nonviolent insurgency. Complex peace operations try, on one hand, to establish a nonviolent space where conflict is solved through rules and institutions.[122] As they try to do so, they will face attempts by groups to challenge power within this space. These attempts may be pursued through legitimate means. Therefore, not all forms of competition and resistance within these spaces can be equated to insurgency. Denying administrative authorizations or blocking laws in parliament are the daily business of liberal democratic battles. The fact that nonviolent competition over power is occurring is a sign of success for any peace operation and is also a sign that this very space is holding.

Second, the objective at the center of nonviolent insurgency is key. To qualify as nonviolent insurgent action, a given action needs to challenge the very existence of a given nonviolent space.

Third, to qualify as nonviolent insurgent actions, such actions must entertain a particularly close relationship with generalized violence. The mere existence of a secessionist discourse does not necessarily equate to nonviolent insurgency. Calling into question the existence of a given constitutional order is an action protected by various public liberties in most liberal democracies. It would indeed be somewhat counterintuitive to qualify those who argued for the dissolution of Czechoslovakia in the early 1990s as "insurgents." Context therefore matters. One needs to distinguish between the dissolution of Czechoslovakia on one hand and secessionist actions that are in violation of a peace process seeking to end a war marked by genocide, ethnic cleansing, generalized murder, and rape.

Finally, nonviolent insurgency is fluid. Political confrontations follow tortuous paths and evolve organically. A group that may accept the maintenance of a nonviolent space may suddenly resort to nonviolent insurgent action under certain circumstances. It may therefore be inappropriate to ascribe the label of nonviolent insurgent to a specific group. Bosnian Croat and Bosnian Serb nationalists both resorted to nonviolent insurgent actions during the peace implementation process in BiH. On the other hand, both the SNSD and HDZ – leading Bosnian Serb and Bosnian Croat nationalist parties – supported a constitutional reform process in 2006 that would have increased the competencies of the central state in BiH.

It is with these qualifications in mind that I propose the following definition: a nonviolent insurgency consists of *nonviolent actions that seek, in violation of a peace process, to undermine or overthrow the existence of authorities that are essential for preventing a slide back into a state of generalized violence.*

Diplomatic counterinsurgency, on the other hand, consists of *nonviolent actions undertaken by actors responsible for implementing a peace process in order to prevent nonviolent insurgency from succeeding.* Diplomatic counterinsurgency's objective is not to counter any type of opposition or resistance. Similar to military counterinsurgency, a peace operation may, in the face of a challenge, be forced to adopt nonviolent actions to erode the connectivity between forces of resistance and the general population in its efforts to secure popular consent vis-à-vis new power arrangements. These actions flow from the responsibility conferred upon an international authority to maintain and restore international peace and order. Its sole objective must be to protect the state of nonviolence it is mandated to maintain and/or restore.

Peace Spoilers or Actors in Nonviolent Wars?

Some of the academic literature on peace agreements has focused on the notion of "spoilers."[123] According to a model developed by scholar John Stedman, the greatest source of risk for peacemaking would come from "spoilers – leaders and parties who believe that peace emerging from negotiations threatens their power, worldview, and interests, and use violence to undermine attempts to achieve it."[124] This model considers that international actors make a crucial difference in the success and failure of peace processes. By identifying the type of spoilers to be confronted and by adopting strategies to prevent them from disrupting peace processes, international actors increase the chances of successful peace implementation.

The model is both useful and insightful, but direct personal experience with concrete aspects of peace implementation leads me to believe that it has significant limits. By their very nature, models oversimplify complex and multidimensional realities. The categorization of actors in a peace process does not fully capture their constant adaptation to changing circumstances. Opposition to an agreement may vary depending on subject matters and time. For example, despite being generally supportive of the Dayton peace agreement, a faction of the Bosnian Muslim leadership sought to undermine parts of the agreement guaranteeing the existence of a Serb entity during its implementation phase. While boycotting the agreement initially, the Bosnian Serb leadership insisted on the strict application of several of the agreement's components many years later.

Moreover, parties to a conflict are not monolithic entities, and the interests and positions they claim to represent change over time. They are subjected to internal sub-conflicts over power amongst different factions embracing different objectives and interests. The position of these groups is shaped by constituencies. All these factors make the behaviors of parties in conflict highly unpredictable and subject to several mutations. These organic mutations of interests and positions inevitably affect the accuracy of models. Stedman himself acknowledges and alerts policy makers to the existence of complexities associated with categorizing a party as a specific type of spoiler.[125]

Another limitation of the spoiler model lies in its assumption that peace processes are necessarily threatened through violent means. Events in Bosnia, Kosovo, and Northern Ireland, to name only a few examples, illustrate that resistance to peace initiatives are often carried out through nonviolent means.[126] As such, the model leaves unaddressed a significant range of threats to peace processes.

But the biggest problem with the spoiler model lies with its initial focus. The model tends to examine violent conflict through the prism of peace processes. For example, the very notion of a "spoiler" is contingent on the existence of a peace process, and the strategies proposed to handle spoilers aim at preserving the integrity of that process. As such, the model seems to be based on some of the same assumptions that led us astray in Bosnia and Herzegovina. It assumes that the context within which one operates in a foreign theater is primarily set by the internationals. This leads us to an important consideration. Rather than asking ourselves whether, and how, violent challenges may disrupt peace processes, is it not more appropriate to ask ourselves how *peace processes interfere with a given conflict?*

This distinction is more than purely semantic. The experience in Bosnia and Herzegovina teaches that it may indeed be misleading to assume that the potential for peace resides in peace processes designed

Nonviolent Insurgency 149

and managed by internationals. This potential resides instead in the will of parties to stop pursuing objectives at the heart of conflict. The willingness of parties in conflict to take part in peace initiatives does not mean that they have necessarily decided to stop pursuing conflict.

Experience bears out this contention. Several unsuccessful peace initiatives sought to stop violence between 1992 and 1995 in Bosnia. The Oslo peace process was one of many attempts to solve the ongoing Israeli-Palestinian conflict. Six peace initiatives were undertaken in Northern Ireland between 1973 and 1998.[127] Despite agreeing to a six-point plan brokered by former UN Secretary-General Kofi Annan, the Syrian regime intensified its crackdown on opponents in 2012. Peace initiatives come and go. Conflicts, on the other hand, are strongly rooted in the environment.

Decisions made by belligerent groups to end or pursue conflict are not made within the confines of a peace process designed by outsiders. These decisions are made amidst conflicts in which groups have engaged for a long period of time. Stedman's premise acknowledges this. His definition of spoilers is based on the impact of peace initiatives on the power interests of parties. The focus of his model, however, tends to shift toward international actors and strategies to protect peace processes.[128] While valid and insightful, by focusing our attention on peace processes, we are partially taking our focus away from conflict. Forgetting the existence of conflict is what some of us did in Bosnia. This led us to lose track of crucial shifts on the ground.

Adopting a conflict-centered perspective allows us to better understand why belligerent parties may have an interest in switching their resistance from violence to nonviolence. The next chapter will illustrate how the dynamics of interventions, resistance, and nonviolent insurgency and diplomatic counterinsurgency played out in Bosnia and Herzegovina during the peace implementation process that followed the signature of the Dayton peace agreement in 1995.

7 Diplomatic Counterinsurgency

> We saved this area militarily ... but we lost it at Dayton.
> –Milenko Karisik, Republika Srpska Deputy Minister of Interior.[1]

Dayton was the starting point of Bosnia-Herzegovina's nonviolent war. The international military presence deployed to Bosnia in the aftermath of the Dayton peace agreement constrained the capacity of belligerent parties to resort to violence and pushed conflict to evolve within a nonviolent space. The ensuing peace implementation process, led by the Office of the High Representative, destabilized positions and interests of parties engaged in the nonviolent extension of war and engendered resistance. This resistance in turn pushed intervention to increase in intensity. As the international community intervened more assertively, its actions triggered fears amongst Bosnian Croats and Bosnian Serbs that the peace implementation process would ultimately strengthen the capacity of Bosniaks to impose their will on the rest of the country.[2] These fears led nationalist forces within both communities to challenge the foundations of Bosnia's fragile state. These actions finally led the international community to embark on a campaign of *diplomatic counterinsurgency* to protect the space of nonviolence agreed to at Dayton. This chapter chronicles this story.

Resistance to International Intervention in Bosnia and Herzegovina

Foreign interventions occurred during all phases of the Bosnian conflict, each time triggering reactions from parties on the ground. Bosnian Serb

Diplomatic Counterinsurgency

military forces tied United Nations Protection Force (UNPROFOR) soldiers to targets they wanted to protect in reaction to NATO air strikes in 1995.[3] Dynamics of resistance permeated peace negotiations at Dayton as well. While Bosniaks were mostly favorable to negotiations aimed at preserving Bosnia and Herzegovina's existence, its president, Alija Izetbegović, nevertheless refused to sign the peace agreement until the very last minute. He considered the agreement unjust.[4] In Izetbegović's eyes, the agreement favored peace over justice and enshrined gains achieved through war crimes and crimes against humanity. Bosnian Croats and Bosnian Serbs were, on the other hand, keen to preserve gains they had made in their failed attempt to secede by force. Their desires for secession were, however, tampered by another form of foreign intervention: one that came from Bosnia's neighboring states. While present at Dayton, the interests of Bosnian Serbs and Croats were ultimately negotiated through Tuđman and Milošević, the respective leaders of neighboring Croatia and Yugoslavia (now Serbia).

While keen to preserve power for Bosnian Croats, Tuđman was willing to trade his support for Bosnia and Herzegovina's territorial integrity in exchange for Croatia's control over Eastern Slavonia – a Croatian region bordering Serbia that had been under Serb control during the war in Croatia.[5] Under the prospect of even more international sanctions, Milošević had an interest in agreeing to a peace agreement that guaranteed Bosnia's territorial integrity. While both Milošević and Tuđman were keen to abandon plans to carve up Bosnia – at least in the short run – they knew that any power-sharing agreement in Bosnia had to preserve the power of Bosnian Croats and Serbs to the largest possible extent. This is the context within which the Dayton peace agreement was negotiated. The Bosniaks' desire for power in a united Bosnia would be simultaneously resisted by the desire of Bosnian Croats and Bosnian Serbs to preserve their autonomy.

Resistance at the negotiating table in Dayton led to the creation of a highly decentralized federal structure where power was mostly allocated to Bosnia's two entities and their subdivisions. Moreover, the power of the common central institutions would emerge from the Dayton negotiations constrained by numerous ethnic and territorial vetoes designed to ensure that no party could impose its will on the others.

Vetoes as a Product of Resistance

One of the best ways to understand the extent to which resistance affected the efficiency of the central institutions is to examine the budget adoption process of Bosnia's central level of government. Those who already considered Bosnia complex may have to brace themselves as we take a closer look at the process. The following demonstration may indeed appear painfully convoluted to some. The reason is simple: the arrangements negotiated at Dayton are painfully complex. Analyzing them is important. It provides a concrete measure of the impact of resistance at the negotiating table in Dayton.

In Bosnia, a budget proposal must first be forwarded by the Ministry of Finance to the Council of Ministers (Bosnia's central government). The Council of Ministers, on which members of each constituent people (Bosniaks, Bosnian Croats, and Bosnian Serbs) are represented, must approve the budget by majority vote and forward the adopted proposal to Bosnia's tripartite presidency.[6]

The tripartite presidency (composed of one Bosniak and one Croat, each directly elected from the territory of the Federation of Bosnia and Herzegovina, and one Serb directly elected from the territory of the Republika Srpska) must then consult with the chair of Bosnia's Council of Ministers and Bosnia's Ministry of Treasury.[7] The presidency must also consult the prime ministers of Bosnia's two federal entities (namely Republika Srpska and the Federation of Bosnia and Herzegovina).[8] After such consultations, the Bosniak, Croat, and Serb members of the tripartite presidency must vote to adopt the budget proposal. A dissenting member may declare the decision taken by the two other members to be destructive of a vital interest of the entity from which he or she was elected. The Serb member of the presidency can, for example, declare the budget proposal adopted by the two other members to be destructive of the vital national interest of Republika Srpska. A Bosniak or Croat member can do the same with respect to the Federation.

If declared to be in violation of an entity vital interest by a member, the issue is then referred to a legislative body of the relevant entity. Should the mechanism be activated by the Serb member of the presidency, the matter is referred to the National Assembly of

Diplomatic Counterinsurgency

Republika Srpska (the equivalent of a state legislature in the United States). Should the Bosniak or Croat member of the presidency activate the mechanism, the matter will be referred respectively to the Bosniak or Croat delegates of the House of Peoples of the Federation of Bosnia and Herzegovina (the equivalent of a caucus in the Senate of a state legislature in the United States). If the declaration by a member of the presidency is confirmed by a two-thirds vote of the competent entity legislative body, the challenged decision shall not take effect.[9]

It is as if the presidency of the United States were a tripartite institution composed of two members elected from California and one elected from Texas. Each decision of the U.S. presidency would need to be agreed upon by the three members. Each member could, each time, declare a decision taken by the two other members to be in violation of a vital interest of the state from which the member was elected. The issue would then need to be referred to the legislative body of Texas or California. Should a two-thirds majority in the concerned body support the member's declaration of state interest violation, the decision of the U.S. presidency would be blocked.

From the Presidency to the Parliamentary House of Representatives

The budgetary adoption process of Bosnia and Herzegovina does not stop with the presidency. Once the budget proposal has left the presidency, it must be adopted by the Parliamentary Assembly. The Parliamentary Assembly is composed of two houses: the *House of Representatives* and the *House of Peoples*.

The House of Representatives must adopt the budget by a majority vote with efforts to ensure that this majority consists of one-third of members from the territory of each federal entity.[10] If the majority does not include one-third of members from the territory of an entity, a commission will then need to be created to obtain approval.[11] If no approval is obtained, the budget will need to be approved by a majority of the House members who are present and voting, provided that dissenting votes do not include two-thirds or more of the members elected from an entity.[12]

It is as if the House of Representatives in the U.S. Congress had to adopt a proposed federal budget by a majority vote that needed to include, according to the constitution, the vote of one-third of the representatives from each state. In the event that the majority in Congress failed to include such votes, the budget proposal would be sent to a commission. Should this commission fail to reach agreement, the budget would need to be approved by a vote that satisfies two cumulative conditions. First, the budget proposal would need to be adopted by a majority vote of the representatives of the House who are present and voting. Second, the dissenting votes would need not to include two-thirds or more members elected from each state. The scale of the American federal system and the country's demography may distort the analogy, but the constitutional mechanics at the basis of the analogy are the same.

The budget proposal also needs to be adopted by the House of Peoples of Bosnia's Parliamentary Assembly. The House of Peoples is composed of three caucuses: one representing the interests of the Bosniak people, one representing those of the Croat people, and one representing those of the Serb people in Bosnia. The process is subjected to the same entity-based veto as that of the House of Representatives. However, members of the House of Peoples may also opt to declare a proposed budget to be destructive of a vital interest of the Bosniak, Croat, or Serb people. A majority of members in a given caucus may indeed declare that the proposed budget is in violation of the "vital national interest" of the people it represents. If there are no objections to such an invocation, the majority will need to be supported by a majority in each caucus. If a majority in another caucus objects to such a declaration, a commission will need to be formed to resolve the issue. Should the commission be unable to resolve it, the matter is then referred to the Constitutional Court of Bosnia and Herzegovina. The budget will need to be adopted by a majority in each caucus.[13]

Resistance to concede power at Dayton pushed Bosnian structures of governance into a complex system of checks and balance seeking to ensure that no party could impose its will on any other. Resistance did not stop at the negotiating table. It would, as we will now see, permeate life after Dayton.

Diplomatic Counterinsurgency

Resistance after Negotiations

International efforts to implement Dayton would also provoke resistance. In the weeks that followed the ratification of the peace agreement, the Bosnian Serb leadership ordered Serbs in Sarajevo to burn their apartments and leave the part of the city that had been under Bosnian Serb control during the siege. The exodus came as a response to provisions agreed upon at Dayton stipulating that Sarajevo had to come under the jurisdiction of the Federation of Bosnia and Herzegovina (the entity of Bosnia inhabited by a majority of Bosniaks and Bosnian Croats). "We saved this area militarily ... but we lost it at Dayton," said a Bosnian Serb official.[14]

A significant part of the Dayton agreement reversed gains achieved through armed conflict. Parties sought to resist the implementation of those provisions affecting their interests through nonviolent means. The implementation of the right of refugees and displaced persons to return to their homes of origin guaranteed by the Dayton agreement illustrates the dynamic of this resistance.

Resisting Returns

The Dayton agreement guaranteed all refugees and displaced persons the right to freely return to their homes of origin in Bosnia.[15] Its implementation threatened gains achieved through ethnic cleansing. It would thus be either encouraged or resisted by nationalist elites, depending on whether such returns increased or decreased electoral support in a given jurisdiction.

Legislative and administrative measures adopted by the nationalist parties regarding the right to return are a good illustration of nonviolent war in action. Immediately after the end of armed conflict, authorities on all sides adopted legislation that sought to crystallize the effects of ethnic cleansing. The Federation of Bosnia and Herzegovina set arbitrary deadlines for refugees and displaced persons to reoccupy their property. Failure to repossess property within these deadlines irreversibly extinguished one's rights to return to his or her home of origin under such legislation. Republika Srpska also adopted legislation similarly restricting people's effective capacity to exercise their right to return.[16] People returning to their prewar homes often found other people occupying their property. Administrative and judicial obstruction prevented many from returning. Exorbitant "reconnection fees" for utilities were charged. Payments for pension funds managed by another entity would not be accessible in the entity to which persons had returned. Access to education and health care would be limited. Threatening graffiti and explosive devices left on doorsteps often welcomed returnees.

Frustrated by the resistance it was encountering, the international community decided to increase the intensity of its intervention in Bosnia. Meeting in Bonn in December 1997, the Peace Implementation Council consented to a more robust use of international power. It acquiesced to the intention of the High Representative to tackle resistance more aggressively. The council welcomed the intention of the High Representative to make "binding decisions" regarding the "timing, location and chairmanship of meetings of the common institutions" and to impose "interim measures to take effect when parties are unable to reach agreement." It also supported the High Representative in taking other measures to ensure implementation of the peace agreement, including "actions against persons holding public office or officials who are absent from meetings without good cause or who are found by the High Representative to be in violation of legal commitments made under the Peace Agreement or the terms of its implementation."[17]

Under increasing pressure, the Federation and Republika Srpska adopted new legislation to facilitate the implementation of the right to return during the course of 1997–8. Problems with the newly adopted legislation became quickly apparent to international officials monitoring the return process.[18] Taking a more proactive approach, the High Representative then adopted twenty-eight decisions that either enacted or amended property legislation between April and December 1999.[19] A Reconstruction and Return Task Force (RRTF) was established to oversee their implementation.[20] Lawyers, political officers, refugee protection experts, soldiers, and police officers were by now intervening daily in the minute details of Bosnia and Herzegovina's nonviolent war fought over the details of the right of persons to return to their homes.[21]

The international community adopted several measures to tackle constraints on freedom of movement more systemically. The United Nations International Police Task Force and SFOR ended arbitrary controls by local police at the internal boundary line between Bosnia's two entities. In 1998, the High Representative pushed for the adoption of new neutral license plates.[22] The previous license plates bore territorial identifications and were a common source of harassment and vandalism. When Bosnian Croat truck drivers refused to adopt the new Bosnian license plate, states sitting on the Peace Implementation Council instructed their respective border control authorities to refuse access to Bosnian vehicles without the new license plates. These measures "broke the truckers' resistance overnight" according to an international official involved with this process.[23] When a police force in the city of Stolac – a town in western Bosnia with a postwar Bosnian Croat majority population – refused to change its license plates, the international military force towed the police cars away.[24]

These efforts increased the number of property restitutions in Bosnia, but their impact on the balance of power between parties engaged in Bosnia's nonviolent conflict remained limited. While UNHCR has registered more than 1 million returns in Bosnia since 1995 – an impressive number – patterns of returns have proved unpredictable. Preferring to live in areas where they formed the majority, many returnees sold or exchanged restituted property. Reassured that restituting property to displaced persons would not necessarily lead to an erosion of their electoral base, nationalist politicians lowered their resistance.[25]

Entering Fully Into Bosnia's Nonviolent War

Efforts to enforce the right to return were not the only ways the international community interfered with Bosnia's nonviolent war. The implementation of Bosnia's new constitutional arrangements was a powerful source of disruption for parties. Viewed from the prism of Bosnia's conflict over power, the provisions of Bosnia's new constitution agreed to at Dayton delineated the very conditions under which parties would continue to pursue conflict. Implementing Bosnia's new constitutional structure implied the establishment of limited central authorities. The establishment of central authorities became a core component of international efforts to restore peace and security. Between 2000 and 2011, the United Nations Security Council adopted more than ten resolutions explicitly calling upon the authorities in Bosnia to "strengthen joint institutions" and to "foster the building of a fully functioning self-sustaining state."[26]

International support for a functioning central level of government favored those in Bosnia who had fought for the maintenance of a united Bosnia during the war. International "state building" – as it came to be known – was thus embraced by large segments of the Bosniak population. The implementation of Bosnia's new constitutional provisions, however, threatened the secessionist aspirations of many nationalists within the Bosnian Croat and Bosnian Serb communities. In response to increasing international pressure to rebuild the central institutions, these forces challenged the foundations of the Bosnian state primarily through nonviolent means.

Bosnian Croat Resistance

The first attempts to undermine the power of the Bosnian state emerged from ultranationalist factions within the HDZ. Shortly after the end of the armed conflict, the regime of President Tuđman in neighboring Croatia had supported parallel Bosnian Croat armed forces and institutions in Bosnia and Herzegovina. After the war, regions under the effective control of the HDZ had retained links with neighboring Croatia. Some regions were displaying official Croatian state symbols and using the Croatian currency. Croatia contributed to paying salaries and pensions of persons working within these Bosnian Croat parallel structures.

Part of the financial revenues that allowed the HDZ to pay the salaries of police officers, civil servants, and judges working for the Bosnian Croat parallel institutions came from Tuđman's regime in Croatia. However, other revenues came from public companies controlled by the HDZ reportedly generating money from the illegal smuggling of goods across Bosnia and Herzegovina's borders.[27] These

Diplomatic Counterinsurgency

revenues were processed through Hercegovačka Banka – a financial institution established in western Mostar under the control of HDZ ultranationalists.[28]

The power of the HDZ came increasingly under pressure in 2000. Tuđman's loss in the elections in Croatia had ended Croatia's financial support of Bosnian Croat parallel structures. The establishment of a state border service in Bosnia made it more difficult to generate revenues through smuggling. Moreover, the Provisional Election Commission, an interim body responsible for organizing elections in Bosnia under the authority of the Organization for Security and Cooperation in Europe (OSCE), decided to enact interim election rules perceived by some within the HDZ as detrimental to Bosnian Croats. The amendments pertained to the election of delegates to the House of Peoples of the Federation of Bosnia and Herzegovina. The rules allowed each member of a cantonal assembly to participate in the election of Bosniak, Croat, or other representatives to the Federation House of Peoples. The HDZ viewed the new rules as a direct challenge to previously agreed power-sharing mechanisms. Bosniak representatives were now entitled to participate in the election of Bosnian Croat representatives in the House of Peoples. This instilled fear in the minds of HDZ officials that proxy Bosnian Croat representatives controlled by outside parties could now be elected and undermine their power.

The HDZ reacted by announcing plans to hold a referendum on the rights of Croats in the fall of 2000. High Representative Petritsch and the OSCE immediately warned that such an initiative would have no legal validity. Then, on March 3, 2001, Bosnian Croat nationalists from several political parties conveyed a session of a self-proclaimed "Croat National Congress" to declare the establishment of a separate "Croat Self Government."

The response from the international community came quickly. In a bold move, High Representative Wolfgang Petritsch dismissed Ante Jelavić from his position in the tripartite presidency of Bosnia and Herzegovina on March 7, 2001. Jelavić was also removed from his position as president of the HDZ.[29] Petritsch also removed three other prominent members behind the March 3 declaration: Ivo Andrić Lozanski, vice president of the HDZ and delegate in the House of

Representatives of Bosnia and Herzegovina, as well as Zdravko Batinić and Marko Tokić, both vice presidents of the HDZ.[30]

Stjepan Mesić, Croatia's new president, publicly distanced himself from the actions of the HDZ in Bosnia and stressed Croatia's commitment to the territorial integrity of Bosnia.[31] This was a crucial development. Conscious of its European integration prospects, the new government in Croatia refused to support Jelavić in Bosnia and, by doing so, ended the irredentist policies of the Tuđman era.

On March 22, 2001, the United Nations Security Council condemned, by way of a presidential statement, the "recent unilateral moves by the so-called Croat National Congress to establish Croat self-rule in open contradiction of the provisions of the Peace Agreement."[32] The Security Council further called on all parties "to work within the legal institutions and constitutional framework of Bosnia and Herzegovina and the entities" and expressed "its support for the High Representative in taking actions against persons holding public office who are found to be in violation of legal commitments made under the Peace Agreement or the terms for its implementation."[33]

In a dramatic escalation of events, several thousand Bosnian Croat soldiers left the army of the Federation of Bosnia and Herzegovina at the end of March 2001. HDZ politicians established their own separate defense headquarters and promised soldiers to continue paying their salaries.

The response from the international community would be swift. "Any attempt to establish parallel structures is illegal and anti-Dayton. We call on all members of the federation army to remain loyal to their legally appointed commanders," the OHR spokesperson indicated after the move by Bosnian Croat soldiers.[34] Then, soldiers from NATO's stabilization force in BiH (SFOR) immediately intervened to secure weapons storage facilities.[35] On April 5, High Representative Petritsch went on the offensive and targeted the financial nucleus of the Bosnian Croat resistance by appointing an international provisional administrator of the Hercegovačka Banka. Petritsch's decision suspended the powers of all of the bank's officers, directors, and shareholders and transferred these powers to an international provisional administrator. According to the terms of his decision, the international administrator was "authorized, required and empowered to take all such measures

Diplomatic Counterinsurgency

as necessary and appropriate in order to secure the assets and records of the bank and its branches and subsidiaries ... so as to prevent their dissipation by theft or other improper action."[36]

On April 6, 2001, the international provisional administrator launched a surprise audit of Hercegovačka Banka. Supported by SFOR soldiers, international officials from the OHR, American banking specialists, and Bosnian financial inspectors entered the premises of Hercegovačka Banka branches to conduct a comprehensive audit. "There were helicopters flying around us as we entered.... Once inside the bank, I told the staff 'I am now the manager of this bank. Please take your hands off the keyboards and step away from everything. This bank is now under international control,'" an international official leading a team into one of the bank's branches recalled.[37] The operation did not go as smoothly in other divisions of the bank. In Mostar, Široki Brijeg, and Grude, the presence sent by SFOR was insufficient and failed to contain angry mobs that had been dispatched on sight to prevent the audit. Violent protesters burned vehicles and managed to penetrate into some of the branches. Once inside, they beat up inspectors and held others hostage at gunpoint.[38]

The crisis finally came to an end when the minister of defense of the federation reached an agreement with the Bosnian Croat generals who had led the mutiny. The arrangement provided for the return and reregistering of the seven thousand soldiers who had left the federation army.[39] The secessionist push by ultranationalist factions within the Bosnian Croat community had not succeeded. Divisions between moderates and nationalists within the Bosnian Croat political community combined with the withdrawal of support from the Croatian regime in Zagreb helped quash the insurgency.

The newly established constitutional order of Bosnian and Herzegovina had been challenged. Slowly being rebuilt with international support, the central institutions of Bosnia were hardly in a position to protect the territorial integrity of the state. The armed forces of Bosnia were still heavily divided along ethnic lines. Bosnian Croat representatives were in a position to trigger the numerous vetoes available to them within the presidency, the Council of Ministers, and the Parliamentary Assembly to block any legislative and executive counteractions. The High Representative and NATO filled the vacuum.

Later during the summer of 2001, Ante Jelavić appeared before a court in Sarajevo in relation to his involvement in the Bosnian Croat resistance. His comments were indicative of a new dynamic to come. Speaking to a crowd of supporters outside the court, he accused High Representative Petritsch of running a "protectorate which took the darkest form of neo colonialism" and refused "to accept a system in which one man was prosecutor, judge and jury."[40]

The crisis had not only shed light on the inability of Bosnia's central institutions to resist direct challenges against the sovereignty of the state. It had also highlighted the existence of a democratic deficit in Bosnia's postwar dynamics. The country's integrity and sovereignty was still heavily dependent on the support of foreigners. While accountable to members of the Peace Implementation Council, the High Representative remained nevertheless an unelected foreign official with significant powers to intervene in Bosnia's internal affairs. Jelavić's comments were a prelude to dynamics to come. As the High Representative would act more assertively to protect the nonviolent space established by Dayton, challenges against his authority would also increase.

Bosnian Serb Resistance

Just like their counterparts in the Bosnian Croat community, Bosnian Serb nationalists resisted attempts to further unite Bosnia under an effective central level of government. Immediately after the signature of the Dayton agreement, their resistance took the form of denial and boycott. Despite having a delegation present at the negotiations, the Dayton agreement had been effectively negotiated by Milošević. Back in Bosnia, the Bosnian Serb leadership was in no particular hurry to participate in new institutions provided for by a peace agreement they had not designed.

Efforts to establish the country's first postwar government would directly collide with Bosnian Serb resistance. Under the new constitution agreed to at Dayton, the nomination of the chair of Bosnia's Council of Ministers was dependent on a consensus decision within the tripartite presidency. Momčilo Krajišnik, the Bosnian Serb member

Diplomatic Counterinsurgency 163

of the tripartite presidency and cofounder of the SDS with Radovan Karadžić, was fully aware of this. "Krajišnik just refused to meet. He would refuse to meet in Sarajevo.... We spent the first half year just trying to get the Presidency to meet as a body. It was almost impossible, primarily because of Krajišnik," an official from the U.S. State Department recalled.[41] Krajišnik ended up being sentenced to twenty years in prison by the International Criminal Tribunal for the former Yugoslavia (ICTY) in 2009.

Despite heavy resistance, international pressure gradually succeeded in securing Bosnian Serb participation in the common institutions. But such participation did not imply the end of wartime objectives. Forced to join common institutions against their will, many Bosnian Serb nationalists did so on the basis of a narrative that helped them preserve future secessionist aspirations. According to their narrative, sovereignty was primarily vested with Republika Srpska and Republika Srpska had consented to transfer a limited number of authorities to common institutions through Dayton. Republika Srpska was therefore not, according to this narrative, an emanation or a subdivision of Bosnia and Herzegovina. Rather, Bosnia and Herzegovina had emanated from an agreement between Republika Srpska and the federation. Drawing heavily on the position Yugoslav republics enjoyed within the former Yugoslav constitutional system, this narrative allowed Bosnian Serb nationalists to justify participation in Bosnia's institutions while preserving self-proclaimed entitlements to secede at a later stage.[42] If Republika Srpska could agree to join, it could very well decide to opt out one day, according to them.

The narrative helps explain some of the legal confrontations between Republika Srpska and Bosnia's central institutions in the aftermath of the armed conflict. In 1998, Alija Izetbegović, the Bosniak member of the tripartite presidency, challenged the constitutionality of numerous provisions of the entities' constitutions before Bosnia's Constitutional Court. The Bosnian constitutional system allows entities to have their own constitutions, but their provisions must be consistent with those of Bosnia's constitution. Izetbegović's submissions argued, among others, that the preamble of Republika Srpska's constitution – which explicitly referred to Republika's Srpska's "sovereignty" and "state independence" – was incompatible with Bosnia's constitution.

The Constitutional Court declared such references unconstitutional in 2000.[43]

In 1999, Bosnia's central level of government adopted laws pertaining to foreign policy, direct foreign investments, and customs. While such laws fell within the field of competencies allocated to the central state under the constitution, Republika Srpska lawmakers reacted to their adoption by enacting legislation purporting to authorize their application in Republika Srpska. It was as if the state of Texas were to claim that laws adopted by the United States Congress could only apply in Texas once endorsed by Texas's legislature. High Representative Petritsch struck down Republika Srpska's legislation. His decision stipulated that the laws of Bosnia and Herzegovina had entered into force and were thus applicable throughout Bosnia's entire territory. Petritsch's decision further underlined that entities were not competent under the constitution to adopt legislation on the applicability of state laws in their territory.[44]

Resistance to state building by Republika Srpska followed a recurring pattern. As legislation seeking to reestablish or strengthen common institutions supported by the international community would be introduced before the Parliamentary Assembly, representatives of Republika Srpska would almost immediately block its adoption. The High Representative would then impose the legislation to overcome this blockage and Republika Srpska officials would almost immediately challenge the law imposed by the High Representative before the Constitutional Court. For example, representatives of the National Assembly of Republika Srpska challenged the constitutionality of a decision of the High Representative that amended state legislation on travel documents in 2000.[45] A few months later, after a working group composed of state and entity representatives had negotiated and agreed upon draft legislation seeking to establish a court of Bosnia and Herzegovina, the draft legislation was blocked in the Parliamentary Assembly. Soon after, the High Representative imposed the law and twenty-five representatives of the National Assembly of Republika Srpska attacked its constitutionality before the Constitutional Court.[46] Similar scenarios repeated themselves in relation to legislation pertaining to public broadcasting[47] and statistics,[48] for example.

Parliamentary blockages and judicial challenges are part of democratic life. Most federal units in the world protect their interests through similar tactics. Not all Republika Srpska representatives necessarily supported a secessionist agenda. Some were indeed willing to evolve within the Bosnian constitutional framework, albeit one that preserved high levels of autonomy for Republika Srpska. The decision of Republika Srpska leaders to transfer several responsibilities to the central state structures in the field of defense and indirect taxation between 2002 and 2007 reflect such dynamics.[49]

On the other hand, there is little doubt that some of these legal challenges formed part of a protracted struggle to undermine Bosnia's common institutions. From a substantive point of view, many of them attacked legislation that was intimately linked to Bosnia's statehood and that clearly fell within the central state's competencies under the constitution. The legislation on travel documents that Republika Srpska representatives had blocked in parliament and challenged before the Constitutional Court in 2000 specified, among other things, that the cover of Bosnian passports needed to contain the words "Bosnia and Herzegovina," the coat of arms of Bosnia and Herzegovina, as well as the word "Passport." These challenges were neither merely seeking, as many Bosnian Serb officials persisted in claiming, to limit an unforeseen expansion of the central state. The central state's authorities had been rejected with violence between 1992 and 1995 and Dayton inevitably called for the partial reestablishment of such authorities. Qualifying this reestablishment process as "an expansion" implicitly delegitimized the existence of central state structures. Finally, these challenges occurred within a specific context. Bosnian Serb nationalists had tried to secede from Bosnia through violence between 1992 and 1995. Some of them were still publically embracing secession as a political objective during the peace implementation process. Proceeding incrementally, they were seeking to transform Republika Srpska into a mini-state within a dysfunctional Bosnian structure to make secession easier to justify at a later date. Neighboring Montenegro had incrementally decimated the common institutions of Serbia and Montenegro before securing its independence from "Serbia and Montenegro" through referendum in 2006. Many believe secessionist forces were pushing Republika Srpska to do the same in Bosnia.

More Intervention, More Resistance

Bosnian Serb resistance extended beyond attempts to strengthen common institutions in Bosnia. Several provisions of the Dayton peace agreement provided for clear obligations to cooperate and assist authorities responsible for investigating and adjudicating violations of international humanitarian law committed during Bosnia's armed conflict.[50] The UN Security Council had called upon all states to cooperate with the ICTY while establishing the international tribunal in 1993.[51] The Council also called upon parties to the Dayton agreement to do so through numerous resolutions.[52]

By 2003, international pressure to cooperate with the investigation of war crimes converged more specifically on Republika Srpska. Nine years after the war, Republika Srpska had not transferred one single person indicted by the ICTY. The two most wanted Bosnian Serb fugitives, Radovan Karadžić and Ratko Mladić, were still hiding. In August 2003, the UN Security Council adopted a resolution that called upon Serbia and Montenegro, Croatia, and Bosnia and Herzegovina to intensify cooperation with the ICTY to bring Karadžić and Mladić to the ICTY.[53] The resolution specifically called upon Republika Srpska, a subdivision of Bosnia, to intensify its cooperation. It reiterated this specific demand in March 2004.[54]

To overcome the resistance of Republika Srpska, High Representative Paddy Ashdown imposed a number of measures directly targeting the SDS, the main party in power in Republika Srpska at the time. On April 2, 2004, Ashdown suspended the payment of public party funding destined for the SDS and ordered the party to file financial reports with the Office of the High Representative. These reports needed to include information such as the territorial structure of the party, an account of its cash transactions, its income, a list of contributions of physical and legal persons, and an account of expenditures and debt.[55]

A few weeks later, members of the Steering Board of the Peace Implementation Council expressed dissatisfaction with Bosnia and Herzegovina's cooperation with the ICTY. Their communiqué noted Republika Srpska's "failure to locate or apprehend even one war-crimes

Diplomatic Counterinsurgency

indictee in the nine years since the Dayton Accord." The communiqué added that Republika Srpska was "failing to carry out a key obligation under Dayton and international law" and that the relevant individuals and institutions had to "be held accountable."[56]

The diplomatic pressure on Republika Srpska increased even more a few days later. On June 28, 2004, while attending a summit in Istanbul, the heads of NATO member states refused Bosnia's membership to NATO's Partnership for Peace (PfP) program (a bilateral cooperation arrangement reached between NATO and individual states). Their final communiqué indicated that they were "concerned that Bosnia and Herzegovina, particularly obstructionist elements in the Republika Srpska entity" had "failed to live up to its obligation to cooperate fully with ICTY, including the arrest and transfer to the jurisdiction of the Tribunal of war crimes indictees, a fundamental requirement for the country to join PfP. We also look for systemic changes necessary to develop effective security and law enforcement structures."[57]

Only two days later, Ashdown announced one of the most comprehensive set of measures ever adopted by the international community in Bosnia. The measures directly targeted officials and institutions in Republika Srpska suspected of obstructing cooperation with the ICTY. More than fifty individuals were removed from public or party functions. The interior minister of Republika Srpska, as well as many individuals working within the local police force structures in Republika Srpska, was among those removed.[58] The European Union and the United States imposed visa bans on persons suspected of obstructing efforts to cooperate with the ICTY.

Several of these measure targeted the SDS directly. Its president Dragan Kalinić, also chairman of the National Assembly of Republika Srpska, was removed.[59] Five of the party's vice presidents were also removed.[60] The measures blocked all sixty municipal accounts of the party[61] and redirected nearly 1 million KM (500,000 euros) of public money slated for the SDS as part of Bosnia's political party funding system to the budget of the central state institutions.[62] The measures also ordered an audit of a company suspected of channeling funds to support indicted war criminals.

"The SDS is a party like no other in the RS. It was founded by Europe's most wanted fugitive, Radovan Karadžić.... Nearly a decade after the war, it is still linked to the organized crime that robs this country, and to the man who founded it. This is not a contested view. It is the consensus opinion of intelligence agencies, of the international organizations operating in BiH, of many individuals in BiH's own law enforcement agencies. It is also the common daily experience of tens of thousands of people living in the RS," noted Ashdown during a press conference held in June.[63]

Despite their comprehensive nature, the measures yielded few results. At the end of 2004, Ashdown adopted another comprehensive series of measures. His decisions removed individuals from the board of the SDS, the police, and intelligence structures of Republika Srpska. He also ordered the special auditor of Republika Srpska to conduct a series of special audits in six organizations suspected of channeling financial resources to support persons indicted for war crimes.[64] His measures amended criminal procedure codes to restrict family member exemptions to assist investigation and adjudication of war crimes.[65] The U.S. government supported Ashdown's measures by freezing the assets of the SDS on its territory and by prohibiting American nationals from entering into any financial transaction with the SDS. It also imposed travel restrictions on the leadership of the SDS and the Party of Democratic Progress (PDP) – the SDS's coalition partner in the Republika Srpska government.[66]

The Bosnian Serb refusal to cooperate with the ICTY also led the international community to consider the numerous, disconnected elements of the Bosnian police system to be at the source of the country's incapacity to effectively investigate and prosecute serious criminal activity such as war crimes. The rejection of Bosnia's membership to NATO's Partnership for Peace program gave political momentum for Paddy Ashdown to launch a police reform process.[67] He established a Police Restructuring Commission to be chaired by former Belgian prime minister Wilfried Martens. The commission was responsible for proposing "a single structure of policing for Bosnia and Herzegovina under the overall political oversight of a ministry or ministries in the Council of Ministers."[68] In December 2004, the Martens commission report recommended the establishment of a single structure of police under the exclusive constitutional authority of the state of Bosnia and Herzegovina.[69]

In reaction to the measures imposed by the international community, the prime minister of Republika Srpska, the foreign minister of Bosnia and Herzegovina, and the Serb member of Bosnia's presidency resigned from their functions in December 2004 and boycotted the central institutions. "I am not prepared to accept the threats and ultimatums," said Prime Minister Dragan Mikerević following his resignation.[70] "We do not want to take part in a process that would lead to the creation of Bosnia without the Serb Republic. This is an attack on us and it is a direct consequence of our opposition to unconstitutional changes," noted Mladen Ivanić after resigning from his position as foreign minister a few days later.[71]

These developments connect us directly to the events described in the first part of this book. For the crisis in 2007 was the product of the interaction of intervention and resistance. Seeking to strengthen Bosnia's central institutions through police reform, the international community had engendered stiff resistance from representatives of Republika Srpska. The measures Miroslav Lajčák enacted in 2007 were seeking to address this very resistance as well as preventing a repetition of the 2004 attempts to block Bosnia's parliamentary and executive organs through boycott.

By the end of 2007, strong international support for peace implementation had put the secessionist aspirations of Bosnian Croat and Bosnian Serb nationalists on the defensive. The Office of the High Representative, positioned as a foreign leviathan in Bosnia, was not only helping rebuild Bosnia's fragile central institutions, but was also protecting them from political, legal, and administrative challenges from those who opposed such efforts. While occasionally relying on the support of the international military presence, the efforts to protect the state were primarily diplomatic in nature. The international community was indeed using NATO and EU integration processes and sanctions from the EU and the United States to support its actions in Bosnia. The High Representative was intervening on a daily basis in Bosnia's nonviolent wars by removing officials and imposing financial sanctions on political parties and legislation. The international leviathan was leading what appeared to be an effective diplomatic counterinsurgency campaign.

But things were about to change. Despite its appearances of power and stability, this entire arrangement was on the verge of collapsing. By 2007, Republika Srpska was about to successfully mount a nonviolent campaign that would lead to the partial collapse of the authority of the High Representative. How was this possible? The next chapter seeks to answer that question.

★ ★ ★

8 The Avalanche

> The North Vietnamese and Viet Cong, fighting in their own country, needed merely to keep in being forces sufficiently strong to dominate the population after the United States tired of the war. We fought a military war; our opponents fought a political one. We sought physical attrition; our opponents aimed for our psychological exhaustion. In the process, we lost sight of one of the cardinal maxims of guerilla war: the guerilla wins if he does not lose. The conventional army loses if it does not win.
> –Henry Kissinger, commenting on the United States' war in Vietnam[1]

Avalanches are a common point of reference for those studying complex systems. Their dynamics are useful for those seeking to better understand, anticipate, and manage sudden shifts in markets, for example. Avalanches are also useful to better understand some of the dynamics of foreign intervention and peace processes.

Avalanches have the potential to kill people and destroy property. They are devastating and unpredictable affairs. Despite the illusion of stability they project, there is nothing stable about masses of snow lying on a mountain. These masses are not passively lying in isolated conditions. Elements within them are interconnected to their environment and are constantly mutating. Avalanches are indeed triggered on the basis of topographic conditions to which they are exposed.[2] The steepness of a given mountain, its elevation and orientation, and the shape of the terrain all play a role in triggering avalanches. Slope orientation can influence the amount of wind and solar radiation that interacts with snow. This, in turn, may either increase or decrease the likelihood of avalanches.³ Meteorological conditions also play an important role. More than 80 percent of avalanches fall during or shortly after snowfalls. Snowfalls add weight and pressure to the existing snow cover, which contributes to triggering avalanches. Other factors such as sudden changes of temperature, rain, and wind conditions can also play a role in triggering avalanches.⁴

Efforts to protect people require that we look at avalanches within a broad framework, one that acknowledges that snow is neither static nor isolated. Analyzing interconnections of snow masses, placing them within their wider environment, and examining their potential interactions allows us to better predict possible outcomes. This broader approach allows us to see more clearly how pressure from the environment can activate interconnected elements in the system and engender simultaneous retroactions that lead the mass to suddenly collapse.

This chapter explains why we ought to adopt a similar perspective on peace operations and conflict systems. We can make a number of parallels between avalanches and the power of complex peace operations. While mandates, headquarters, equipment, and staff project an appearance of stability, peace operations evolve in complex interconnected environments and are unstable. Their power may, just like snow on a mountain, collapse under certain conditions. The defeat of the High Representative in 2007 acts as an illustration.

Ephemeral Foreign Presences

Historical precedents highlighting the ephemeral nature of foreign presences abound. The British and French colonial outposts looked stable at the beginning of the twentieth century. Their footprint may still be visible in many countries' political, economic, and social structures, but for all intents and purposes, colonial regimes are gone. The U.S. military maintained a force of several hundred thousand soldiers during the war in Vietnam. Its barracks, helicopters, and soldiers have since vanished. Modern complex peace operations are certainly very different from the military or colonial enterprises of the past. But, when we examine these operations at a higher level of abstraction, we can identify similarities that help us understand their evolution through time.

All forms of foreign presence, be they military or peace operations, evolve in interconnected systems. The systems in which they evolve are in constant evolution. Time and action will, among other things, affect a system's mutations. Foreign presences seek to effect change in the environment to which they are deployed. Their actions will, therefore, inevitably disturb elements of the system in which they operate. As we have seen in the previous chapter, some elements in the system will resist the impact of intervention. At some point the forces supporting a foreign presence will be lesser than those resisting it. Just like snow on a mountain that is beginning to take the form of an avalanche, the power of the foreign mission will abruptly shift away at this point.

We have drawn some parallels between violent and nonviolent insurgencies in the previous chapter by illustrating that power can be challenged – and protected – through violent or nonviolent means. While diplomatic counterinsurgency differs in many respects from military counterinsurgency, some of the military thinking that explains how a stronger military force can be defeated by a smaller one provides valuable insight into understanding the dynamics of nonviolent insurgent action.

How the Weak Defeats the Powerful

How can weaker opponents defeat more powerful ones? That question has challenged everyone from historians to military strategists. It is especially intriguing because since the Second World War, weaker opponents have been generally successful in defeating powerful states – or at least in denying them a decisive victory. Hitler was unable to tame Tito's partisans in Yugoslavia. The United States was unable to secure decisive victory in Vietnam. Going further back in time, Napoléon's Grande Armée could not defeat the guerilla forces in Spain. How can a military power fail to secure victory against a weaker opponent?

In 1975, scholar Andrew Mack published a seminal article that tried to answer this question. In an article entitled "Why Big Nations Lose Small Wars: The Politics of Asymmetric Conflict," Mack argued that success for an insurgent engaged in guerilla warfare does not necessarily arise from military victory on the ground.[5] Success, according to Mack, will often arise from the incremental attrition of a powerful actor's *political capability* to wage war. Mack noted: "the Vietnam conflict has demonstrated how, under certain conditions, the theatre of war extends well beyond the battlefield to encompass the polity and social institutions of the external power. The Vietnam War may be seen as having been fought on two fronts – one bloody and indecisive in the forests and mountains of Indochina, the other essentially nonviolent – but ultimately more decisive – within the polity and social institutions of the United States. The nature of the relationship between these two conflicts – which are in fact different facets of the same conflict – is critical to an understanding of the outcome of the war."[6]

More recent scholarly research has proposed that weaker actors win wars against more powerful opponents when they adopt and maintain a counterstrategy that can divide the power of their powerful enemy.[7] These findings seem to confirm the long-held view that the best way for insurgents to avoid defeat is to refuse to confront a more powerful enemy on its own terms. Confronting a more powerful opponent on its own terms will simply offer it an opportunity to convert its superiority into concrete gains on the battlefield. By opting for an opposite approach, the weak can, however, deflect and divide the power of its enemy and inflict increasing costs on a stronger opponent.[8]

Others have argued that outcomes in asymmetric conflict can be influenced by the governing structures of the stronger country. Democratic states, it is suggested, would "fail in small wars because they find it extremely difficult to escalate the level of violence and brutality to that which can secure victory."[9] As accounts of brutality and casualties increase, the population will withdraw its support from the war effort, which will, in turn, deprive the state of the means necessary to secure victory.[10]

While tactical considerations about counterinsurgency certainly affect outcomes, battlefield considerations only take one so far. The significance of Mack's approach lies in its conception of asymmetric warfare within a complex system of interconnected fronts. Weaker opponents are conscious of the importance of interconnections. Reflecting on the dynamics of China's war with Japan, Mao noted:

"Thus through a study of the interconnections of all the factors on the enemy's side and our own, we have reached the conclusion that the Anti-Japanese War is a protracted war. The enemy is strong and we are weak, so we are facing the danger of subjugation. But in other respects the enemy has shortcomings and we have advantages. The enemy's advantages can be reduced, and his shortcomings be aggravated, by our efforts."[11]

Broader interconnections can be underestimated – if not ignored – by those on the battlefield. Direct involvement with events on the ground blurs one's perceptions. There is a tendency amongst those deployed on the ground to underestimate the importance of the home front. Proximity to action creates a sense of superior understanding and autonomy, and those in the field tend to look at people back home with contempt. Ministers, representatives, staffers, and scholars come for a few days, receive briefings, and go back home. To those stationed in the field, most of these visitors seem disconnected from what is really going on. In 2010, *Rolling Stone* magazine published a piece that quoted U.S. General Stanley McChrystal and his advisors making fun of President Obama and Vice President Biden's understanding of their military operations in Afghanistan.[12] In what must have felt like a brutal reminder of the importance of the home front, McChrystal resigned from his job a few days later.

Despite McChrystal's team's missteps, the U.S. military seems institutionally very conscious of the fact that wars are fought over several fronts. Since the Vietnam War, information transiting from one front to the other is carefully managed. Journalists are embedded with the troops; pictures of bodies returning home are prohibited from publication. The military is conscious that effective management of public opinion at home may extend its capacity to wage war abroad. A recent study that examined whether reports of insurgent deaths from Iraq improved public perceptions of military success during the U.S.-led intervention in Iraq after 2003 seem to confirm this.[13] Part of the study was based on an experiment in which participants were randomly exposed – through a mock newspaper article on a hypothetical battle in Iraq – to a body count frame ("twenty-five Americans were killed") or a casualty ratio frame ("twenty-five Americans and one hundred and twenty five insurgents were killed"). The participants were then asked to what extent they thought the hypothetical battle was a success. The study showed that almost 65 percent of participants exposed to a casualty ratio frame labeled the battle "very much a success" or "somewhat a success," compared to only 38 percent of those exposed to a body count frame. Moreover, 30 percent of participants exposed to the body count frame labeled the battle "very much a failure" or "somewhat a failure," compared to 17.5 percent in the casualty ratio frame.[14] Information framing has an impact on one's political capability to wage war.

Public opinion is not only framed by casualty accounts. Asymmetric confrontations are also fought on a conceptual field delineated by norms and values. U.S. Colonel Charles Dunlop argued in 2001 that weaker opponents have been increasingly successful in neutralizing American military power by resorting to the law; a process Dunlop defined as *lawfare*.[15] According to Dunlop, international law has been increasingly used as a weapon to achieve military objectives against the United States. Those who wage *lawfare* seek to use the law to gain political ground within the public opinion of a more powerful opponent's population. Framing their opponent's military actions as violations of international law, enemy forces seek to weaken their powerful opponent at home.[16] Using the example of a U.S. military attack on a bunker in Baghdad during the First Gulf War, Dunlop notes: "Some experts concluded that the post-attack pictures of the bodies of family members of high Iraqi officials (who evidently used the bunker as a bomb shelter) being excavated from the wreckage achieved politically what the Iraqi air defenses could not do militarily: rendering downtown Baghdad immune from attack."[17]

Democratic states must wage war within the legal and institutional boundaries imposed by their liberal democratic nature. Acknowledging the connection between rules, institutions, and political confrontations at home and operations on the battlefield allows us to better understand how weak opponents can ultimately defeat powerful ones. Insurgent resilience increases political costs for the opponent. It is also because of these interconnections that those at home who oppose the war abroad are often perceived as playing the game of the insurgents. As Mack noted: "The guerilla strategists understand perfectly that the war they fight takes place on two fronts and the conflict must be perceived as an integrated whole. From this perspective, those who oppose the war in the metropolis act *objectively* – regardless of their subjective political philosophies – as strategic resources for the insurgents."[18]

Peace Operations

This overview allows us to better understand the dynamics faced by states involved in complex peace operations abroad and their capacity to manage resistance through diplomatic counterinsurgency. There are significant differences between military and peace operations. While armed counterinsurgency, such as the U.S.-led operations that took place in Vietnam, Iraq, and Afghanistan, often rely on civilian means to win popular support, opponents pursue objectives primarily through the application of force. Given the extent to which armed confrontation affects human life, public opinion at home tends to be generally familiar with the broad evolution of the war.

Peace operations, on the other hand, are focused on promoting, establishing, or strengthening a state of nonviolence. While the actions of those seeking to establish or strengthen peace – as in Bosnia and Kosovo – may have important military components, their operations primarily rely on civilian and diplomatic means to address nonviolent components of conflict. Unlike military campaigns, public opinion back home hardly follows the daily evolution of peace operations.

Despite these differences, both types of operations are seeking to effect change in a foreign theater. Both evolve in interconnected systems where the theater of operations is linked to home fronts. As seen in the previous chapters, they both have an impact on conditions on the ground and engender resistance. While public opinion back home may ignore many of the daily outcomes of peace operations, the home front does not completely ignore what is happening in the field. By and large, it takes something exceptional for public opinion to pay attention to peace operations. The deaths of American and Belgian soldiers involved in UN-mandated peace operations in Somalia and Rwanda in 1994 spurred outrage at home, followed by decisions to withdraw troops. But peace operations are nevertheless constantly monitored and followed at the bureaucratic level in each contributing country.

As such, peace operations, like military operations abroad, evolve in organic environments composed of interconnected fronts.

Like other foreign presences, peace operations maintain *internal* and *external* interconnections. They are internally interconnected to elements within the state. Power depends, to a large extent, on the levels of consent and cooperation given by the local population and administration. A peace operation will inevitably need to draw upon these internal resources to effect outcomes. Peace operations are also *externally* interconnected to states or organizations that provide money, staff, and other forms of support. These external resources often coexist with local ones as many peacekeeping missions operate alongside international soldiers, judges, prosecutors, and police officers. Analyzing a peace operation by placing it at the intersection of its internal and external interconnections allows us to better understand potential mutations of the operation's power.

Looking at the evolution of complex peace operations in Bosnia, Kosovo, or East Timor through this lens suggests that, as with other forms of foreign presences, complex peace operations are destined to fall over time. The reason for this lies in the interaction of support and resistance. As time passes and as manifest signs of violence fade away, the levels of support of a given peace operation will inevitably decrease while levels of resistance within a conflict system may increase, decrease, or be maintained. Given the stronger long-term trends of decreasing support, there will come a point in time when levels of support will fall below those of resistance. When this is the case, the peace operation enters what we could call a *zone of vulnerability*. Transition to this zone may go unnoticed by those working for the peace operation or those resisting it. But just like a skier may trigger an avalanche, a specific event within a conflict system may trigger actions and counteractions that will ultimately lead the power of a peace operations to suddenly shift away.

Decreasing Support

Interests in peace operations tend to decline quickly. Peace operations are indeed often linked to secondary or tertiary sets of interests.

Typically deployed amidst concerns over refugee flows, regional stability, or the credibility and cohesion of international organizations such as NATO or the EU, they compete against core interests on the home front soon after being established. These secondary sets of interests also clash against more intense interests on the ground. Peace operations deploy amidst groups fighting to protect their existence, power, and standing after the end of armed conflict. International officials that invoke bureaucratic standards during their meetings tend to face counterparts more disposed to refer to their people's resistance against the Ottomans in 1389, or to point out that their Illyrian ancestors occupied southeast Europe before Slav populations arrived there. Local actors are operating on a much higher level of intensity. Complex peace operations are therefore established on the basis of a systemic deficit of interests, a deficit destined to increase over time.

Declining interest affects resources and accentuates the relative decrease of support. Looking back at the international presence in Bosnia after 1995, the trend seems clear. Since the initial deployment of the NATO-led implementation force (IFOR) in Bosnia at the end of 1995, the military presence morphed into a stabilization force (SFOR), which then subsequently transitioned to a European Union force (EUFOR). Mandates were reduced along the way. The number of troops passed from an initial sixty thousand in 1995 to approximately twelve hundred EUFOR troops in 2012.[19] The United Nations' two thousand-strong International Police Task Force deployed at the end of 1995 – responsible for monitoring, advising, and training law enforcement authorities in BiH – was replaced by a smaller European Union Police Mission (EUPM) of 433 police officers in 2003.[20] The mandate of the EUPM ended in 2012. The budget of the OSCE mission in BiH went from $794,765,222.8 USD in 1999 to $19,874,725.1 USD in 2010.[21] From 2002 until 2010, the staff of OSCE in BiH was reduced by an additional 30 percent.[22] As far as the resources of the OHR are concerned, the office had, in 1999, a budget of 31,926,000 euros and employed 232 international and 474 national contractors. By 2011, its staff had been reduced to 19 international contractors and 131 national contractors. Its budget had been reduced to 9,376,000 euros by 2012.[23]

In Kosovo, similar trends affected the operations of UNMIK and the OSCE. At the outset of the international interim administration in 2000, the OSCE mission in Kosovo (OMIK) had a budget of $113,405,708.70 USD.[24] By 2010, its budget had been reduced to $30,285,707.10 USD.[25] As far as UNMIK resources were concerned, the United Nations General Assembly appropriated 427,061,800 USD for UNMIK in 2000.[26] That amount had been reduced to 220,897,200 USD in 2007[27] and to 47,802,200 USD by 2011[28] – a reduction of approximately 89 percent of its resources since 2000.

The United Nations involvement in East Timor followed a similar pattern. The United Nations Transitional Administration Mission in East Timor (UNTAET) – established to temporarily administer the territory between 1999 and 2002 – comprised 6,281 international troops, 1,288 civilian police, and 737 international civilian personnel in 2002.[29] Its mandate ended in May 2002 as East Timor acceded to statehood. It was replaced by a new United Nations Mission (UNMISET) responsible for supporting East Timor as it assumed control over its own affairs.[30] The transition from UNTAET to UNMISET came with a reduction in mandate and resources. On August 31, 2002, UMISET relied on 4,776 international troops, 771 civilian police, and 465 international civilian staff.[31] By the end of its mandate in 2005, the mission was composed of 469 international troops, 135 civilian police, and 264 international civilian staff.[32] UNMISET was then replaced by a third United Nations mission in 2005 (UNMIT).[33] By 2012, UNMIT relied on 1,242 international police, 33 international military liaison officers, and 288 international civilian staff.[34] The trend in East Timor clearly highlights a consistent reduction of resources over time. While the violence that erupted in East Timor in 2006 and 2008 led the UN Security Council to temporarily reinforce law enforcement components within UNMIT operations,[35] resources and mandates were never readjusted anywhere near the initial UN presence levels of 1999.[36]

The decline in external resources is not simply quantitative. It is also qualitative. Political and diplomatic support – a resource difficult to measure – suffers from horizontal and vertical erosion with time. External powers and organizations tend to be less united. Bureaucratic involvement back home slowly slides down the hierarchy. Administration change and new interests interfere. Russia's alignment with the Clinton administration in Bosnia in 1995 bears little resemblance to the more divergent policies the Medvedev administration pursued in 2007. The fragile international unity behind UNMIK in 1999 had crumbled by the time Kosovo declared its independence in 2008.

Lack of resilience behind foreign presences seems to go back a long way. Recent scholarly work comparing modern complex peace operations – such as those undertaken in Bosnia, Kosovo, and East Timor – to the colonial occupations of liberal democratic states at the beginning of the twentieth century illustrates how both have not been particularly successful in transforming societies.[37] While initially giving appearances of strong resolve to effect change, both liberal democratic colonial projects and modern complex peacekeeping operations have shown a lack of will to follow through on such plans.[38]

The weakening of external interests and resources has significant consequences for an organization like UNMIK or the OHR. As time passes, the organization becomes increasingly more dependent on – and thus more vulnerable to – changes in internal support. When complex peace operations evolve alongside high numbers of international troops, police officers, prosecutors, and judges, it is significantly easier for them to implement their will. Not only can they implement their decisions more easily, but their capacity to coerce consent and cooperation in the domestic theater is increased. But as military and law enforcement contingents diminish, so does the capacity of complex peace operations to autonomously coerce behavior. They become more dependent on the willingness of domestic administrations to cooperate.

Resistance

Resistance against foreign intervention fluctuates. It may increase, maintain itself, or decrease depending on various factors, including the intensity of actions pursued by foreign interveners. The experience with the peace implementation process in Bosnia sheds light on a number of possible fluctuations for resistance. Increased pressure by the international community triggered the Bosnian Croat nationalist nonviolent insurgency of 2001. Once countered, levels of resistance within the Bosnian Croat nationalist political representation diminished. The resistance of Republika Srpska followed a different path. Initial opposition to Dayton morphed into partial acceptance of the agreement's terms which, by 2007, morphed into intense resistance in the face of increased international attempts to strengthen Bosnia's common institutions. The evolution of resistance to foreign intervention in Bosnia offers good insight as to how factions may be able, over time, to escalate their resistance to a level where counteractions by a peace operation become counterproductive – something to which we will now turn.

The Liberal Democratic Conundrum

A foreign presence seeking to maintain a nonviolent space acts both as an actor and an arbitrator in conflict systems. On one hand, it seeks to ensure that parties respect obligations and boundaries of the peace process. In doing so its role tends to resemble that of an arbitrator. It is usual for rules to protect arbitrators in systems. Sport referees cannot be tackled or targeted as they perform their functions. Judges benefit from immunities in order to control power of other branches of government in democratic systems. In the same way, peace operations benefit from immunities in order to enforce and maintain boundaries.

But the role of a peace operation exceeds that of an arbitrator. Regardless of proclaimed intentions and objectives, its mere presence affects positions and interests of parties in a conflict system. Peace operations are also neither objective nor neutral. They are deployed by states promoting a specific set of interests destined to clash with those of factions on the ground. The authorities of the peace operation will consequently likely come under attack over time. Going back to our wrestling analogy, if a wrestler starts to feel that a referee is indirectly helping the opponent, the wrestler will start questioning the referee's authority and standing in the arena.

Factions resisting complex peace operations will increasingly ask: *Who are you? Why should we listen to you? Why can't we control your decisions?* The capacity to challenge and control power is a fundamental feature of any liberal democratic system. In overseeing the establishment of such a space, peace operations are therefore bound to evolve within these parameters. When facing a specific challenge against their authority, it is almost impossible to determine whether the challenge forms part of an attempt to overthrow the system they are trying to uphold, or is simply seeking to protect rights within that system. This is a key conundrum of diplomatic counterinsurgency. As peace operations are helping to build a space where power is challenged through nonviolent means, they must accept that their power will be challenged by forces working against the establishment of this space. Moreover, by escalating their resistance, factions may force a peace operation to adopt counteractions that will put it increasingly at odds with the liberal democratic standards it tries to establish. There will be a point where such counteractions may cause resistance against a peace operation to increase and its support to decrease. Factions can therefore push a peace operation further into its zone of vulnerability by increasing their resistance. The legal, administrative, and political challenges against the OHR in Bosnia are good illustrations of such dynamics.

Legal Challenges against the Powers of the High Representative

Acts of the High Representative were challenged in court as soon as his powers were used more assertively to overcome resistance. The first significant case brought against an act of the High Representative pertained to legislation establishing a national service to manage and protect the borders of Bosnia and Herzegovina. In the war's aftermath, the country's border had been ineffectively secured by a myriad of local police forces. Following the decision of members of the Parliamentary Assembly to block the adoption of legislation to establish a state border service, the High Representative decided to enact the law. The law enacted by the High Representative was challenged before Bosnia's Constitutional Court shortly after. One of the questions the court had to address in this case pertained to whether or not it was competent to review acts adopted by the High Representative. The court decided it was.

In its decision, the court noted that the powers of the High Representative were not unprecedented. Its decision stressed that sovereign states such as Germany and Austria had been placed under international supervision after the Second World War. During such supervision, the court noted, foreign authorities – acting on behalf of the international community – substituted themselves for domestic authorities and enacted norms. According to the court's majority decision: "The same holds true for the High Representative: he has been vested with special powers by the international community and his mandate is of an international character. In the present case, the High Representative ... intervened in the legal order of Bosnia and Herzegovina substituting himself for the national authorities. In this respect, he therefore acted as an authority of Bosnia and Herzegovina and the law which he enacted is in the nature of a national law and must be regarded as a law of Bosnia and Herzegovina."[39]

According to the court's decision, certain acts of the High Representative could be reviewed under certain conditions. Its decision made an important distinction between the types of acts adopted by the High Representative. It stipulated that when the High Representative substituted for a national authority, the constitutionality of the High Representative's act could be reviewed as if it had directly emanated from the national authority itself. The court noted, however, that certain elements of the High Representative's mandate were of an "international character" and, as such, could not be reviewed by the court. While the constitutionality of norms enacted through substitution powers – such as legislation – could be reviewed, acts of an "international character" – such as removals from office – were deemed to fall outside the purview of the Constitutional Court. The High Representative consented to the Constitutional Court's exercise of jurisdiction vis-à-vis legislation it enacted. Such legislation would be routinely challenged before the court. The court maintained this position for a number of years.[40]

This point of equilibrium would, however, be challenged. In 2004, several persons removed from their functions by the High Representative requested that the court examine whether such removals violated their rights under the constitution. While the court declared the cases inadmissible, its decisions nevertheless signaled the court's willingness to revisit its previous position regarding acts of international character of the High Representative.[41]

It was a simple matter of time before an admissible request raising similar points would end up before the court. It did reach the court in April 2005. In this case, Milorad Bilbija and Dragan Kalinić, both removed from public functions by the High Representative for failure to cooperate with the ICTY, argued that their removal from office violated their constitutional rights.[42] Partially reversing its previous position, the court declared itself competent to hear the merits of the case (something it had refused to do until then), and concluded that the rights of the appellants had been violated, not by the High Representative, but by the authorities of Bosnia and Herzegovina. While the court refused to directly examine the constitutionality of the High Representative's decisions, it nevertheless called for an indirect form of control. The court had indeed concluded that Bosnia had failed to ensure that the appellants had access to an effective legal remedy against the decisions of the High Representative.[43]

The decision triggered a shockwave within the international community. Not only had the court declared itself competent to review the case, it had called upon Bosnian authorities to take measures to secure an effective legal remedy against decisions of the High Representative. Bosnian authorities would gain, it was feared, the means to determine to what extent they had to comply with their own international obligations.

The ensuing debates within the Office of the High Representative and the Peace Implementation Council reflected fundamental tensions inherent to the peace implementation process. Some questioned how national authorities could be entitled to establish domestic mechanisms allowing them to overturn, or at least modulate, their own obligations under international law. Other members of the international community called upon the OHR to annul the court's decision. Others called for a suspension of the decision's legal validity. Other members of the PIC were, however, bitterly opposed to the very idea of interfering with the independence of the court. How could the international community promote judicial independence and then interfere so bluntly with the judiciary when its interests were at stake? Legal challenges had pushed the OHR close to a breaking point. If it annulled or suspended the decision of the court, it would inevitably erode support within its international constituency. If it did not react, its power could be quickly constrained by ad hoc domestic review mechanisms.

The response from the OHR came in March 2007. Several of us, in the Legal Department of the OHR, had been pushing for a solution that, in our opinion, struck a balance between the need to protect the authorities of the High Representative and the need to respect judicial independence. We recommended that the High Representative stay clear of any direct interference with the Constitutional Court. Instead, the High Representative could issue a decision that steered actions of the Bosnian authorities responsible for implementing the court's decision in a direction that prevented them from overturning our decision. This could be done by instructing the presidency of Bosnia – responsible for foreign affairs – to raise the issue of remedies with the High Representative as chair of the Steering Board of the Peace Implementation Council. High Representative Schwarz-Schilling decided to follow our recommendation. To satisfy those in the international community calling for more robust actions, it was agreed that the decision would be called an "order."

On March 23, 2007, Schwarz-Schilling issued an order pertaining to the implementation of the decision of the Constitutional Court. The order stipulated, among other things, that the presidency of Bosnia and Herzegovina had to address all the matters raised in the court's decision to the High Representative.[44] This solution was in line with our view that, given the immunities of the High Representative and Bosnia's obligations under international law, it belonged to the High Representative to establish a mechanism to review his decision rather than domestic authorities. Our position was aligned with previous opinions of the European Commission for Democracy through Law (Venice Commission), the Council of Europe's advisory body on constitutional matters,[45] and would subsequently be supported by the European Court for Human Rights.[46] The decision of the High Representative essentially steered the actions of the Bosnian authorities back to the chair of the Steering Board of the Peace Implementation Council: namely the High Representative.[47] This circular arrangement was certainly not optimal, but was, in our opinion, the least disruptive way to manage the situation engendered by the court's decision. We had been pushed into nearly impossible territory.

This would, however, not be the end. Another important case concerning the powers of the High Representative would soon be lodged before the European Court for Human Rights. While the case pertained, again, to removal decisions by the High Representative for noncooperation with the ICTY, the application had not been brought against the High Representative himself (the High Representative is not a party to the European Convention on Human Rights). The case had been lodged, instead, against the state of Bosnia. Bosnia had become party to the European convention in 2002 and the applicants' legal strategy was therefore seeking to hold Bosnia responsible for actions taken by the High Representative.[48] The court allowed the High Representative to make submissions in this case.[49] Our submissions mainly argued that the High Representative's powers derived from international law; that the High Representative was not an organ of any state and that his actions could therefore not engage the responsibility of any state, including Bosnia and Herzegovina.

The European Court reached its decision in October 2007. Noting that Bosnia and Herzegovina could not be responsible for acts taken by the High Representative, it declared the application inadmissible.[50] A year later, the court would also reject an application from Bilbija and Kalinić, who had complained, among others, that the March 2007 order of the High Representative violated their rights under the European convention. The court maintained its previous position to the effect that Bosnia could not be held responsible for acts taken by the High Representative, and declared their complaint inadmissible.[51]

These examples show how legal challenges can place a peace operation in a position that is increasingly more difficult to reconcile with the liberal democratic norms and values it seeks to promote and establish. But, as we will now see, opportunities to resist power extend beyond the realm of legal challenges.

Administrative Resistance

Factions resisting the impact of a peace operation may also erode its support through administrative noncooperation – something some of us at the OHR witnessed firsthand in 2004. In June 2004, High Representative Paddy Ashdown removed Radomir Lukić from the main board of the SDS for noncooperation with the ICTY. His decision also barred Lukić from holding any official, elective, or appointed public office.[52] A few weeks later, the law school of East Sarajevo University asked the OHR to clarify whether Lukić could continue working as dean of the Law School. The OHR notified the university that Lukić was barred from holding such a position.

Lukić refused to step down. In June 2005, the OHR wrote to the rector of the University of East Sarajevo and to the minister of education of Republika Srpska requesting that they forward to the OHR evidence of Lukić's removal, as well as written explanations as to why Lukić had not yet vacated his position. Republika Srpska Minister of Education Milovan Pecelj informed the OHR that he refused to intervene in this matter. His letter indicated that the authority to remove Lukić from his position was vested, under the law, with the university, and that he had therefore no power to remove Lukić. The OHR wrote back to the minister stressing that Lukić had already been dismissed from his position and that the minister's responsibility to supervise the work of the university implied a responsibility to ensure that its work was carried out in accordance with the law.

The minister refrained from intervening, and Lukić did not step down. Ashdown then wrote to the prime minister of Republika Srpska in September 2005. His letter stressed that Lukić's continued employment at the law school was in direct violation of his removal decision of June 2004, and urged the government of Republika Srpska to terminate all remuneration to Lukić. In October 2005, the government of Republika Srpska instructed the Ministry of Finance to halt salary payment to Lukić. Despite the government's action, Lukić continued to work at the law school and the minister of education persisted in his refusal to intervene.

His resistance triggered another flurry of letters from the OHR asking the minister to issue a public statement declaring that Lukić was barred from working at the university and asking that any accreditation of students for a class taught by him be declared null and void. The minister refused to do so. On October 28, 2005, Ashdown removed Minister Pecelj from his functions for failure to cooperate with the High Representative.[53]

The Lukić case shows how individuals and groups can use administrative noncooperation to trigger escalations that will ultimately place a peace operation in a position that is at odds with the liberal democratic

Political and Public Resistance

Political and public pressure can also lead to further erosions of support. Political challenges against the High Representative appeared as soon as the OHR asserted its powers more aggressively. By 2007, attacks in the local media against the legitimacy of the High Representative were routine. The powers of the High Representative were not only criticized in Bosnia and Herzegovina. Members of the international media, think tanks, and academia also condemned the High Representative. A column published in *The Spectator* in 2001 noted, for example: "the powers now vested in the UN administrator of Bosnia and Herzegovina are as close to pure tyranny as anything which has existed in recent European history. The decisions of the UN High Representative are neither democratically legitimized nor subject to the rule of law. Sniggering admissions that Bosnia and Herzegovina is in reality 'a protectorate' fail to capture the sheer lawlessness of the UN's power there, which goes way beyond the powers enjoyed, say, by a British colonial official in the last century."[54]

In 2003, two members of the European Stability Initiative published a piece in which they compared the High Representative to a European Raj. The authors criticized the lack of control over the power of the international community in Bosnia, and more specifically the power of the High Representative. Their report noted: "Six years after the end of the fighting in BiH, and despite possibly the largest amount of democratization assistance per capita ever spent in one country, the international mission to BiH has arrived at this paradoxical conclusion: What Bosnia and Herzegovina needs is not democratic domestic politics, but government by international experts. In Bosnia and Herzegovina, outsiders do more than participate in shaping the political agenda – something that has become the norm throughout Eastern Europe, as governments aspire to join the European Union. In BiH, outsiders actually set that agenda, impose it, and punish with sanctions those who refuse to implement it. At the center of this system is the OHR, which can interpret its own mandate and so has essentially unlimited legal powers. It can dismiss presidents, prime ministers, judges, and mayors without having to submit its decisions for review by any independent appeals body. It can veto candidates for ministerial positions without needing publicly to present any evidence for its stance. It can impose legislation and create new institutions without having to estimate the cost to Bosnian taxpayers."[55]

Increasing concerns over human rights led the Venice Commission to examine the compatibility of measures enacted by the High Representative with human rights norms in 2005. The commission's report noted that: "The High Representative is not an independent judge and he has no democratic legitimacy deriving from the people of BiH. He pursues a political agenda, agreed by the international community, which serves the best interests of the country and contributes to the realisation of Council of Europe standards. As a matter of principle, it seems unacceptable that decisions directly affecting the rights of individuals taken by a political body are not subject to a fair hearing or at least the minimum of due process and scrutiny by an independent court."[56] While the commission's opinion noted that it would have been unrealistic to insist on immediate full compliance with international standards in a postconflict situation, it nevertheless stressed that "This situation can however not last forever" and that "the day must come when such decisions are made subject to full judicial control and made the responsibility of the proper national institutions."[57]

A piece published in *The Guardian* during the 2007 crisis observed: "The international community has a pivotal role to play in Bosnia and Herzegovina, but articulating political crises as a means through which to recover lost credibility and legitimacy undermines its capacity to act as a reform mediator.... Former High Representative Lord Ashdown once remarked that the people of Bosnia and Herzegovina 'have to decide who to vote for in the elections. This country has to mature.' In regularly pinning blame on the people and their politicians for reform failures, the international community has sought to exclude itself from scrutiny and responsibility."[58] Another piece published during the same period in *The Guardian* accused the High Representative of running Bosnia like a feudal fiefdom: "Twelve years after the Bosnian conflict was apparently resolved with the Dayton agreement, the international high representative still runs Bosnia as if it was a feudal fiefdom. He has the power to impose legislation and dismiss elected politicians without any right of appeal."[59]

Unlike colonial structures, the OHR had not been deployed to subjugate a population or to exploit its resources. The OHR was part of a multilateral peace operation exercising powers stemming from an international agreement agreed by the parties and endorsed by UN Security Council resolutions. But despite their limits,[60] the colonial analogies highlighted the growing dissonance between the actions of the OHR and the liberal democratic values it claimed to be supporting. The analogies also tapped into growing frustrations. Foreign interventions almost inevitably engender local resentment. Complex peace operations do not escape this dynamic. Appealing international slogans and logos soon give way to disillusions and resentment for people on the ground. The experience in Yugoslavia's successor states certainly confirms this. Yugoslavia had expelled the Nazis during the Second World War, stood up to the Soviet Union in 1948, and helped form the nonaligned movement. Its people had the highest living standards of the socialist bloc and could travel both east and west with their passports during the Cold War. The country produced several Nobel Prize winners. Many of the films, books, and art produced in Yugoslavia in the twentieth century represented major international contributions. The majority of people in Yugoslavia watched this world go down in flames during the war. Clinging to hopes of decisive international help, they witnessed confusion, hesitation, and half measures from the outside world. In the immediate aftermath of the armed conflict, they found themselves evolving in environments controlled by former warlords, nationalists, and organized crime gang leaders.

It is in this context that a wave of international bureaucrats and NGO workers came to their country and energetically tried to impose foreign norms with a sense of superiority. People had to contend with agendas and processes imposed by foreigners. For years, the OHR had been perceived as an umbrella that allowed expatriates living in relative isolation from the rest of the local population to impose new norms and models with little regard to those in place. By pointing to unfairness, arrogance, and ignorance, there is little doubt that colonial analogies fueled existing resentment and resistance against the international effort.

Self-Reinforcing Loops

Domestic factions are often conscious of the strategic advantage of dividing the international bureaucratic consensus behind a foreign actor. From their point of view, forces that resist the mandate of the foreign presence act as a strategic resource. The experience in Bosnia shows how internal and external resistance came to feed each other in a self-reinforcing retroactive loop. The interaction between the resistance of Milorad Dodik's government in Republika Srpska against the OHR, and that of certain members of the international community, acts as a good illustration.

After its election in 2006, Milorad Dodik's government in Republika Srpska realized that it had strategic resources in the international constituency behind the OHR. Dodik's government hired Washington, DC lobbyists and lawyers to represent its interest. It publicized its own narrative through a website – maintained by its law firm – called "BiH Dayton Project."[61] During the crisis in 2007, representatives of Republika Srpska actively courted EU member states in Brussels to denounce Lajčák's measures, including Lajčák's own government. By February 2009, Republika Srpska started sending regular reports to the presidency of the United Nations Security Council in an attempt to counteract the impact of the High Representative's briefing to the Security Council. Its communication was crafted in a way that accentuated points of divergence amongst the international constituency of the OHR.

Some powerful EU member states, such as France and Germany, had been increasingly willing to reduce the role of the OHR to strengthen their position in BiH. As an EU official involved with EU policy in the western Balkans observed: "For the EU, the OHR logic no longer works.... We are trying to move on to a Brussels philosophy. This transition went through several phases. In 2006, we tried to close the OHR. It did not work. Then we tried to change instruments, to focus more on the EU pull factor.... This did not work either." The EU was now pursuing a new "phase in – phase out" strategy. Its new approach sought, first, to establish a stronger European Union Special Representative in BiH to subsequently open the way for reducing the presence of the OHR in three steps. "The idea is to start a discussion with international partners in order to decrease the funding of the OHR, then relocate it outside of Bosnia, and then close it," according to the EU official.[62]

Republika Srpska's reports to the Security Council took such factors into account. They stressed, for example, that the situation in Bosnia no longer posed a threat to international peace and security, that the presence of the High Representative hindered further domestic progress, and that Republika Srpska and Bosnian officials were working toward Bosnia's EU integration.[63]

Russia's willingness to reassert itself on the international scene also offered strategic opportunities for Republika Srpska. Since taking power in 2006, Dodik's government allowed increased Russian investments in banking, oil, and natural gas in Republika Srpska. Its public messaging has, at times, been particularly supportive of Russia's interests. In May 2009, Dodik called upon Bosnian Serb members of the BiH armed forces to boycott a NATO-led military exercise in Georgia.[64] Returning from a trip to Russia in early 2013, Dodik declared his intention to submit any decision regarding Bosnia's accession to NATO to a referendum in Republika Srpska.[65]

The statements made by Russia, Germany, and the European Union following the report of High Representative Inzko to the UN Security Council in November 2011 show how external and internal resistance against the OHR came to interact and reinforce each other. Commenting on Inzko's remarks before the Security Council, the Russian representative indicated: "Unfortunately, we have no choice but to recognize that High Representative Inzko's analysis of the situation in Bosnia and Herzegovina can hardly be called objective. His report ... again reflects considerable prejudice against the Bosnian Serb leadership. In order to gain a more balanced idea of the events taking place in Bosnia, we recommend that members of the Council also read the letter from the President of the Republika Srpska, Mr. Dodik, to the Secretary-General on 10 November, and the sixth report of the Republika Srpska to the Security Council."[66] The Russian statement indicated further : "we continue to believe that an important task for the international community at the current stage of the Bosnian settlement is the transfer of responsibility for the future of the country to Bosnians themselves. In practical terms, that means abolishing the Office of the High Representative for Bosnia and Herzegovina."[67]

The statement of the German representative before the Security Council reflected similar dynamics: "Our focus should be on employing instruments that are better suited to initiate positive developments. Obsolete approaches should be discontinued. Decoupling the High Representative and the EU Special Representative and endowing the latter with a sound mandate was an important step. Further steps must follow. The European Union and Bosnia and Herzegovina's EU perspective should become the only game in town.... In addition, we are of the view that the Office of the High Representative should be downsized and relocated abroad. Its staff levels should be commensurate with its remaining tasks."[68]

The position of the European Union representative followed similar lines and was consistent with an identifiable trend.[69] In March 2011, the Council of the European Union had adopted conclusions stressing that its members were looking forward to "discussions of the international community on the reconfiguration of the international presence, including consideration of the possible relocation of the OHR."[70] In August 2011, French Minister for Foreign Affairs Alain Juppé and his German counterpart Guido Westerwelle had sent a joint letter to EU High Representative for Foreign Affairs and Security Policy Catherine Ashton in which they stressed their firm conviction that the OHR had to be downsized and relocated outside of Bosnia and Herzegovina.[71] Their letter also argued for a significant reduction in EU financial support to the OHR.[72]

Just like other foreign presences, complex peace operations evolve in interconnected and unstable systems. This brief overview shows how levels of resistance within conflict systems may, over time, surpass those supporting a peace operation and lead its power to suddenly shift away.

The Defeat of the OHR in 2007

Our reflections opened with a general question: How to explain the defeat inflicted on the OHR in the fall of 2007? We can now propose a few answers.

I continue to believe that the defeat in 2007 could have been averted. While there may have been divisions within the Peace Implementation Council, important members, including the United States and the United Kingdom, firmly supported the actions of the OHR. Had the OHR coordinated with its international and domestic partners more closely before enacting changes to parliamentary and government decision-making rules, it would have been in a better position to decide whether it was appropriate to proceed with such changes at that point in time. It would also have been able to harness the power of a broad coalition as it went along.

Moreover, several means – short of removing the leadership of Republika Srpska from office – remained available to solve the crisis. The international community could have temporarily suspended economic assistance to Republika Srpska or imposed visa bans and asset freezes on its leadership. It could have used NATO and EU accession processes as leverage to overcome Republika Srpska's obstruction to police reform. This leverage could also have been used to invite the government in Serbia to distance itself from Dodik's actions in Bosnia. While none of these measures could have guaranteed an easy way out of the crisis, they would have, at a minimum, helped the international community emerge from the crisis in a much stronger position than it did in 2007.

But even if we are ready to accept that the international community could have come out of the crisis in a better position, had it not shown that the capacity of the international community to manage intense forms of resistance was no longer as strong as it once was?

The fact is that we were working under inaccurate assumptions in 2007. These assumptions led us to believe that the OHR could still operate as an international leviathan in Bosnia, while it was, in fact, acting within a zone of vulnerability. Our failure to identify profound changes in external and internal levels of support and resistance over the years led us not only to downplay our vulnerabilities, but to launch ourselves into an ambitious confrontation against Milorad Dodik, a skilled politician with tremendous popular support in Republika Srpska, while being in a vulnerable position.

Had we been more conscious of conflict's extraordinary capacity to adapt, we would have acknowledged more readily that we were not simply amending peripheral elements of power-sharing arrangements in 2007. We were actually intervening in Bosnia's nonviolent war. We were certainly aware of the existence of continuing conflict dynamics in Bosnia. But our failure to contextualize this conflict within its broader evolution led us to underestimate the fact that its actors were still operating at very high levels of intensity. Acknowledging this intensity more accurately would have helped us better anticipate the decision of the leadership of Republika Srpska to face the risks associated with challenging the international community. For them, such risks were justified when measured against what they perceived as threats to core interests and positions.

The crisis also sheds light on our failure to fully acknowledge that our power ultimately depended on the consent of the population in Bosnia. Perceiving the power of the High Representative as a fixed capacity inherent to its mandate, we sought to reactivate his authorities through a policy of forceful reassertion. Had we conceived power as a more fluid capacity, dispersed within the population, we would have been more conscious of a number of key factors. First, that our power depended on our relationship with the population. Second, that we were competing against more effective local actors in trying to secure popular consent to achieve our objectives. Third, and more important, that this very consent could ultimately be withdrawn, either by the population as a whole or by some of its key segments. It was Bosnians who, at the end of the day, consented to the authorities of the High Representative, published the High Representative's decisions in the *Official Gazettes* and enforced them though judicial and administrative action. It was those living and working in Republika Srpska who withdrew their consent to our authority in 2007.

Finally, as we assessed potential reactions to our measures, we failed to position the OHR within its broader set of interconnections and to acknowledge crucial shifts in levels of support and resistance. More than a decade had passed since armed conflict had ended in Bosnia. Manifest signs of violence had disappeared from daily life. There were divisions in the Peace Implementation Council. Russia was increasingly willing to break ranks. The European Union was actively seeking to replace the OHR with an EU presence. Far from passive, Republika Srpska was acting in ways that accentuated such divisions. Moreover, its resistance had, over time, triggered escalations that had placed the OHR in a position of increasing dissonance with the liberal democratic values held by its constituents.[73]

As far as our internal levels of support were concerned, while the presence of sixty thousand troops in Bosnia in 1995 certainly contributed to the capacity of the international community to ensure high levels of consent and cooperation – through direct enforcement or through its capacity to coerce consent – the small EUFOR force in place in 2007 left us much more dependent on the cooperation of Republika Srpska's administrative structures and population. Consent could be withdrawn more easily. All of these points were clear indications that our levels of support were far below those we had enjoyed in the past. This helps to explain why the international community was able to successfully counter the nonviolent insurgency of Bosnian Croat nationalists in 2001, but failed to manage that launched by the leadership of Republika Srpska in 2007.

The consequences of such mutations should have been clearer: we were in a zone of vulnerability and our actions forced counter-actions by Republika Srpska that we were not able to fully contain. Their actions had not been directed against the powers of Bosnia's common institutions. They had targeted those of their main international supporter: the OHR. The credibility of the international community – including that of the European Union – has greatly suffered as a consequence. While able to rely on the cooperation and consent of other levels of government in Bosnia, the authorities of the High Representative have almost been entirely rejected in Republika Srpska since 2007 and secessionist aspirations have been emboldened. The defeat of the OHR in 2007 illustrates a strategic failure, one during which international interveners failed to push Bosnia's conflict system to bifurcate away from disruptive and counterproductive avenues. Reflecting further on this failure, the next chapter offers a number of thoughts and recommendations for other interventions.

9 Looking Forward

> War systems are similar to sieges, one must concentrate all his fire against one single point. Once the breach is created, the equilibrium is disrupted, and all the rest becomes irrelevant.
> —Napoléon Bonaparte[1]

This book makes three main suggestions. First, it suggests that we were not merely implementing a peace process after the end of armed conflict in Bosnia and Herzegovina. We were managing a nonviolent war. While successfully ending armed conflict, international military intervention in Bosnia and Herzegovina did not extinguish conflict per se. Using limited means to achieve limited objectives, NATO's intervention in 1995 established a space for diplomacy to manage the nonviolent continuation of war. Akin to culture wars, nonviolent wars are intense forms of conflict fought over power through parliaments, ministries, media, and courts. Although fought primarily through nonviolent means, they maintain a particularly close relationship with violence insofar as their developments can disrupt fragile peace processes.

Second, when foreign actors intervene to reestablish a state's capacity to protect those within its reach, they inevitably disturb positions and interests of parties engaged in a competition over power on the ground. Interveners are therefore never merely rebuilding parliaments, courts, and police forces. As they engage in "state building," "capacity building," or "technical assistance," they have an impact on ongoing conflicts. This is why belligerent groups may attack foreigners as they try to rebuild courthouses. If the capacity for violence has been neutralized, belligerent groups may still seek to challenge the power of foreign interveners through nonviolent means. Given that power can indeed be challenged and protected through nonviolent means, peace operations may be called upon to counter such challenges through diplomacy – a process this book suggests to call *diplomatic counterinsurgency*.

Finally, the book argues that, as important as it may appear, the power of peace operations to effect change in conflict systems is limited and ephemeral. While the experience in Bosnia suggests that international interveners can address and counter nonviolent resistance, including nonviolent insurgencies, their capacity to do so is, however, limited. Neither permanent nor stable, peace operations evolve in interconnected systems that are in constant motion. As they try to establish or maintain a space of nonviolence, factions engaged in conflict can trigger escalations that will ultimately lead to the peace operations' levels of support to decrease, and their power to suddenly collapse. The defeat of the Office of the High Representative in 2007 is an illustration of such dynamics.

The events chronicled in the first part of this book highlight the consequences of overestimating international power in a post–armed conflict context, and invite us to ask ourselves serious questions about how power can be applied more efficiently. After more than fifteen years and several billion dollars dedicated to the peace implementation process in Bosnia and Herzegovina, the state is still unable to autonomously maintain itself. Even the more optimistic voices regarding Bosnia and Herzegovina's progress are not calling for a withdrawal of the international presence stationed on its territory. Despite having reduced the size, mandates, and composition of the military presence, the United Nations Security Council continues to authorize a small military force in Bosnia twenty years after the beginning of the armed conflict in 1992.[2] Almost two decades after secessionist forces violently challenged its authorities, the country's central government is unable to protect the state against secessionist threats without the daily support of the European Union, the United States, and other countries of the Peace Implementation Council. The peace implementation process in Bosnia and Herzegovina reveals painful lessons about the limits of international power.

So what does that teach us as we look forward? This chapter outlines a number of thoughts and considerations examining ways foreign intervention can optimize its impact on conflict. It suggests that foreign interveners can do so (1) by proactively embracing the inherent confusion and uncertainty of complex environments in which they intervene; (2) by setting more attainable and realistic objectives; and (3) by applying power more efficiently. I examine each point in turn.

Embracing Confusion and Uncertainty

Policy makers ought to define the end point of intervention from the very outset, and elaborate plans defining the manner in which they intend to reach their objective. Plans are essential tools to manage complex environments. But by adhering too closely to them, interveners tend to isolate themselves from the complex environments in which they intervene, and decrease their capacity to effect change within these environments. The most precise model only partially encapsulates the complex reality it seeks to understand. Taking refuge in models will inevitably lead interveners to be surprised.[3]

Nothing is entirely certain or predictable about conflict. No model or framework can fully anticipate or manage conflict outcomes, let alone outcomes sought through foreign intervention. It is presumptuous to assume that we can fully understand or predict outcomes within these environments. Instead of succumbing to dangerous illusions of certainty and predictability, strategy should be designed in a way that *proactively embraces confusion and uncertainty*.

Speaking before the Council of Foreign Relations in October 2011 about his time in Afghanistan, U.S. General Stanley McChrystal said: "We didn't know enough and we still don't know enough. Most of us, me included, had a very superficial understanding of the situation and history, and we had a frighteningly simplistic view of recent history, the last 50 years."[4] Edgar Morin, a leading thinker on complexity, cautions against the limits of blind intelligence as we evolve in complex environments.[5] For Morin, knowledge is the product of a rationalization process that, like a translation process, inherently betrays complex realities. He argues that as we approach these complex realities through disjointed linear models, we inevitably isolate elements from each other and lose the capacity to observe complexity for what it is:

a vast, unpredictable, nonlinear, and interconnected reality that is a constant source of uncertainty. "We are blind to the problem of complexity.... This blindness is part of our barbarism. It makes us realize that in the world of ideas, we are still in the age of barbarism. We are still in the prehistory of the human mind."[6]

A recent essay on intervention argues that "the foreigners who comprise 'the international community' are usually much weaker than they imagine. They are inevitably isolated from local society, ignorant of local culture and context, and prey to misleading abstract theories. 'The international community' often lacks legitimacy and local support because it is amorphous, unelected, and foreign.... Local political leaders are often more competent and powerful than the international theories ... suggest."[7] The authors of the essay rightly denounce the arrogance of many international officials intervening in foreign theaters and wisely invite them to proceed with a sense of moderation and incrementalism. But, by focusing on the existence of illusions, contradictions, and adjustments of international interveners, their work chronicles the self-correcting trajectories of those who navigate complex realities without tackling a more important set of questions: Have they improved along the way? How could they have improved? As interesting as our strengths and weaknesses may be, our thinking needs to break away from our own reflection in the water.[8] Acting in complex environments inevitably leads to mistakes and corrections. Tolstoy wondered in *War and Peace* why historians focused so much attention on decisions and actions of generals and emperors to explain the outcomes of military battles when such battles depended on complex and unpredictable interactions unable to be fully determined in advance. To better grasp the lessons of history, Tolstoy believed, one needs to leave aside kings, ministers, and generals and focus on movement. Abraham Lincoln wrote in April 1864: "I claim not to have controlled events, but confess plainly that events have controlled me."[9]

So how can interveners better manage movement? First, while complexity should inject humility into the minds of policy makers, it should not paralyze them with a sense of powerlessness. Though it is true that most elements in complex systems are interconnected and that a specific action targeting one element may trigger reactions elsewhere in the system, it is equally true that not all elements are connected with the same intensity. Some elements and connections may be more significant than others. As they conceptualize these complex realities, interveners ought therefore to identify – and seek to address – critical points and interconnections within them.

Second, policy makers can better manage uncertainty by recognizing that they are not distinct from the realities in which they intervene. They are part of them. This implies, among other things, that as soon as they start acting in these environments, their actions will immediately escape their intentions. Absorbed by larger open environments, their actions will trigger multiple reactions. While relying on models and plans may allow them to understand more clearly some of the potential mutations within these environments, they will only navigate them more effectively by displaying constant vigilance, humility, and flexibility as they proceed. Acting with humility and vigilance implies that they readjust, correct, or even torpedo their own actions as they move along.[10] Mistakes are indeed much more than the measures of one's own illusions; they are also signals through which complex systems partially reveal themselves to us. Far from being a sign of weakness, proactively embracing confusion and uncertainty reflects a more profound, richer, and more responsible way to approach the inherently complex realities of conflict.[11]

Attainable and Realistic Objectives

Building on these considerations, foreign interveners may gain in designing strategy around realistic and attainable objectives that embrace *the central role of conflict*, seek to *steer* conflict rather than to *solve* it, and *focus on conflict's critical points*.

The centrality of conflict: While this may appear counterintuitive and difficult for nonpractitioners to conceive, the existence of conflict in itself is, at times, one of the most underestimated factors in theaters of foreign intervention such as Bosnia or Kosovo. Projects, deliverables, and schedules provide a distorted sense of control. Interests and mandates blur perceptions and can make conflict seem more a distant abstraction than a practical reality. But relying too closely on plans and timelines comes at a cost. The danger lies in losing sight of the

Looking Forward 203

very reason why one has intervened in the first place: the existence of conflict.

This book opens with the story of a bomb exploding in front of the International Civilian Office in Kosovo in November 2008. Given that the organization was mandated to support Kosovo's accession to statehood, many of us working there could hardly understand why we had been bombed in the middle of Pristina. The answer was to be found in Kosovo's conflict. As many of us were working in the office that evening, Pieter Feith, the head of the ICO, was trying, together with other international officials, to facilitate arrangements between the European Union, the United Nations, and the governments of Kosovo and Serbia regarding the deployment of a European Union rule of law–led mission in Kosovo (called EULEX).

While the intricacies of this bureaucratic deployment process may have appeared removed from conflict to some, they were not. Serbia had conditioned its consent to the deployment of EULEX. It would consent to the deployment only if the United Nations Interim Administration Mission in Kosovo (UNMIK) retained several responsibilities in Kosovo. By doing so, Belgrade had sought to make gains in its confrontation with Pristina over Kosovo's status. Kosovo authorities found Serbia's proposal intolerable. They perceived UNMIK as a potential threat to Kosovo's newly declared sovereignty. UNMIK could, in their eyes, be used as a Trojan horse by Serbia and other nonrecognizing countries to erode the effectiveness of Kosovo's newly declared independence. They feared that UNMIK could be pressured to adopt laws or run administrative agencies in Kosovo. Therefore, while ICO had been deployed to support Kosovo's sovereignty, its attempts to convince Kosovo leaders to accept the deployment of EULEX made some wonder whether it had become an instrument of Belgrade's maneuverings. It is within this context that the bomb exploded. Some in Kosovo had presumably decided to send ICO a message. For those of us in the office, the blast appeared to come from nowhere. It did not. It had its source in the long-lasting conflict over Kosovo's status.[12]

The more one compartmentalizes conflict, the more likely one may be surprised by its manifestations. Placing and maintaining conflict at the center of our focus allows us to better identify potential mutations in the environment. Interveners are not merely implementing peace agreements or establishing refugee camps. Willingly or not, they disturb positions and interests of groups engaged in conflict. By identifying parties, constituencies, and interconnections with external and internal actors, they can better understand a given conflict's potential reactions. Mapping out conflict, closely monitoring its evolution, and maintaining it at the center of strategic considerations is key to increase one's capacity to navigate complex environments.[13] The events chronicled in the first part of the book illustrate how some of us in the Office of the High Representative had lost sight of Bosnia's ongoing conflict in 2007. This led us to significantly underestimate the impact of our actions while overestimating our capacity to manage potential reactions.

Steering conflict: It is not realistic to seek to stop or halt conflict through international intervention. As this book illustrates, conflict is fluid and resilient and, consequently, has an extraordinary capacity to adapt and survive. As we neutralize armed conflict, it morphs into nonviolent confrontation. Armed attacks against occupying forces can metamorphose into nonviolent challenges. But how realistic is it to seek to stop conflict in Bosnia, Kosovo, or Syria when conflict thrives on a daily basis in Belgium or Canada? By pursuing elusive objectives such as "halting," "solving," or "ending" conflict, are we not restricting the definition of conflict in ways that prevent us from acting more effectively?

Seeking to solve or end conflict is often the product of the very illusions we entertain about the power we can project. Strategic discussions should, instead, start with an honest assessment of the extent and nature of the power we can project through intervention. The experience in Bosnia and Kosovo suggests that, even in cases where significant resources can be mobilized, international power is almost inevitably limited. Seeking to solve conflict in such contexts may therefore be an elusive quest that distracts us and lead us to squander limited resources.

We cannot afford to design strategy based on premises that overestimate the power of foreigners and underestimate the resilience of conflict. A scholar examining the work of complex peace operations rightly noted that peace operations ought to limit their goals and proposed that peace operations focus their attention on restoring basic security where "commerce can be practiced, and the arts can flourish."[14] Her work argued that peace operations should not try to create perfect societies but ones that are functional; societies where "[b]orders are controlled, terrorism is curtailed and the government does not face constant threats of violent overthrow."[15] She further suggested that peacekeeping and occupation operations should focus on providing security "while the politics are sorting themselves out."[16] Another scholar who examined international efforts to build peace after war noted that foreign intervention can exacerbate conflict and argued for a more nuanced approach to intervention. Examining the propensity of international interveners to promote liberal democratic models of governance in postwar environments, his work argued that peace operations ought to acknowledge that democratization and marketization exacerbate conflict. Instead of rushing forward with elections and economic reforms, peacekeepers should seek to establish domestic institutions capable of managing democratization and marketization's conflict-inducing effects and phase in political and economic reforms.[17] The author calls this proposed strategy "Institutionalization Before Liberalization."[18]

Although many of these perspectives are commendable, some aspects of them are problematic from a practical standpoint. The suggestion to "let politics sort themselves out" while peacekeeping forces focus on maintaining basic security fails to recognize that politics and security are intimately linked and that the reestablishment of security may very well depend on politics. Post–armed conflict politics entertain very close links with violence. The mere presence of the NATO-led force in Kosovo (KFOR) did not prevent subsequent resurgence of violence in 2004 or 2011, for example. Recommendations to design electoral systems that reward moderation[19] or to approach economic reforms in ways that reduce conflict rather than exacerbate it[20] are certainly sound. But, as this book argues, it is outside intervention itself – as opposed to specific processes such as liberalization or marketization – that disturbs conflict and triggers reactions.

The problem with these approaches is that they are partially based on the misleading assumption that interveners have the capacity to suspend or compartmentalize conflict. The suggestion that peace operations should "permit the postponement of elections for as long as it takes to establish the right institutional and political conditions for a constructive vote that advances, rather than hinders, efforts to consolidate a stable and lasting peace"[21] is an illustration of such problematic assumptions. Parties in conflict are active, not passive. They influence most components of the environments in which foreigners intervene and do not feel compelled to abide by distinctions or timetables drawn by outsiders. They do not wait until institutions are built to engage opponents or foreign actors. On the contrary, they often immediately seek to prevent institutions and competencies from falling into the hands of their opponents. State building does not occur within a parallel space created by foreigners. State building is an *integral part* of conflict after the cessation of armed confrontation. Internationals who support the establishment of state institutions do not operate in a vacuum. Their projects require laws, regulations, permits, administrative approvals, and construction workers. Each of these elements provides opportunities for opponents to block each other's relative advance in conflict. It took international officials years to secure rights to rent premises for some of the new state institutions in Bosnia and Herzegovina. In Afghanistan, the Taliban has not interrupted its activities as outsiders rebuild the country's military and police forces. They have attacked those rebuilding them.[22]

Commenting on a law enacted by the OHR to establish a court of Bosnia and Herzegovina, Milorad Dodik noted in a speech before the National Assembly of Republika Srpska in April 2011: "The aim of the first phase was disciplining the Serb and Croat officials, by arrests, detentions and judicial prosecutions without adequate evidence. Intimidation was the message to others, as well, what would befall them if they opposed the remapping of the Dayton Agreement and the centralisation in favour of Bosniaks."[23] On the same day, the members of the National Assembly decided to ask the population of Republika Srpska, by way of referendum, whether it supported laws imposed by the High Representative in Bosnia – in particular the laws that had established Bosnia's court and prosecutors office.[24]

The manner in which UNMIK's "Standards before Status" policy[25] was rejected in March 2004 acts as another reminder of the dangers of assuming that outsiders can build institutions away from conflict. General violence erupted in Kosovo in March 2004 as a consequence of deep frustration with the international community's attempt to strengthen institutional safeguards before establishing a process to solve Kosovo's final status. Commenting on the violence in Kosovo in 2004, the International Crisis Group observed: "After the two-day rampage of partly coordinated arson, looting, shooting, and stone, petrol bomb, and grenade-throwing that left nineteen dead, nearly 900 injured (more than twenty gravely), over 700 Serb, Ashkali and Roma homes, up to 10 public buildings and 30 Serbian churches and two monasteries damaged or destroyed, and some 4,500 Kosovo Serbs displaced, that 'standards before status' policy looks threadbare and sorely in need of repair."[26]

Peace implementation strategies need to be based on a more realistic and humble assessment of international capacities. Because international power is both limited and ephemeral, we cannot afford objectives that seek to *completely solve or compartmentalize* conflict. Rather, we ought to apply power in a way that recognizes that interveners are constantly interacting with actors in conflict. Strategy must acknowledge that conflict will continue to permeate daily life *during* and *after* international intervention. International efforts should focus on ensuring that such competitions take place in a self-sustainable nonviolent space. Rather than seeking to suspend or compartmentalize conflict, interveners should seek to modulate its intensity at levels that prevent it from throwing society back into violence. Strategy should be anchored on a more realistic objective: one that seeks to *steer conflict toward a sustainable nonviolent space.*

But how? The events chronicled in this book allow for a number of suggestions to guide intervention in that regard. First, rather than approaching conflict indiscriminately, strategy ought to address conflict's critical points. Second, interveners can manage conflict systems more effectively by applying military force in a focused way; by better coordinating the interaction of force and diplomacy; by approaching negotiations more strategically; and by deploying power more strategically during the peace implementation phase. The following section examines each point in turn.

More Effective Application of International Power

In cases where international power can be mobilized, its application is often rigid and ephemeral. As time passes, the interveners' power tends to diminish. Competing priorities on the domestic front gradually reduce levels of support. Local actors on the ground improve their capacity to resist and dilute the power of interveners. While it may take minutes for local groups to shift from conventional warfare to insurgency, from violent to nonviolent resistance, the response from the foreign intervening force will inevitably be slower. Tactical shifts from local actors activate tensions between divisions, departments, ministries, and coalition partners on the international side. As domestic actors switch tactics, they create new opportunities to dilute the impact of foreign interveners. This is how losses at war are recuperated at the negotiating table and how concessions made in peace treaties are neutralized through resistance in the implementation phase. Time is therefore a strategic resource for local actors. If managed well, they can resist the impact of foreign intervention. Local actors benefit from a longevity advantage. When intervening in conflicts such as those in Bosnia or Kosovo, foreign actors ought, therefore, to consider ways to apply power earlier, more densely, and against critical points in conflict systems. The application of power at a critical juncture early on will lead to longer-term gains and will reduce opportunities to dilute the impact of intervention.

Focusing on critical points: While international efforts to steer conflict away from its violent potential should address multiple variables at once, not all variables and interconnections are equally important. No conflict is configured similarly, therefore no action will have the same impact.

A 2000 UN report on peace operations considered, for example, that peace building "includes but is not limited to reintegrating former combatants into civilian society, strengthening the rule of law (for example, through training and restructuring of local police, and judicial and penal reform); improving respect for human rights through the monitoring, education and investigation of past and existing abuses; providing technical assistance for democratic development (including electoral assistance and support for free media); and promoting conflict resolution and reconciliation techniques."[27] The report further noted that "[e]ssential complements to effective peacebuilding include support for the fight against corruption, the implementation of humanitarian demining programmes, emphasis on human immunodeficiency virus/acquired immunodeficiency syndrome (HIV/AIDS) education and control, and action against other infectious diseases."[28]

Multidimensional approaches to conflict are essential. But working on all aspects of conflict with no regard to its interconnections can lead to counterproductive results. As aqueducts, school, courts, and homes are rebuilt and as NGOs bring children from different communities closer through football, arts, and theater, international intervention must prioritize its actions and ensure that it decisively addresses critical points of conflict.

The collapse of the former Yugoslavia and its subsequent peace processes provide valuable insight as to what may act as critical points in conflict systems. The collapse and its aftermath have illustrated how interferences with power arrangements (which we can define as rules and institutions governing the distribution of power) quickly disturb collective feelings of self-worth, status, and fears of domination and engender wide systemic reverberations in the environment – including violent ones. Milošević's attempt to increase Serbia's power over other Yugoslav republics pushed Slovenia, Croatia, and Bosnia and Herzegovina to secede in 1991 and 1992. Within Bosnia and Herzegovina and Croatia, fears of subjugation fueled Serb minorities' violent challenges against the newly independent states. Milošević's revocation of Kosovo's special status triggered Ibrahim Rugova's campaign of passive resistance and the subsequent violent attacks from the Kosovo Liberation Army (KLA) in Kosovo. More recently, attempts by Kosovar authorities to take control of border checkpoints in northern Kosovo have triggered a resurgence of violence as the majority Kosovo Serb population in the north fear more assertive Kosovo Albanian control.[29] The peace implementation process in Bosnia and Herzegovina has illustrated similar reactions. Changes to electoral rules by the international community triggered the attempt by a faction of the Bosnian Croat community to secede from Bosnia and Herzegovina in 2001. High Representative Miroslav Lajčák's amendments to governmental and parliamentary decision-making procedures in 2007 increased fears of further centralization that pushed the leadership of Republika Srpska to directly challenge Lajčák's authority and allude to the secession of Republika Srpska.

Power arrangements act as key points in conflict systems. Interference with them is likely to disturb powerful collective feelings of self-worth, ignite fears of domination and subjugation, and trigger self-reinforcing counteractions that can ultimately lead some factions to challenge the very foundations of the nonviolent space in which they evolve. As they seek to manage the evolution of conflict, foreign interveners would therefore be wise to focus their attention on power arrangements. Applying power to secure arrangements guaranteeing that groups can exercise power in a manner that is commensurate with their importance, and that adequately protect them from domination, may contribute to the stability of the system as it evolves.

Better coordination of force and diplomacy: When intervening militarily to manage armed conflict in places such as Bosnia and Herzegovina or Kosovo, foreign interveners are not fighting the large interstate wars of the past century. Rather than inflicting decisive outcomes on the battlefield, these types of military intervention create, instead, opportunities for diplomacy. As British General Rupert Smith rightly notes in *The Utility of Force: The Art of War in the Modern World*, when intervening in places such as Bosnia and Kosovo we "do not intervene in order to take or hold territory; in fact once an intervention has occurred a main preoccupation is how to leave the territory rather than keep it. Instead, we intervene in, or even decide to escalate to, a conflict in order to establish a condition in which the political objective can be achieved by other means and in other ways."[30]

If we are – as we intervene in such conflicts – returning to the wars of diplomacy that preceded Napoléon and Clausewitz, the efficiency of international interventions is therefore linked to our capacity to effectively combine force and diplomacy. Clausewitz observed that "[t]he main lines along which military events progress, and to which they are restricted, are political lines that continue throughout the war into the subsequent peace."[31] If the objective of international intervention is to reestablish states' capacity to protect those within their reach, and if the reestablishment of such a capacity requires belligerent groups to abandon absolutist claims to power, then military power and diplomacy must be closely aligned toward that end.

If we acknowledge that conflict, as this book argues, is likely to survive international military interventions, then we ought to deploy military force in ways that affect to the greatest possible extent the capacity of parties to continue pursuing war objectives through nonviolent means. Force ought to shape conflict in ways that allow diplomacy to secure decisive gains at the negotiating table. Instead of merely seeking to end violence, military force ought to achieve objectives that directly feed into diplomacy. If a given intervention – such as that in Bosnia and Herzegovina – seeks to put an end to the secessionist aims of certain groups, then military action ought to be deployed in ways that will make such claims difficult to promote with credibility in the subsequent phases of conflict. By confining secessionist forces to non-contiguous zones and/or allowing governmental forces to control larger and more strategic portions of territory, international military force can certainly increase diplomacy's chances of securing power arrangements that effectively constrain future secessionist threats. Examining civil war terminations since 1940, recent scholarly work concluded, for example, that civil wars ended by military victory are less likely to recur.[32]

Effecting decisive outcomes through diplomacy: Diplomacy must take full advantage of the opportunities created by military intervention. Rather than approaching negotiations as a process seeking to end armed conflict, it must look further ahead and approach the design of power arrangements as critical points of transition where parties set the conditions under which they will pursue conflict. As war continues to be waged at the negotiating table, foreign interveners ought to resist the temptation of securing loose agreements. Resilient application of power at the negotiating table increases our capacity to steer conflict more effectively for three main reasons.

First, given that nonviolent conflict is waged through rules and institutions, it follows that one's ability to influence the design of such rules and institutions is a crucial conflict management asset. Diplomacy gains in harnessing the systemic force of power arrangements.

Second, diplomacy can, during negotiations, achieve in days or weeks what would otherwise require months or years to accomplish at a later stage. It took those of us working at the Office of the High Representative several years, several million dollars, numerous political commissions, and rounds of negotiations to bring entities to transfer some of their constitutional competencies to Bosnia's central level of government several years after the Dayton agreement. These transfers triggered challenges before courts and threats of referendums. Compromises led to dysfunctions and blockages within state institutions that required endless hours and efforts to overcome. These dysfunctions provided significant political ammunition for those seeking to discredit any subsequent reinforcement of the central state. Certain provisions are cheaper to secure at the negotiating table.

Finally, as time passes, international unity erodes. It becomes increasingly more difficult for interveners to marshal diplomatic support to change core provisions of power arrangements. Recent scholarly work examining seventeen reform efforts undertaken in Bosnia and Herzegovina, Kosovo, and East Timor illustrate, for example, that reform efforts in these environments only fully succeed when the international community is unified and its demands threaten neither nationalist goals nor informal power networks.[33]

Applying power more acutely at the negotiating table can increase the impact of interveners. Much can be learned from the strengths and weaknesses of the Dayton peace process in that regard.

Addressing self-reinforcing loops: Power arrangements must find a delicate point of equilibrium between efficiency and protection. Too much power may trigger challenge from groups fearing domination. Too much protection fuels quests for more power. This point of equilibrium is unique to each conflict. There are no ready-made models for power arrangements. The Dayton agreement illustrates problems engendered by power arrangements that lean too heavily on protection. The executive and legislative branch of Bosnia's central government are clogged with vetoes. While the agreement's numerous vetoes and protection mechanism certainly helped convince parties to share power in a nonviolent space, their objective to ensure that no group can ever impose its will on the others comes at a cost for the system's functionality and stability.

Functionality and stability are interlinked. By establishing a weak central state clogged by a myriad of vetoes, Dayton's constitutional architecture denied the legitimate desire of many Bosnians to evolve in a minimally functioning state. These dysfunctions have legitimized calls to reinforce central authorities and increase their effectiveness – igniting a form of political security dilemma.[34] Calls for more effectiveness have in turn galvanized internal fears of domination and engendered countercalls to secede from Bosnia and Herzegovina. Bosnia and Herzegovina's system of governance, as designed, fails to effectively contain the self-reinforcing loop between power and fears of subjugation and is potentially self-destructive.[35]

Granting each group the capacity to prevent other groups from imposing their will may appear to some as an equal accommodation at first glance. It nevertheless produces unequal outcomes by granting numerically smaller groups the same amount of power as larger ones. Such a system fuels resentment of numerically more important groups and legitimizes calls for more power within their constituencies.

Designing power-sharing mechanisms that allocate power in accordance with a group's relative importance may contribute to more sustainable outcomes. In assessing protection mechanisms, rather than focusing on "whether" groups can impose their will on others, it may be wiser to assist parties in determining in relation to "what" they ought to be able to do so. Interveners may consider, for example, inviting parties to refrain from subjecting competencies over matters such as trade, telecommunications, and transportation to veto constraints. By doing so, they promote the design of arrangements that encourage systemic centripetal forces. They may also consider bringing parties to consider protection mechanisms in relation to competencies that pertain to matters more intimately linked to notions of self-worth and identity such as education, culture, language, and religion.

Shaping actors' behavior through systemic incentives: The Dayton peace implementation experience leads us to ask ourselves hard questions about the wisdom of designing electoral systems that continuously consolidate ethnic loyalties and polarize opponents' positions after a war. Electoral rules and institutions shape behavior within systems.[36] As designed, the current electoral system in Bosnia and Herzegovina allows parties established along ethnic lines to appeal exclusively to their own constituencies and elect representatives at the municipal, cantonal, entity, and state levels of government. Rather than rewarding cooperation and compromise, the current electoral system provides incentives for political polarization and invites some groups to continuously take aim at the foundations of the nonviolent space agreed to at Dayton. Bosniak nationalist politicians tend to win election on promises to further unify the country. Bosnian Croat nationalist parties win election on promises of establishing a Croat majority entity while Bosnian Serb nationalist parties promote secession as an adequate response to further centralization. Rather than rewarding cooperation and compromise, the electoral rules fuel the very self-reinforcing loops that threaten the stability of Bosnia's constitutional system.

Diplomats involved with electoral engineering ought to consider systems providing electoral incentives that favor cooperation and compromise between groups and that condition electoral access to power on a political actor's capacity to gain support across various constituencies. By enlarging electoral constituencies, designers can encourage more moderate positions articulated around areas of consensus among groups or entities. Under certain conditions, vote pooling can, for example, engender political moderation amongst ethnic groups.[37] Preferential voting systems such as those used in Australia, Fiji, Papua New Guinea, and Northern Ireland illustrate the potential moderating impact of electoral incentives and ought to be considered in the future.[38]

Designing self-sustaining arrangements: While outsiders can play a role in maintaining the system in the aftermath of armed conflict, the experience in Bosnia and Herzegovina illustrates that power arrangements whose functionality primarily depends on the presence and input of foreign actors are unsustainable. For many years after the conclusion of the Dayton agreement, the capacity of the High Representative to intervene in Bosnia's domestic sphere acted as a functionality valve for Bosnia's system of governance. International substitution overcame blockages in the country's parliamentary and executive branches of power. The withdrawal of the international community and the defeat inflicted on the High Representative in 2007 has revealed often insurmountable blockages.

The failure to establish a more efficient, functional central government at Dayton has left belligerent groups to evolve in a constitutionalized state of nature that fails to discourage the pursuit of absolutist claims to power. Dayton's system steered conflict into a nonviolent

Looking Forward 215

space but maintained conflict at a level of intensity that generated continuous challenges against the foundations of the state and required continuous external protection. Because the capacity of foreigners to effect outcome in foreign theaters is ephemeral, a system whose cohesion depends on foreigners is unsustainable.

Interveners ought to steer the design of power arrangements in ways that maintain the integrity and cohesion of the system. In addition to effectively constraining self-reinforcing destructive loops and providing electoral incentives that favor cooperation, interveners ought to consider the inclusion of other systemic centripetal forces as they facilitate negotiations over power arrangements. The central level of government ought to be able to autonomously exercise its competencies. Granting it powers to raise taxes and allocating ownership over public property should be considered a priority. It took the international community many years to bring parties to reform the indirect taxation system ensuring that the state level of government could finance its activities more autonomously in Bosnia and Herzegovina. Bosnia's entities still refuse to recognize ownership by the central state over a wide range of public property. For many years, the central state has been required to rent property from the entities. Interveners should also seek to allocate competencies in ways that allow institutions to gradually push centrifugal forces back toward the center. Providing the central state with competencies over peace and security, trade and commerce, the responsibility to nominate and appoint judges to the constitutional court, and residual competencies are all examples of mechanisms that can contribute to self-sustainability.

By approaching negotiations strategically, diplomacy increases its capacity to steer conflict. But applying power more efficiently also requires interveners to consolidate and protect power arrangements more effectively once agreed. The experience in Bosnia and Herzegovina has shown that diplomacy can achieve impressive results in recalibrating power arrangements and in protecting them from resistance. The international community successfully supported the reestablishment of core elements of Bosnia's central government after the war. It also managed to bring Bosnia's entities to transfer constitutional responsibilities over defense, taxation, and judicial and prosecutorial appointments to the central level of government many years after the conclusion of Dayton. It was successful in countering the nonviolent insurrection of Bosnian Croat nationalists in 2001. Diplomacy can thus manage nonviolent wars and can also protect power from nonviolent challenges. It cannot, however, do so forever.

Acknowledging the limits of foreign actors to manage resistance: The experience in Bosnia and Herzegovina illustrates that interveners can manage nonviolent wars and protect power arrangements from nonviolent challenges primarily through diplomatic means in contexts where armed conflict has been neutralized. Through the use of NATO and EU integration processes, assets freezes, travel bans, removals from public office, and financial sanctions on political parties, international interveners were able to counter nonviolent challenges against the fragile central authorities of Bosnia and Herzegovina.

Although diplomatic counterinsurgency can be effective, the experience in Bosnia and Herzegovina highlights important limits to its effectiveness. The defeat of the Office of the High Representative in 2007 is a powerful indictment of attempts to recalibrate power arrangements late in a peace process. Perceived by the Bosnian Serb leadership as an interference with power-sharing arrangements agreed to at Dayton, the measures the OHR enacted in 2007 triggered powerful reactions that the international community was no longer able to effectively address. These events teach us that foreign actors should not interfere with power arrangements unless they are in a position to manage the reactions they may trigger. By relying too extensively on the Office of the High Representative to bring Bosnia and Herzegovina's nonviolent war to a more decisive end twelve years after the conclusion of the Dayton peace agreement, the international community overestimated its power and underestimated that of local actors and was forced to withdraw under conditions set by those who opposed its objectives rather than withdrawing under conditions it controlled.

Heavy consolidation and adjustment earlier: Acknowledging that their power is a diminishing resource, interveners should consider tackling the heaviest part of their mandate at the stage of intervention where their power is at its highest. Rather than seeking to achieve heavy lifting at a later stage, peace operations ought to tackle their heaviest challenges earlier, when their levels of external and internal support tend to be higher.

Looking Forward 217

Maintaining conflict at the center of strategy: There are limits to the effectiveness of categorizing resistance into linear models and assigning simplifying labels to groups. Conflict and resistance are fluid phenomena. Yesterday's "spoilers" may turn into tomorrow's supporters. Resistance to a given peace process may shift from one group or subgroup to another. Resistance can spread between different groups. Relying too closely on linear models and categorizations may lead interveners to simplify complex realities in ways that omit several variables and ultimately fail to embrace unpredictability. Rather than asking themselves whether, and how, resistance may disturb peace processes, it seems more appropriate for interveners to ask themselves how a given *peace process may affect conflict*. By constantly keeping conflict at the center of their strategy – by continuously monitoring its evolution and evaluating how their actions may disturb positions and interests of parties in it – interveners will better prevent triggering counteractions they are not able to manage and will increase their capacity to manage conflict more effectively.

Interconnections: Shuttling between Belgrade, Sarajevo, and Zagreb in 1995, U.S. diplomat Richard Holbrooke and his team worked hard to make sure that Bosnia's two neighboring states were part of the solution to the Bosnian conflict. Their calculations proved right. Not only were both neighboring countries instrumental in securing the peace agreement at Dayton, but they also were crucial assets during the agreement's implementation phase. The international community often relied on Zagreb and Belgrade to manage resistance within Bosnia after the conclusion of the peace agreement. Zagreb's decision to end its support to Bosnian Croat parallel structures during the spring of 2001 was a crucial factor that contributed to the international community's successful management of the Bosnian Croat nonviolent insurgency. The capacity to effectively leverage external connections is a crucial component of diplomatic management of nonviolent wars. As it seeks to bring groups to agree on and implement power arrangements, diplomacy gains in strategically managing interconnections.[39]

Addressing resistance through accountability: Accountability strengthens the ability of interveners to manage nonviolent wars and nonviolent insurgency. By making themselves more accountable, peace operations reduce their potential to infringe upon rights, which in turn limits the capacity of opponents to mount political and legal challenges against them. A foreign presence that seeks to maintain a nonviolent space acts both as a systemic actor and systemic arbitrator. Factions that resist a foreign actor's attempt to consolidate levels of popular consent to power arrangements are likely to seize institutions and ask: *Who are you? Why should we listen to you? Why can't we control your decisions?*

Power can – and ought – to be challenged through nonviolent means in the nonviolent space that foreign intervention seeks to establish. Unaccountability prevents interveners from proactively managing resistance and ultimately concedes ground to their opponents. Through judicial activism, nonviolent insurgents can neutralize the power of interveners. Measures of the High Representative were consistently challenged before the Constitutional Court of Bosnia and Herzegovina and the European Court for Human Rights during the peace implementation process.

The decision by the High Representative to consent to the review of his acts by Bosnia's Constitutional Court reduced the extent to which opponents could frame him as an unaccountable authority. Judicial review over other measures – such as removals, audits, and reporting obligations – was more sensitive and problematic as it directly touched upon the capacity of the High Representative to act as a system arbitrator. While allowing for such measures to be reviewed by domestic judicial authorities often controlled by local actors is problematic (especially at the earliest stage of a peace implementation process), there are ways foreign presences can – and should – increase their accountability.[40]

Harnessing endogenous systemic power. Interveners can also increase their capacity to manage resistance by harnessing the power of authorities within the system in which they intervene rather than pitting themselves against them. The consequences of failing to do so can be significant. The United Nations Mission's failure to ensure the existence of a clear legal basis to implement its acts in Bosnia and Herzegovina led to several hundred of its decisions to be successfully challenged before domestic courts in the weeks that followed the end of its mandate.[41] Rather than acting on the belief that domestic courts will consent to interpreting domestic legislation in accordance with the country's international obligations, interveners ought to clearly enshrine their power in the domestic legal system in which they act. By doing so, they harness the power of authorities in that system. The transitional provisions enshrined in the Kosovo Constitution in 2008 are relevant developments in that regard.[42]

Exiting under controlled conditions: Though the experience chronicled in this book highlights that interveners can manage nonviolent wars and insurgency through diplomacy, it also highlights that they cannot do so forever. By continuously recalibrating power arrangements, foreign actors inevitably fuel or maintain resistance. As levels of support decrease over time, they reach a point where levels of resistance overcome those supporting them. Misunderstanding these dynamics is what led us at the OHR to be defeated in 2007. Blindly pushing peace operations toward this point forces interveners to relinquish power under conditions determined by others. Intervention ought to better anticipate and manage these points of rupture in order for foreign actors to exit under conditions they control.

Looking Forward in Bosnia

Looking ahead, it is difficult to conceive how the international community can rely on the OHR to recalibrate power arrangements in Bosnia. The defeat of the OHR in 2007 marked the end of an era. The center of gravity within the international community has since shifted – and will continue to shift – toward the European Union. While the role of the OHR should continue to diminish, all of its authorities and powers ought to remain fully available to act as an insurance policy in case the international community needs to reengage more assertively in the future.

The European Union is in a good position to steer Bosnia's conflict. Bosnia is in the initial phase of a process to integrate into the EU. The EU allocates significant resources to reform and strengthen Bosnia's institutions and will continue to do so for many years to come. Using the integration process as leverage, the EU has successfully managed to steer Serbia and Croatia away from irredentism vis-à-vis Bosnia – a powerful stabilization tool it ought to continue to use. EU diplomacy has successfully leveraged the power of the EU integration process to broker a historic agreement between Belgrade and Pristina in 2013 by which both parties agreed to normalize their relations – a prospect very few people would have imagined possible just a few years ago.

Looking forward, the EU can do a number of things to increase its capacity to manage Bosnia's conflict. First, it should base some of EUFOR's operations in the District of Brčko to help constrain secessionist dynamics in Bosnia. Second, it should define more precisely where Bosnia ought to be legally and institutionally to enter the European Union. While it is known that the country needs to meet the Copenhagen criteria to become a member of the EU, there are many unknowns as to what Bosnia needs to accomplish to join.[43] The Copenhagen criteria require, among others, that a country intending to join the EU needs to have "stable institutions guaranteeing democracy, the rule of law, human rights and respect for and protection of minorities" as well as "the ability to take on and implement effectively the obligations of membership, including adherence to the aims of political, economic and monetary union."[44] It is difficult to conceive how the current attempts of Republika Srpska to decimate Bosnia's weak central institutions are compatible with such requirements.

There is a tendency amongst certain member states to believe that EU integration prospects alone will ultimately prove capable of managing Bosnia's conflict. Some voices have optimistically noted, for example: "In the case of the Balkans, one of the most powerful sources of soft power for the international interveners was the attraction of European Union membership as a goal for elites and populations in all Balkan countries. It was this promise of joining a community of prosperous and stable democracies as equal members that gave reformers in all countries powerful arguments to leave the nationalist visions of the previous decade."[45] It is common for outsiders, as this book suggests, to carry idealized perspectives about their capacity to effect peace outcomes. While it is true that European and NATO memberships have been attractive prospects, they have certainly not convinced politicians from the former Yugoslavia to abandon all nationalist interests and positions. As Robert Cooper, special advisor to the EU high representative for foreign affairs and security policy, more realistically observed: "We have tried to use the prospect of accession as leverage with Bosnia. Until recently, they left us with the feeling that they care more about their quarrels than EU accession."[46] Despite the prospect of a Stabilization and Association Agreement, the political situation in Bosnia has indeed worsened since 2007. In its 2012 report on enlargement to the European Council, the European Commission stated: "A shared vision among the political representatives on the overall direction and future of the country and its institutional set-up for a qualitative step forward on the country's EU path remains absent."[47]

As this book argues, there is little point in building strategy around linear assumptions that conflict can be suspended or compartmentalized. Bosnia's conflict and European integration evolve simultaneously and interact with each other. Factions in Bosnia use the process to make gains. Bosniak nationalist factions use European aspirations to promote a unitary state. Secessionist advocates in Republika Srpska seek to create as many inter-entity structures as possible to prevent any strengthening of the central state, thus preserving their chances to opt out at a later stage. Milorad Dodik noted in February 2013: "A couple of months ago the EU financed a study stating that 70 per cent of the competences for [Bosnia's] EU path lie with entities, in our hands, and we do not want to lose that, but strengthen it.... The ultimate goal of our movement towards the EU is strengthening our autonomy."[48]

European integration is destined to exacerbate Bosnia's conflict regardless of attempts by the EU to present this process as "neutral" or "technical." As an EU official working on enlargement noted: "As soon as we touch a technical issue, we touch politics. The political problem transcends all issues."[49] Rather than taking refuge in the belief that EU integration will either extinguish or sideline conflict, EU strategy must directly address conflict and acknowledge that its integration process will be highly destabilizing for Bosnia. EU strategy ought to break away from the misleading assumption that its power to steer conflict will be felt as soon as the parties start negotiating the modalities of EU accession. Power arrangements are crucial points in conflict system. The European accession process directly interferes with the distribution and allocation of power within Bosnia, and will consequently be highly destabilizing. The current political deadlock in Bosnia reflects the existence of a profound reluctance to abandon rigid wartime aspirations. The challenge for EU diplomacy is therefore not to neutralize or compartmentalize conflict, but to address it directly by channeling it in the right direction. To do so, it must define the parameters of Bosnia's integration more precisely from the very outset.

There is a tendency amongst some EU officials in Brussels to refrain from imposing any specific constitutional or institutional model on Bosnia – a tendency that is both understandable and legitimate. For any such arrangement to be sustainable, it must be designed and agreed upon by Bosnians. But this cannot come at the expense of the EU's capacity to project soft power. Soft power rhetoric must be translated into effective action. Setting the agenda is an integral part of soft power.[50] Setting the conditions under which Bosnia will be deemed eligible to enter the EU is a prerogative of the EU – not Bosnian political factions.

The EU's formal framework should make clear at a minimum that, in the specific context of Bosnia, the Copenhagen criteria imply that (1) only a united Bosnia will be eligible to enter into the EU and (2) the stability of the country's institutions and its ability to undertake and implement the obligations of membership require the existence of an efficient state-level government that, in addition to all of its current responsibilities, must be vested with responsibilities and institutions that are necessary to implement and enforce the *acquis communautaire*.

EU diplomacy must then be frank with its Bosnian counterpart and must stress that while the precise modalities of Bosnia's constitutional and institutional arrangements are a matter for Bosnians to decide, wartime objectives such as the establishment of a unitary state, abolishing Republika Srpska, or seceding from Bosnia and Herzegovina are directly incompatible with EU membership. Making these positions clear and known publically at the outset of the process will discredit nationalist electoral platforms promoting wartime objectives and will allow European diplomacy to manage political conflict more effectively. The positions expressed by Brussels so far fall short of setting clear conditions for eligibility.[51] Worse, the EU's willingness to dilute its own conditionality regarding the SAA since 2007 has seriously undermined its capacity to effect outcomes.

Once a formal framework is defined with more precision, EU diplomacy will be in a better position to directly engage with Bosnians and accompany them as they gradually abandon wartime objectives. The EU's current dialogue with Bosnian authorities is conducted without a clear framework. Few people in Bosnia understand the nature and conditions of the integration process. Brussels sends ambiguous signals and has given the impression that current state institutions may be open to negotiations.

Engaging with Bosnians will imply direct and sustained engagement with those in Bosnia wishing to establish unitary state structures and invite them to work on a more realistic objective that maintains decentralized federal structures similar to those that prevail in numerous EU member states. It will also require to engage with Republika Srpska officials and make clear to them that the EU will not acquiesce to the gradual decimation of Bosnia. EU diplomacy must urge Republika Srpska to negotiate the establishment of additional state institutions while making very clear that it is not harboring any plan to dismantle Republika Srpska. It ought to highlight to Republika officials that calls for secession give credence to the more assertive unitary voices within Bosnia and are ultimately counterproductive. It is in Republika Srpska's interest to control the design of additional state institutions through negotiations rather than having to react to a potential backlash against its resistance.

None of these measures will allow the EU and its international partners to extinguish conflict in Bosnia. Conflict will exist for a long time. The European integration process will even exacerbate it. The challenge for the EU will be to modulate the intensity of this conflict and ensure that Bosnia emerges out of the integration process as a more stable and sustainable political space.

Even by setting more attainable, realistic objectives and by applying power more efficiently, interveners cannot fully control the environment in which they intervene or fully predict its mutations. But by proactively embracing confusion and uncertainty, interveners can better navigate them and achieve more sustainable outcomes. If we are to accept Edgar Morin's contention that our blindness to complexity keeps us in the prehistoric age of the human mind, I hope that these thoughts can modestly contribute to our ability to better evolve in the prehistory of international peace intervention. Our mistakes are more than the mere reflection of our own illusions.

Epilogue

I returned to Bosnia and Herzegovina in September 2010. During my visit, I arranged to meet with Jovan Divjak, a former Bosnian Serb officer in the Yugoslav armed forces. Divjak's decision to defend Sarajevo against Bosnian Serb forces during the war transformed him into a hero to those supporting the existence of a multiethnic Bosnia and Herzegovina. We had agreed to meet at the office of the association he established after the war: Udruzenje Obrazovanje Gradi BiH (Education Builds Bosnia and Herzegovina), which supports children affected by the conflict. The offices of the association are located on the upper part of one of the many hills surrounding Sarajevo. We met in front of the association's office on a chilly morning.

"I walk every morning from my home in the center of town. It takes me approximately forty-five minutes," he says as we make our way through corridors filled with names of children that the association supports.

He offers me coffee as we sit down. I wanted to meet him because I was particularly interested in his vision of Bosnia's future. Divjak is a man in his early seventies with a sharp mind, piercing eyes, and generous shock of white hair – a countenance not unlike an old fox. He insists on addressing me in French, my native tongue and a language he learned at the Yugoslav School of Foreign Languages in Belgrade during his training as a military officer. Born in Belgrade in 1937 to a Serbian mother and a father of Bosnian Serb origin, Divjak completed his military studies in Belgrade at the end of the 1950s. After his studies, he served in Tito's personal guard – an elite group responsible for the protection of the former leader. A portrait of Tito still hangs in Divjak's office. Divjak guards a favorable recollection of Tito and the Communist Party: "It was a party more modern than many other parties in Europe. Sure, it was not good to have a single party. But the party sought to guarantee that each citizen had the same rights; the right to education, health, work, the right to travel. The party was hard but had the interests of all citizens at heart."

Promised to a brilliant career, Divjak was sent to the École d'état-major in Paris in 1965 – a rare privilege for a young military officer in Yugoslavia during the Cold War. It was upon his return from France that Divjak was deployed to Bosnia and Herzegovina. By 1984, he was an officer within Bosnia's Territorial Defense Force. Under the Yugoslav system, each republic had its own territorial defense force to assist in times of natural disasters and to act as reserve for the Yugoslav National Army. As Yugoslavia spiraled down into armed conflict in the 1990s, these territorial defense forces morphed into armies defending newly independent republics. Bosnia and Herzegovina was no exception. At the outbreak of armed conflict in Yugoslavia, Divjak, then a colonel in the Territorial Defense Force based in Sarajevo, was still very much attached to Yugoslavia.

"At the beginning of the war in Yugoslavia, I was frustrated, as a military, to see the Yugoslav National Army withdraw from Slovenia."

But by the time conflict had reached Bosnia and Herzegovina, Divjak had lost any illusion about the neutrality of the Yugoslav National Army: it had become the instrument of Milošević's policies in Belgrade. As tensions rose in Sarajevo in the spring of 1992, Divjak chose to join Bosnia and Herzegovina's nascent, disorganized, and inexperienced armed forces. A decision, he says, that was motivated both by professional and personal reasons.

"Some say that I left the Yugoslav National Army, but I continued my role in the Territorial Defense Force."

After a brief pause, he adds: "Nationalists on all sides were saying that we could not live together. It was not true. I live today in a building in the center of Sarajevo where Muslims, Catholics, Orthodox and Jews have lived together peacefully. My father was a Serb born in Bosnia. This is why I stayed. It was the continuation of a family story that started in Bosnia and Herzegovina.... I sensed that I belonged to all this. I had no problem with continuing my life – not changing it – but continuing my life in Sarajevo as a military person."

Divjak has remained committed to the idea of a multiethnic Bosnian state throughout the conflict, despite many disillusions. As the war progressed, the armed forces of Bosnia became less multiethnic and gradually transformed themselves into an instrument of the Bosnian Muslim leadership. Seen as traitors by Bosnian Serb and Bosnian Croat nationalists and treated with suspicion by Bosnian Muslim nationalists, Bosnian Serbs and Bosnian Croats occupied an increasingly tenuous position within the army. Divjak's relationship with Bosnia's leadership was affected as a consequence. While relatively close to President Izetbegović at the outset of the war, Divjak became gradually marginalized as the conflict evolved. "I was a bit removed from the overall command. I did not react … I visited all the brigades, the soldiers, taught them how to dig trenches.… I was with the soldiers. I was also touring the hospital to give courage to the wounded, the doctors and medical staff."

His marginalization was further accentuated in 1993 as Divjak wrote to Izetbegović to denounce atrocities committed by Mušan Topalović – a Sarajevo gangster who had been integrated in the Bosnian army during the war. Divjak's communication pointed to the fact that Topalović had terrorized Bosnian Serb and Bosnian Croat civilians in Sarajevo and called on the Bosnian leadership to take appropriate actions. Izetbegović's handling of Topalović had been suboptimal.[1] In 1994, Izetbegović abruptly suggested that Divjak retire.[2] Other members of the Bosnian presidency blocked Izetbegović's attempt to exclude him from the army. Saddened, Divjak stayed in the army until the end of the war, fulfilling peripheral tasks. He visited units on the ground and liaised with the International Red Cross. In 1996, Divjak learned about his retirement though the media. Crushed, he refused to attend the official ceremony.[3] His relationship with Izetbegović soured further after 1996. Learning that suspected war criminals had been promoted to his rank, Divjak wrote to Izetbegović in November 1998 and gave back the rank of "brigadier general" to which he had been promoted in 1993. "Surely, I do not belong to that list, next to the names of such persons," his letter indicated.[4] A few weeks before Izetbegović's death, Divjak paid him a visit. At the end of what would turn out to be their last encounter, Izetbegović told him "I was honored by your visit."

"Maybe it was a late gesture, at the end of his life. Maybe a signal from God," Divjak tells me looking down at his coffee cup.

Divjak was awarded the Légion d'honneur by the French government in 2001. Since his retirement, he runs his association for children from Sarajevo. The association gives financial and moral support to children whose parents were injured or killed during the war. The association had by 2010, provided assistance to nearly thirty-seven hundred children across Bosnia.

"The fauna of Bosnia and Herzegovina. The towns of Bosnia and Herzegovina. These are the themes of calendars for each year," he tells me while flipping through the association calendars drawn by children.

As we look through them, we start talking about the future of the country.

"Do you think it is possible for Bosnia and Herzegovina to plunge back into armed conflict?" I ask.

"A conflict between armed forces? No. Maybe local forms of violence with light weapons.... The tanks, the heavy artillery are stored in one place, the ammunitions elsewhere. Everything is monitored by NATO and EUFOR. The probabilities of a new military conflict are low," he says.

"But what if EUFOR and NATO were to leave Bosnia?"

Interrupting me before I can complete my question, Divjak says:

"Never! They can never leave! Have the troops left Germany after the Second World War?"

"Yes, but I ask you the question purely hypothetically. In the event that ... "

Interrupting me again, Divjak says:

"I know. I know. But my answer is that NATO will not leave."

Divjak tried to be reassuring. He thought there were no reasons to fear a return to armed conflict.

"In any case, NATO will not leave," he stresses once more.

As our meeting draws to an end, a friend of Divjak knocks at his office door. He is celebrating the end of Ramadan and decided to pay a visit to Divjak. They tease each other. They explain to me that they had bet on the Euro 2012 qualifying match between France and Bosnia and Herzegovina. The Bosnian side had lost 0–2 a few days before.

Epilogue

"I bet on Bosnia. He bet on France. He is coming to get paid!" Divjak says. They both start laughing.

I said goodbye to both of them and thanked Divjak for his time. As I walked through streets on my way back to the central part of town, I could not help thinking about how the country's stability was still closely intertwined with the presence of outsiders. Having lost many illusions about the resilience of international missions abroad, I thought Divjak was wrong to assume that the international military presence was a quasi-permanent fixture in Bosnia.

★ ★ ★

In March 2011, I received an e-mail informing me that Divjak had been arrested at the airport in Vienna on his way to Italy. His arrest by the Austrian authorities had been carried out pursuant to an extradition request from Serbia in relation to his involvement in what became known as the "Dobrovoljačka street" affair.

The Dobrovoljačka street incidents occurred at the early stage of the armed conflict in Bosnia. On May 2, 1992, as Izetbegović was flying back to Sarajevo after unsuccessful peace negotiations in Lisbon, soldiers of the Yugoslav National Army detained him as he landed at the airport.[5] His detention was linked to other events in Sarajevo. In the days preceding Izetbegović's return, a large group of militiamen in Sarajevo had surrounded the Yugoslav National Army barracks in the center of town. General Kukanjac and 400 of his soldiers stationed there were trapped in barracks surrounded by hostile militiamen. Izetbegović had become a bargaining chip to help the Yugoslav National Army secure the release of General Kukanjac and his soldiers trapped in Sarajevo.

The strategy yielded results. After many hours in detention, Izetbegović struck a deal with General Kukanjac. According to their agreement, the Yugoslav National Army would release Izetbegović. In exchange, Kukanjac and his men would be allowed to safely leave their barracks in Sarajevo. General MacKenzie, the Canadian commander of the UN force in Sarajevo, agreed to assist the parties in implementing their agreement. It was agreed that a convoy would lead Izetbegović back to the presidency and escort Kukanjac and his men out of the central part of town.[6] As the convoy slowly made its way through the narrow streets, it was ambushed. Militiamen cut the convoy in half, shot several Yugoslav National Army soldiers, and ran away with equipment and ammunition. Divjak arrived on site amid generalized confusion. Video footage included in the BBC documentary *The Death of Yugoslavia* shows Divjak next to Izetbegović ordering the militiamen to stop shooting.[7] His orders were ignored. Several soldiers of the Yugoslav National Army were killed and injured as a result of the attack.[8]

The death of these soldiers formed, many years later, the basis of the Serbian extradition request against Divjak. In 2009, an investigative judge in Serbia had issued arrest warrants against nineteen officials allegedly implicated in the Dobrovoljačka street events. Serbia and Bosnia and Herzegovina were now different states. Serbia was trying to prosecute nationals of Bosnia and Herzegovina in relation to events that had occurred in Sarajevo in 1992 in what appeared to some as retaliation. In 2010, Ejup Ganić, the acting member of the Bosnian presidency during the incident in 1992, had been arrested in London in relation to the Dobrovoljačka street events. A few months later, the British judge in charge of the case released Ganić.[9] His decision noted that the extradition proceedings had been used for political purposes and amounted to an abuse of the process of the court.[10]

Divjak's arrest in Vienna was the latest episode in this string of Serbian extradition requests. The arrest of Divjak, a well-known figure, triggered a flurry of reactions both inside and outside of Bosnia and Herzegovina. In a demonstration of support, Željko Komšić, the Croat member of the presidency, and Sven Alkalaj, Bosnia and Herzegovina's minister of foreign affairs, visited Divjak in Austria after his arrest.[11] Demonstrators gathered in front of the Austrian embassy in Sarajevo in protest.[12] Intellectuals and advocacy groups in neighboring Serbia denounced the arrest. Many European public intellectuals came out publically in support of Divjak.[13] In an op-ed published by *Le Monde*, some of them wrote: "We share the disgust of those who demonstrate in Sarajevo.... We urge the European diplomacies to put an end to this shameful situation so that those, like General Divjak, who were and remain the honor of Europe, will never be disturbed again."[14] Bosnian Serb officials, led by Milorad Dodik, saw things differently

Epilogue

and strongly criticized public support for Divjak. "He participated in and commanded war crimes." For Serbs, the ex-general "is definitively responsible," Dodik indicated.[15]

On July 29, 2011, citing concerns about Serbia's capacity to guarantee Divjak's right to a fair trial, Austrian judicial authorities rejected the Serbian extradition request and released Divjak.[16]

After having reviewed[17] evidence related to Divjak's role during the Dobrovoljačka street events, the prosecutor's office of the ICTY determined in 2002 that there was insufficient evidence to initiate proceedings against him.[18] In early 2012, the state prosecutor's office of Bosnia and Herzegovina reached similar conclusions. It decided to terminate its investigation into the case as it found no evidence of involvement in any criminal action on the part of Divjak and thirteen other persons involved in the events.[19] The proceeding nevertheless reactivated tensions in Bosnia at each step.

Soon after Divjak's arrest in March 2011, Milorad Dodik called for a special session of the Republika Srpska National Assembly to discuss an action plan to arrest Bosnian citizens charged with crimes in neighboring Serbia.[20] During a press conference, Dodik condemned the support given to Divjak by the Bosnian political establishment and the international community. Despite the fact that the country's prosecutorial authorities had dropped the investigation against Divjak, Dodik made clear that he considered Divjak a war criminal and that the authorities of Republika Srpska would not hesitate to arrest him and hand him to the neighboring state of Serbia in the event he came to Republika Srpska. The "Bosnia-Herzegovina court and prosecution are unconstitutional and anti-Dayton institutions whose only task is to judge Serbs," Dodik said.[21] "It is incredible that Bosniaks ... say they want to live together with Republic of Srpska while blaming Serbs for everything." "It would be better for them, too, if Republic of Srpska were to withdraw from Bosnia-Herzegovina," he added.[22]

The war is not over.

Notes

Introduction

1 In a somewhat bizarre turn of events, authorities in Kosovo arrested three German citizens suspected of working for the German secret services, all of whom were later released. See "Germans Held in Kosovo over Blast," *BBC News*, November 23, 2008, http://news.bbc.co.uk/2/hi/europe/7744535.stm; See also Neil Macdonald, "UN Judge Orders Release of German Spies," *Financial Times*, November 30, 2008, http://www.ft.com/intl/cms/s/0/1cdeccaa-bf0d-11dd-ae63-0000779fd18c.html#axzz1fPbDA82W.
2 Carl von Clausewitz, *On War* (Princeton, NJ: Princeton University Press, 1976), 87.

1. We Fired First

1 Robert Jervis, *System Effects: Complexity in Political and Social Life* (Princeton, NJ: Princeton University Press, 1997), 17–18, referring to "Arthur Daley, 'Out of the Hat,'" *New York Times*, March 26, 1969.
2 Louis Sell, *Slobodan Milosevic and the Destruction of Yugoslavia* (Durham, NC & London: Duke University Press, 2002), 65–94.
3 Laura Silber and Allan Little, *The Death of Yugoslavia* (New York: Penguin Books, 1995), 147–68.
4 Noel Malcolm, *Bosnia: A Short History* (London: Papermac, 1996), 222–3. The number of Bosniak, Serb, and Croat representatives broadly reflected the ethnic composition of Bosnia's society. The SDA won 86 of the 240 available parliamentary seats in the 1990 elections. The SDS and the HDZ won respectively 72 and 44 seats.
5 Ibid., 240 1.
6 Josip Glaurdić, *The Hour of Europe: Western Powers and the Breakup of Yugoslavia* (New Haven, CT: Yale University Press, 2011), 148–72.
7 On the United States' initial reluctance to intervene in Bosnia, see Wayne Bert, *The Reluctant Superpower: United States Policy in Bosnia, 1991–1995*

233

(New York: St. Martin's Press, 1997). See also Mark Danner, *Stripping Bare the Body: Politics, Violence, War* (New York: Nation Books, 2009), 125–44.

8 On divisions within European policy at the outset of armed conflict in Yugoslavia, see Glaurdić, *The Hour of Europe*, 215–48.

9 Bildt continued to play a central role in formulating EU Balkan policy after his appointment as Sweden's minister for foreign affairs in 2006.

10 United Nations High Commissioner for Refugees, *Statistics Package*, Sarajevo, September 30, 2007, www.unhcr.ba.

11 Lawrence Weschelr, "Letter from the Republika Srpska: High Noon at Twin Peaks," *The New Yorker*, August 18, 1997, 28–35, http://www.newyorker.com/archive/1997/08/18/1997_08_18_028_TNY_CARDS_000378246.

12 "Order Seizing Travel Documents of Persons Who Obstruct or Threaten to Obstruct the Peace Implementation Process," Office of the High Representative, July 10, 2007, http://www.ohr.int/decisions/war-crimes-decs/default.asp?content_id=41138.

13 According to Bosnia's constitution, a majority of the elected members of the House of Representatives of the Parliamentary Assembly needs to be present for the House to hold a session. Subsequent parliamentary rules of procedures required that such a majority needed to include a specific number of members from each constituent people, namely Bosnian Serbs, Bosnian Croats, and Bosniaks. As a matter of consequence, if a certain number of representatives from a given constituent people decided to boycott a session, the House of Representatives could not convene, even if a majority of its members were present.

14 According to Article 18 (2) and (3) of the law on the Council of Ministers of Bosnia and Herzegovina applicable at the time, the Council had to decide by consensus with respect to issues that did not need to be referred to the Parliamentary Assembly (such as regulations, nominations, and appointments by the Council of Ministers). In cases where consensus could not be reached in relation to such issues, the chair of the Council was required to hold a meeting with the dissenting member(s) of the Council to find a solution. In cases where consensus could still not be reached on the basis of such discussions, a decision needed to be supported by a majority that included the votes of two members of each constituent people in order to be adopted. Therefore, a certain number of representatives from a constituent people could ultimately block such decisions in the Council simply by being absent.

15 The constitution of Bosnia and Herzegovina is an annex of the Dayton peace agreement (i.e., Annex 4). See *General Framework Agreement for Peace in Bosnia Herzegovina*, December 14, 1995, 35 I.L.M. 75.

2 They Fire Back

1 Milovan Djilas, *Conversations with Stalin* (New York: Harcourt, Brace & World, 1962); See also Vladimir Dedijer, *The Battle Stalin Lost: Memoirs of*

Yugoslavia 1948–1953 (New York: The Viking Press, 1970). Vladimir Dedijer, another close advisor to Tito, wrote an entire book on the 1948 split with Moscow at Tito's request. Dedijer had been a director of the Government Information Office as well as the head of the Press and Agitation Section of the Agitation and Propaganda Administration in the Yugoslav Communist Party's Central Committee. I am indebted to Felix Martin for pointing my attention to the excerpt in Djilas's work cited in the text.

2 Djilas, *Conversations with Stalin*, 180–1.
3 Milovan Djilas, *Tito: The Story from Inside* (New York & London: Harcourt Brace Jovanovich, 1980), 169.
4 Ibid., 170.
5 Ibid., 171.
6 Explanatory Note on the High Representative's Decision from October 19th," Office of the High Representative, October 24, 2007, http://www.ohr.int/ohr-dept/presso/pressr/default.asp?content_id=40710.
7 "Statement by the Deputy High Representative and Head of Banja Luka Office, Ivan Busniak, during the Delivery of the Explanatory Note," Office of the High Representative, October 24, 2007, http://www.ohr.int/ohr-dept/presso/pressr/default.asp?content_id=40718.
8 "Kostunica: Serbia's Top Priorities – Kosovo, RS," *B-92 News*, October 25, 2007, http://www.b92.net/eng/news/politics-article.php?yyyy=2007&mm=10&dd=25&nav_id=44862.
9 United Nations Security Council (SC), S/2007/168/Add.1, "Comprehensive Proposal for the Kosovo Status Settlement," March 26, 2007, http://www.unosek.org/docref/Comprehensive_proposal-english.pdf.
10 For a detailed overview of the Ahtisaari process, see Henry H. Perritt Jr., *The Road to Independence for Kosovo: A Chronicle of the Ahtisaari Plan* (New York: Cambridge University Press, 2010).
11 UN Security Council, Security Council Resolution 1244 (1999), June 10, 1999, S/RES/1244 (1999), Articles 10 & 11.
12 The final report of the International Commission on Kosovo had noted in 2000: "The Commission's view is that the international community cannot defer Kosovo's final status in expectation of positive change in the FRY. The essential reality that the international community must face is that, because of the FRY's systematic violation of Kosovar rights, substantial autonomy and self-government for Kosovo have become incompatible with continued Yugoslav sovereignty of the province, and will remain so even if Yugoslavia eventually makes a transition to democratic rule. The simple truth is that no Kosovar will accept to live under Serb rule, however notional, ever again." See Independent International Commission on Kosovo, *The Kosovo Report: Conflict, International Response, Lessons Learned* (Oxford: Oxford University Press, 2000), 271.
13 "Bosnia Faces Turmoil," *Balkan Insight*, November 1, 2007, http://www.balkaninsight.com/en/article/bosnia-faces-turmoil.

14 "Bosnian Serb Crowd Beats Muslims at Mosque Rebuilding," *New York Times*, May 8, 2001, http://query.nytimes.com/gst/fullpage.html?res=9A07E 4D9163BF93BA35756C0A9679C8B63.
15 United Nations High Commissioner for Refugees, *Statistics Package*, Sarajevo, September 30, 2007, www.unhcr.ba. Since the signature of the Dayton peace agreement, the UNCHR office in Bosnia had registered 167,943 returns by members of minority ethnic groups in Republika Srpska, including more than 12,000 in the broader municipality of Banja Luka.
16 The government of Republika Srpska has moved to a new building since then.
17 The PIC is composed of Canada, France, Germany, Italy, Japan, Russia, the United Kingdom, the United States, the presidency of the European Union, the European Commission, and the Organization of the Islamic Conference (OIC) represented by Turkey.
18 His words would prove premonitory. Several years later, Bosnian Serb forces, under the command of Ratko Mladić, entered the town of Srebrenica. In the worst episode of mass violence to occur in Europe since World War II, Mladić's forces separated men from women and massacred thousands of Bosnian Muslim men.
19 John Zaritsky, dir., *Romeo and Juliet in Sarajevo* (Canadian Broadcasting Corporation, National Film Board of Canada, PBS *Frontline*, 1994), TV documentary.
20 "Lessons and Conclusions on the Execution of IFOR Operations and Prospects for a Future Combined Security System: The Peace and Stability of Europe after IFOR," Foreign Military Studies Office (FMSO) and Center for Military-Strategic Studies (CMSS), November 2000, http://fmso.leavenworth.army.mil/documents/IFOR/English.pdf.
21 Kevin Ryan, U.S. General (retired). Interview by author. Cambridge, Massachusetts, August 17, 2010.
22 "Declaration by the Steering Board of the Peace Implementation Council," Peace Implementation Council, October 31, 2007, http://www.ohr.int/pic/default.asp?content_id=40758.
23 "Press Conference by the High Representative Miroslav Lajčák, following the PIC meeting," Office of the High Representative, October 31, 2007, http://www.ohr.int/ohr-dept/presso/pressb/default.asp?content_id=40767.
24 "Bosnia Prime Minister Resigns Amid Tension," *Financial Times*, November 2, 2007, http://www.ft.com/cms/s/0/088de29c-88c5-11dc-84c9-0000779fd2ac.html#axzz16JwPy8HQ.

3 The Battle

1 Général Beaufre, *Le drame de 1940* (Paris: Plon, 1965), 232–3 (author's translation). The original text in French reads: "Quand nous arrivons, vers 3 heures du matin peut-être, tout est éteint sauf cette pièce qui n'est qu'à

moitié éclairée. Au téléphone, le commandant Navereau répète d'une voix douce les renseignements qu'il reçoit. Les autres se taisent. Le général Roton, chef d'État-Major, est affalé dans un fauteuil. L'atmosphère est celle d'une famille ou l'on veille un mort. Georges se lève vivement et vient au devant de Doumenc. Il est terriblement pâle: 'Notre front est enfoncé à Sedan! Il y a eu des défaillances.'"

2 "Declaration by the Steering Board of the Peace Implementation Council," October 31, 2007. The PIC had welcomed the High Representative's efforts to work on a note and had encouraged Republika Srpska legal experts "to engage constructively with OHR legal experts on the explanatory note."

3 Such concerns were linked to the fact that Lajčák's decision had amended Article 16 (2) of the law on Council of Ministers. The law, as amended, provided that sessions of the Council of Ministers had to be held at least once per week. It allowed, however, for derogations in justified cases (such as holidays). These justified cases had to be determined by rules of procedure. Representatives of Republika Srpska were concerned that this provision, read together with another new provision that stipulated that deputy chairs could jointly convene a session of the Council in cases where the chair had failed to convene two consecutive sessions, opened the possibility to convene sessions of the Council by surprise. Our amendments explicitly allowed for such a possibility to occur *only* in cases where the chair of the Council of Ministers had failed to convene a session *in a manner that contravened the provisions of the law and the provisions of the rules of procedure.* Therefore, by specifying in the rules of procedures that sessions could not be held on days during which Bosnian Serbs were celebrating a specific holiday, there was no possibility to convene a session by surprise.

4 Alija Izetbegović, *Islamska Deklaracija* (Sarajevo: Bosnia, 1990).

5 Noel Malcolm, *Bosnia: A Short History* (London: Papermac, 1996), 219.

6 Laura Silber and Allan Little, *The Death of Yugoslavia* (New York: Penguin Books, 1995), 207–8.

7 Alija Izetbegović, *Izetbegovic of Bosnia and Herzegovina: Notes from Prison, 1983–1988* (Westport, CT & London: Praeger, 2002).

8 Ibid., 82.

9 Ibid., 87.

10 Richard Holbrooke, *To End a War* (New York: The Modern Library, 1999), 97–8.

11 Malcolm, *Bosnia: A Short History*, 221.

12 "Russia, the Bosnian Serbs Are Making Trouble Again," *The Economist*, October 25, 2007, http://www.economist.com/node/10026370.

13 Silber and Little, *The Death of Yugoslavia*, 283–289.

14 Between 1992 and the signature of the Dayton Accords in November 1995, numerous plans had been designed to put an end to armed conflict. There was the Cutileiro Plan in 1992, the Vance-Owen Peace Plan in 1993, the

Owen-Stoltenberg Plan in 1993, and the Contact Group Plan in 1994. See Leo Tindemans et al., *Unfinished Peace: Report of the International Commission on the Balkans* (Washington, DC: Carnegie Endowment for International Peace, 1996), 47–55.

15 Silber and Little, *The Death of Yugoslavia*, 276.
16 Ibid., 277–81.
17 Ibid., 281–83.
18 Ibid., 284–87.
19 The Republika Srpska proposal of November 8, 2007 sought to introduce a dual system of ethnic and territorial qualifications to quorum and decision making in the Council of Ministers. Prior to Lajčák's amendments, the law defined *quorum* as a majority of members that *needed to include* at least two members of each constituent people. Our amendment had removed such a condition and defined *quorum* as a majority of the Council's members. Under the terms suggested by the November 8 proposal, quorum rules required that a majority of members that *included* at least one member of each constituent people and one member from each entity (i.e., the Federation of BiH and Republika Srpska) be present. The proposal sought to extend the same qualifications to decision-making rules in the Council.
20 "RS Proposal: No Basis for Further Discussion," Office of the High Representative, November 9, 2007, http://www.ohr.int/ohr-dept/presso/pressr/default.asp?content_id=40821.
21 Ibid.
22 "Cracking Up: Spurred by Russia, the Bosnian Serbs Are Making Trouble Again," October 25, 2007; "Bosnia Prime Minister Resigns Amid Tension," *Financial Times*, November 2, 2007; "La démission du premier ministre serbe ouvre une crise à Sarajevo," *Le Monde*, November 3, 2007.
23 Gerald Knaus and Felix Martin, "Travails of the European Raj," *Journal of Democracy*, **14**, no. 3 (2003), http://www.journalofdemocracy.org/articles/gratis/KnausandMartin.pdf.
24 "The Worst in Class: How the International Protectorate Hurts the European Future of Bosnia and Herzegovina," European Stability Initiative, November 8, 2007, http://www.europarl.europa.eu/meetdocs/2004_2009/documents/dv/dsee_20080121_10_/DSEE_20080121_10_en.pdf.
25 Ibid.
26 "Thirty-Second Report of the High Representative for Implementation of the Peace Agreement on Bosnia and Herzegovina to the Secretary-General of the United Nations," Office of the High Representative, November 15, 2007, http://www.ohr.int/otherdoc/hrreports/default.asp?content_id=40835.
27 United Nations Security Council (SC), S/PV.5780, "Official Communiqué of the 5780th (closed) Meeting of the Security Council," November 15, 2007, http://daccess-dds-ny.un.org/doc/UNDOC/GEN/N07/600/60/PDF/N0760060.pdf?OpenElement.

28 Milorad Dodik, "Krizu Proizveo OHR," *Nezavisne Novine*, November 18, 2007, http://www.nezavisne.com/komentari/kolumne/Krizu-proizveo-OHR-17052.html.
29 Ibid. Translation from original text.
30 The op-ed exposed in more detail an argument that would become the cornerstone of Republika Srpska's opposition to our amendments. The argument stated that Article IX (3) of Bosnia's constitution required that officials appointed to positions in Bosnia's institutions had to be generally representative of the country's constituent peoples. It then noted that the provisions of the previous law on the Council of Ministers that defined the Council's quorum (which Lajčák had amended) referred explicitly to Article IX (3) of the constitution. It concluded that by brushing aside the need for two members of each constituent people to be present, Lajčák's amendments to the law violated the constitution. This argument was, in our opinion, based on an invalid premise. The text of Article IX (3) did not regulate quorum or decision-making processes in Bosnia's institutions: it simply imposed a number of constraints on the power to *appoint* officials in Bosnia's institutions (i.e., the appointing authority had to ensure that institutions remained generally representative of Bosnia's constituent peoples). It did not impose any restriction on the manner in which quorum or decision making could be regulated in a specific institution. The mere fact that a regular statute (such as the law on the Council of Ministers) referred to provisions of the constitution did not confer any constitutional status to this statute. To put it more simply, if the regulations of a fishing club referred to conditions set in a country's constitution to regulate its decision-making process, a subsequent change in the fishing club's rules would not be considered in violation of the constitution.
31 The proposal discussed would have made it more difficult for the Council of Ministers to convene and decide. The law, as amended by Lajčák, required that a majority of the Council's members be present for the Council to hold a session. It also provided that final decisions of the Council (such as appointments and nominations) needed to be adopted by a majority of members who were present and voting, and that such a majority needed to include the votes of at least one member of each constituent people. The proposal discussed would have changed this system. By requiring that the majority include the votes of the chair and cochairs, the proposal would have made the Council's decisions contingent upon stricter requirements. There were two deputy chairs and one chair of the Council – reflecting the three constituent peoples of Bosnia. While several members of each constituent people were appointed to the Council, only one Bosniak, one Bosnian Croat, and one Bosnian Serb member were meant to be acting as either the chair or one of the deputy chairs of the Council. By making decision making in the Council contingent upon their vote, the proposal was granting them an exclusive veto power.

4. The Defeat

1. Olli Rehn, "Initialing of the Stabilisation and Association Agreement" (speech, Sarajevo, Bosnia and Herzegovina, December 4, 2007), http://europa.eu/rapid/press-release_SPEECH-07-802_en.htm?locale=FR.
2. "Lajčák Expects Party Leaders to Make Progress on EU Agenda," Office of the High Representative, November 21, 2007, http://www.ohr.int/ohr-dept/rule-of-law-pillar/prc/prc-pr/default.asp?content_id=40872.
3. The EU conditions were defined as follows: (1) all legislative and budgetary competencies for all police matters shall be vested at the state level; (2) no political interference with the operational work of the police; (3) functional local police areas shall be determined in accordance with technical criteria for the police work, while the operational command shall be vested at the local level. The three conditions had been established on the basis of a letter from EU Commissioner Christopher Patten to Adnan Terzic, chair of Bosnia and Herzegovina's Council of Ministers, on November 16, 2004.
4. The relevant part of the agreement, titled *Action Plan for the Implementation of the Mostar Declaration*, stipulated that the relationships between the coordinating state bodies and the local police bodies "shall be regulated through a new and single police structure of BiH, on the basis of the three principles of the European Commission, and which shall be established pursuant to the provisions of the Constitution of BiH to be elaborated in a constitutional reform process." The text of the agreement is available at: http://www.ohr.int/ohr-dept/rule-of-law-pillar/prc/prc-other/default.asp?content_id=40959.
5. Richard Holbrooke, "Back to the Brink in the Balkans," *Washington Post*, November 25, 2007, http://www.washingtonpost.com/wp-dyn/content/article/2007/11/23/AR2007112301237.html.
6. Ian Bancroft, "An Unhealthy State," *The Guardian*, November 26, 2007, http://www.guardian.co.uk/commentisfree/2007/nov/26/anunhealthystate.
7. Pursuant to Article X of the constitution of Bosnia and Herzegovina, constitutional amendments could be adopted only if two cumulative conditions were met. First, an amendment needed to be adopted by a decision of the Parliamentary Assembly. Second, such a decision needed to include a two-thirds majority of those present and voting in the House of Representatives. While it is true that the changes to the parliamentary rules of procedure proposed by Miroslav Lajčák on October 19 would have made it possible for the House of Representatives to adopt a decision without members of Republika Srpska attending, it would have nevertheless been impossible for the House of Peoples to adopt such a decision without the vote of at least three Serb members from Republika Srpska. According to Article IV (1) b) of the constitution, nine members of the House of Peoples comprise a quorum, provided that at least three Bosniak, three Croat, and three Serb delegates are present.

8 Olli Rehn, "Bosnia and Herzegovina in 2007: A Year of Opportunities" (speech, Sarajevo, Bosnia and Herzegovina, March 16, 2007), http://europa.eu/rapid/press-release_SPEECH-07-152_en.htm.

9 "Decision Enacting the Law on Changes and Amendments to the Law on the Council of Ministers of Bosnia and Herzegovina," Office of the High Representative, October 19, 2007, http://www.ohr.int/decisions/statemattersdec/default.asp?content_id=40687; "Decision Enacting the Authentic Interpretation of the Law on Changes and Amendments to the Law on the Council of Ministers of Bosnia and Herzegovina Enacted by the Decision of the High Representative of 19 October 2007," Office of the High Representative, December 3, 2007, http://www.ohr.int/decisions/statemattersdec/default.asp?content_id=40931. Before the changes enacted by the High Representative on October 19, Article 18 (3) of the Law on the Council of Ministers provided that in cases where consensus could not be reached in relation to decisions that needed not to be referred to the Parliamentary Assembly, such decisions needed to be adopted by a majority that included the votes of at least two members of each constituent people. Article 5 of the Decision Enacting the Law on Changes and Amendments to the Law on the Council of Ministers of Bosnia and Herzegovina enacted by the High Representative on October 19 amended Article 18 (3) of the law on the Council of Ministers by requiring, inter alia, that such decisions be adopted by a majority vote *of those present and voting* that included the *vote of at least one member of each constituent people*. This new decision-making process was effectively changed by the last paragraph of the Decision Enacting the Authentic Interpretation of the Law on Changes and Amendments to the Law on the Council of Ministers of Bosnia and Herzegovina Enacted by the Decision of the High Representative of 19 October 2007 enacted on December 3, 2007. The last paragraph of the authentic interpretation stipulated more restrictive conditions insofar as it effectively required that the vote of a member of a constituent people be cast by the chair and deputy chairs of the Council of Ministers (or a member mandated by them in case of absence or incapacity to vote). The last paragraph of the authentic interpretation provides: "Article 18, Paragraph 3 of the Law on Council of Ministers shall be interpreted as requiring that best efforts be made in order to ensure that the vote of at least one member of each constituent people referred to in the said provision be cast by the Chair of the Council of Ministers and the Deputy Chairs of the Council of Ministers. In the event that the Chair or Deputy Chairs are absent or otherwise unable to cast the said votes, they shall mandate a member of the Council of Ministers belonging to the same constituent people to cast their vote on their behalf. In the event that the Chair or Deputy Chairs fail to duly mandate a member of the Council of Ministers or in the event that a duly mandated member of the Council of Ministers is absent or otherwise unable to cast the said vote, any other member of the Council of

Ministers belonging to the concerned constituent people shall be entitled to cast the said vote."
10 "Proposed Changes and Amendments to the Rules of Procedure of the House of Representatives of the Parliamentary Assembly of Bosnia and Herzegovina (Article 10)," Office of the High Representative, October 24, 2007, http://www.ohr.int/decisions/statemattersdec/default.asp?content_id=40716; "Proposed Changes and Amendments to the Rules of Procedure of the House of Peoples of the Parliamentary Assembly of Bosnia and Herzegovina (Article 11)," Office of the High Representative, October 24, 2007, http://www.ohr.int/decisions/statemattersdec/default.asp?content_id=40715. A central component of the proposed changes and amendments to the rules of procedures of the House of Representatives and the House of Peoples sought to clarify the manner in which Article IV (3) d) of the constitution ought to be applied. Article IV (3) d) stipulates: "All decisions in both chambers shall be by majority of those present and voting. The Delegates and Members shall make their best efforts to see that the majority includes at least one-third of the votes of Delegates or Members from the territory of each Entity. If a majority vote does not include one-third of the votes of Delegates or Members from the territory of each Entity, the Chair and Deputy Chairs shall meet as a commission and attempt to obtain approval within three days of the vote. If those efforts fail, decisions shall be taken by a majority of those present and voting, provided that the dissenting votes do not include two-thirds or more of the Delegates or Members elected from either Entity." The proposed changes issued by the High Representative in October 2007 provided that the "one third of the votes" requirement should be calculated based on members or delegates from the territory of each entity who are *present and voting*. They also stipulated that the dissenting votes should *be calculated based on the total number of members elected from either entity and shall not be calculated based on the dissenting votes of the number of members elected from either entity who are present and voting*. Copying the integral text of Article IV (3) d) of the constitution into the rules of procedures therefore failed to specify the manner in which such requirements ought to be procedurally calculated.
11 Rehn, "Bosnia and Herzegovina in 2007: A Year of Opportunities."
12 Unofficial translation. For original text, see "Džerard Selman: Nema preglasavanja," *Nezavisne Novine*, December 4, 2007; available at: http://www.nezavisne.com/novosti/bih/Dzerard-Selman-Nema-preglasavanja-17631.html.
13 "A Stuck Region: How Troubles in Bosnia and Elsewhere Obstruct the Balkans' Path to Europe," *The Economist*, February 12, 2009, http://www.economist.com/node/13110080.
14 Elvira Jukic, "Breakthrough on Bosnia Impasse," *Balkan Insight* (Sarajevo, Bosnia and Herzegovina), December 28, 2011, http://www.balkaninsight.com/en/article/end-of-political-stalemate-in-bosnia.

15 "Bosnia: State Institutions under Attack: Europe Briefing No. 62," *International Crisis Group*, May 6, 2011, http://www.crisisgroup.org/en/regions/europe/balkans/bosnia-herzegovina/b062-bosnia-state-institutions-under-attack.aspx; Ian Traynor, "Bosnia in Worst Crisis since War as Serb Leader Calls Referendum," *The Guardian*, April 28, 2011, http://www.guardian.co.uk/world/2011/apr/28/bosnia-crisis-serb-leader-referendum; Eldin Hadzovic, "Bosnian Croats Form National Assembly," *Balkan Insight*, April 19, 2011, http://www.balkaninsight.com/en/article/bosnian-croats-to-form-the-national-assembly.

16 Malcolm, *Bosnia: A Short History*, 240–1; "Turning Strife to Advantage: A Blueprint to Integrate the Croats in Bosnia and Herzegovina: Europe Report No. 106," *International Crisis Group*, March 15, 2001, http://www.crisisgroup.org/en/regions/europe/balkans/bosnia-herzegovina/106-turning-strife-to-advantage-a-blueprint-to-integrate-the-croats-in-bosnia-and-herzegovina.aspx. Mate Boban, leader of the BiH HDZ, had declared the establishment of a "Croat Community of Herzeg-Bosnia" in July 1992. In March 2001, a meeting of the "Croat National Congress" had declared the establishment of a separate "Croat Self Government."

17 Republika Srpska National Assembly, *Conclusion 01–613/11* (O.G. Republika Srpska no. 45/11), April 13, 2011, http://www.narodnaskupstinars.net/.

18 Republika Srpska National Assembly, *Conclusion 01–610/11* (O.G. Republika Srpska no. 45/11), April 13, 2011, http://www.narodnaskupstinars.net/.

19 Constitutional Court of Bosnia and Herzegovina, *U 16/08*, Sarajevo, Bosnia and Herzegovina, March 28, 2009, http://www.ccbh.ba/eng/; Philippe Leroux-Martin, "Article III.5: Additional Responsibilities," in *Constitution of Bosnia and Herzegovina: A Commentary*, ed. Christian Steiner and Nedim Ademović (Berlin: Konrad-Adenauer-Stiftung, 2010), 594–5. When the central government of Bosnia and Herzegovina adopts legislation on the basis of responsibilities prescribed under the constitution, it occupies its own fields of responsibilities. These responsibilities are not the result of a transfer by the entities. They fall within the exclusive domain of Bosnia and Herzegovina. The specific argument over "transferred responsibilities" that formed the basis of the conclusions of the assembly has been rejected by the Constitutional Court of Bosnia and Herzegovina. In its case U 16/08, the court examined amendments to legislation on the Court of Bosnia and Herzegovina. The applicant had argued that some provisions of the law were the result of an unconstitutional transfer of responsibilities from the entities to the central government and that this "silent transfer" endangered the trust of peoples and entities in constitutional changes. The court rejected the applicant's argument and concluded that Bosnia and Herzegovina had acted within its field of competencies. Referring to its earlier decisions, the court confirmed that Bosnia and Herzegovina was authorized to establish additional institutions for the exercise of its responsibilities.

20 Unofficial translation. For the original text, see section II: Republika Srpska National Assembly, *Decision to Announce the RS Entity-Wide Referendum* (O.G. Republika Srpska no. 45/11), April 13, 2011, http://www.narodnaskupstinars.net/.
21 Milorad Dodik, president of Republika Srpska, "Address by the President of the Republic at 4th Session of RSNA," April 13, 2011, http://predsjednikrs.net/index.php?option=com_content&view=article&id=8128%3A - - 4 - -&Itemid=144&lang=en.
22 Bruno Waterfield, "Bloodshed to Return to Bosnia, Paddy Ashdown Fears," *The Telegraph*, May 27, 2011, http://www.telegraph.co.uk/news/worldnews/europe/serbia/8541578/Bloodshed-to-return-to-Bosnia-Paddy-Ashdown-fears.html.
23 Ibid.
24 "Bosnia: State Institutions under Attack," International Crisis Group.

5. Nonviolent Wars

1 Carl von Clausewitz, *On War* (Princeton, NJ: Princeton University Press, 1976), 80.
2 Ivo Andric, *Bosnian Chronicle* (New York: Arcade Publishing, 1963), 5–6.
3 Friedrich Dürrenmatt, translated by James Kirkup, *The Physicists* (New York: Grove Weidenfeld, 1991), 95. I am indebted to Bonnie Campbell for the reference.
4 Peace Implementation Council, "Declaration by the Steering Board of the Peace Implementation Council," The Office of the High Representative, October 31, 2007, http://www.ohr.int/pic/default.asp?content_id=40758.
5 Clausewitz, *On War*, 75. Clausewitz notes that, to overcome an enemy, "you must match your effort against his power of resistance, which can be expressed as the product of two inseparable factors, ... *the total means at his disposal* and *the strength of his will*" (77), emphasis in original.
6 Ibid., 77.
7 Rupert Smith, *The Utility of Force: The Art of War in the Modern World* (London: Penguin-Allen Lane, 2005), 29–63.
8 Clausewitz, *On War*, 595–6. In his words: "if the enemy is thrown off balance, he must not be given time to recover. Blow after blow must be aimed in the same direction: the victor, in other words, must strike with all his strength and not just against a fraction of the enemy's. Not by taking things the easy way ... but by constantly seeking out the center of his power, by daring all to win all, will one really defeat the enemy" (596).
9 Smith, *The Utility of Force*, 30.
10 On the transition from dynastic to national warfare, see Larry H. Addington, *The Patterns of War since the Eighteenth Century* (Bloomington & Indianapolis: Indiana University Press, 1994), 1–42.

11 Hubert Camon, *La Guerre Napoléonienne: Les Systèmes d'Opérations Théorie et Technique* (Paris: Economica, 1997), 23–4.
12 Clausewitz, *On War*, 591–2.
13 Smith, *The Utility of Force*, 30–3; Addington, *The Patterns of War*, 19–29.
14 Camon, *La Guerre Napoléonienne*, 24–5.
15 Smith, *The Utility of Force*, 30–3.
16 Ibid., Addington, *The Patterns of War*, 27–9.
17 Smith, *The Utility of Force*, 34.
18 Ibid., 39.
19 Ibid., 59. Clausewitz noted that war under Napoléon became "the concern of the people as a whole, took on an entirely different character, or rather closely approached its true character, its absolute perfection. There seemed no end to the resources mobilized; all limits disappeared in the vigor and enthusiasm shown by governments and their subjects. Various factors powerfully increased that vigor: the vastness of available resources, the ample field of opportunity, and the depth of feeling generally aroused. The sole aim of war was to overthrow the opponent. Not until he was prostrate was it considered possible to pause and try to reconcile the opposing interests. War, untrammeled by any conventional restraints, had broken loose in all its elemental fury." See Clausewitz, *On War*, 592–3.
20 According to Clausewitz, the means available "were fairly well defined, and each could gauge the other side's potential in terms of both of numbers and time. War was thus deprived of its most dangerous feature – its tendency toward the extreme, and of the whole chain of unknown possibilities which would follow." See Clausewitz, *On War*, 589.
21 Ibid., 590. See also Addington, *The Patterns of War*, 7.
22 Smith, *The Utility of Force*, 39.
23 Clausewitz, *On War*, 590.
24 Smith, *The Utility of Force*, 39.
25 Ibid., 29–30. According to Smith, modern Western armies, navies, and air forces "still carry much of the structure and organization Napoléon created when he remodeled the armies of France and set out to conquer Europe."
26 Martin Shaw, *The New Western Way of War* (Cambridge: Polity, 2005), 42. Martin Shaw notes: "Industrial total warfare combined 'total' social mobilization – extensive reorganization of national societies for war – with 'total' destruction – targeting of civilian populations as well as mass armies. These two elements of total war were crucially linked: social mobilization incorporated economy and society into the 'supply' side of war, which in turn created the demand to treat them as 'targets.' Technological dynamism supplied ever more destructive means, enabling this military 'logic' to be realized, while mass politics and thinking supplied the rationale for treating civilian populations as part of the 'enemy.'"

27 James M. McPherson, "From Limited War to Total War in America," in *On the Road to Total War: The American Civil War and the German Wars of Unification, 1861–1871*, ed. Stig Forster and Jorg Nagler (Cambridge: Cambridge University Press, 1997), 309.
28 Max Hastings, *Winston's War: Churchill, 1940–1945* (New York: Alfred A. Knopf, 2010), 14.
29 Charles Eade, *The War Speeches of the Right Hon. Winston Churchill*, vol.1 (London: Cassell, 1951), 181.
30 Morton Halperin, Joseph Siegle, and Michael Weinstein, *The Democracy Advantage: How Democracies Promote Prosperity and Peace* (New York & London: Routledge, 2005), 94.
31 Smith, *The Utility of Force*, 267.
32 Shaw, *The New Western Way of War*, 50.
33 Ibid., 52.
34 Smith, *The Utility of Force*, 267. Shaw, *The New Western Way of War*, 51–2. Shaw notes: "Most wars are fought primarily among local and regional actors rather than between these and the West. The West is usually involved, to a greater or lesser degree, in the political conflicts surrounding these wars, but they are invariably rooted most directly in local and regional power cleavages. In this sense, war is produced as well as fought in the local political structures of the non-Western world."
35 Shaw, *The New Western Way of War*, 17.
36 United States Office of War Information, United States Department of Agriculture, *U.S. Government Campaign to Promote the Production, Sharing and Proper Use of Food: Book IV The Victory Gardens Campaign* (Washington, DC: United States Government Printing Office, 1943), 4.
37 Gladwin Hill, "Rail City Blasted – 500 U.S. 'Heavies' Bomb Town in the Direct Path of Red Army Troops – Dresden Nears Ruin – RAF Rips Berlin, Mainz, Chemnitz, Nuremberg, Duisburg, Dessau," *New York Times*, February 16, 1945, XCIV, No. 31800, 1 and 6.
38 "Syria Crisis: Valerie Amos Describes Homs 'Devastation,'" *BBC News*, March 7, 2012, http://www.bbc.co.uk/news/world-middle-east-17290058.
39 David Kennedy, "The Wages of a Mercenary Army: Issues of Civil Military Relations," *Bulletin of the American Academy*, Spring 2006, 13, http://www.amacad.org/publications/bulletin/spring2006/8mercenary.pdf.
40 Pew Research Center, *The Military-Civilian Gap: War and Sacrifice in the Post-9/11 Era*, October 5, 2011, 73, http://www.pewsocialtrends.org/files/2011/10/veterans-report.pdf.
41 Shaw, *The New Western Way of War*, 55. According to Shaw, contemporary warfare tends to become "dominant in war zones, and even globally dominant for brief periods, but it cannot override social relations fully or widely as total war could."

42 Ibid., 55. See also Andrew Mack, "Why Big Nations Lose Small Wars: The Politics of Asymmetric Conflict," *World Politics* **27**, no. 2 (1975): 184. Mack makes a similar point about the dynamics of asymmetric wars such as those fought by the United States in Vietnam and by France in Algeria.

43 Eliot Cohen, "Kosovo and the New American Way of War," in *War Over Kosovo: Politics and Strategy in a Global Age*, ed. Andrew Bacevich and Eliot Cohen (New York: Columbia University Press, 2001,) 46–8. Shaw, *The New Western Way of War*, 34.

44 Cohen, "Kosovo and the New American Way of War," 51.

45 United Nations, *Charter of the United Nations*, October 24, 1945, 1 UNTS XVI, articles 42 and 51.

46 Clausewitz, *On War*, 603. One may wonder whether this characteristic of modern wars is truly modern. Clausewitz had already noted the following regarding military alliances: "One country may support another's cause, but will never take it so seriously as it takes its own." He added further: "Even when both share a major interest, action is clogged with diplomatic reservations, and as a rule the negotiators only pledge a small and limited contingent, so that the rest can be kept in hand for any special ends the shift of policy may require."

47 UN Security Council, *Resolution 770 (1992)*, August 13, 1992, S/RES/770.

48 UN Security Council, *Resolution 781 (1992)*, S/RES/781, October 9, 1992; UN Security Council, *Resolution 816 (1993)*, March 31, 1993, S/RES/816 (1993).

49 UN Security Council, *Resolution 824 (1993)*, May 6, 1993, S/RES/824 (1993).

50 UN Security Council, *Resolution 836 (1993)*, June 4, 1993, S/RES/836 (1993).

51 Smith, *The Utility of Force*, 358. Referring to the international military interventions in Bosnia, Smith noted: "No nation that sent forces to join UNPROFOR, or for that matter NATO in support of UNPROFOR, had any intention of committing those forces to battle or indeed of risking them at all."

52 Richard Holbrooke, *To End a War* (New York: The Modern Library, 1999), 107.

53 Ibid., 113.

54 Ibid., 143.

55 Ibid.

56 As one U.S. general noted while answering questions about the role of NATO allies: "They all have a vote on everything. They can vote on whether we start this or not. They can vote on whether we continue. They can vote on everything.... I will tell you that as we go down this campaign, the mission that's been given to General Clark has been given by 19 nations to execute.

That's who we answer to." See Cohen, "Kosovo and the New American Way of War," 51, referring to remarks from U.S. General Wald taken from U.S. Department of Defense News Briefing of April 19, 1999 available at: http://www.defense.gov/Transcripts/Transcript.aspx?TranscriptID=594.
57 Wesley Clark, *Waging Modern War: Bosnia, Kosovo and the Future of Combat* (New York: Public Affairs, 2001), 119–20.
58 Ibid., 260.
59 Ibid., 264.
60 Ibid., 137–8, 166. Clark also illustrates how Richard Holbrooke came to face fierce resistance against the presence of NATO ground troops from the U.S. Department of Defense. "And, Holbrooke complained to me: 'Your Secretary of Defense warned me that under no circumstances was I to offer NATO ground troops as peacekeepers.' I was not surprised that the Secretary was firmly against U.S. troops – the Congress would have been extremely skeptical, and it would have become an immediate and divisive issue in the midterm elections in November." See also Michael Ignatieff, *Virtual War: Kosovo and Beyond* (London: Chatto & Windus, 2000), 62–3.
61 Clark, *Waging Modern War*, 166.
62 Ibid., 124.
63 Tim Judah, *Kosovo: War and Revenge* (New Haven, CT & London: Yale University Press, 2002), 266.
64 Clark, *Waging Modern War*, 255–6.
65 Ibid., 270.
66 Ibid., 274.
67 Some may dispute the categorization of military intervention in Afghanistan in 2001 as a *management war*. While the primary motive of the military intervention by the United States was based on self-defense, the United States, and subsequently NATO, nevertheless intervened in an ongoing conflict between the Taliban and opposing factions in Afghanistan. In that sense, it can be argued that the intervention was a particular form of management war, one in which the United States and its allies sought to recalibrate the dynamics of an ongoing domestic conflict in accordance with their security interests.
68 White House, Office of the Press Secretary, "Remarks by the President in Address to the Nation on the Way Forward in Afghanistan and Pakistan" (speech, West Point, NY, December 1, 2009), http://www.whitehouse.gov/the-press-office/remarks-president-address-nation-way-forward-afghanistan-and-pakistan.
69 While the U.S. military actions were undertaken on the basis of the United States' right to self-defense, NATO's operations were carried out on the basis of a decision of the United Nations Security Council authorizing NATO troops to assist in stabilizing the country. NATO's troops were, pursuant to the authorization, primarily responsible for assisting

Afghan authorities in establishing and training Afghan security and armed forces and for maintaining security; see UN Security Council, *Security Council Resolution 1386 (2001)*, December 20, 2001, S/RES/1386; See also Annex 1, *Agreement on Provisional Arrangements in Afghanistan Pending the Re-Establishment of Permanent Government Institutions ("Bonn Agreement")* [Afghanistan], S/2001/1154, December 5, 2001, http://www.unhcr.org/refworld/docid/3f48f4754.html.

70 The alliance had previously deployed ground troops in Bosnia and Kosovo. Such forces had, however, been deployed to help implement peace processes in the aftermath of armed conflict.
71 UN Security Council, *Security Council Resolution 1386 (2001)*.
72 UN Security Council, *Security Council Resolution 1510 (2003)*, October 13, 2003, S/RES/1510.
73 On NATO's "political room to maneuver," see, inter alia, Dag Henriksen, "Inflexible Response: Diplomacy, Airpower and the Kosovo Crisis, 1998–1999," *The Journal of Strategic Studies* **31**, no. 6 (December 2008): 850–1.
74 Peter Baker and Ann Scott Tyson, "Bush to Meet NATO Allies Divided over Adding Troops in Afghanistan," *Washington Post*, March 31, 2008, http://www.washingtonpost.com/wp-dyn/content/article/2008/03/30/AR2008033001835.html.
75 David Ljunggren, "Canada Threatens to Pull Soldiers from Afghanistan," *Reuters*, January 28, 2008, http://www.reuters.com/article/2008/01/28/us-afghan-idUSN2248709020080128.
76 Jon Lee Anderson, "Sons of the Revolution: Can a Ragtag Civilian Army Defeat a Dictator," *The New Yorker*, May 9, 2011, 49.
77 UN Security Council, *Security Council Resolution 1973 (2011) [on the situation in the Libyan Arab Jamahiriya]*, March 17, 2011, S/RES/1973, http://www.unhcr.org/refworld/docid/4d885fc42.html.
78 Ibid., see par. 4, which explicitly excludes the presence of "a foreign occupation force of any form on any part of Libyan territory."
79 The White House, Office of the Press Secretary, "Remarks by the President in Address to the Nation on Libya" (speech, Washington, DC, March 28, 2011), http://www.whitehouse.gov/the-press-office/2011/03/28/remarks-president-address-nation-libya.
80 Ibid.
81 "US Examines Legality of Libya War," *BBC News*, May 20, 2011, http://www.bbc.co.uk/news/world-us-canada-13475159.
82 See *War Powers Resolution of 1973*, 50 U.S.C. § 1541, 1544 (1973).
83 HR Res 292, 112th Cong., (June 2, 2011), http://www.house.gov/young/news/6-3-11/BILLS-112hres292eh.pdf.
84 John A. Boehner, Speaker of the House of Representatives, letter to the President of the United States, June 14, 2011, http://www.speaker.gov/UploadedFiles/Letter_to_POTUS_Libya_061411.PDF.

85 Charlie Savage, "2 Top Lawyers Lost to Obama in Libya War Policy Debate," *New York Times*, June 17, 2011, http://www.nytimes.com/2011/06/18/world/africa/18powers.html?_r=2&pagewanted=print.

86 Charlie Savage, "War Powers Act Does Not Apply to Libya, Obama Argues," *New York Times*, June 15, 2011, http://www.nytimes.com/2011/06/16/us/politics/16powers.html?ref=global-home&pagewanted=print.

87 Susan Cornwell, "House to Vote on Bill Cutting Funds for Libya," *Reuters*, June 23, 2011, http://www.reuters.com/article/2011/06/23/us-usa-libya-funds-idUSTRE75M25J20110623.

88 Jennifer Steinhauer, "House Deals Obama Symbolic Blow with Libya Votes," *New York Times*, June 24, 2011, http://thecaucus.blogs.nytimes.com/2011/06/24/house-takes-up-a-rebuke-to-obamas-libya-policy/.

89 Ibid.

90 Jennifer Steinhauer, "Obama Adviser Defends Libya Policy to Senate," *New York Times*, June 28, 2011, http://www.nytimes.com/2011/06/29/us/politics/29powers.html?_r=1&src=rechp. The "defunding resolution" in the House of Representatives had also failed to pass despite being supported by the Republican leadership in the House. See Steinhauer, "House Deals Obama Symbolic Blow with Libya Votes."

91 "Italy's Foreign Minister Calls for End to Hostilities in Libya," *Voice of America*, June 21, 2011, http://www.voanews.com/content/italy-arab-league-head-call-for-end-of-hostilities-in-libya-124342279/141113.html.

92 Savage, "2 Top Lawyers Lost to Obama in Libya War Policy Debate." Some lawyers in the Obama administration had reportedly advocated stopping drone attacks in Libya to reinforce the administration's claim that its activities in Libya did not amount to "hostilities" under the War Powers Resolution.

93 Nicolas Pelham, "Bogged Down in Libya," *The New York Review of Books* LVIII, no.8, May 12, 2011, 16.

94 Peter W. Singer, "Do Drones Undermine Democracy?" *New York Times*, January 22, 2012, http://www.nytimes.com/2012/01/22/opinion/sunday/do-drones-undermine democracy.html?pagewanted=all.

95 Ibid.

96 On the increasing presence of drones in modern military arsenals, see Peter Singer, *Wired for War: The Robotics Revolution and Conflict in the 21st Century* (New York: Penguin Press, 2009).

97 Eade, *The War Speeches of the Right Hon. Winston Churchill*, 181.

98 Ibid.

99 Smith, *The Utility of Force*, 270.

100 Clark, *Waging Modern War*, 345–74.

101 Henriksen, "Inflexible Response: Diplomacy, Airpower and the Kosovo Crisis, 1998–1999," 826.

102 Barry Cunliffe, "The Roots of Warfare," in *Conflict*, ed. Martin Jones and A. C. Fabian (Cambridge: Cambridge University Press, 2006), 71. Systemic

evidence of violent conflict has been found, for example, in the Upper Paleolithic cemetery of Gebel Sahaba in Egyptian Nubia. Forty percent of the fifty-nine men, women, and children buried there were found to have projectile points either embedded or closely associated with their skeletons.

103 Richard E. Rubenstein, "Sources," in *Conflict: From Analysis to Intervention*, ed. Sandra Cheldelin, Daniel Druckman, and Larissa Fast (London & New York: Continuum, 2003): 55.

104 Sports, for example, are highly regulated forms of conflict in which one side tries to establish its dominance over the other in a protracted process made public. See Randall Collins, *Violence: A Micro-sociological Study* (Princeton, NJ & Oxford: Princeton University Press, 2008), 283 and 296.

105 See, for example, Matthew Levinger, *Conflict Analysis: Understanding Causes, Unlocking Solutions* (Washington, DC: United States Institute of Peace Press, 2013), 29–34. Levinger examines a proposed conceptualization of conflict through curves that move through different levels of conflict intensity such as peace, instability, violent conflict and war. See also Dennis J. D. Sandole, "Typology," in *Conflict: From Analysis to Intervention*, ed. Sandra Cheldelin, Daniel Druckman, and Larissa Fast (London & New York: Continuum, 2003), 40. Sandole distinguishes among three categories of conflicts. The first category, *latent conflicts*, refers to conflicts that are developing, but that have not yet expressed themselves in an observable manner. The second type, *manifest conflict processes*, comprises those that have developed to the extent that they are observable, but that have not yet been expressed violently. The last category, called *aggressive manifest conflict processes*, regroups conflicts that have escalated to a violent level of expression and that are destructive to parties, resources, and others.

106 See, for example, Barbara Walter, "Does Conflict Beget Conflict? Explaining Recurring Civil War," *Journal of Peace Research* **41**, no. 3 (2004): 372–3. See also Chaim Kaufman, "Possible and Impossible Solutions to Ethnic Civil Wars," *International Security* **20**, no. 4 (1996): 139 and 145.

107 Some scholars have, for example, suggested looking at civil conflicts within the broader framework of persistent "enduring internal rivalries." See Karl R. De Rouen and Jacob Bercovitch, "Enduring Internal Rivalries: A New Framework for the Study of Civil War," *Journal of Peace Research* **45**, no. 1 (2008): 55–74. The authors' central hypothesis examines whether civil wars associated with enduring internal rivalries are more intractable than other wars. De Rouen and Bercovitch define "enduring internal rivalries" as "internal conflicts between a government and an insurgency with at least 10 years of armed conflict in which there are at least 25 deaths – regardless of whether or not these years are consecutive" (59). Their study lists enduring internal rivalries that have taken place between 1946 and 2004 in Afghanistan, Algeria, Angola, Bangladesh, Burma, Burundi, Cambodia, China, Colombia, El Salvador, Ethiopia, Georgia, Guatemala, India, Indonesia, Iran, Iraq, Israel,

Laos, Malaysia, Morocco, Mozambique, Peru, Philippines, Russia, Senegal, Sierra Leone, Somalia, South Africa, South Vietnam, Spain, Sri Lanka, Sudan, Turkey, Uganda, and the United Kingdom (62–3). The author's perspective on conflict proposed in this chapter differs from De Rouen and Bercovitch's definition of "enduring internal conflict" insofar as it does not require the existence of ten years of armed conflict. This difference explains why conflicts in Bosnia and Herzegovina and Kosovo do not fall within De Rouen and Bercovitch's list of "enduring internal conflict" but nevertheless constitute illustrations of conflicts that have oscillated from nonviolence to violence according to this book.

108 World Bank, *World Development Report 2011: Conflict, Security and Development*, April 11, 2011, 57–8.
109 Clausewitz, *On War*, 87.
110 Ibid., 87 and 605. Elaborating further on his contention, Clausewitz argues that while the "political object is the goal, war is the means of reaching it, and means can never be considered in isolation from their purpose" (87). Later in his work, he notes: "war is only a branch of political activity; that it is in no sense autonomous," and "war is simply a continuation of political intercourse, with the addition of other means," or "war in itself does not suspend political intercourse or change it into something entirely different. In essentials that intercourse continues, irrespective of the means it employs. The main lines along which military events progress, and to which they are restricted, are political lines that continue throughout the war and into the subsequent peace. How could it be otherwise? Do political relations between peoples and between their governments stop when diplomatic notes are no longer exchanged? Is war not just another expression of their thoughts, another form of speech or writing? Its grammar, indeed, may be its own, but not its logic" (605).
111 The contention that management wars – given their lower intensity and impact – make it more likely for conflict to survive in a nonviolent form seems indirectly supported by recent studies. See Daniel S. Morey, "Conflict and the Duration of Peace in Enduring Internal Rivalries," *Conflict Management and Peace Science* **26**, no. 4 (2009): 331–45. Morey's work suggests that "high-concentration conflicts weaken support for future conflict, creating longer periods of peace" while "low-concentration conflicts do not have this pacifying effect, leading to shorter pauses in fighting" (332). The focus of Morey's study relates, however, to the likelihood of armed conflict resuming (rather than being followed by nonviolent conflict).
112 Jill Lepore, "Birthright: What's Next for Planned Parenthood," *The New Yorker*, November 14, 2011, 44–55.
113 Ibid., 44.
114 Ibid., 47.
115 Ibid., 46–7.

Notes to Pages 110–114

116 Ibid., 46.
117 Ibid., 47–8. See also Erik Eckholm, "Anti-Abortion Groups Are Split on Legal Tactics," *New York Times*, December 5, 2011, at p. 1, section A.
118 Lepore, "Birthright: What's Next for Planned Parenthood, 46.
119 Eckholm, "Anti-Abortion Groups Are Split on Legal Tactics."
120 James Davison Hunter, *Culture Wars: The Struggle to Define America* (New York: Basic Books, 1991).
121 Ibid., 42.
122 Ibid., 52.
123 Ibid., 173–5.
124 Ibid., 251–2.
125 International military forces remain a component of the international presence in Kosovo and Bosnia today. Similarly, the United Nations peacekeeping force mandated by the Security Council in 1964 to prevent a return to armed conflict between the Turkish Cypriot and Greek Cypriot communities in Cyprus are still on the ground almost fifty years later. The force was initially deployed in 1964 pursuant to UN Security Council, *Resolution 186 (1964)*, UN doc. S/5575, March 4, 1964.
126 Donald L. Horowitz, *Ethnic Groups in Conflict* (Berkeley & Los Angeles: University of California Press, 1985), 185.
127 Ibid., 186–7.
128 See, for example, Mary Kaldor, *New and Old Wars: Organized Violence in a Global Era* (Stanford, CA: Stanford University Press, 1999), 51–2. During the Bosnian armed conflict, exclusion was achieved by directly targeting civilians belonging to another ethnic group in a given territory. Entire villages were shelled; paramilitary forces were sent to terrorize residents belonging to other ethnic groups. Once residents had been expelled from the territory, exclusive control over the local administration was established.
129 Paul Koring, "An Encounter with the Butcher of Srebrenica," *The Globe and Mail*, May 27, 2011, A10.
130 On the emotional dynamics of ethnic conflict, see Roger D. Petersen, *Understanding Ethnic Violence: Fear, Hatred, and Resentment in Twentieth Century Eastern Europe* (Cambridge: Cambridge University Press, 2002).
131 Ashutosh Varshney, "Nationalism, Ethnic Conflict, and Rationality," *Perspectives on Politics* **1**, no. 1 (2003): 85–99. Varshney argues, inter alia, that rational-choice theories cannot answer a number of fundamental questions regarding ethnicity and nationalism.
132 Horowitz, *Ethnic Groups in Conflict*, 187.
133 Kenan Trebincevic, "Marshal Tito in Queens," *New York Times*, May 3, 2012, http://www.nytimes.com/2012/05/04/opinion/marshal-tito-in-queens.html?pagewanted=1&hpw.
134 "Water Polo Riots Spark Balkans Row," *BBC News*, June 16, 2003, http://news.bbc.co.uk/2/hi/europe/2994008.stm.

135 Mark Tallentire, "Violence Erupts between Serbs and Bosnians after Djokovic's Win," *The Guardian*, January 23, 2009, http://www.guardian.co.uk/sport/2009/jan/23/australian-open-violence-djokovic.

136 Judah, *Kosovo: War and Revenge*, 39–40.

137 Ibid.

138 Independent International Commission on Kosovo, *The Kosovo Report: Conflict, International Response, Lessons Learned* (Oxford: Oxford University Press, 2000), 70–5; See also Henry Perritt, *The Road to Independence for Kosovo: A Chronicle of the Ahtisaari Plan* (New York: Cambridge University Press, 2010), 37.

139 The proposed agreement stipulated that three years after its entry into force, an international meeting would be convened to: "determine a mechanism for a final settlement for Kosovo, on the basis of the will of the people, opinions of relevant authorities, each Party's efforts regarding the implementation of this Agreement, and the Helsinki Final Act." See more generally U.S. State Department, *Rambouillet Agreement: Interim Agreement for Peace and Self-Government in Kosovo*, http://www.state.gov/www/regions/eur/ksvo_rambouillet_text.html.

140 Judah, *Kosovo: War and Revenge*, 217–19; see also Independent International Commission on Kosovo, *The Kosovo Report*, 155–8.

141 The armed conflict in Kosovo ended following a decision by the Milošević government in Belgrade to comply with the modalities of an arrangement proposed by former Finnish President Ahtisaari, former Russian Prime Minister Chernomyrdin, and U.S. Deputy Secretary of State Talbott on June 2, 1999. The modalities of Belgrade's military withdrawal from Kosovo were specified in a military technical agreement reached in Kumanovo (FYROM) on June 9, 1999. The following day, the Security Council of the United Nations adopted a resolution that demanded, inter alia, that the Federal Republic of Yugoslavia put an end to violence and repression in Kosovo. It also agreed on the deployment of international civil and security presences in Kosovo. See UN Security Council, *Resolution 1244 (1999)*; See also Judah, *Kosovo: War and Revenge*, 269.

142 UN Security Council, *Resolution 1244 (1999)*.

143 Ibid., Article 10.

144 Ibid., Article 11e.

145 Perritt, *The Road to Independence for Kosovo*, 71–3.

146 Ibid., 74.

147 "Collapse in Kosovo: Europe Report No. 155," *International Crisis Group*, April 22, 2004, http://www.crisisgroup.org/~/media/Files/europe/155_collapse_in_kosovo_revised.ashx.

148 UN Security Council, *Main Provisions of the Comprehensive Proposal for the Kosovo Status Settlement* annexed to *Letter dated 26 March 2007 from the Secretary-General addressed to the President of the Security Council*, March

26, 2007, S/2007/168/Add.1, paragraph 4, http://www.unosek.org/docref/Comprehensive_proposal-english.pdf.
149 International Civilian Office (ICO), Kosovo, *Report of the International Civilian Office*, Vienna, Austria, February 27, 2009, http://www.ico-kos.org/d/ISG%20report%20finalENG.pdf.
150 World Bank, World Development Report 2011, 60–1.

6. Nonviolent Insurgency

1 Government of India, *India in 1930–31: A Statement Prepared for Presentation to Parliament in Accordance with the Requirements of the 26th Section of the Government of India Act (5&6 Geo. V, Chap.61)* (Calcutta: Government of India Central Publication Branch, 1932), 80. Reference taken from Gene Sharp, *Politics of Nonviolent Action* (Boston, MA: Extending Horizons Books Porter Sargent Publishers, 1973), 41.
2 Jeronim Perović, "The Tito-Stalin Split," *Journal of Cold War Studies* **9**, Issue 2 (2007): 52–7. See also Ivo Banac, *With Stalin against Tito: Cominformist Splits in Yugoslav Communism* (Ithaca, NY & London: Cornell University Press, 1988), 40–1.
3 Stalin was apparently keen to live up to an agreement he had reached with Churchill according to which Great Britain was meant to retain a 90 percent political interest in Greece. See Banac, *With Stalin against Tito*, 32–3. See also Perović, "The Tito-Stalin Split," 53–4.
4 Banac, *With Stalin against Tito*, 43–4.
5 Ibid., 117–18.
6 Ibid., 118.
7 Perović, "The Tito-Stalin Split," 60.
8 The conference was attended by representatives of the communist parties of Bulgaria, Czechoslovakia, France, Hungary, Italy, Poland, Romania, and the Soviet Union. See Giuliano Procacci et al., *The Cominform: Minutes of the Three Conferences 1947/1948/1949* (Milano: Feltrinelli Editore, 1994), 607.
9 Paragraph 1 of the Resolution on the Situation in the Communist Party of Yugoslavia. See ibid., 611.
10 Paragraph 2 of the Resolution on the Situation in the Communist Party of Yugoslavia. See ibid., 611.
11 Paragraph 7, *in fine*, of the Resolution on the Situation in the Communist Party of Yugoslavia. See ibid., 619.
12 See the concluding section of the Resolution on the Situation in the Communist Party of Yugoslavia in Procacci, *The Cominform*, 621. The resolution also regarded the expulsion of members of the Yugoslav Communist Party who had been advocating for friendship between Yugoslavia and the Soviet Union as "disgraceful." It stressed that this "*à la turque*, terrorist regime" was "intolerable in a Communist Party" and that for the "sake

of the very existence and development of the Yugoslav Communist party, this regime" had to "be ended." See Paragraph 5 of the Resolution on the Situation in the Communist Party of Yugoslavia.

13 Banac, *With Stalin against Tito*, 130.
14 Ibid., 130–1.
15 Perović, "The Tito-Stalin Split," 59.
16 John Lewis Gaddis, *Strategies of Containment: A Critical Appraisal of American National Security Policy during the Cold War* (Oxford: Oxford University Press, 2005), 66.
17 The Soviet Union had a plan to intervene militarily in Yugoslavia. See Banac, *With Stalin against Tito*, 131.
18 Perović, "The Tito-Stalin Split," 60; Perović refers to a report Stalin had sent to Czechoslovak leader Klement Gottwald just two weeks after Yugoslavia's expulsion from the Cominform in which Stalin had stressed: "I have the impression that you ... are counting on the defeat of Tito and his group at the next congress of the KPJ. You suggest publishing compromising material against the Yugoslav leaders.... We in Moscow are not counting on the defeat of Tito and have never counted on it. We have achieved the isolation of Yugoslavia. Hence the gradual decline of Tito's Marxist groups is to be expected. This will require patience and the ability to wait. You seem to be lacking in patience.... There can be no doubt that Marxism will triumph in due course."
19 Tony Judt, *Postwar: A History of Europe since 1945* (New York: Penguin Press, 2005), 179.
20 Ibid., 180–1.
21 Robert Jervis, *System Effects: Complexity in Political and Social Life* (Princeton, NJ: Princeton University Press, 1997), 25.
22 Gaddis, *Strategies of Containment*, 62.
23 Referred to in ibid., 62; see also Jervis, *System Effects*, 25.
24 S. Neil MacFarlane, *Intervention in Contemporary World Politics* (Oxford: Oxford University Press for the International Institute for Strategic Studies, 2002), 20–1.
25 UN Security Council, *Resolution 1973 (2011)*, March 17, 2011 authorized UN member states to take all necessary measures "to protect civilians and civilian populated areas under threat of attack" in Libya.
26 United Nations, *Charter of the United Nations*, articles 2(4), 42, and 51.
27 Unipolarity also meant that the United Nations could be bypassed when threats of vetoes in the Security Council became an obstacle. The NATO-led intervention in Kosovo in 1999 occurred without prior authorization from the United Nations Security Council.
28 See UN Security Council, *Resolution 678 (1990)*, November 29, 1990, S/RES/678, at par. 2.
29 UN Security Council, *Security Council Resolution 1244 (1999)*. The resolution recognized that the repression of civilian populations in Iraq "threatened

international peace and security in the region" (at par. 1). The resolution further demanded that "Iraq, as a contribution to removing the threat to international peace and security in the region, immediately end this repression" (at par. 2).

30. This international human rights regime is composed of the following main instruments: Universal Declaration of Human Rights, G.A. res. 217A (III), UN Doc A/810 at 71 (1948); International Covenant on Civil and Political Rights, G.A. res. 2200A (XXI), 21 UN GAOR Supp. (No. 16) at 52, UN Doc. A/6316 (1966), 999 U.N.T.S. 171, entered into force March 23, 1976; International Covenant on Economic, Social and Cultural Rights, G.A. res. 2200A (XXI), 21 UN GAOR Supp. (No. 16) at 49, UN Doc. A/6316 (1966), 993 U.N.T.S. 3, entered into force January 3, 1976; European Convention for the Protection of Human Rights and Fundamental Freedoms, ETS 5, 213 U.N.T.S. 222, entered into force September 3, 1953, as amended by Protocols No. 3, 5, and 8, which entered into force on September 21, 1970, December 20, 1971, and January 1, 1990 respectively; African Charter on Human and Peoples' Rights, adopted June 27, 1981, OAU Doc. CAB/LEG/67/3 rev. 5, 21 I.L.M. 58 (1982), entered into force October 21, 1986; American Convention on Human Rights, O.A.S. Treaty Series No. 36, 1144 U.N.T.S. 123, entered into force July 18, 1978, reprinted in *Basic Documents Pertaining to Human Rights in the Inter-American System*, OEA/Ser.L.V/II.82 doc.6 rev.1 at 25 (1992).

31. References can be made, for example, to the European Court of Human Rights or the Inter-American Court of Human Rights.

32. MacFarlane, *Intervention in Contemporary World Politics*, 51–5.

33. The commission's proposed threshold principles for humanitarian intervention stipulated: "[t]here are two valid triggers of humanitarian intervention. The first is severe violations of international human rights or humanitarian law on a sustained basis. The second is the subjection of a civilian society to great suffering and risk due to the 'failure' of their state, which entails the breakdown of governance at the level of the territorial sovereign state." See Independent International Commission on Kosovo, *The Kosovo Report: Conflict, International Response, Lessons Learned* (Oxford: Oxford University Press, 2000), 193.

34. International Commission on Intervention and State Sovereignty, *The Responsibility to Protect: Report of the International Commission on Intervention and State Sovereignty* (Ottawa: International Development Research Centre, 2001), http://responsibilitytoprotect.org/ICISS%20Report.pdf.

35. Ibid.

36. In September 2005, the United Nations General Assembly adopted the "2005 World Summit Outcome," which endorsed the notion of responsibility to protect. See UN General Assembly, *Integrated and Coordinated Implementation of and Follow-Up to the Outcomes of the Major United Nations*

Conferences and Summits in the Economic, Social and Related Fields / Follow-up to the Outcome of the Millennium Summit, September 15, 2005, A/60/L.1, par. 138–9.

37 Robert A. Pape, "When Duty Calls: A Pragmatic Standard of Humanitarian Intervention," *International Security* **37**, no. 1 (Summer 2012): 43. Pape argues, for example, that the responsibility to protect has set the bar for intervention too low. Pape suggests an alternative standard – "pragmatic humanitarian intervention" – to guide future intervention decisions. He proposes a standard with three requirements: "(1) an ongoing campaign of mass homicide sponsored by the local government in which thousands have died and thousands more are likely to die; (2) a viable plan for intervention with reasonable estimates of casualties not significantly higher than in peacetime operations and near zero for the intervening forces during the main phase of the operation; and (3) a workable strategy for creating lasting local security, so that saving lives in the short term does not lead to open-ended chaos in which many more are killed in the long term."

38 "Joint UK, French and German statement on Syria," HM Government, August 18, 2011, http://www.number10.gov.uk/news/joint-uk-french-and-german-statement-on-syria/.

39 Ibid.

40 Stephen Harper, "Statement by the Prime Minister of Canada on the Situation in Syria" (speech, Ottawa, Ontario, August 18, 2011), http://pm.gc.ca/eng/media.asp?category=3&featureId=6&pageId=49&id=4266.

41 The White House, Office of the Press Secretary, "Statement by President Obama on the Situation in Syria" (speech, Washington, DC, August 18, 2011), http://www.whitehouse.gov/the-press-office/2011/08/18/statement-president-obama-situation-syria.

42 Ibid.

43 "France's Alain Juppe: Syria committing 'grave crimes,'" *BBC News*, September 7, 2011, http://www.bbc.co.uk/news/world-middle-east-14822636.

44 Despite confirming that President Obama had asked the Pentagon to prepare initial military options for Syria in their testimony before the United States Senate Armed Services Committee in March 2012, U.S. Defense Secretary Leon Panetta and Joint Chiefs of Staff Chairman General Dempsey stated that diplomatic and economic pressure were the best means to protect civilians in Syria at the time. See Elisabeth Bumiller, "U.S. Defense Officials Say Obama Reviewing Military Options in Syria," *New York Times*, March 7, 2012, http://www.nytimes.com/2012/03/08/world/middleeast/united-states-defense-officials-stress-nonmilitary-options-on-syria.html?ref=global-home. See also Karen DeYoung, "U.S. Officials Warn against Intervention in Syria," *Washington Post*, March 7, 2012, http://www.washingtonpost.com/world/national-security/us-officials-warn-against-syrian intervention/2012/03/07/gIQA1t39wR_story.html.

45 The United Nations Protection Force (UNPROFOR) was initially deployed in Croatia pursuant to UN Security Council, *Resolution 743 (1992)*, February 21, 1992, S/RES/743. Its deployment was subsequently extended to Bosnia and Herzegovina pursuant to UN Security Council, *Resolution 758 (1992)*, June 8, 1992, S/RES/758 and to the Former Yugoslav Republic of Macedonia (FYROM) pursuant to UN Security Council, *Resolution 795 (1992)*, December 21, 1992, S/RES/795.

46 See, inter alia, Michael W. Doyle and Nishkala Suntharalingam, "The UN in Cambodia: Lessons for Complex Peacekeeping," *International Peacekeeping* 1, no. 2 (1994): 117–47; Kimberly Zisk Marten, *Enforcing the Peace: Learning from the Imperial Past* (New York: Columbia University Press, 2004).

47 "Citizen Journalism in Syria," CBC, *The Current*, January 4, 2011 (Rami Jarah interviewed by Anna Maria Tremonti).

48 UN Security Council, *Resolution 713 (1991)*, September 25, 1991, S/RES/713 (1991), par. 6.

49 Steven L. Burg and Paul S. Shoup, *The War in Bosnia-Herzegovina: Ethnic Conflict and International Intervention* (New York: M. E. Sharpe, 1999), 134–5. See also Noel Malcolm, *Bosnia: A Short History* (London: Papermac, 1996), 248–9.

50 Mark Cutts, "The Humanitarian Operation in Bosnia, 1992–1995: Dilemmas of Negotiating Humanitarian Access," *UNHCR Policy Research Unit*, May 1999, 13–16, 24–5, http://www.unhcr.org/3ae6a0c58.pdf. Cutts highlights that UNHCR delivered approximately nine hundred fifty thousand metric tons of humanitarian assistance to 2.7 million persons in Bosnia between 1992 and 1995 but argues that, while impressive in terms of quantity delivered, a significant amount of the assistance was provided to people who could have survived without it or was diverted for military purpose.

51 Tarek Amara, "Violent Unrest Breaks Out in Tunisian Capital," *Reuters*, January 11, 2011, http://www.reuters.com/article/2011/01/11/us-tunisia-protests-idUSTRE70A2GO20110111.

52 Anthony Shadid, "Syrian Leader Vows 'Iron Fist' to Crush 'Conspiracy,'" *New York Times*, January 11, 2012, http://www.nytimes.com/2012/01/11/world/middleeast/syrian-leader-vows-to-crush-conspiracy.html?ref=globalhome.

53 David D. Kirkpatrick, "Egypt Defies U.S. by Setting Trial for 19 Americans," *New York Times*, A1, February 6, 2012.

54 Neil MacFarquhar, Nada Bakri, and Liam Stack, "Isolating Syria, Arab Group Sets Broad Sanctions," *New York Times*, A1, November 28, 2011; Neil MacFarquhar and Hwaida Saad, "Syria Calls the Arab League's Sanctions 'Economic War,'" *New York Times*, A6, November 29, 2011.

55 David Galula, *Counterinsurgency Warfare: Theory and Practice* (New York: Frederick A. Prager, 1964), 4. Galula defined *revolution* as an explosive, sudden, brief, spontaneous, unplanned upheaval such as those that occurred

in France in 1789 and in Russia in 1917. He defines a *plot* as a clandestine action – that excludes the masses – directed at the overthrow of the top leadership in a country (4).
56 U.S. Army & Marine Corps, *Counterinsurgency Field Manual*, (Chicago and London: The University of Chicago Press, 2007) 2.
57 Ibid.
58 John A. Nagl, *Learning to Eat Soup with a Knife: Counterinsurgency Lessons from Malaya and Vietnam* (Chicago, IL & London: University of Chicago Press, 2005), 19–20.
59 Ibid.
60 David Kilcullen, *Counterinsurgency* (Oxford: Oxford University Press, 2010), 1.
61 Ibid.
62 U.S. Army & Marine Corps, *Counterinsurgency Field Manual*, 2.
63 Kilcullen, *Counterinsurgency*, 8.
64 Ibid., 9.
65 ISAF, *Commander's Counterinsurgency Guidance*, Kabul, Afghanistan, August 2009, 1, http://www.nato.int/isaf/docu/official_texts/counterinsurgency_guidance.pdf.
66 Ibid., 3.
67 Kilcullen, *Counterinsurgency*, 11–12.
68 Molly Moore, "NATO Confronts Surprisingly Fierce Taliban," *Washington Post*, February 26, 2008, http://articles.washingtonpost.com/2008-02-26/world/36779338_1_taliban-fighters-uruzgan-coalition-forces.
69 Ben Farmer, "Life under the Taliban: How a Boy of Seven was Hanged to Punish his Family," *The Telegraph*, June 12, 2010, http://www.telegraph.co.uk/news/worldnews/asia/afghanistan/7823404/Life-under-the-Taliban-how-a-boy-of-seven-was-hanged-to-punish-his-family.html.
70 Galula himself partially recognizes this possibility. See Galula, *Counterinsurgency Warfare*, 31–2 and 43–7. According to Galula, a revolutionary war can be divided into a period of "cold revolutionary war" and "hot revolutionary war" (43–7). During the "cold revolutionary war" period, the insurgents' actions remain legal and nonviolent. It is a period during which insurgents would traditionally (1) create a party and (2) build a united front (31–2). This period generally acts as a prelude to "hot revolutionary war," a period during which the insurgents' actions become illegal and violent (32 and 43–7). While Galula's notion of "cold revolutionary war" seems conceived merely as a prelude to a violent revolutionary phase, Galula nevertheless recognizes that power can be seized through nonviolent means. He notes, while highlighting the transition between cold and hot revolutionary wars, that an insurgent "may seize power merely by political play and subversion. If not, then an armed struggle is the logical continuation" (32). The

U.S. Army & Marine Corps *Counterinsurgency Field Manual* also recognizes that "government can be overthrown in a number of ways" and notes that "an unplanned, spontaneous explosion of popular will, for example, might result in a revolution like that in France in 1789." On the prevalence of nonviolent insurrection, see generally Sharp, *Politics of Nonviolent Action*, 4; Kurt Schock, *Unarmed Insurrection: People Power Movements in Nondemocracies* (Minneapolis: University of Minnesota Press, 2005), 13–15.

71 The ruling class is said to have made a number of concessions to the Plebeians as a consequence of the revolt. See Sharp, *Politics of Nonviolent Action*, 4. See Andrew Lintott, *The Constitution of the Roman Republic* (Oxford: Clarendon Press, 1999), 32–3. See additionally Tim Cornell, *The Beginnings of Rome: Italy and Rome from the Bronze Age to the Punic Wars* (New York: Routledge, 1995), 242–71.

72 Schock, *Unarmed Insurrection*, 16–17 and 22.

73 Ibid., 4–5. Schock lists thirty-one cases of "major unarmed insurrections" that occurred in the "Second and Third Worlds" between 1978 and 2001. Listed chronologically, these countries are: Iran, Bolivia, El Salvador, Poland, Pakistan, Philippines, Chile, South Africa, Haiti, Sudan, South Korea, Tibet, Palestine (West Bank and Gaza Strip), Burma, Bulgaria, China, Czechoslovakia, East Germany, Hungary, Kenya, Bangladesh, Mongolia, Mali, Nepal, Niger, Thailand, Madagascar, Indonesia, Nigeria, Yugoslavia, and Philippines.

74 Ibid., 2.

75 Erica Chenoweth and Maria Stephan, *Why Civil Resistance Works: The Strategic Logic of Nonviolent Conflict* (New York: Columbia University Press, 2011), 6–10.

76 Ibid., 7.

77 Ibid., 39–41. Recognizing that numbers alone do not guarantee victory in resistance campaigns, Chenoweth and Stephan note: "Over space and time, large campaigns are much more likely to succeed than small campaigns. The trend is clear that as membership increases, the probability of success also increases" (39).

78 On physical barriers to participation, see ibid., 34–5.

79 Ibid., 10–11 and 35–9.

80 Joseph Nye, *Soft Power: The Means to Success in World Politics* (New York: Public Affairs, 2004), 1.

81 This definition of power is based on Peter Morris's analysis of power. See Peter Morris, *Power: A Philosophical Analysis* (Manchester & New York: Manchester University Press, 2002). Morris suggests that power must be understood as a dispositional property, a *capacity* (13). It must also be distinguished from the notion of *influence*. While *influence* is linked to *affecting*, power pertains to *effecting* (29–30). Power is thus the capacity to effect outcomes (32 and 35).

82 Sharp, *Politics of Nonviolent Action*, 9; Gene Sharp, *Waging Non Violent Struggle: 20th Century Practice and 21st Century Potential* (Boston, MA: Extending Horizons Books, 2005), 27–8.
83 Sharp, *Politics of Nonviolent Action*, 11–12.
84 Ibid. See also Sharp, *Waging Non Violent Struggle*, 29–30.
85 Sharp, *Politics of Nonviolent Action*, 11.
86 Robert Helvey, *On Strategic Nonviolent Conflict: Thinking about the Fundamentals* (Boston, MA: The Albert Einstein Institution, 2004), 9–18. Helvey identifies nine pillars of support: the police, the military, civil servants, media, business community, youth, workers, religious organizations, and non-governmental organizations. The strategy of nonviolent conflict should, he argues, seek to pull these pillars of support away from a ruling authority.
87 Sharp, *Politics of Nonviolent Action*, 16; Sharp, *Waging Non Violent Struggle*, 32–3.
88 Sharp, *Waging Non Violent Struggle*, 33–5.
89 David Bell, *Resistance and Revolution* (Boston, MA: Houghton Mifflin Company, 1973), 45–6.
90 Sharp, *Waging Non Violent Struggle*, 52.
91 Ibid., 54.
92 Ibid., 60.
93 Ibid., 61.
94 Ibid., 64.
95 Schock, *Unarmed Insurrection*, 30–1.
96 See United Nations Human Rights Council, *Report of the United Nations High Commissioner for Human Rights on the Situation of Human Rights in the Syrian Arab Republic*, September 15, 2011, A/HRC/18/53, par. 33.
97 Schock, *Unarmed Insurrection*, 32.
98 Andrew England, Heba Saleh, and Michael Peel, "Egypt Stands Divided as Mubarak Supporters Launch Assault on Protest," *Financial Times*, February 3, 2011.
99 Sharp, *Politics of Nonviolent Action*, 12.
100 Sharp, *Waging Non Violent Struggle*, 31–3.
101 While the assumption is that repression acts as a constraint on mobilization, studies have found support for three different types of relationships between repression and dissent: (1) some studies associate repression with a decrease in dissent; (2) some studies associate repression with an increase in dissent; (3) some studies suggest the existence of an inverted U-shaped relationship between the two variables. Namely, dissent will be low at low levels of repression, high at medium levels of repression, and low again at high levels of repression. See Schock, *Unarmed Insurrection*, 32.
102 Schock, *Unarmed Insurrection*, 32.
103 Adam Michnik, *Letters from Prison and Other Essays* (Berkeley: University of California Press, 1985), 10.

Notes to Pages 140–141

104 Ibid., 14–15.
105 Schock, *Unarmed Insurrection*, 33–4.
106 Sharp calls this phenomenon "political ju-jitsu." See Sharp, *Waging Non Violent Struggle*, 47–8.
107 See United Nations Human Rights Council, *Report of the United Nations High Commissioner for Human Rights on the Situation of Human Rights in the Syrian Arab Republic*, par. 46:

> A large-scale military operation was launched on 25 May in the town of Ar Rastan, where "armed gangs" were still allegedly operating, and demonstrators had reportedly toppled the statue of the late President Assad. Highly consistent accounts given by witnesses described the events there. The armed forces surrounded the town, controlling all points of access with tanks and armoured vehicles to prevent the entry of food and medical supplies. The town was divided into two operational zones. Inside each zone, rows of soldiers pushed through the different areas, preceded by officers. Behind each unit there were groups of six to eight *Shabbiha* members, allegedly ready to shoot any soldier who looked back or refused to obey orders. Soldiers broke into homes and looted, shooting indiscriminately at cars and passers-by, and damaging property. Many of the inhabitants of Ar Rastan fled to nearby fields to hide, but were pursued, and numerous people were killed. Several of the witness accounts also referred to the killing of army officers by unidentified sniper fire during the operation.

108 Schock, *Unarmed Insurrection*, 52.
109 Sharp, *Waging Non Violent Struggle*, 45–6.
110 Adam Roberts, "Introduction," in *Civil Resistance and Power Politics*, ed. Adam Roberts and Timothy Garton Ash (Oxford: Oxford University Press, 2009), 3–4.
111 Ibid., 2–3.
112 Adam Roberts, "Civil Resistance to Military Coups," *Journal of Peace and Research*, **12**, no.1 (1975): 22–3.
113 Ibid., 23–30.
114 Author's translation. The original version of de Gaulle's speech reads: "j'ordonne que tous les moyens, je dis tous les moyens, soient employés partout pour barrer la route à ces hommes-là, en attendant de les réduire. J'interdis à tous Français, et d'abord à tous soldats, d'exécuter aucun de leurs ordres." De Gaulle's speech of April 23, 1961 can be accessed on the website of the French National Audiovisual Institute. See "Discours du 23 avril 1961," *Institut National de l'Audiovisuel*, April 23, 1961, http://www.ina.fr/fresques/de-gaulle/fiche-media/Gaulle00071/discours-du-23avril1961?video=Gaulle00071.
115 Ibid. Author's translation. The original text in French reads: "Francaises, Francais, aidez-moi."
116 Roberts, "Civil Resistance to Military Coups," 27–8.

117 Schock, *Unarmed Insurrection*, 15. According to this line of thinking, the power of noninstitutional politics lies in its indeterminateness and disruptiveness. This power would inevitably be decreased were actions taken through institutions where outcomes could be procedurally predetermined. Shock writes: "While the outcome of institutional political action is determinate, that is, prescribed by some procedure, practice or norms, noninstitutional political action is indeterminate, that is, it is not prescribed by any such existing rules or regulations, and its outcome is a function of contentious interactions between opposing forces.... The power of noninstitutional politics inheres in its indeterminateness and disruptiveness. When noninstitutional political action loses its uncertainty and disruptiveness and becomes institutionalized, as in highly choreographed and regulated protest demonstrations at the Mall in Washington, DC, its effectiveness in promoting political change decreases."

118 Schock, *Unarmed Insurrection*, 6, 7, and 15; Chenoweth and Stephan, *Why Civil Resistance Works*, 12.

119 UN Security Council, *Report of the Secretary General on the United Nations Interim Administration in Kosovo*, November 24, 2008, S/2008/692, par. 21, http://daccess-dds-ny.un.org/doc/UNDOC/GEN/N08/518/31/PDF/N0851831.pdf?OpenElement.

120 This challenge is not regulated anywhere and is certainly disruptive. Its outcome is uncertain and may trigger negative consequences for the domestic actors.

121 Andrew Mack, "Why Big Nations Lose Small Wars: The Politics of Asymmetric Conflict," *World Politics* **27**, no. 2 (1975): 176.

122 Modern peace operations often import liberal democratic standards to the space in which they intervene. The peace operations deployed to Haiti, Bosnia, Kosovo, or East Timor have sought to reshape these environments along liberal democratic standards. See Roland Paris, "International Peacebuilding and the 'Mission Civilisatrice,'" *Review of International Studies* **28** (2002): 637–6; Paris suggests that peace-building missions are more than exercises in conflict management. According to his suggestion, they should be conceived within a larger phenomenon by which powerful states seek to transfer values and norms to a less developed periphery.

123 John Stedman, "Spoiler Problems in Peace Process," *International Security* **22**, no. 2 (Fall 1997): 5–53.

124 Ibid., 5.

125 Ibid., 6 and 8–12.

126 For nonviolent opposition to peace initiatives in Northern Ireland, see Christopher Farrington, "Non-Violent Opposition to Peace Processes: Northern Ireland's Serial Spoilers," *University College Dublin Geary Institute Discussion Paper Series*, February 28, 2006, http://hdl.handle.net/10197/1845.

127 Ibid., 6 and 15.
128 A number of scholars have recently examined some of the limits of Stedman's spoiler model. See, for example, Kelly M. Greenhill and Solomon Major, "The Perils of Profiling Civil War Spoilers and the Collapse of Intrastate Peace Accords," *International Security* 31, no. 3 (Winter 2006/07): 7–40. See also Marie-Joelle Zahar, "Reframing the Spoiler Debate in Peace Processes" in *Contemporary Peacemaking: Conflict, Peace Processes and Post-War Reconstruction*, ed. John Darby and Roger MacGinty (New York: Palgrave Macmillan, 2008), 159–77; See also Farrington, "Non-Violent Opposition to Peace Processes: Northern Ireland's Serial Spoilers." Zahar and Farrington's views come closest to some of the views expressed in this book. Zahar acknowledges, for example, that "not all would-be spoilers resort to violence in their opposition to the negotiations of a given peace process" (163). Farrington notes: "Most of the research conducted on peace agreements has looked at the relationship between parties to the agreement, how they analyse the costs and benefits of negotiations and how those incentives can be altered by third parties. However, the politics of implementing peace agreements involve all the relationships between the parties to the *conflict* and not just the relationships between those who conclude the agreement" (3). He also stresses: "'Non-violent spoilers' do not seem to arise within Stedman's research because of the type of conflicts and peace processes he has examined.... Violent and non-violent spoilers differ only in their methods and not in their intentions, position, type or locus" (4).

7. Diplomatic Counterinsurgency

1 Richard Holbrooke, *To End a War* (New York: The Modern Library, 1999), 335.
2 On the self-reinforcing interaction between resistance and international intervention in Bosnia, see Susan L. Woodward, "Bosnia and Herzegovina: How Not to End Civil War," in *Civil Wars, Insecurity, and Intervention*, ed. Barbara F. Walter and Jack Snyder (New York: Columbia University Press, 1999), 104–8.
3 See Noel Malcolm, *Bosnia: A Short History* (London: Papermac, 1996), 262. See Holbrooke, *To End a War*, 63–4.
4 Holbrooke, *To End a War*, 308–9. See also Derek Chollet, *The Road to the Dayton Accords: A Study of American Statecraft* (New York: Palgrave Macmillan, 2005), 178–9.
5 See Holbrooke, *To End a War*, 238–9.
6 See Article 48 (1) and Article 84 of the *Rules of Procedure of the Council of Ministers of Bosnia and Herzegovina* (O.G. BiH 22/03).
7 On the composition of Bosnia's tripartite presidency, see Article V of the Constitution of Bosnia and Herzegovina; the European Court of Human

Rights found the eligibility requirements for election to the presidency to be in violation of Article 1 of Protocol No. 12 to the European Convention on Human Rights in 2009. See App. Nos. 27996/06 and 34836/06, *Sejdić and Finci v. Bosnia and Herzegovina*, Eur.Ct. H.R., judgment of December 22, 2009, at par. 52–6; available at: http://hudoc.echr.coe.int/sites/eng/pages/search.aspx?i=001-96491.

8 See Article 45 (2) of the *Rules of Procedure of the Presidency of Bosnia and Herzegovina* (O.G. BiH 25/01).
9 Article V (2) d) of the Constitution of Bosnia and Herzegovina.
10 Article IV.3 d) of the Constitution of Bosnia and Herzegovina.
11 Article IV.3 d) of the Constitution of Bosnia and Herzegovina.
12 Article IV.3 d) of the Constitution of Bosnia and Herzegovina.
13 Article IV.3 d) and e) of the Constitution of Bosnia and Herzegovina.
14 Holbrooke, *To End a War*, 335.
15 See Article 1(1) of Annex 7 of the *General Framework Agreement for Peace*. Article 1 (1) stipulates: "All refugees and displaced persons have the right freely to return to their homes of origin. They shall have the right to have restored to them property of which they were deprived in the course of hostilities since 1991 and to be compensated for any property that cannot be restored to them. The early return of refugees and displaced persons is an important objective of the settlement of the conflict in Bosnia and Herzegovina. The Parties confirm that they will accept the return of such persons who have left their territory, including those who have been accorded temporary protection by third countries."
16 See, inter alia, Rhodri C. Williams, "Post-Conflict Property Restitution and Refugee Return in Bosnia and Herzegovina: Implications for International Standard-Setting and Practice," *New York University Journal of International Law and Politics* 37, no. 3 (2005): 441–553. See also Reconstruction and Return Task Force, *Report April 1997*, April 30, 1997, section 3.2, http://www.ohr.int/ohr-dept/rrtf/key-docs/reports/default.asp?content_id=5565.
17 Peace Implementation Council, *PIC Bonn Conclusions*, December 10, 1997, Section XI, http://www.ohr.int/pic/default.asp?content_id=5182#11.
18 Williams, "Post-Conflict Property Restitution," 489–96.
19 Ibid., 498.
20 See also Carl Dahlman and Gearoid O. Tuathail, "The Legacy of Ethnic Cleansing: The International Community and the Returns Process in Post-Dayton Bosnia-Herzegovina," *Political Geography* 24, (June 2005): 586–90.
21 On international efforts to implement the right to return enshrined in Annex 7 of the Dayton agreement, see generally Gerard Toal and Carl T. Dahlman, *Bosnia Remade: Ethnic Cleansing and Its Reversal* (Oxford: Oxford University Press, 2011).
22 "Decision on the Deadlines for the Implementation of the New Uniform License Plate System," *Office of the High Representative*, May 20, 1998, http://www.ohr.int/decisions/statemattersdec/default.asp?content_id=347.

Notes to Pages 157–160

23 International official involved with the implementation of new license plates in 1998. Interview with the author, 2010.
24 Ibid.
25 See Rhodri C. Williams, "Post-Conflict Property Restitution in Bosnia: Balancing Reparations and Durable Solutions in the Aftermath of Displacement," TESEV International Symposium on 'Internal Displacement in Turkey and Abroad,' Istanbul, Turkey, December 5, 2006, p. 9, http://www.brookings.edu/~/media/Files/rc/speeches/2006/1205property/200612_rcw_TESEVpresentation.pdf.
26 See, inter alia, UN Security Council, *Resolution 1423 (2002)*, S/RES/1423 (2002), July 12, 2002, at par. 2; UN Security Council, *Resolution 1491 (2003)*, S/RES/1491 (2003), July 11, 2003, at par. 2; UN Security Council, *Resolution 1551 (2004)*, S/RES/1551 (2004), July 9, 2004, at par. 2; UN Security Council, *Resolution 1575 (2004)*, S/RES/1575 (2004), November 22, 2004, at par. 2; UN Security Council, *Resolution 1639 (2005)*, S/RES/1639 (2005), November 21, 2005, at par. 2; UN Security Council, *Resolution 1722 (2006)*, S/RES/1722 (2006), November 21, 2006, at par. 2; UN Security Council, *Resolution 1785 (2007)*, S/RES/1785 (2007), November 21, 2007, at par. 2; UN Security Council, *Resolution 1845 (2008)*, S/RES/1845 (2008), November 20, 2008, at par. 2; UN Security Council, *Resolution 1895 (2009)*, S/RES/1895 (2009), November 18, 2009, at par. 2; UN Security Council, *Resolution 1948 (2010)*, S/RES/1948 (2010), November 18, 2010, at par. 2; UN Security Council, *Resolution 2019 (2011)*, S/RES/2019 (2011), November 16, 2011, at par. 2.
27 "Turning Strife to Advantage: A Blueprint to Integrate the Croats in Bosnia and Herzegovina: Balkans Report No. 106," International Crisis Group, March 15, 2001, 8–9, http://www.crisisgroup.org/~/media/Files/europe/Bosnia%2038.pdf.
28 Ibid.
29 "Decision Removing Ante Jelavić from his Position as the Croat Member of the BiH Presidency," Office of the High Representative, March 7, 2001, http://www.ohr.int/decisions/removalssdec/default.asp?content_id=328.
30 "Decision Removing Ivo Andrić Lozanski from his post as a Delegate to the BiH House of Representatives and Banning Him from Holding Public and Party Office," Office of the High Representative, March 7, 2001, http://www.ohr.int/decisions/removalssdec/default.asp?content_id=327; "Decision Removing Zdravko Batinić from Holding Public and Party Office," Office of the High Representative, March 7, 2001, http://www.ohr.int/decisions/removalssdec/default.asp?content_id=324; "Decision Removing Marko Tokić from Holding Public and Party Office," Office of the High Representative, March 7, 2001, http://www.ohr.int/decisions/removalssdec/default.asp?content_id=326.
31 Amra Kebo, "Bosnian Croat Separatism Threat: The Beleaguered HDZ Party in Bosnia Appears to be Preparing the Ground for the Establishment of

a Bosnian Croat State," Institute for War and Peace Reporting, November 2, 2000, http://iwpr.net/report-news/bosnian-croat-separatism-threat.

32 UN Security Council, *Statement by the President of the Security Council*, S/PRST/2001/11, March 22, 2001.

33 Ibid.

34 Nick Thorpe, "Croatian Soldiers Mutiny in Bosnia," *The Guardian*, March 28, 2001, http://www.guardian.co.uk/world/2001/mar/29/1; Amra Kebo, "Croat Troops Mutiny," Institute for War and Peace Reporting, March 23, 2011, http://iwpr.net/report-news/croat-troops-mutiny.

35 "No Early Exit: NATO's Continuing Challenge in Bosnia: Balkans Report No. 110," International Crisis Group, May 22, 2001 at p. 4, http://www.crisisgroup.org/~/media/Files/europe/Bosnia%2040.pdf.

36 "Decision appointing a Provisional Administrator for the Hercegovačka Banka," Office of the High Representative, April 5, 2001, http://www.ohr.int/decisions/econdec/default.asp?content_id=60.

37 International official involved with leading an international team of auditors. Interview by the author, 2010.

38 International official held hostage. Interview by the author, 2012; Janez Kovac, "Bank Closure Provokes Croat Wrath: Bosnian Croat Hardliners are Furious over Attempts to Severe their Financial Lifelines," Institute for War and Peace Reporting, April 11, 2001, http://iwpr.net/report-news/bank-closure-provokes-croat-wrath; "No Early Exit: NATO's Continuing Challenge in Bosnia: Balkans Report No. 110," pp. 4–6, http://www.crisisgroup.org/~/media/Files/europe/Bosnia%2040.pdf.

39 "Deal Ends Bosnian Croat Mutiny," *BBC News*, May 16, 2001, http://news.bbc.co.uk/2/hi/europe/1334353.stm.

40 "Former Bosnian Croat Leader in Court," *BBC News*, August 29, 2001, http://news.bbc.co.uk/2/hi/europe/1515447.stm.

41 U.S. State Department official. Interview by author, 2012.

42 There is debate as to whether former Yugoslav republics enjoyed an explicit right to secede under Yugoslav constitutional law. The former constitution stipulated, at a minimum, that the Socialist Yugoslav Federation was the product of a common agreement of nations that enjoyed the right to self-determination and the right to secession at the time of its creation. "Basic Principle I" in the "Introductory Part" of the constitution of the Socialist Federal Republic of Yugoslavia provided: "The nations of Yugoslavia, proceeding from the right of every nation to self-determination, including the right to secession, on the basis of their will freely expressed in the common struggle of all nations and nationalities in the National Liberation War and Socialist Revolution, and in conformity with their historic aspirations, aware that the further consolidation of their brotherhood and unity is in the common interest, have, together with nationalities with which they live, united in a federal republic of free and equal nations and nationalities."

See *The Constitution of the Socialist Federal Republic of Yugoslavia* (New York: Cross Cultural Communications, 1976), 13. See also Richard F. Iglar, "The Constitutional Crisis in Yugoslavia and the International Law of Self-Determination: Slovenia's and Croatia's Right to Secede," *Boston College International and Comparative Law Review* **15**, no. 1 (1992): 218–19.

43 See *Case U 5/98 (Partial Decision Part 3)*, Constitutional Court of Bosnia and Herzegovina, July 1, 2000. The decision of the court indicated, inter alia: "The Constitutional Court thus finds that all the references in the provisions of the Preamble of the Constitution of RS to sovereignty, independent decision-making, state status, state independence, creation of a state, and complete and close linking of the RS with other States of the Serb people violate Article I.1 taken in conjunction with Article I.3, Article III.2 (a), and Article 5 of the Constitution of BiH which provide for the sovereignty, territorial integrity, political independence, and international personality of Bosnia and Herzegovina." (par. 32).

44 "Decision Annulling Five RS laws Concerning State-Level Competencies, Which Were Passed in Violation of the BiH Constitution," Office of the High Representative, October 1, 1999, http://www.ohr.int/decisions/statematters-dec/default.asp?content_id=356.

45 *Case U 25/00*, Constitutional Court of Bosnia and Herzegovina, March 23, 2001.

46 *Case U 26/01*, Constitutional Court of Bosnia and Herzegovina, September 28, 2001.

47 *Case U 42/03*, Constitutional Court of Bosnia and Herzegovina, December 17, 2004. Bosnian Serb member Nikola Špirić, deputy chair of the House of Representatives of the Parliamentary Assembly of Bosnia and Herzegovina, requested the Constitutional Court to assess the constitutionality of provisions of the Law on the Basis of the Public Broadcasting System and on the Public Broadcasting Service of Bosnia and Herzegovina (O.G. BiH, no. 29/02).

48 *Case U 9/07*, Constitutional Court of Bosnia and Herzegovina, October 4, 2008. Bosnian Serb member Milorad Živković, deputy chairman of the House of Representatives of the Parliamentary Assembly of Bosnia and Herzegovina, requested the Constitutional Court to review the Law on Statistics of Bosnia and Herzegovina (O.G. of BiH, nos 26/04 and 42/04). The High Representative had imposed the law on October 21, 2002.

49 These responsibilities were transferred pursuant to Article III.5 of the Constitution of Bosnia and Herzegovina.

50 Article IX of the General Framework Agreement for Peace stipulates: "The Parties shall cooperate fully with all entities involved in implementation of this peace settlement, as described in the Annexes to this Agreement, or which are otherwise authorized by the United Nations Security Council, pursuant to the obligation of all Parties to cooperate in the investigation and

prosecution of war crimes and other violations of international humanitarian law." Article II (8) of the Constitution of Bosnia and Herzegovina provides: "All competent authorities in Bosnia and Herzegovina shall cooperate with and provide unrestricted access to any international human rights monitoring mechanisms established for Bosnia and Herzegovina; the supervisory bodies established by any of the international agreements listed in Annex I to this Constitution; the International Tribunal for the Former Yugoslavia (and in particular shall comply with orders issued pursuant to Article 29 of the Statute of the Tribunal); and any other organization authorized by the United Nations Security Council with a mandate concerning human rights or humanitarian law."

51 UN Security Council, *Resolution 827 (1993)*, S/RES/827, May 25, 1993, par. 4.

52 See UN Security Council, *Resolution 1031 (1995)*, S/RES/1031, December 15, 1995, at par. 4; UN Security Council, *Resolution 1088 (1996)*, S/RES/1088, December 12, 1996, at par. 7; UN Security Council, *Resolution 1423 (2002)*, S/RES/1423 (2002), July 12, 2002, at par. 3; UN Security Council, *Resolution 1491 (2003)*, S/RES/1491, July 11, 2003, at par. 3; UN Security Council, *Resolution 1551 (2004)*, S/RES/1551, July 9, 2004, at par. 3; UN Security Council, *Resolution 1575 (2004)*, S/RES/1575, November 22, 2004, at par. 3; UN Security Council, *Resolution 1639 (2005)*, S/RES/1639, November 21, 2005, at par. 3; UN Security Council, *Resolution 1722 (2006)*, S/RES/1722, November 21, 2006, at par. 3; UN Security Council, *Resolution 1785 (2007)*, S/RES/1785, November 21, 2007, at par. 3; UN Security Council, *Resolution 1845 (2008)*, S/RES/1845, November 20, 2008, at par. 3; UN Security Council, *Resolution 1895 (2009)*, S/RES/1895, November 18, 2009, at par. 3; UN Security Council, *Resolution 1948 (2010)*, S/RES/1948, November 18, 2010, at par. 3; UN Security Council, *Resolution 2019 (2011)*, S/RES/2019, November 16, 2011, at par. 3.

53 The resolution also referred specifically to Ante Gotovina, a Croatian national. See UN Security Council, *Resolution 1503 (2003)*, S/RES/1503 (2003), August 28, 2003, par. 2: "Calls on all States, especially Serbia and Montenegro, Croatia, and Bosnia and Herzegovina, and on the Republika Srpska within Bosnia and Herzegovina, to intensify cooperation with and render all necessary assistance to the ICTY, particularly to bring Radovan Karadzic and Ratko Mladic, as well as Ante Gotovina and all other indictees to the ICTY and calls on these and all other at-large indictees of the ICTY to surrender to the ICTY."

54 UN Security Council, *Resolution 1534 (2004)*, S/RES/1534 (2004), March 26, 2004, par. 1.

55 "Decision Suspending All Disbursements of Budgetary Itemizations for Party Funding to the SDS and Ordering the SDS to Submit a Financial Plan for the Period from 1 January 2003 until 31 March 2004," Office of the High

Notes to Pages 166–168

Representative, April 2, 2004, http://www.ohr.int/decisions/war-crimes-decs/default.asp?content_id=32208.
56. "Communiqué by the PIC Steering Board," Office of the High Representative, June 25, 2004, http://www.ohr.int/pic/default.asp?content_id=32727.
57. "Istanbul Summit Communiqué: Issued by the Heads of States and Government Participating in the Meeting of the North Atlantic Council," North Atlantic Treaty Organization, June 28, 2004, par. 34, http://www.nato.int/docu/pr/2004/p04-096e.htm.
58. "Decision Removing Mr. Zoran Djerić from his Position of Minister of Interior of Republika Srpska," Office of the High Representative, June 30, 2004, http://www.ohr.int/decisions/war-crimes-decs/default.asp?content_id=32753.
59. "Decision Removing Dr. Dragan Kalinić from his Positions as Chairman of the National Assembly of Republika Srpska and as President of the SDS," Office of the High Representative, June 30, 2004, http://www.ohr.int/decisions/war-crimes-decs/default.asp?content_id=32750.
60. "Decision Removing Nedjeljko Djekanović from his Position as Vice President of the SDS and from Other Public and Party Positions he Currently Holds," Office of the High Representative, June 30, 2004, http://www.ohr.int/ohr-dept/presso/pressb/default.asp?content_id=32749; "Decision Removing Cvjetan Nikić from his Position as Vice President of the SDS and from Other Public and Party Positions he Currently Holds," Office of the High Representative, June 30, 2004, http://www.ohr.int/decisions/war-crimes-decs/default.asp?content_id=32759; "Decision Removing Slobodan Saraba from his Position(s) as Vice President of the SDS and Director of Hydroelectric Power Plants Trebisnjica and from other Public and Party Positions he Currently Holds," Office of the High Representative, June 30, 2004, http://www.ohr.int/decisions/war-crimes-decs/default.asp?content_id=32758; "Decision Removing Pantelija Curguz from his Position as Vice President of the SDS and from other Public and Party Positions he Currently Holds," Office of the High Representative, June 30, 2004, http://www.ohr.int/decisions/war-crimes-decs/default.asp?content_id=32757.
61. "Decision Blocking All Bank Accounts Held by and/or in the Name of the SDS and Requiring the SDS to Establish one Bank Account," Office of the High Representative, June 30, 2004, http://www.ohr.int/decisions/war-crimes-decs/default.asp?content_id=32752.
62. "Directive Reallocating Budgetary Itemisations Intended to Fund the SDS," Office of the High Representative, June 30, 2004, http://www.ohr.int/decisions/war-crimes-decs/default.asp?content_id=32751.
63. "Press Conference 30 June: High Representative Announces Measures against ICTY Obstructionists," Office of the High Representative, June 30, 2004, http://www.ohr.int/ohr-dept/presso/pressb/default.asp?content_id=32749.
64. "Decision Enacting the Conclusion Ordering the Auditor General of Republika Srpska to Conduct Special Audits," Office of the High

Representative, December 16, 2004, http://www.ohr.int/decisions/warcrimes-decs/default.asp?content_id=33809.
65 "Decision Enacting the Law on Amendments to the Criminal Procedure Code of Bosnia and Herzegovina," Office of the High Representative, December 16, 2004, http://www.ohr.int/decisions/judicialrdec/default.asp?content_id=33791.
66 "U.S. Press Statement for Joint Press Conference: The U.S. Announces Sanctions against the SDS and PDP," Office of the High Representative, December 16, 2004, http://www.ohr.int/print/?content_id=33755.
67 Ashdown's remarks during his press conference on June 30, 2004 act as an illustration. See "Press Conference 30 June: High Representative Announces Measures against ICTY Obstructionists": "However, it is clear that the very structure of the police in BiH hinders effective action being taken not only against dangerous and influential indicted war criminals, but against high level crime figures more generally, many of whom are abusing their positions in government to steal money from the citizens and taxpayers of the RS and BiH. NATO's Istanbul communiqué specifically mentions this area and calls on BiH to strengthen its police structures in order to join PfP. The Prime Minister and I will give a separate press conference on this on Friday, with the new Chairman of the Police Restructuring Commission that will shortly be established, and EUPM Police Commissioner Carty. But, responding to the Istanbul Summit statement, the remit I will set for the Police Restructuring Commission will now call for the substantial strengthening of state police structures in order to enable us more effectively to catch war criminals. Nothing will be ruled in, and nothing ruled out. But let me underline that our priority will be to ensure that the law-abiding citizens of this country get a police force that is structured in order to serve their interests, not the interests of a corrupt few."
68 "Decision Establishing the Police Restructuring Commission," Office of the High Representative, July 2, 2004, at article 1 (1), http://www.ohr.int/decisions/statemattersdec/default.asp?content_id=32888.
69 See Police Restructuring Commission of Bosnia and Herzegovina, *Final Report on the Work of the Police Restructuring Commission of Bosnia and Herzegovina*, Sarajevo, December 2004, (unpublished). Although recommending that the state of Bosnia and Herzegovina be vested with exclusive competency for all police matters, the report nevertheless recommended the establishment of a decentralized police structure. The proposed structure was composed of a state and local level. The state level would have comprised police agencies with authorities over national, international, and inter-entity matters. The proposed local level would have been composed of local police bodies responsible to prevent, detect, and investigate common crimes, provide rapid intervention, traffic control and safety, crowd control, and public order within local police areas.

Notes to Pages 169–176

70 "Bosnian Serb Leader Resigns," *The Guardian*, December 17, 2004, http://www.guardian.co.uk/world/2004/dec/18/balkans.
71 "Bosnian Serb Officials Quit Over Police Reforms," *Los Angeles Times*, December 19, 2004, http://articles.latimes.com/2004/dec/19/world/fg-bosnia19.

8. The Avalanche

1 Henry A. Kissinger, "The Viet Nam Negotiations," *Foreign Affairs* **47**, no. 2 (January 1969): 214.
2 Shiva P. Pudasaini and Kolumban Hutter, *Avalanche Dynamics: Dynamics of Rapid Flows of Dense Granular Avalanches* (Verlag, Berlin, Heidelberg: Springer, 2007), 72.
3 Ibid., 73–4.
4 Ibid., 74–5.
5 Andrew Mack, "Why Big Nations Lose Small Wars: The Politics of Asymmetric Conflict," *World Politics* **27**, no. 2 (1975): 175–200.
6 Ibid., 177–8.
7 Ivan Areguin-Toft, *How the Weak Win Wars: A Theory of Asymmetric Conflict* (Cambridge: Cambridge University Press, 2005), 200.
8 Ibid., 204–5.
9 Gil Merom, *How Democracies Lose Small Wars* (Cambridge: Cambridge University Press, 2003), 15.
10 Ibid., 19, 21–2. Merom writes: "I submit that modern democracies lose protracted small wars because in situations of deep *instrumental dependence*, the *politically most relevant* citizens create a *normative difference* of insurmountable proportions" (19). Merom recognizes that democratic states can increase their capacity to wage war by adjusting their instrumental dependence on society or by controlling the level of normative difference between the state and the population. They would, however, be unable to effectively affect the political relevance of its citizens without encroaching upon their democratic foundations.
11 Mao Tse-Tung, *On the Protracted War* (Peking: Foreign Language Press, 1954), 39.
12 Michael Hastings, "The Runaway General," *Rolling Stone*, July 8, 2010 (Issue 1108/1109): 90–121.
13 William A. Boettcher and Michael D. Cobb, "Echoes of Vietnam: Casualty Framing and Public Perceptions of Success and Failure in Iraq," *Journal of Conflict Resolution* **50**, no. 6 (December 2006): 832.
14 Ibid., 841 and 848–9.
15 Colonel Charles J. Dunlop, Jr., USAF, "Law and Military Interventions: Preserving Humanitarian Values in 21st Century Conflicts" (Carr Center for Human Rights Policy Working Paper, Harvard Kennedy School Program on National Security and Human Rights, 2001).

16 Ibid., 10–11.
17 Ibid., 5.
18 Mack, "Why Big Nations Lose Small Wars," 187.
19 IFOR troops numbered sixty thousand and were deployed from December 1995 until December 1996. IFOR's replacement, SFOR, was deployed from January 1996 until December 2005. SFOR's initial force was thirty-one thousand troops. Its troops were reduced to nineteen thousand in 2002, twelve thousand by the end of 2004, and seven thousand by the end of 2005; http://www.nato.int/cps/en/natolive/topics_52122.htm; SFOR's replacement, EUFOR, maintained an initial force of seven thousand troops in December 2005. Its force had been reduced to twelve hundred troops by 2012 (http://www.euforbih.org/). NATO remained involved in BiH after the deployment of EUFOR. It provided assistance to BiH authorities regarding the reform of their defense forces. It also maintained responsibilities for a number of operational tasks regarding counterterrorism and the apprehension of persons indicted for war crimes.
20 The United Nations International Police Task Force was established at the end of 1995. By November 1997, it comprised 2,047 civilian police and military liaison personnel. See http://www.un.org/en/peacekeeping/missions/past/unmibh/. The European Union Police Mission (EUPM) deployed from 2003 until 2012. In 2003, EUPM relied on 431 police officers. By the end of the mission in 2012, the number of police officers had been reduced to 13. See www.eupm.org; the EUPM mission was terminated in 2012.
21 Center on International Cooperation, *Review of Political Missions 2011*, New York, 2011, 257, http://cic.nyu.edu/content/review-political-missions-2011; A significant amount of the budget of the OSCE in BiH was reduced from 1999 to 2000 due to a transfer of responsibilities for the organization of elections to BiH authorities. The mission's budget continued to continuously decrease from 2000 to 2010, passing from 49,924,948,50 USD in 2000 to 19,874,725,10 USD in 2010.
22 The number of staff at OSCE BIH passed from 708 in 2002 to 507 in 2010. For OSCE BiH 2002 staff figures, see OSCE, *Financial Report and Financial Statement for the Year Ended 31 December 2002*, available at: www.osce.org. For OSCE BIH 2010 staff figures, see OSCE, *2010 Audited Financial Statements*, available at: www.osce.org
23 For OHR staff and budget figures, see www.ohr.int.
24 Center on International Cooperation, *Review of Political Missions 2011*, 251.
25 Ibid.
26 UN General Assembly, *Resolution 54/245*, A/RES/54/245, February 2, 2000.
27 UN General Assembly, *Resolution 61/285*, A/RES/61/285, August 1, 2007.
28 UN General Assembly, *Resolution 65/300*, A/RES/65/300, September 1, 2011.

Notes to Pages 180–184

29 UN Security Council, *Resolution 1272 (1999)*, S/RES/1272, October 25, 1999. For facts and figures on UNTAET, see: http://www.un.org/en/peacekeeping/missions/past/etimor/etimor.htm.
30 UNMISET was established pursuant to UN Security Council, *Resolution 1410 (2002)*, S/RES/1410, May 17, 2002. The mission's mandate was subsequently extended by UN Security Council, *Resolution 1480 (2003)*, S/RES/1480, May 19, 2003; UN Security Council, *Resolution 1543 (2004)*, S/RES/1543, May 14, 2004; and UN Security Council, *Resolution 1573 (2004)*, S/RES/1573, November 16, 2004.
31 For UNMISET staffing facts and figures, see http://www.un.org/en/peacekeeping/missions/past/unmiset/background.html.
32 Ibid.
33 UNMIT was established pursuant to UN Security Council, *Resolution 1704 (2006)*, S/RES/1704 (2006), August 25, 2006.
34 For UNMIT staffing facts and figures, see www.unmit.org (accessed on June 22, 2012).
35 See, for example, UN Security Council, *Resolution 1704 (2006)*, S/RES/1704, August 25, 2006.
36 See, inter alia, UN Security Council, *Resolution 1802 (2008)*, S/RES/1802, February 25, 2008; UN Security Council, *Resolution 1867 (2009)*, S/RES/1867, February 26, 2009; UN Security Council, *Resolution 1912 (2010)*, S/RES/1912, February 26, 2010; and UN Security Council, *Resolution 1969 (2011)*, S/RES/1969 (2011), February 24, 2011.
37 Kimberly Zisk Marten, *Enforcing the Peace: Learning from the Imperial Past* (New York: Columbia University Press, 2004).
38 Ibid., 17, 93–118, 146–9.
39 *Case U 9/00*, Constitutional Court of Bosnia and Herzegovina, November 3, 2000, at paragraphs 5–6: "The Law on State Border Service was enacted by the High Representative on 13 January 2000 following the failure of the Parliamentary Assembly to adopt a draft law proposed by the Presidency of Bosnia and Herzegovina on 24 November 1999. Taking into account the prevailing situation in Bosnia and Herzegovina, the legal role of the High Representative, as agent of the international community, is not unprecedented, but similar functions are known from other countries in special political circumstances. Pertinent examples are the mandates under the regime of the League of Nations and, in some respect, Germany and Austria after the Second World War. Though recognized as sovereign, the States concerned were placed under international supervision, and foreign authorities acted in these States, on behalf of the international community, substituting themselves for the domestic authorities. Acts by such international authorities were often passed in the name of the States under supervision. Such a situation amounts to a sort of functional duality: an authority of one legal system intervenes in another legal system, thus making its functions dual. The

same holds true for the High Representative: he has been vested with special powers by the international community and his mandate is of an international character. In the present case, the High Representative – whose powers under Annex 10 to the General Framework Agreement, the relevant resolutions of the Security Council and the Bonn Declaration as well as his exercise of those powers are not subject to review by the Constitutional Court – intervened in the legal order of Bosnia and Herzegovina substituting himself for the national authorities. In this respect, he therefore acted as an authority of Bosnia and Herzegovina and the law which he enacted is in the nature of a national law and must be regarded as a law of Bosnia and Herzegovina." The Human Rights Chamber of Bosnia and Herzegovina reached similar conclusions in *Miholič et al.*, Case CH/97/60, 7 December 2001, at par 127–32; The Chamber declared itself incompetent *ratione personae* in relation to individual acts of the High Representative. See additionally Christian Steiner and Nedim Ademović, "Article VI – Constitutional Court of Bosnia and Herzegovina" in *Constitution of Bosnia and Herzegovina: Commentary*, ed. Christian Steiner and Nedim Ademović (Sarajevo: Konrad-Adenauer-Stiftung, 2010), 797–8.

40 See, inter alia, *Case U 41/01*, Constitutional Court of Bosnia and Herzegovina, January 30, 2004, par. 20, www.ccbh.ba.

41 The court indicated, inter alia, that it had competence to review all legal acts in Bosnia and Herzegovina regardless of who adopted them. It also noted that the removal decisions of the High Representative raised possible violations of fundamental rights and freedoms protected by the constitution. The court nevertheless rejected the cases as inadmissible for procedural reasons. See *AP 777/04*, Constitutional Court of Bosnia and Herzegovina, September 29, 2004, par. 7–8; See also *AP 759/04*, Constitutional Court of Bosnia and Herzegovina, September 29, 2004; *AP 784/04*, Constitutional Court of Bosnia and Herzegovina, September 29, 2004; *AP 347/04*, Constitutional Court of Bosnia and Herzegovina, November 30, 2004, and *AP 905/04*, Constitutional Court of Bosnia and Herzegovina, November 30, 2004 available at: www.ccbh.ba. See additionally Steiner and Ademović, "Article VI – Constitutional Court of Bosnia and Herzegovina," 799–803.

42 The decision of the High Representative removed Milorad Bilbija from his position as deputy head of the Administration of the Intelligence and Security Agency in Banja Luka. See "Decision Removing Milorad Bilbija from his Position of Deputy Head Operative Administration of the Intelligence and Security Agency in Banja Luka and from other Public and Party Positions he Currently Holds," Office of the High Representative, December 16, 2004, www.ohr.com. Dragan Kalinić was removed from his position as chairman of the Republika Srpska National Assembly and from his position as president of the SDS; "Decision Removing Dr. Dragan Kalinić from his Positions as Chairman of the National Assembly of Republika Srpska and as President

of the SDS," Office of the High Representative, June 29, 2004. Both decisions further barred Bilbija and Kalinić from standing for elections and holding public office.

43 See *Case AP 953/05*, Constitutional Court of Bosnia and Herzegovina, July 8, 2006, www.ccbh.ba. The court concluded that the appellants' right to a legal remedy had been violated and that Bosnia and Herzegovina had failed to comply with its obligation to protect their constitutional rights. The court's decision noted that there was no effective legal remedy against decisions of the High Representative affecting individual rights in the legal system of Bosnia and Herzegovina. It concluded that Bosnia and Herzegovina had failed to undertake any activities to secure such a remedy.

44 "Order on the Implementation of the Decision of the Constitutional Court of Bosnia and Herzegovina in the Appeal of Milorad Bilbija et al, No. AP-953/05," Office of the High Representative, March 23, 2007. The order stipulated: "Article 1: In order to implement the Decision of the Court, the Presidency of Bosnia and Herzegovina shall address to the High Representative, as Chair of the Steering Board of the Peace Implementation Council, all matters raised in said Decision that ought to be considered by the international authorities referenced in the said Decision. Article 2: Any step taken by any institution or authority in Bosnia and Herzegovina in order to establish any domestic mechanism to review the Decisions of the High Representative issued pursuant to his international mandate shall be considered by the High Representative as an attempt to undermine the implementation of the civilian aspects of the General Framework Agreement for Peace in Bosnia and Herzegovina and shall be treated in itself as conduct undermining such implementation. Article 3: Notwithstanding any contrary provision in any legislation in Bosnia and Herzegovina, any proceeding instituted before any court in Bosnia and Herzegovina, which challenges or takes issue in any way whatsoever with one or more decisions of the High Representative, shall be declared inadmissible unless the High Representative expressly gives his prior consent. Any proceeding referred to in Paragraph 1 of this Article shall be effectively and formally notified to the High Representative by the concerned court without delay. For the avoidance of any doubt or ambiguity, and taking into account the totality of the matters aforesaid, it is hereby specifically ordered and determined, in the exercise of the said international mandate of the High Representative and pursuant to its interpretation hereinunder and by virtue of the said Annex 10, that no liability is capable of being incurred on the part of the Institutions of Bosnia and Herzegovina, and/or any of its subdivisions and/or any other authority in Bosnia and Herzegovina, in respect of any loss or damage allegedly flowing, either directly or indirectly, from such Decision of the High Representative made pursuant to his or her international mandate, or at all. Article 4: For the avoidance of doubt, it is hereby specifically declared and provided that the provisions of the Order contained herein

are, as to each and every one of them, laid down by the High Representative pursuant to his international mandate and are not, therefore, justiciable by the Courts of Bosnia and Herzegovina or its Entities or elsewhere, and no proceedings may be brought in respect of duties in respect thereof before any court whatsoever at any time hereafter. Article 5: This Order shall enter into force immediately and shall be published without delay in the Official Gazette of Bosnia and Herzegovina, the Official Gazette of the Brcko District of Bosnia and Herzegovina, the Official Gazette of the Federation of Bosnia and Herzegovina and the Official Gazette of Republika Srpska."

45 In an opinion issued in 2005, the Venice Commission had considered, for example, that neither Bosnian courts nor any other BiH authorities were competent to review or reverse decisions taken by the United Nations regarding the certification of police officers in BiH. The commission considered that such decisions had to be reviewed by the United Nations. See European Commission for Democracy through Law, *Opinion on a Possible Solution to the Issue of Decertification of Police Officers in Bosnia and Herzegovina*, CDL-AD (2005)024, Venice, Italy, October 21–2, 2005, par. 61–2, www.venice.coe.int. The commission reached similar views in another opinion issued in 2005 in which it examined the powers of the High Representative. The commission observed that the practice by which the High Representative removed officials from public office did not correspond to democratic principles when exercised without due process and the possibility of judicial control. While understandable in an immediate postwar period, its justification became more questionable over time, according to the commission. Its opinion called for a progressive phasing out of these powers and for the establishment of an advisory panel of independent lawyers regarding such decisions until the authorities of the High Representative were transferred to domestic institutions. See European Commission for Democracy through Law, *Opinion on the Constitutional Situation in Bosnia and Herzegovina and the Powers of the High Representative*, CDL-AD (2005)004, Venice, Italy, March 11–12, 2005, par. 92–100, www.venice.coe.int.

46 See App. Nos. 36357/04, 36360/04, 38346/04, 41705/04, 45190/04, 45578/04, 45579/04, 45580/04, 91/05, 97/05, 100/05, 101/05, 1121/05, 1123/05, 1125/05, 1129/05, 1132/05, 1133/05, 1169/05, 1172/05, 1175/05, 1177/05, 1180/05, 1185/05, 20793/05, and 25496/05, *Berić and Others v. Bosnia and Herzegovina*, European Court of Human Rights, October 16, 2007, par. 28; available at www.echr.coe.int. The court held, inter alia: "Contrary to the applicants' submissions, a decision by the Constitutional Court of Bosnia and Herzegovina (or, indeed, any authorities of the host State) which seeks to establish a review mechanism in respect of the acts of the High Representative cannot change the legal nature of those acts, unless the High Representative consents to such changes (as he had done in the past in respect of legislation imposed by him)."

47 See *Case AP 953/05*, Constitutional Court of Bosnia and Herzegovina, par. 73. The court noted that: "Bosnia and Herzegovina, through the Steering Board of the Peace Implementation Council and the Security Council of the United Nations, a body in charge of nominating and confirming the appointment of the High Representative, was obliged to make an effort in pointing to the alleged violations of constitutional rights of individual rights on the ground of lack of an effective legal remedy and thus ensure the protection of constitutional rights of its citizens."

48 Although the provisions of the European Convention for the Protection of Human Rights and Fundamental Freedoms and those of its protocols are directly applicable and have priority over all other law in BiH pursuant to Article II (2) of Bosnia's constitution, the jurisdiction of the European Court for Human Rights over cases concerning Bosnia and Herzegovina became effective after Bosnia's ratification of the European Convention in July 2002.

49 The government of the United Kingdom also intervened in this case.

50 The court considered that the High Representative was exercising "lawfully delegated UNSC Chapter VII powers." Following positions taken in an earlier case, the court further argued that the European Convention could not be interpreted in a way that subjected acts and omissions taken pursuant to such powers to the scrutiny of the European Court. Such scrutiny would, in the opinion of the court, interfere with the fulfillment of the United Nations' key mission. See App. Nos. 36357/04, 36360/04, 38346/04, 41705/04, 45190/04, 45578/04, 45579/04, 45580/04, 91/05, 97/05, 100/05, 101/05, 1121/05, 1123/05, 1125/05, 1129/05, 1132/05, 1133/05, 1169/05, 1172/05, 1175/05, 1177/05, 1180/05, 1185/05, 20793/05, and 25496/05, *Berić and Others v. Bosnia and Herzegovina*, European Court of Human Rights, October 16, 2007, par. 29–30. See also the court's similar reasoning in relation to complaints against states participating in the NATO-led force in Kosovo (KFOR) under UN Security Council *Resolution 1244 (1999)*. See App. Nos. 71412/01 and 78166/01, *Behrami and Behrami v. France*, and *Saramati v. France, Germany and Norway*, European Court of Human Rights, May 5, 2007, available at www.echr.coe.int.

51 See App Nos. 45541/04 and 16587/07, *Dragan Kalinic and Milorad Bilbija v. Bosnia and Herzegovina*, European Court of Human Rights, May 13, 2008, www.echr.coe.int. The court held: "The Court recalls that removals from office ordered by the High Representative pursuant to his 'Bonn powers' are, in principle, attributable to the United Nations and that Bosnia and Herzegovina could not be held responsible for such removals.... The applicants' complaints concerning the decisions of 29 June 2004 and 16 December 2004 must accordingly be declared incompatible *ratione personae* within the meaning of Article 35 § 3 of the Convention. Notwithstanding the fact that the decision of 23 March 2007 did not concern removals from office

directly, but prevented the introduction of an effective remedy with regard to such removals into the legal system of Bosnia and Herzegovina, the Court considers that the reasoning outlined in *Berić and Others* (cited above) also applies to that decision. The applicants' complaints concerning the decision of 23 March 2007 must likewise be declared incompatible *ratione personae* within the meaning of Article 35 § 3 of the Convention."

52 "Decision to Remove Radomir Lukić from His Position as Member of the Main Board of the SDS and from Other Public and Party Positions," Office of the High Representative, June 30, 2004, http://www.ohr.int/decisions/war-crimes-decs/default.asp?content_id=32797.

53 "Decision Removing Mr. Milovan R. Pecelj from his Position as Minister of Education and Culture of Republika Srpska," Office of the High Representative, October 28, 2005, http://www.ohr.int/decisions/removalss-dec/default.asp?content_id=35815.

54 John Laughland, "UN Tyranny in Bosnia," *The Spectator*, May 5, 2001.

55 Gerhard Knaus and Felix Martin, "Travails of the European Raj," *Journal of Democracy* **14**, no. 3 (July 2003): 61.

56 Ibid.

57 Ibid.

58 Ian Bancroft, "An Unhealthy State," *The Guardian*, November 26, 2007.

59 David Chandler, "The High Representative for Bosnia Still Runs it Like a Feudal Kingdom," *The Guardian*, November 19, 2007, www.guardian.co.uk.

60 On differences between peacekeeping and colonialism, see Marten, *Enforcing the Peace*, 7 and 61–4.

61 See www.bihdaytonproject.com.

62 EU official. Interview by author, 2011.

63 See, inter alia, Milorad Dodik, Prime Minister of Republika Srpska, letter to H.E. Ambassador Thomas Mayr-Harting, President of the United Nations Security Council, 04/1–2229/09, November 16, 2009, www.vladars.net; Prime Minister Milorad Dodik's letter of November 16, 2009 summarized the content of the RS government's November 2009 report as follows: "the significant political progress that has been made this year in BiH by BiH's elected officials. The Report also takes note of the conclusions of experts that there is no threat to international peace and security in BiH. Next, the Report explains how progress in BiH has been hindered by serious heightened intervention of the High Representative and certain States into internal BiH affairs. The Report then describes the relevant law, including that which applies to the Peace implementation Council and the High Representative, and the need for adherence to the law and a mechanism for redress when breached. Finally, the Report outlines the Government's response to the High Representative's unlawful actions and the Government's commitment and program for achieving EU integration and constitutional reform. The

Notes to Pages 193–197

Government believes firmly that, in the absence of unlawful international interference, BiH's elected leaders can accelerate political progress and build a better future for BiH." See also Government of Republika Srpska, *Republika Srpska's Seventh Report to the UN Security Council*, May 2012, www.vladars.net.

64 Srecko Latal, "Bosnian Serbs Called Off from NATO Drill," *Balkan Insight*, May 8, 2009, http://www.balkaninsight.com/en/article/bosnian-serbs-called-off-from-nato-drill.

65 Ratka Babic, "Bosnia Serbs Will Call Referendum on NATO," *Balkan Insight*, February 12, 2013, http://www.balkaninsight.com/en/article/bosnia-serb-leader-announces-referendum-over-nato.

66 See UN Security Council, *Report of the United Nations Security Council 6,659th Meeting (The Situation in Bosnia and Herzegovina)*, S/PV.6659, November 15, 2011.

67 Ibid.

68 Ibid.

69 Ibid. The representative of the European Union indicated, inter alia: "As regards to its overall strategy for Bosnia and Herzegovina, the European Union looks forward to the discussions with the international community on the reconfiguration of the international presence, including its downsizing and the possible relocation of the Office of the High Representative in the appropriate forum. The European Union regularly encourages Bosnia and Herzegovina's political representatives to act with a greater spirit of compromise, to step up consultations and to work for the long-term interests of the country. We also stand fully behind the authority of the High Representative and welcome the close cooperation between him and the new European Union Special Representative."

70 Council of the European Union, *Council Conclusions on Bosnia and Herzegovina: Extract from 3,078th Council Meeting (Foreign Affairs)*, Brussels, Belgium, March 21, 2011, https://www.consilium.europa.eu/uedocs/cms_data/docs/missionPress/files/BosnieHEN210311.pdf.

71 French Foreign Affairs Minister Alain Juppé and German Foreign Affairs Minister Guido Westerwelle, letter to EU High Representative for Foreign Affairs and Security Policy Catherine Ashton, August 26, 2011.

72 Ibid.

73 Reflecting on his work in Bosnia several years later, Ashdown reflected on the difficulty engendered by this dissonance: "One of the most frightening aspects of my job was that, in order to get things moving, I often had to challenge the opinions of elected representatives – and sometimes use my powers to overrule them.... This is, on the face of it, an undemocratic thing to do.... It is also a very scary thing to do. Because, when a politician representing an ethnic interest threatened that his people would be out on the streets if we did X, we had to have sufficient confidence in our own judgment about what

the people of Bosnia really wanted, or at least were prepared to tolerate, to be able to push ahead nevertheless." See Paddy Ashdown, *A Fortunate Life* (London: Aurum, 2009), 352–3.

9. Looking Forward

1 Author's translation. The original text in French reads: "Il en est des systèmes de guerre comme des sièges de place, il faut réunir ses feux contre un seul point. La brèche faite, l'équilibre est rompu, tout le reste devient inutile." Taken from Napoléon's report of July 19, 1794 to Augustin Robespierre, representative of the French people to the army in Italy, quoted in Hubert. Camon, *La guerre Napoléonienne: Les systèmes d'opérations théorie et technique* (Paris: Economica, 1997), 25.
2 See inter alia UN Security Council, *Resolution 2019 (2011)*, S/RES/2019, November 16, 2011.
3 Donella Meadows suggests that systems always surprise us because they always fall short of representing the world fully. She notes: "Everything we think we know about the world is a model. Every word and every language is a model. All maps and statistics, books and databases, equations and computer programs are models.... Our models usually have a strong congruence with the world.... However, and conversely, our models fall short of representing the world fully. That is why we make mistakes and why we are regularly surprised." See Donella H. Meadows, *Thinking in Systems: A Primer* (White River Junction, VT: Chelsea Green Publishing, 2008), 86.
4 Declan Walsh, "US Had 'Frighteningly Simplistic' View of Afghanistan, Says McChrystal," *The Guardian*, October 7, 2011, http://www.guardian.co.uk/world/2011/oct/07/us-frighteningly-simplistic-afghanistan-mcchrystal.
5 See, inter alia, Edgar Morin, *Introduction à la pensée complexe* (Paris: Éditions du Seuil, 2005). See also Edgar Morin, *On Complexity* (Cresskill, NJ: Hampton Press, 2008). On Morin's reflections regarding humans' knowledge of knowledge, see Edgar Morin, *La Connaissance de la connaissance: Livre premier, anthropologie de la connaissance* (Paris: Éditions du Seuil, 1986).
6 Morin, *On Complexity*, 6.
7 Rory Stewart and Gerald Knaus, *Can Intervention Work?* (New York: W. W. Norton & Company, 2011), xix and xx.
8 The introduction to their work concludes by noting: "these essays aim to offer not an anthropology of the country into which the West is intervening, but an anthropology of the West – an anthropology of ourselves." See ibid., xxvi.
9 The phrase appears in Abraham Lincoln's letter of April 4, 1864 to Albert G. Hodges. See Abraham Lincoln, *The Collected Works of Abraham Lincoln*, Vol. VII, ed. Roy P. Basler (New Brunswick, NJ: Rutgers University Press, 1953), 282–3.

Notes to Pages 202–204

10 Morin, *On Complexity*, 54–7.
11 On complexity theory and systems thinking see, inter alia, Meadows, *Thinking in Systems*; Morin, *On Complexity*; Morin, *Introduction à la pensée complexe*; Robert Jervis, *Complexity in Political and Social Life* (Princeton, NJ: Princeton University Press, 1997); Stuart Kauffman, *At Home in the Universe: The Search for Laws of Self-Organization and Complexity* (New York & Oxford: Oxford University Press, 1995); Jack Snyder and Robert Jervis, ed. *Coping with Complexity in the International System* (Boulder, CO: Westview Press, 1993); Roger Lewin, *Complexity: Life at the Edge of Chaos* (New York: Collier Books/Macmillan Publishing Company, 1992).
12 The UN secretariat had proposed to reconfigure UNMIK to take account of the new realities set by Kosovo's declaration of independence. According to the secretary-general's proposal, the reconfigured UNMIK was to retain responsibilities for facilitating practical arrangements between Serbia and Kosovo in six main areas (namely police, customs, justice, transportation, boundaries, and Serbian patrimony). This proposal became known as the "six-point plan." Kosovo finally consented to the deployment of EULEX. However, Kosovo insisted that the report of the UN secretary-general recommending the reconfiguration of UNMIK include an annex that explicitly registered its rejection of the six-point plan and that asserted the sovereignty and territorial integrity of Kosovo. See UN Security Council, *Report of the Secretary General on the United Nations Interim Administration in Kosovo*, S/2008/692, November 24, 2008, http://daccess-dds-ny.un.org/doc/UNDOC/GEN/N08/518/31/PDF/N0851831.pdf?OpenElement, in Annex 1. The text of the statement reproduced in Annex 1 of the report reads as follows:

1. We are in favour of a quick deployment of EULEX in Kosovo in accordance with the mandate foreseen in the Declaration of Independence, the Comprehensive Proposal for a Kosovo Status Settlement, the Constitution of the Republic of Kosovo, Kosovo legislation, the European Union Joint Action of 4 February 2008 and Kosovo's institutions' invitation to EULEX.
2. Kosovo's institutions reject the whole six-point document.
3. Kosovo's institutions will cooperate with EULEX on its deployment throughout the entire territory of Kosovo, based on the mandate foreseen in the documents mentioned in (1) above, respecting the sovereignty and territorial integrity of the Republic of Kosovo.
4. The institutions of the Republic of Kosovo will, as always, continue the close cooperation with the United States, the European Union and NATO.

13 On conflict mapping and systems mapping see, inter alia, Matthew Levinger, *Conflict Analysis: Understanding Causes, Unlocking Solutions* (Washington, DC: United States Institute of Peace Press, 2013), 135–46.

14. Kimberly Zisk Marten, *Enforcing the Peace: Learning from the Imperial Past* (New York: Columbia University Press, 2004), 157.
15. Ibid.
16. Ibid., 156.
17. Roland Paris, *At War's End: Building Peace after Civil Conflict* (Cambridge: Cambridge University Press, 2004), ix and 179–211.
18. See, inter alia, ibid., 179.
19. Ibid., 191.
20. Ibid., 199–205.
21. Ibid., 191.
22. Thomas Harding, "NATO Moves to Thwart Taliban Infiltration of Afghan Police and Army," *The Telegraph*, August 16, 2012, http://www.telegraph.co.uk/news/worldnews/asia/afghanistan/9480307/Nato-moves-to-thwart-Taliban-infiltration-of-Afghan-police-and-army.html. See also Richard A. Oppel and Graham Bowley, "Attacks on Afghan Troops by Colleagues are Rising, Allies Say," *New York Times*, August 23, 2012, http://www.nytimes.com/2012/08/24/world/asia/afghan-troops-killing-colleagues-in-greater-numbers.html?pagewanted=all.
23. Address by Milorad Dodik, President of Republika Srpska, during 4th Special Session of the Republika Srpska National Assembly, April 13, 2011, http://predsjednikrs.net/index.php?option=com_content&view=article&id=8128%3A – – 4 – – &Itemid=144&lang=en.
24. Republika Srpska National Assembly, *Decision to Announce the RS Entity-Wide Referendum* (O.G. Republika Srpska no. 45/11), April 13, 2011, http://www.narodnaskupstinars.net/. See also "Bosnia: State Institutions under Attack: Europe Briefing No. 62." *International Crisis Group*, 3.
25. See UNMIK, *The Kosovo Status Process 2003–2007*, UNMIK/StratCo 070420 http://www.unmikonline.org/standards/docs/KSP2003-2007.pdf.
26. "Collapse in Kosovo: Europe Report No. 155," International Crisis Group, April 22, 2004, p. 1. http://www.crisisgroup.org/~/media/Files/europe/155_collapse_in_kosovo_revised.ashx.
27. See par. 13 of *Report of the Panel on United Nations Peace Operations*, A/55/305 – S/2000/809, August 17, 2000, http://www.un.org/peace/reports/peace_operations/.
28. Ibid., par. 14.
29. See, inter alia, Mark Lowen, "Kosovo Tense after Deadly Clash on Serbian Border," *BBC News*, July 26, 2011, http://www.bbc.co.uk/news/world-europe-14303165.
30. See Rupert Smith, *The Utility of Force: The Art of War in the Modern World* (London: Penguin-Allen Lane, 2005), 270.
31. Carl von Clausewitz, *On War* (Princeton, NJ: Princeton University Press, 1976), 605.

32 See Monica Duffy Toft, *Securing the Peace: The Durable Settlement of Civil Wars* (Princeton, NJ & Oxford: Princeton University Press, 2010), 1–18 and 53–8. On the basis of her empirical findings, Duffy Toft recommends the adoption of hybrid strategies that build on the strengths of negotiated settlements and military victories to end civil wars more effectively (4). See also Monica Toft, "Peace through Security: Making Negotiated Settlements Stick," Working Paper no. 23, Research Group in International Security, November 2006, http://www.cepsi.umontreal.ca/uploads/gersi_publications.filename/CIPSS_WorkingPaper_23.pdf.

33 Andrew Radin, "The Limits of State Building: The Politics of War and the Ideology of Peace," Massachusetts Institute of Technology, June 2012 (unpublished thesis).

34 Some scholars have suggested the existence of similar self-reinforcing loops in other phases of ethnic conflict. Scholar Barry Posen has argued, for example, that the concept of *security dilemma* can be applied to ethnic conflict. As security collapses, groups compete to ensure their respective security. As one group amasses power to ensure its own security, it ignites counter-actions from other groups, which will seek to amass more power to ensure their own security. See Barry R. Posen, "The Security Dilemma and Ethnic Conflict," *Survival* 35, no. 1 (1993): 27–47. See also Jack Snyder and Robert Jervis, "Civil Wars and the Security Dilemma," in *Civil Wars, Insecurity, and Intervention*, ed. Barbara F. Walter and Jack Snyder (New York: Columbia University Press, 1999): 15–37.

35 Ethnic conflict is shaped by systemic factors. Donald Horowitz distinguishes between two main types of ethnic systems: *ranked* and *unranked* systems, for example. *Ranked* systems are those in which one ethnic group is subordinated to another such as the relationships between Tutsis and Hutus in Rwanda. On the other hand, *unranked* systems are systems in which no group is definitely ranked vis-à-vis another. Horowitz's basic distinction allows one to better predict the type of conflict that may emerge between ethnic groups. Because ethnic boundaries tend to follow class boundaries in ranked systems, conflict will tend to take the form of a social revolution in ranked systems. On the other hand, conflict in unranked systems (such as Bosnia) resembles that between states on the international plane. There is often no sufficient authority to stabilize the elements within unranked systems. There will thus be a constant competition for power and a constant fear of seeing opponents gain power. Unranked systems consequently contribute to protracted conflicts over power. See Donald L. Horowitz, *Ethnic Groups in Conflict* (Berkeley & Los Angeles: University of California Press, 1985), 21–4 and 30–2.

36 There seems to be a consensus amongst scholars that electoral engineering shapes political behavior. There is, however, disagreement as to the types of electoral systems that are most suited for divided environments. Two

predominant schools of thought – *consociationalism* and *centripetalism* – seem to have emerged. Consociationalism, often associated with scholar Arend Lijphart, argues that, for democracy to work in divided societies, such societies should develop elite power-sharing arrangements such as coalition governments, proportional representation in the legislature and civil service, federal arrangements over power, and veto power for minority groups over important decisions. On the other hand, centripetalists, often associated with scholar Donald Horowitz, argue that the best way to mitigate the negative forces of ethnic confrontation is to design electoral systems that encourage cooperation amongst groups. See Benjamin Reilly, *Democracy in Divided Societies: Electoral Engineering for Conflict Management* (Cambridge: Cambridge University Press, 2001), 20–1. The experience in Bosnia and Herzegovina suggests that interveners ought to consider centripetal electoral systems in contexts of ethnic or national divisions. These electoral systems can coexist with some of the federal arrangements and minority protection mechanisms advocated by consociationalism. On the suitability of centripetal electoral incentives for divided societies, see Reilly, *Democracy in Divided Societies*, 167–93. See also Paris, *At War's End*, 191–4; Donald L. Horowitz, "Constitutional Design: Proposals Versus Processes," in *The Architecture of Democracy: Constitutional Design, Conflict Management and Democracy*, ed. Andrew Reynolds (Oxford University Press: Oxford, 2002), 23–4; Donald Horowitz, "Making Moderation Pay: The Comparative Politics of Ethnic Conflict Management," in *Conflict and Peacemaking in Multiethnic Societies*, ed. Joseph V. Montville (Toronto: Lexington Books, 1990), 451–75. On consociationalism, see, inter alia, Arend Lijphart, *Democracy in Plural Societies: A Comparative Exploration* (New Haven, CT: Yale University Press, 1977).

37 Reilly, *Democracy in Divided Societies*, 167–71.
38 In Australia, when voting for candidates for the House of Representatives in a given district, voters are required to rank all candidates running in their electoral district. To be elected, a candidate must secure more than half of the votes cast. In the event that no candidate can secure a majority through first preference votes, the candidate with the fewest votes is excluded and his or her votes are transferred to the other candidates according to the second preferences indicated on each ballot – a process that continues until a given candidate can secure a majority of votes. The electoral system encourages moderation and compromise by attributing value to votes cast by secondary or tertiary groups of support. See Reilly, *Democracy in Divided Societies*, 18–19.
39 Looking back at the implementation process in Bosnia and Herzegovina, former High Representative Paddy Ashdown noted: "There are not many really golden rules in peacemaking and post-conflict reconstruction. But one is that these operations have a much greater chance of success if the neighboring countries constructively participate in the process. We began to succeed in Bosnia, only after Zagreb and later Belgrade shifted from wreckers

to helpers in the process." See Paddy Ashdown, *Swords and Ploughshares: Bringing Peace to the 21st Century* (London: Weidenfeld & Nicolson, 2007), 139–40.

40 UNMIK's establishment of a human rights advisory panel is an example of a step in that direction.

41 After having registered and reviewed the background of law enforcement officials in Bosnia, the UN International Police Task Force had denied several hundred of them the right to work as law enforcement officials in Bosnia. Pursuant to agreements reached between the UN and Bosnian authorities, the employment of persons who had been denied certification by the UN had to be terminated by the competent domestic authorities. The United Nations Mission in Bosnia and Herzegovina nevertheless failed to secure a clear legal basis in Bosnia's domestic legal sphere for Bosnian authorities to implement its decision. Within weeks of the UN's departure from Bosnia, hundreds of local administrative decisions that purported to terminate the employment of decertified police officials were challenged before domestic judicial authorities for lack of a legal basis. On the issue of decertification of police officers by the United Nations in Bosnia, see Venice Commission, *Opinion on a Possible Solution to the Issue of Decertification of Police Officers in Bosnia and Herzegovina*, Opinion no. 326 / 2004, CDL-AD(2005)024, October 24, 2005, http://www.securitycouncilreport.org/atf/cf/%7B65BFCF9B-6D27-4E9C-8CD3-CF6E4FF96FF9%7D/Venice%20Commission.pdf. See also European Stability Initiative, *On Mount Olympus: How the UN Violated Human Rights in Bosnia and Herzegovina, and Why Nothing has Been Done to Correct It*, February 10, 2007, http://www.esiweb.org/pdf/esi_document_id_84.pdf.

42 See, for example, Articles 146, 147, and 153 of the transitional provisions of the Constitution of the Republic of Kosovo adopted in 2008. The provisions provided:

> Article 146
>
> Notwithstanding any provision of this Constitution:
> 1. The International Civilian Representative and other international organizations and actors mandated under the Comprehensive Proposal for the Kosovo Status Settlement dated 26 March 2007 have the mandate and powers set forth under the said Comprehensive Proposal, including the legal capacity and privileges and immunities set forth therein.
> 2. All authorities in the Republic of Kosovo shall cooperate fully with the International Civilian Representative, other international organizations and actors mandated under the Comprehensive Proposal for the Kosovo Status Settlement dated 26 March 2007 and shall, inter alia, give effect to their decisions or acts.
>
> Article 147
>
> Notwithstanding any provision of this Constitution, the International Civilian Representative shall, in accordance with the Comprehensive Proposal for

the Kosovo Status Settlement dated 26 March 2007, be the final authority in Kosovo regarding interpretation of the civilian aspects of the said Comprehensive Proposal. No Republic of Kosovo authority shall have jurisdiction to review, diminish or otherwise restrict the mandate, powers and obligations referred to in Article 146 and this Article.

Article 153

Notwithstanding any provision of this Constitution, the International Military Presence has the mandate and powers set forth under the relevant international instruments including United Nations Security Council Resolution 1244 and the Comprehensive Proposal for the Kosovo Status Settlement dated 26 March 2007. The Head of the International Military Presence shall, in accordance with the Comprehensive Proposal for the Kosovo Status Settlement dated 26 March 2007, be the final authority in theatre regarding interpretation of those aspects of the said Settlement that refer to the International Military Presence. No Republic of Kosovo authority shall have jurisdiction to review, diminish or otherwise restrict the mandate, powers and obligations referred to in this Article.

43 The criteria commonly referred to as the "Copenhagen criteria" were stipulated by the European Council during its June 1993 session held in Copenhagen. See European Council, *Conclusions of the Presidency*, SN 180/1/93 REV 1, Copenhagen, Denmark, June 21–2, 1993, http://www.consilium.europa.eu/uedocs/cms_data/docs/pressdata/en/ec/72921.pdf; Section 7 (a) iii) of the conclusions of European Council stipulates, inter alia:

The European Council today agreed that the associated countries in Central and Eastern Europe that so desire shall become members of the European Union. Accession will take place as soon as an associated country is able to assume the obligations of membership by satisfying the economic and political conditions required. Membership requires that the candidate country has achieved stability of institutions guaranteeing democracy, the rule of law, human rights and respect for and protection of minorities, the existence of a functioning market economy as well as the capacity to cope with competitive pressure and market forces within the Union. Membership presupposes the candidate's ability to take on the obligations of membership including adherence to the aims of political, economic and monetary union.

44 Ibid.
45 Stewart and Knaus, *Can Intervention Work?* 191.
46 Robert, Cooper, Counsellor to EU High Representative for Foreign Affairs and Security Policy. Interview by author, Brussels, October 18, 2011.
47 European Commission, *Communication from the Commission to the European Parliament and the Council: Enlargement Strategy and Main Challenges 2012–2013*, October 10, 2012, p. 15, http://ec.europa.eu/enlargement/pdf/key_documents/2012/package/strategy_paper_2012_en.pdf.

48 Ratka Babic, "Bosnia Serbs Will Call Referendum on NATO," *Balkan Insight*, February 12, 2013, http://www.balkaninsight.com/en/article/bosnia-serb-leader-announces-referendum-over-nato.
49 EU official. Interview by author, 2011.
50 Joseph Nye, *Soft Power: The Means to Success in World Politics* (New York: Public Affairs, 2004), 7–9.
51 While some of the past conclusions of the Council and the European Council have alluded to Bosnia and Herzegovina's territorial integrity and the efficiency of its state institutions, they have so far fallen short of incorporating them into a clear and specific set of conditions for Bosnia's eligibility. See Council of the European Union, *Council Conclusions on Enlargement and Stabilisation and Association Process: 3,210th General Affairs Council Meeting*, December 11, 2012, http://www.consilium.europa.eu/uedocs/cms_data/docs/pressdata/EN/genaff/134234.pdf; Paragraph 50 of the Council's conclusions stipulates: "The Council reiterates its unequivocal support for Bosnia and Herzegovina's EU perspective as a sovereign and united country enjoying full territorial integrity." The Council's conclusions were subsequently endorsed by the European Council. See European Council, *Conclusions: 13/14 December 2012*, December 14, 2012, par. 27, http://www.consilium.europa.eu/uedocs/cms_data/docs/pressdata/en/ec/134353.pdf; See also Council of the European Union, *Council Conclusions on Bosnia and Herzegovina: Extract from 3,078th Council Meeting (Foreign Affairs)*, March 21, 2011, https://www.consilium.europa.eu/uedocs/cms_data/docs/missionPress/files/BosnieHEN210311.pdf; Paragraph 1 of the conclusions provides that: "The Council reaffirms its unequivocal commitment to the territorial integrity of Bosnia and Herzegovina as a sovereign and united country." Paragraph 3 stipulates: "The Council stresses the importance of improving and strengthening the efficient functioning of the state and the institutions, including through necessary constitutional changes. In particular, the country will need to be in a position to adopt, implement and enforce laws and rules of the EU."

Epilogue

1 In the fall of 1993, Bosnian authorities tried to arrest Topalović. During his arrest, Topalović was shot and died under unclear circumstances. On Divjak's communication with Izetbegović regarding Topalović, see Jovan Divjak, *Sarajevo mon amour: Entretiens avec Florence La Bruyère* (Paris: Buchet/Chastel, 2004), 228–9.
2 Ibid., 231.
3 Ibid., 233.
4 Ibid., 277–80.
5 See Laura Silber and Allan Little, *The Death of Yugoslavia* (New York: Penguin Books, 1995), 232.

6. See Canadian General MacKenzie's account of the agreement in Lewis MacKenzie, *Peacekeeper: The Road to Sarajevo* (Vancouver/Toronto: Douglas&McIntyre, 1993), 166.
7. Norma Percy, dir. *The Death of Yugoslavia [Part 4 – The Gates of Hell]* (London: British Broadcasting Corporation, 1995) TV Documentary, at around forty-four minutes.
8. Silber and Little, *The Death of Yugoslavia*, 241; See also MacKenzie, *Peacekeeper: The Road to Sarajevo*, 166–7.
9. Damien McElroy, "Extradition of Former Bosnian President Ejup Ganic Thrown Out," *The Telegraph*, July 27, 2012, http://www.telegraph.co.uk/news/worldnews/europe/bosnia/7913326/Extradition-of-former-Bosnian-president-Ejup-Ganic-thrown-out.html.
10. See *The Government of the Republic of Serbia v. Ejup Ganic*, City of Westminster Magistrates' Court, Judge Tim Workman, July 27, 2010, http://www.judiciary.gov.uk/NR/rdonlyres/63FBA6BB-59F4-4BAF-BA78-95FED04AAEC2/0/serbiavganic27072010.pdf.
11. Piotr Smolar, "Divjak, héros à Sarajevo, criminel pour la Serbie," *Le Monde*, March 10, 2011, 9.
12. Ibid. See also Georhe Jahn, "Austria Detains Ex-Bosnian General on Serb Warrant," *Washington Post*, March 4, 2011, http://www.washingtonpost.com/wp-dyn/content/article/2011/03/04/AR2011030401384.html. See also "Austria Holds Ex-Bosnia General Divjak on Serb Warrant," *BBC News*, March 4, 2011, http://www.bbc.co.uk/news/world-europe-12654192.
13. See Antoine Garapon et al., "Lettre ouverte au gouvernement autrichien," *Le Monde*, July 7, 2011, http://www.lemonde.fr/idees/article/2011/07/07/lettre-ouverte-au-gouvernement autrichien_1545827_3232.html?xtmc=divjak&xtcr=1.
14. Translation from the author. See original text in French. Agnes b. et al., "Jovan Divjak et l'honneur de l'Europe," *Le Monde*, March 3, 2011, http://www.lemonde.fr/idees/article/2011/03/11/jovan-divjak-derriere-des-barreaux-de-prison_1491483_3232.html.
15. "Bosnian War General Faces Austrian Extradition," *Agence France Press*, March 4, 2011, http://www.google.com/hostednews/afp/article/ALeqM5gd9_yQ1ETJFV1i01zRQhHD74waxA?docId=CNG.0dc8667c1044e69c192df3be444c31bf.941.
16. Edin Hadzovic, "Austria Refuses to Extradite Divjak to Serbia," *Balkan Insight*, July 29, 2011, http://www.balkaninsight.com/en/article/jovan-divjak-released-by-austrian-court; See also Edin Hadzovic, "Return of Freed General Divides Bosnia," *Balkan Insight*, July 29, 2011, http://www.balkaninsight.com/en/article/jovan-divjak-to-be-welcomed-in-sarajevo.
17. Until October 2004, no person could be arrested and prosecuted for war crimes in Bosnia and Herzegovina in the absence of a decision by the office of the prosecutor of the ICTY stating that there were credible charges to

Notes to Page 231

do so. Bosnia and Herzegovina had consented to this procedure as a safeguard against politically motivated arrests and prosecution for war crimes. This procedure, known as the "Rules of the Road procedure," required Bosnian authorities to submit case files to the office of the ICTY prosecutor for review. Under the procedure, the ICTY prosecutor's office was then required to review case files and determine whether they contained credible charges. Bosnian authorities could neither arrest nor prosecute persons for war crimes in the absence of such a determination. See, inter alia, http://www.icty.org/sid/96.

18 In July 2002, the prosecutor's office of the ICTY received a file in relation to the Dobrovoljačka Street events in which Jovan Divjak was identified as one of the suspects. After having reviewed the information submitted to it, the office concluded that there was insufficient evidence for the prosecution of war crimes. See comments of special adviser to the Prosecutor of the ICTY Frederick Swinnen, during ICTY Weekly Press Briefing of March 9, 2011, available at http://www.icty.org/sid/10613/en.

19 Elvira Jukic, "Bosnia Serbs Demand New Dobrovoljacka Probe," *Balkan Insight*, February 1, 2012, http://www.balkaninsight.com/en/article/bosnia-s-serbs-demand-dobrovoljacka-probe-again.

20 Edin Hadzovic, "Bosnia's Dodik Threatens to Arrest General Divjak," *Balkan Insight*, March 11, 2011, http://www.balkaninsight.com/en/article/bosnia-s-dodik-threatens-to-arrest-general-divjak.

21 "RS Parliament to Hold Divjak Session," *B92 News*, March 11, 2011, http://www.b92.net/eng/news/region-article.php?yyyy=2011&mm=03&dd=11&nav_id=73172.

22 "RS Parliament to Hold Divjak Session," *B92 News*, March 11, 2011, http://www.b92.net/eng/news/region-article.php?yyyy=2011&mm=03&dd=11&nav_id=73172.

Bibliography

Books

Addington, Larry H. *The Patterns of War since the Eighteenth Century.* Bloomington & Indianapolis: Indiana University Press, 1994.

Andrić, Ivo. *Bosnian Chronicle.* New York: Arcade Publishing, 1963.

—— *The Damned Yard and Other Stories.* London: Forest Books, 1992.

Areguin-Toft, Ivan. *How the Weak Win Wars: A Theory of Asymmetric Conflict.* Cambridge: Cambridge University Press, 2005.

Ashdown, Paddy. *Swords and Ploughshares: Bringing Peace to the 21st Century.* London: Weidenfeld & Nicolson, 2007.

—— *A Fortunate Life.* London: Aurum, 2009.

Banac, Ivo. *With Stalin against Tito: Cominformist Splits in Yugoslav Communism.* Ithaca, NY & London: Cornell University Press, 1988.

Basler, Roy P., ed. *The Collected Works of Abraham Lincoln,* Vol. VII. New Brunswick, NJ: Rutgers University Press, 1953.

Beaufre, Général. *Le drame de 1940.* Paris: Plon, 1965.

Bell, David. *Resistance and Revolution.* Boston, MA: Houghton Mifflin Company, 1973.

Bert, Wayne. *The Reluctant Superpower: United States Policy in Bosnia, 1991–1995.* New York: St. Martin's Press, 1997.

Bougarel, Xavier. *Bosnie: Anatomie d'un conflit.* Paris: La Découverte, 1996.

Burg, Steven L., and Shoup, Paul S. *The War in Bosnia-Herzegovina: Ethnic Conflict and International Intervention.* New York: M. E. Sharpe, 1999.

Call, Charles T. and Vanessa Wyeth, eds. *Building States to Build Peace.* Boulder, CO: Lynne Rienner Publishers, 2008.

Camon, Hubert. *La guerre Napoléonienne: Les systèmes d'opérations théorie et technique.* Paris: Economica, 1997.

Chenoweth, Erica and Stephan, Maria. *Why Civil Resistance Works: The Strategic Logic of Nonviolent Conflict*. New York: Columbia University Press, 2011.

Chollet, Derek. *The Road to the Dayton Accords: A Study of American Statecraft*. New York: Palgrave Macmillan, 2005.

Clark, Wesley. *Waging Modern War: Bosnia, Kosovo and the Future of Combat*. New York: Public Affairs, 2001.

Cohen, Eliot. "Kosovo and the New American Way of War." In *War over Kosovo: Politics and Strategy in a Global Age*, edited by Andrew Bacevich and Eliot Cohen. New York: Columbia University Press, 2001, 38–62.

Cornell, Tim. *The Beginnings of Rome: Italy and Rome from the Bronze Age to the Punic Wars*. New York: Routledge, 1995.

Cunliffe, Barry. "The Roots of Warfare." In *Conflict*, edited by Martin Jones and A. C. Fabian. Cambridge: Cambridge University Press, 2006, 63–81.

Danner, Mark. *Stripping Bare the Body: Politics, Violence, War*. New York: Nation Books, 2009.

Dedijer, Valdimir. *The Battle Stalin Lost: Memoirs of Yugoslavia 1948–1953*. New York: The Viking Press, 1970.

Divjak, Jovan. *Sarajevo mon amour: Entretiens avec Florence La Bruyère*. Paris: Buchet/Chastel, 2004.

Djilas, Milovan. *Conversations with Stalin*. New York: Harcourt, Brace & World, 1962.

——— *Tito: The Story from Inside*. New York & London: Harcourt Brace Jovanovich, 1980.

Duffy Toft, Monica. *Securing the Peace: The Durable Settlement of Civil Wars*. Princeton, NJ & Oxford: Princeton University Press, 2010.

Dürrenmatt, Friedrich, translated by James Kirkup. *The Physicists*. New York: Grove Weidenfeld, 1991.

Eade, Charles. *The War Speeches of the Right Hon. Winston Churchill*, vol. 1. London: Cassell, 1951.

Gaddis, John Lewis. *Strategies of Containment: A Critical Appraisal of American National Security Policy during the Cold War*. Oxford: Oxford University Press, 2005.

Galula, David. *Counterinsurgency Warfare: Theory and Practice*. New York: Frederick A. Prager, 1964.

Glaurdić, Josip. *The Hour of Europe: Western Powers and the Breakup of Yugoslavia*. New Haven, CT: Yale University Press, 2011.

Halperin, Morton, Siegle, Josepth, and Weinstein, Michael. *The Democracy Advantage: How Democracies Promote Prosperity and Peace.* New York & London: Routledge, 2005.
Hartzell, Caroline A., and Hoddie, Matthew. *Crafting Peace: Power-Sharing Institutions and the Negotiated Settlement of Civil Wars.* University Park: Pennsylvania State University Press, 2007.
Hastings, Max. *Winston's War: Churchill, 1940–1945.* New York: Alfred A. Knopf, 2010.
Helvey, Robert. *On Strategic Nonviolent Conflict: Thinking about the Fundamentals.* Boston, MA: The Albert Einstein Institution, 2004.
Holbrooke, Richard. *To End a War.* New York: The Modern Library, 1999.
Horowitz, Donald L. *Ethnic Groups in Conflict.* Berkeley, Los Angeles: University of California Press, 1985.
Horowitz, Donald L. "Making Moderation Pay: The Comparative Politics of Ethnic Conflict Management." In *Conflict and Peacemaking in Multiethnic Societies*, edited by Joseph V. Montville. Toronto: Lexington Books, 1990: 451–75.
——— "Constitutional Design: Proposals Versus Processes." In *The Architecture of Democracy: Constitutional Design, Conflict Management and Democracy*, edited by Andrew Reynolds. Oxford University Press: Oxford, 2002: 15–36.
Hunter, James Davison. *Culture Wars: The Struggle to Define America.* New York: Basic Books, 1991.
Ignatieff, Michael. *Virtual War: Kosovo and Beyond.* London: Chatto & Windus, 2000.
Independent International Commission on Kosovo. *The Kosovo Report: Conflict, International Response, Lessons Learned.* Oxford: Oxford University Press, 2000.
International Commission on Intervention and State Sovereignty. *The Responsibility to Protect: Report of the International Commission on Intervention and State Sovereignty.* Ottawa: International Development Research Centre, 2001.
Izetbegović, Alija. *Islamska Deklaracija.* Sarajevo: Bosna, 1990.
——— *Izetbegovic of Bosnia and Herzegovina: Notes from Prison, 1983–1988.* Westport, CT & London: Praeger, 2002.
Jervis, Robert. *System Effects: Complexity in Political and Social Life.* Princeton, NJ: Princeton University Press, 1997.
Judah, Tim. *Kosovo: War and Revenge.* New Haven, CT & London: Yale University Press, 2002.

Judt, Tony. *Postwar: A History of Europe since 1945*. New York: Penguin Press, 2005.
Kaldor, Mary. *New and Old Wars: Organized Violence in a Global Era*. Stanford, CA: Stanford University Press, 1999.
Kauffman, Stuart. *At Home in the Universe: The Search for Laws of Self-Organization and Complexity*. New York & Oxford: Oxford University Press, 1995.
Kilcullen, David. *Counterinsurgency*. Oxford: Oxford University Press, 2010.
Leroux-Martin, Philippe. "Article III.5: Additional Responsibilities." In *Constitution of Bosnia and Herzegovina: A Commentary*, edited by Christian Steiner and Nedim Ademović. Berlin: Konrad-Adenauer-Stiftung, 2010: 592–611.
Levinger, Matthew. *Conflict Analysis: Understanding Causes, Unlocking Solutions*. Washington, DC: United States Institute of Peace Press, 2013.
Lewin, Roger. *Complexity: Life at the Edge of Chaos*. New York: Collier Books / Macmillan Publishing Company, 1992.
Lijphart, Arend. *Democracy in Plural Societies: A Comparative Exploration*. New Haven. CT: Yale University Press, 1977.
Lintott, Andrew. *The Constitution of the Roman Republic*. Oxford: Clarendon Press, 1999.
MacFarlane, S. Neil. *Intervention in Contemporary World Politics*. Oxford: Oxford University Press for the International Institute for Strategic Studies, 2002.
MacKenzie, Lewis. *Peacekeeper: The Road to Sarajevo*. Vancouver/Toronto: Douglas&McIntyre, 1993.
Malcolm, Noel. *Bosnia: A Short History*. London: Papermac, 1996.
Marten, Kimberly Zisk. *Enforcing the Peace: Learning from the Imperial Past*. New York: Columbia University Press, 2004.
McPherson, James M. "From Limited War to Total War in America." In *On the Road to Total War: The American Civil War and the German Wars of Unification, 1861–1871*, edited by Stig Forster and Jorg Nagler. Cambridge: Cambridge University Press, 1997: 295–309.
Meadows, Donella H. *Thinking in Systems: A Primer*. White River Junction, VT: Chelsea Green Publishing, 2008.
Merom, Gil. *How Democracies Lose Small Wars*. Cambridge: Cambridge University Press, 2003.
Michnik, Adam. *Letters from Prison and Other Essays*. Berkeley: University of California Press, 1985.

Bibliography

Morin, Edgar. *La Connaissance de la connaissance: Livre premier, anthropologie de la connaissance.* Paris: Éditions du Seuil, 1986.

———— *Introduction à la pensée complexe.* Paris: Éditions du Seuil, 2005.

———— *On Complexity.* Cresskill, NJ: Hampton Press, 2008.

Morris, Peter. *Power: A Philosophical Analysis.* Manchester & New York: Manchester University Press, 2002.

Nagl, John A. *Learning to Eat Soup with a Knife: Counterinsurgency Lessons from Malaya and Vietnam.* Chicago & London: University of Chicago Press, 2005.

Nye, Joseph. *Soft Power: The Means to Success in World Politics.* New York: Public Affairs, 2004.

Paris, Roland. *At War's End: Building Peace after Civil Conflict.* Cambridge: Cambridge University Press, 2004.

Perritt, Henry H. *The Road to Independence for Kosovo: A Chronicle of the Ahtisaari Plan.* New York: Cambridge University Press, 2010.

Petersen, Roger D. *Understanding Ethnic Violence: Fear, Hatred, and Resentment in Twentieth Century Eastern Europe.* Cambridge: Cambridge University Press, 2002.

Procacci, Giuliano et al. *The Cominform: Minutes of the Three Conferences 1947/1948/1949.* Milano: Feltrinelli Editore, 1994.

Pudasaini, Shiva P. and Hutter, Kolumban. *Avalanche Dynamics: Dynamics of Rapid Flows of Dense Granular Avalanches.* Verlag, Berlin, Heidelberg: Springer, 2007.

Randall, Collins. *Violence: A Micro-sociological Study.* Princeton, NJ & Oxford: Princeton University Press, 2008.

Reilly, Benjamin. *Democracy in Divided Societies: Electoral Engineering for Conflict Management.* Cambridge: Cambridge University Press, 2001.

Roberts, Adams and Garton Ash, Timothy. *Civil Resistance and Power Politics.* Oxford: Oxford University Press, 2009.

Rubenstein, Richard E. "Sources." In *Conflict: From Analysis to Intervention*, edited by Sandra Cheldelin, Daniel Druckman, and Larissa Fast. London & New York: Continuum, 2003, 55–67.

Sandole, Dennis J. D. "Typology." In *Conflict: From Analysis to Intervention*, edited by Sandra Cheldelin, Daniel Druckman, and Larissa Fast. London & New York: Continuum, 2003, 39–50.

Schock, Kurt. *Unarmed Insurrection: People Power Movements in Nondemocracies.* Minneapolis: University of Minnesota Press, 2005.

Sell, Louis. *Slobodan Milosevic and the Destruction of Yugoslavia.* Durham, NC & London: Duke University Press, 2002.

Sharp, Gene. *Politics of Nonviolent Action*. Boston, MA: Extending Horizons Books Porter Sargent Publishers, 1973.

────── *Waging Non Violent Struggle: 20th century practice and 21st century potential*. Boston, MA: Extending Horizons Books, 2005.

Shaw, Martin. *The New Western Way of War*. Cambridge: Polity, 2005.

Silber, Laura and Little, Allan. *The Death of Yugoslavia*. New York: Penguin Books, 1995.

Singer, Peter. *Wired for War: The Robotics Revolution and Conflict in the 21st Century*. New York: Penguin Press, 2009.

Smith, Rupert. *The Utility of Force: The Art of War in the Modern World*. London: Penguin-Allen Lane, 2005.

Snyder, Jack and Robert Jervis, eds. *Coping with Complexity in the International System*. Boulder, CO: Westview Press, 1993.

Snyder, Jack and Jervis, Robert. "Civil Wars and the Security Dilemma." In *Civil Wars, Insecurity, and Intervention*, edited by Barbara F. Walter and Jack Snyder. New York: Columbia University Press, 1999: 15–37.

Steiner, Christian and Ademović, Nedim. "Article VI – Constitutional Court of Bosnia and Herzegovina." In *Constitution of Bosnia and Herzegovina: Commentary*, edited by Christian Steiner and Nedim Ademović. Sarajevo: Konrad-Adenauer-Stiftung, 2010.

Stewart, Rory and Knaus, Gerald. *Can Intervention Work?* New York: W. W. Norton & Company, 2011.

Tindemans, Leo, Cutler, Lloyd, Geremek, Bronislaw, Roper, John, Sommer, Theo, Veil, Simone, and Anderson, David. *Unfinished Peace: Report of the International Commission on the Balkans*. Washington, DC: Carnegie Endowment for International Peace, 1996.

Toal, Gerard and Dahlman, Carl T. *Bosnia Remade: Ethnic Cleansing and Its Reversal*. Oxford: Oxford University Press, 2011.

Tse-Tung, Mao. *On the Protracted War*. Peking: Foreign Language Press, 1954.

U.S. Army & Marine Corps. *Counterinsurgency Field Manual*. Chicago, IL & London: University of Chicago Press, 2007.

Von Clausewitz, Carl, *On War*. Princeton, NJ: Princeton University Press, 1976.

Woodward, Susan L. "Bosnia and Herzegovina: How Not to End Civil War." In *Civil Wars, Insecurity, and Intervention*, edited by Barbara F. Walter and Jack Snyder. New York: Columbia University Press, 1999, 73–115.

Zahar, Marie-Joelle. "Reframing the Spoiler Debate in Peace Processes." In *Contemporary Peacemaking: Conflict, Peace Processes and Post-war*

Reconstruction, edited by John Darby and Roger MacGinty. New York: Palgrave Macmillan, 2008: 114–24.

Cases

Behrami and Behrami v. *France* and *Saramati* v. *France, Germany and Norway*. European Court of Human Rights. May 5, 2007

Berić and Others v. *Bosnia and Herzegovina*. European Court of Human Rights. October 16, 2007.

Case AP 347/04. Constitutional Court of Bosnia and Herzegovina. November 30, 2004.

Case AP 759/04. Constitutional Court of Bosnia and Herzegovina. September 29, 2004.

Case AP 777/04. Constitutional Court of Bosnia and Herzegovina. September 29, 2004.

Case AP 784/04. Constitutional Court of Bosnia and Herzegovina. September 29, 2004.

Case AP 905/04. Constitutional Court of Bosnia and Herzegovina. November 30, 2004.

Case AP 953/05. Constitutional Court of Bosnia and Herzegovina. July 8, 2006.

Case U 5/98 (Partial Decision Part 3), Constitutional Court of Bosnia and Herzegovina, July 1, 2000.

Case U 9/00. Constitutional Court of Bosnia and Herzegovina. November 3, 2000.

Case U 9/07. Constitutional Court of Bosnia and Herzegovina. October 4, 2008.

Case U 16/08. Constitutional Court of Bosnia and Herzegovina. March 28, 2009.

Case U 25/00. Constitutional Court of Bosnia and Herzegovina. March 23, 2001.

Case U 26/01. Constitutional Court of Bosnia and Herzegovina. September 28, 2001.

Case U 41/01. Constitutional Court of Bosnia and Herzegovina. January 30, 2004.

Case U 42/03. Constitutional Court of Bosnia and Herzegovina. December 17, 2004.

Dragan Kalinic and Milorad Bilbija v. *Bosnia and Herzegovina*. European Court of Human Rights. May 13, 2008.

Sejdić and Finci v. *Bosnia and Herzegovina*. European Court of Human Rights. December 22, 2009.

Communiqués, Declarations, and Press Statements

"Communiqué by the PIC Steering Board," *Office of the High Representative*, June 25, 2004.

"Declaration by the Steering Board of the Peace Implementation Council." *Peace Implementation Council*. October 31, 2007.

"Istanbul Summit Communiqué: Issued by the Heads of States and Government Participating in the Meeting of the North Atlantic Council." *North Atlantic Treaty Organization*. June 28, 2004.

"Kosovo: Report of the International Civilian Office." *International Civilian Office*, February 27, 2009.

"Joint UK, French and German statement on Syria." *UK Prime Minister's Office*. August 18, 2011.

"Lajčák Expects Party Leaders to Make Progress on EU Agenda." *Office of the High Representative*. November 21, 2007.

"PIC Bonn Conclusions." *Office of the High Representative*. December 10, 1997.

"Press Conference by the High Representative Miroslav Lajčák, following the PIC meeting." *Office of the High Representative*. October 31, 2007.

"Press Conference 30 June: High Representative Announces Measures against ICTY Obstructionists." *Office of the High Representative*. June 30, 2004.

"RS Proposal: No Basis For Further Discussion." *Office of the High Representative*. November 9, 2007.

"Statement by the Deputy High Representative and Head of Banja Luka Office, Ivan Busniak, during the Delivery of the Explanatory Note." *Office of the High Representative*. October 24, 2007.

"U.S. Press Statement for Joint Press Conference: The U.S. Announces Sanctions Against the SDS and PDP." *Office of the High Representative*. December 16, 2004.

Decisions and Measures of the High Representative for Bosnia and Herzegovina

"Decision Annulling five RS laws Concerning State-Level Competencies, Which Were Passed in Violation of the BiH Constitution." *Office of the High Representative*. October 1, 1999.

"Decision Appointing a Provisional Administrator for the Hercegovačka Banka." *Office of the High Representative*. April 5, 2001.

Bibliography

"Decision Blocking All Bank Accounts Held by and/or in the Name of the SDS and Requiring the SDS to Establish one Bank Account." *Office of the High Representative.* June 30, 2004.

"Decision Enacting the Authentic Interpretation of the Law on Changes and Amendments to the Law on the Council of Ministers of Bosnia and Herzegovina Enacted by the Decision of the High Representative of 19 October 2007." *Office of the High Representative.* December 3, 2007.

"Decision Enacting the Conclusion Ordering the Auditor General of Republika Srpska to Conduct Special Audits." *Office of the High Representative.* December 16, 2004.

"Decision Enacting the Law on Amendments to the Criminal Procedure Code of Bosnia and Herzegovina." *Office of the High Representative.* December 16, 2004.

"Decision Enacting the Law on Changes and Amendments to the Law on the Council of Ministers of Bosnia and Herzegovina." *Office of the High Representative.* October 19, 2007.

"Decision Establishing the Police Restructuring Commission." *Office of the High Representative.* July 2, 2004.

"Decision on the Deadlines for the Implementation of the New Uniform License Plate System." *Office of the High Representative.* May 20, 1998.

"Decision Removing Ante Jelavić from his Position as the Croat Member of the BiH Presidency." *Office of the High Representative.* March 7, 2001.

"Decision Removing Cvjetan Nikić from his Position as Vice President of the SDS and from other Public and Party Positions he Currently Holds." *Office of the High Representative.* June 30, 2004.

"Decision Removing Dr. Dragan Kalinic from his Positions as Chairman of the National Assembly of Republika Srpska and as President of the SDS." *Office of the High Representative.* June 29, 2004.

"Decision Removing Ivo Andrić Lozanski from his post as a Delegate to the BiH House of Representatives and Banning Him from Holding Public and Party Office." *Office of the High Representative.* March 7, 2001.

"Decision Removing Marko Tokić from Holding Public and Party Office." *Office of the High Representative,* March 7, 2001.

"Decision Removing Milorad Bilbija from his Position of Deputy Head Operative Administration of the Intelligence and Security Agency in Banja Luka and from other Public and Party Positions he Currently Holds." *Office of the High Representative.* December 16, 2004.

"Decision Removing Mr. Zoran Djerić from his Position of Minister of Interior of Republika Srpska." *Office of the High Representative.* June 30, 2004.

"Decision Removing Nedjeljko Djekanović from his Position as Vice President of the SDS and from other Public and Party Positions he Currently Holds." *Office of the High Representative.* June 30, 2004.

"Decision Removing Pantelija Curguz from his Position as Vice President of the SDS and from other Public and Party Positions he Currently Holds." *Office of the High Representative.* June 30, 2004.

"Decision Removing Slobodan Saraba from his Position(s) as Vice President of the SDS and Director of Hydroelectric Power Plants Trebisnjica and from other Public and Party Positions he Currently Holds." *Office of the High Representative.* June 30, 2004.

"Decision Removing Zdravko Batinić from Holding Public and Party Office." *Office of the High Representative.* March 7, 2001.

"Decision to Remove Mr. Milovan R. Pecelj from his Position as Minister of Education and Culture of Republika Srpska." *Office of the High Representative.* October 28, 2004.

"Decision to Remove Radomir Lukić from His Position as Member of the Main Board of the SDS and from other Public and Party Positions." *Office of the High Representative.* June 30, 2004.

"Decision Suspending All Disbursements of Budgetary Itemizations for Party Funding to the SDS and Ordering the SDS to Submit a Financial Plan for the Period from 1 January 2003 until 31 March 2004." *Office of the High Representative.* April 2, 2004.

"Directive Reallocating Budgetary Itemizations Intended to Fund the SDS." *Office of the High Representative.* June 30, 2004.

"Explanatory Note on the High Representative's Decision From October 19th." *Office of the High Representative.* October 24, 2007.

"Order on the Implementation of the Decision of the Constitutional Court of Bosnia and Herzegovina in the Appeal of Milorad Bilbija et al., No. AP-953/05." *Office of the High Representative.* March 23, 2007.

"Order Seizing Travel Documents of Persons Who Obstruct or Threaten to Obstruct the Peace Implementation Process." *Office of the High Representative.* July 10, 2007.

"Proposed Changes and Amendments to the Rules of Procedure of the House of Representatives of the Parliamentary Assembly of Bosnia and Herzegovina." *Office of the High Representative.* October 24, 2007.

Bibliography

Interviews

Ashdown, Paddy, *former High Representative for Bosnia and Herzegovina*. Interview by author. London, October 20, 2011.

Braun, Bertram, *U.S. State Department official*. Interview by author. Washington, DC, February 23, 2012.

Burns, R. Nicholas, *former U.S. Undersecretary of State for Political Affairs and U.S. Ambassador to NATO*. Interview by author. Cambridge, Massachusetts, February 7, 2012.

Cooper, Robert, *Counsellor to EU High Representative for Foreign Affairs and Security Policy*. Interview by author. Brussels, October 18, 2011.

Crishock, Louis, *U.S. State Department official*. Interview by author. Washington, DC, January 26, 2012.

D'Aoust, Edouard, *OHR official*. Interview by author. Sarajevo, January 18, 2010.

Divjak, Jovan, *Executive Director of Obrazovanje Gradi BiH*. Interview by author. Sarajevo, September 9, 2010.

Everard, Alix, *Chair of EU Working Party on the Western Balkans Region*. Interview by author. Brussels, October 18, 2011.

Haner, Michael, *OHR official, Sarajevo*. Interview by author. September 14, 2010.

Jonsson, Jonas, *Head of Western Balkans Division, European External Action Service*. Interview by author. Brussels, October 17, 2011.

Korski, Daniel, *former OHR official and current Strategic Adviser to the EU High Representative for Foreign Affairs and Security Policy*. Interview by author. London, October 19, 2011.

Kudelova Dita, *European Commission (DG Enlargement Bosnia)*. Interview by author. Brussels, October 17, 2011.

Lajčák, Miroslav, *former High Representative for Bosnia and Herzegovina and current Foreign Affairs Minister and Deputy Prime Minister of Slovakia*. Interview by author. Bratislava, January 16, 2013.

Lawson, Matthew, *former OHR official*. Interview by author. London, October 19, 2011.

Ryan, Kevin, *U.S. General (retired)*. Interview by author. Cambridge, Massachusetts, August, 17, 2010.

Tuta, Archie, *OHR official*. Interview by author. Sarajevo, January 14, 2010.

Van Den Boogert, Cindy, *European Commission (DG Enlargement Kosovo)*. Interview by author. Brussels, October 17, 2011.

Wisner, Frank G., former U.S. Ambassador to Zambia, Egypt, The Philippines, *India and former U.S Special Representative to the Kosovo Status Talks*. Interview by author. New York, November 12, 2010.

Legislation and Acts of Institutions in Bosnia and Herzegovina

Rules of Procedure of the Council of Ministers of Bosnia and Herzegovina (O.G. BiH 22/03).

Law on the Council of Ministers of Bosnia and Herzegovina (O.G. BiH 38/02, 30/03, 42/03, 81/06, 81/06, 76/07).

Rules of Procedure of the House of Representatives of the Parliamentary Assembly of Bosnia and Herzegovina (O. G. BiH 33/06, 41/06, 81/06 and 91/06).

Rules of Procedure of the House of Peoples of the Parliamentary Assembly of Bosnia and Herzegovina (O.G. BiH. 33/06, 41/06 and 91/06).

Conclusion 01–610/11 (O.G. Republika Srpska 45/11).

Conclusion 01–613/11 (O.G. Republika Srpska 45/11).

Decision to Announce Republika Srpska Entity-Wide Referendum (O.G. Republika Srpska 45/11).

Letters

Boehner, John A., Speaker of the House of Representatives. Letter to the President of the United States. June 14, 2011.

Dodik, Milorad, Prime Minister of Republika Srpska. Letter to H.E. Ambassador Thomas Mayr-Harting, President of the United Nations Security Council. November 16, 2009.

Juppé, Alain, French Foreign Affairs Minister and Westerwelle, Guido, German Foreign Affairs Minister. Letter to EU High Representative for Foreign Affairs and Security Policy Catherine Ashton. August 26, 2011.

Periodicals

Boettcher, William A. and Cobb, Michael D. "Echoes of Vietnam: Casualty Framing and Public Perceptions of Success and Failure in Iraq." *Journal of Conflict Resolution* **50**, no. 6 (December 2006): 831–54.

Dahlman, Carl and Tuathail, Gearoid O. "The Legacy of Ethnic Cleansing: The International Community and the Returns Process in Post-Dayton Bosnia-Herzegovina." *Political Geography* **24** (June 2005): 569–99.

Bibliography

De Rouen, Karl R. and Bercovitch, Jacob. "Enduring Internal Rivalries: A New Framework for the Study of Civil War." *Journal of Peace Research* **45**, no. 1 (2008): 55–74.

Doyle, Michael W. and Suntharalingam, Nishkala. "The UN in Cambodia: Lessons for Complex Peacekeeping." *International Peacekeeping* **1**, no. 2 (1994): 117–47.

Greenhill, Kelly M. and Major, Solomon. "The Perils of Profiling Civil War Spoilers and the Collapse of Intrastate Peace Accords." *International Security* **31**, no. 3 (Winter 2006/07): 7–40.

Henriksen, Dag. "Inflexible Response: Diplomacy, Airpower and the Kosovo Crisis, 1998–1999." *The Journal of Strategic Studies* **31**, no. 6 (December 2008): 825–58.

Iglar, Richard F. "The Constitutional Crisis in Yugoslavia and the International Law of Self-Determination: Slovenia's and Croatia's Right to Secede." *Boston College International and Comparative Law Review* **15**, no. 1 (1992): 213–39.

Kaufman, Chaim. "Possible and Impossible Solutions to Ethnic Civil Wars." *International Security* **20**, no. 4 (1996): 136–75.

Kennedy, David. "The Wages of a Mercenary Army: Issues of Civil Military Relations." *Bulletin of the American Academy* (Spring 2006): 12–16.

Kissinger, Henry A. "The Viet Nam Negotiations." *Foreign Affairs* **47**, no. 2 (January 1969): 211–34.

Knaus, Gerhard and Martin, Felix. "Travails of the European Raj." *Journal of Democracy* **14**, no. 3 (July 2003): 60–74.

Mack, Andrew. "Why Big Nations Lose Small Wars: The Politics of Asymmetric Conflict." *World Politics* **27**, no. 2 (1975): 175–200.

Morey, Daniel S. "Conflict and the Duration of Peace in Enduring Internal Rivalries." *Conflict Management and Peace Science* **26**, no. 4 (2009): 331–45.

Pape, Robert A. "When Duty Calls: A Pragmatic Standard of Humanitarian Intervention." *International Security* **37**, no. 1 (Summer 2012): 41–80.

Paris, Roland. "International Peacebuilding and the 'Mission Civilisatrice.'" *Review of International Studies* **28** (2002): 637–56.

Perović, Jeronim. "The Tito-Stalin Split." *Journal of Cold War Studies* **9**, Issue 2 (2007): 32–63.

Posen, Barry R. "The Security Dilemma and Ethnic Conflict." *Survival* **35**, no. 1 (1993): 27–47.

Roberts, Adam. "Civil Resistance to Military Coups." *Journal of Peace and Research*, **12**, no. 1 (1975): 19–36.

Stedman, John. "Spoiler Problems in Peace Process." *International Security* **22**, no. 2 (Fall 1997): 5–53.

Varshney, Ashutosh. "Nationalism, Ethnic Conflict, and Rationality." *Perspectives on Politics* **1**, no. 1 (2003): 85–99.

Walter, Barbara. "Does Conflict Beget Conflict? Explaining Recurring Civil War." *Journal of Peace Research* **41**, no. 3 (2004): 371–88.

Williams, Rhodri C. "Post-Conflict Property Restitution and Refugee Return in Bosnia and Herzegovina: Implications for International Standard-Setting and Practice." *New York University Journal of International Law and Politics* **37**, no. 3 (2005): 441–553.

Newspapers and Magazines

Agence France Press. "Bosnian War General Faces Austrian Extradition." March 4, 2011.

Agnes b. et al. "Jovan Divjak et l'honneur de l'Europe." *Le Monde*. March 3, 2011.

Amara, Tarek. "Violent Unrest Breaks Out in Tunisian Capital." *Reuters*. January 11, 2011.

Anderson, Jon Lee. "Sons of the Revolution: Can a Ragtag Civilian Army Defeat a Dictator." *The New Yorker*. May 9, 2011.

B-92 News. "Kostunica: Serbia's top priorities – Kosovo, RS." October 25, 2007.

——— "RS Parliament to Hold Divjak Session." March 11, 2011.

Babic, Ratka. "Bosnia Serbs Will Call Referendum on NATO." *Balkan Insight*. February 12, 2013.

Baker, Peter and Tyson, Ann Scott. "Bush to Meet NATO Allies Divided over Adding Troops in Afghanistan." *The Washington Post*. March 31, 2008.

Balkan Insight. "Bosnia Faces Turmoil." November 1, 2007.

Bancroft, Ian. "An Unhealthy State." *The Guardian*. November 26, 2007.

BBC News. "Deal Ends Bosnian Croat Mutiny." May 16, 2001.

——— "Former Bosnian Croat Leader in Court." August 29, 2001.

——— "Water Polo Riots Spark Balkans Row." June 16, 2003.

——— "Austria Holds Ex-Bosnia General Divjak on Serb Warrant." March 4, 2011.

——— "US Examines Legality of Libya War." May 20, 2011.

——— "France's Alain Juppe: Syria Committing 'Grave Crimes.'" September 7, 2011.

——— "Syria Crisis: Valerie Amos Describes Homs 'Devastation.'" March 7, 2012.

Bibliography

Bumiller, Elisabeth. "U.S. Defense Officials Say Obama Reviewing Military Options in Syria." *New York Times*. March 7, 2012.

Chandler, David. "The High Representative for Bosnia Still Runs it Like a Feudal Kingdom." *The Guardian*. November 19, 2007.

Cornwell, Susan. "House to Vote on Bill Cutting Funds for Libya." *Reuters*. June 23, 2011.

DeYoung, Karen. "U.S. Officials Warn against Intervention in Syria." *The Washington Post*. March 7, 2012.

Dodik, Milorad. "Krizu Proizveo OHR." *Nezavisne Novine*. November 18, 2007.

Eckholm, Erik. "Anti-Abortion Groups Are Split on Legal Tactics." *The New York Times*. December 5, 2011.

The Economist. "Cracking Up: Spurred by Russia, the Bosnian Serbs Are Making Trouble Again." October 25, 2007.

——— "A Stuck Region: How Troubles in Bosnia and Elsewhere Obstruct the Balkans' Path to Europe." February 12, 2009.

England, Andrew, Saleh, Heba, and Peel, Michael. "Egypt Stands Divided as Mubarak Supporters Launch Assault on Protest." *Financial Times*. February 3, 2011.

Farmer, Ben. "Life under the Taliban: How a Boy of Seven was Hanged to Punish his Family." *The Telegraph*. June 12, 2010.

Financial Times. "Bosnia Prime Minister Resigns Amid Tension." November 2, 2007.

Garapon, Antoine et al. "Lettre ouverte au gouvernement autrichien." *Le Monde*. July 7, 2011.

The Guardian. "Bosnian Serb Leader Resigns." December 17, 2004.

Hadzovic, Edin. "Austria Refuses to Extradite Divjak to Serbia." *Balkan Insight*. July 29, 2011.

——— "Bosnia's Dodik Threatens to Arrest General Divjak." *Balkan Insight*. March 11, 2011.

——— "Bosnian Croats Form National Assembly." *Balkan Insight* (Sarajevo, Bosnia, and Herzegovina), April 19, 2011.

——— "Return of Freed General Divides Bosnia." *Balkan Insight*. July 29, 2011.

Harding, Thomas. "NATO Moves to Thwart Taliban Infiltration of Afghan Police and Army." *The Telegraph*. August 16, 2012.

Hastings, Michael. "The Runaway General." *Rolling Stone*. July 8, 2010 (Issue 1108/1109).

Hill, Gladwin. "Rail City Blasted – 500 U.S. 'Heavies' Bomb Town in the Direct Path of Red Army Troops – Dresden Nears Ruin – RAF Rips

Berlin, Mainz, Chemnitz, Nuremberg, Duisburg, Dessau." *The New York Times*. February 16, 1945. XCIV, No. 31800.

Holbrooke, Richard. "Back to the Brink in the Balkans." *The Washington Post*. November 25, 2007.

Jahn, Georhe. "Austria Detains Ex-Bosnian General on Serb Warrant." *The Washington Post*. March 4.

Jukic, Elvira. "Bosnia Serbs Demand New Dobrovoljacka Probe." *Balkan Insight*. February 1, 2012.

——— "Breakthrough on Bosnia Impasse." *Balkan Insight*. December 28, 2011.

Kebo, Amra. "Bosnian Croat Separatism Threat: The Beleaguered HDZ Party in Bosnia Appears to be Preparing the Ground for the Establishment of a Bosnian Croat State." *Institute for War and Peace Reporting*. November 2, 2000.

——— "Croat Troops Mutiny." *Institute for War and Peace Reporting*. March 23, 2011.

Kirkpatrick, David D. "Egypt Defies U.S. by Setting Trial for 19 Americans," *The New York Times*, A1, February 6, 2012.

Koring, Paul. "An Encounter with the Butcher of Srebrenica." *The Globe and Mail*. May 27, 2011.

Kovac, Janez. "Bank Closure Provokes Croat Wrath: Bosnian Croat Hardliners are Furious over Attempts to Severe their Financial Lifelines." *Institute for War and Peace Reporting*. April 11, 2001.

Latal, Srecko. "Bosnian Serbs Called Off from NATO Drill." *Balkan Insight*. May 8, 2009.

Laughland, John. "UN Tyranny in Bosnia." *The Spectator*. May 5, 2001.

Le Monde. "La démission du premier ministre serbe ouvre une crise à Sarajevo." November 3, 2007.

Lepore, Jill. "Birthright: What's Next for Planned Parenthood," *The New Yorker*. November 14, 2011.

Ljunggren, David. "Canada Threatens to Pull Soldiers from Afghanistan." *Reuters*. January 28, 2008.

Los Angeles Times. "Bosnian Serb Officials Quit over Police Reforms." December 19, 2004.

Lowen, Mark. "Kosovo Tense after Deadly Clash on Serbian Border." *BBC News*. July 26, 2011.

MacFarquhar, Neil and Saad, Hwaida. "Syria Calls the Arab League's Sanctions 'Economic War.'" *The New York Times*. November 29, 2011.

Bibliography

MacFarquhar, Neil, Bakri, Nada, and Stack, Liam. "Isolating Syria, Arab Group Sets Broad Sanctions." *The New York Times*, A1, November 28, 2011.

McElroy, Damien. "Extradition of Former Bosnian President Ejup Ganic Thrown Out." *The Telegraph*. July 27, 2012.

Moore, Molly. "NATO Confronts Surprisingly Fierce Taliban." *The Washington Post*. February 26, 2008.

The New York Times. "Bosnian Serb Crowd Beats Muslims at Mosque Rebuilding." May 8, 2001.

Oppel, Richard A. and Bowley, Graham. "Attacks on Afghan Troops by Colleagues are Rising, Allies Say." *The New York Times*. August 23, 2012.

Pelham, Nicolas. "Bogged Down in Libya," *The New York Review of Books* LVIII, no. 8, May 12, 2011.

Savage, Charlie. "War Powers Act Does Not Apply to Libya, Obama Argues." *The New York Times*. June 15, 2011.

Shadid, Anthony. "Syrian Leader Vows 'Iron Fist' to Crush 'Conspiracy.'" *The New York Times*. January 11, 2012.

Singer, Peter W. "Do Drones Undermine Democracy?" *The New York Times*, January 22, 2012.

Smolar, Piotr. "Divjak, héros à Sarajevo, criminel pour la Serbie." *Le Monde*. March 10, 2011.

Steinhauer, Jennifer. "House Deals Obama Symbolic Blow with Libya Votes." *The New York Times*. June 24, 2011.

——— "Obama Adviser Defends Libya Policy to Senate." *The New York Times*. June 28, 2011.

Tallentire, Mark. "Violence Erupts Between Serbs and Bosnians after Djokovic's Win." *The Guardian*. January 23, 2009.

Thorpe, Nick. "Croatian Soldiers Mutiny in Bosnia." *The Guardian*. March 28, 2001.

Traynor, Ian. "Bosnia in Worst Crisis since War as Serb Leader Calls Referendum." *The Guardian*. April 28, 2011.

Trebincevic, Kenan. "Marshal Tito in Queens." *The New York Times*. May 3, 2012.

Voice of America. "Italy's Foreign Minister Calls for End to Hostilities in Libya." June 21, 2011.

Walsh, Declan. "US Had 'Frighteningly Simplistic' View of Afghanistan, says McChrystal." *The Guardian*. October 7, 2011.

Waterfield, Bruno. "Bloodshed to Return to Bosnia, Paddy Ashdown Fears." *The Telegraph*. May 27, 2011.

Weschelr, Lawrence. "Letter from the Republika Srpska: High Noon at Twin Peaks." *The New Yorker*, August 18, 1997.

Radio and Television

CBC Radio. "Citizen Journalism in Syria." *The Current*. January 4, 2011.

Percy, Norma. dir. *The Death of Yugoslavia*. British Broadcasting Corporation. 1995. TV Documentary.

Zaritsky, John. dir. *Romeo and Juliet in Sarajevo*. Canadian Broadcasting Corporation, National Film Board of Canada, PBS *Frontline*, 1994. TV Documentary.

Reports

Center on International Cooperation. *Review of Political Missions 2011*. New York, 2011.

European Commission for Democracy through Law. *Opinion on the Constitutional Situation in Bosnia and Herzegovina and the Powers of the High Representative CDL-AD (2005)004*. March 11–12, 2005.

——— *Opinion on a Possible Solution to the Issue of Decertification of Police Officers in Bosnia and Herzegovina CDL-AD (2005)024*, October 21–2, 2005.

European Stability Initiative. *On Mount Olympus: How the UN Violated Human Rights in Bosnia and Herzegovina, and Why Nothing has Been Done to Correct it*. February 10, 2007.

——— *The Worst in Class: How the International Protectorate Hurts the European Future of Bosnia and Herzegovina*. November 8, 2007.

International Crisis Group. *Turning Strife to Advantage: A Blueprint to Integrate the Croats in Bosnia and Herzegovina: Balkans Report No. 106*. March 15, 2001.

———*No Early Exit: NATO's Continuing Challenge in Bosnia: Balkans Report No. 110*. May 22, 2001.

——— *Collapse in Kosovo: Europe Report No. 155*. April 22, 2004.

——— *Bosnia: State Institutions under Attack: Europe Briefing No. 62*. May 6, 2011.

Pew Research Center. *The Military-Civilian Gap: War and Sacrifice in the Post-9/11 Era*. October 5, 2011.

Police Restructuring Commission of Bosnia and Herzegovina. *Final Report on the Work of the Police Restructuring Commission of Bosnia and Herzegovina*. December 2004.

Bibliography 311

Reconstruction and Return Task Force. *Report April 1997.* April 30, 1997.

World Bank. *World Development Report 2011: Conflict, Security and Development.* April 2011.

Research Papers

Cutts, Mark. "The Humanitarian Operation in Bosnia, 1992–1995: Dilemmas of Negotiating Humanitarian Access." *UNHCR Policy Research Unit.* May 1999.

Dunlop, Colonel Charles J. Jr. "Law and Military Interventions: Preserving Humanitarian Values in 21st Century Conflicts." Carr Center for Human Rights Policy Working Paper, Harvard Kennedy School Program on National Security and Human Rights, 2001.

Farrington, Christopher. "Non-Violent Opposition to Peace Processes: Northern Ireland's Serial Spoilers." *University College Dublin Geary Institute Discussion Paper Series.* February 28, 2006.

Toft, Monica. "Peace through Security: Making Negotiated Settlements Stick." Working Paper no. 23, Research Group in International Security. November 2006.

Williams, Rhodri C. "Post-Conflict Property Restitution in Bosnia: Balancing Reparations and Durable Solutions in the Aftermath of Displacement." *TESEV International Symposium on "Internal Displacement in Turkey and Abroad."* Istanbul, Turkey, December 5, 2006.

Speeches

Dodik, Milorad. "Address by the President of the Republic at 4th Session of RSNA." Speech, Banja Luka, April 13, 2011.

Harper, Stephen. "Statement by the Prime Minister of Canada on the Situation in Syria." Speech, Ottawa, August 18, 2011.

Obama, Barack. "Remarks by the President in Address to the Nation on the Way Forward in Afghanistan and Pakistan. Speech, West Point, NY, December 1, 2009.

——— "Remarks by the President in Address to the Nation on Libya." Speech, Washington, DC, March 28, 2011.

——— "Statement by President Obama on the Situation in Syria." Speech, Washington, DC, August 18, 2011.

Rehn, Olli. "Bosnia and Herzegovina in 2007: A Year of Opportunities." Speech, Sarajevo, Bosnia and Herzegovina, March 16, 2007.

——— "Initialing of the Stabilisation and Association Agreement." Speech, Sarajevo, Bosnia and Herzegovina, December 4, 2007.

Treaties and Agreements

American Convention on Human Rights, O.A.S. Treaty Series No. 36, 1144 U.N.T.S. 123, entered into force July 18, 1978, reprinted in Basic Documents Pertaining to Human Rights in the Inter-American System, OEA/Ser.L.V/II.82 doc.6 rev.1 at 25 (1992).

African Charter on Human and Peoples' Rights, adopted June 27, 1981, OAU Doc. CAB/LEG/67/3 rev. 5, 21 I.L.M. 58 (1982), entered into force October 21, 1986.

Agreement on Provisional Arrangements in Afghanistan Pending the Re-Establishment of Permanent Government Institutions ("Bonn Agreement") [Afghanistan]. S/2001/1154. December 5, 2001.

Charter of the United Nations. October 24, 1945, 1 UNTS XVI.

European Convention for the Protection of Human Rights and Fundamental Freedoms, ETS 5, 213 U.N.T.S. 222, entered into force September 3, 1953, as amended by Protocols No. 3, 5, and 8 which entered into force on September 21, 1970, December 20, 1971 and January 1, 1990 respectively.

General Framework Agreement for Peace in Bosnia Herzegovina, December 14, 1995, 35 I.L.M. 75.

International Covenant on Civil and Political Rights, G.A. res. 2200A (XXI), 21 U.N. GAOR Supp. (No. 16) at 52, U.N. Doc. A/6316 (1966), 999 U.N.T.S. 171, entered into force March 23, 1976.

International Covenant on Economic, Social and Cultural Rights, G.A. res. 2200A (XXI), 21 U.N. GAOR Supp. (No. 16) at 49, U.N. Doc. A/6316 (1966), 993 U.N.T.S. 3, entered into force January 3, 1976.

United Nations Resolutions

UN General Assembly. *Resolution 54/245*. A/RES/54/245. February 2, 2000.

——— *Resolution 61/285*. A/RES/61/285. August 1, 2007.

——— *Resolution 65/300*. A/RES/65/300. September 1, 2011.

UN Security Council. *Resolution 186 (1964)*. S/RES/5575. March 4, 1964.

——— *Resolution 678 (1990)*. S/RES/678. November 29, 1990.

——— *Resolution 688 (1991)*. S/RES/688. April 5, 1991.

Bibliography

——— *Resolution 713 (1991)*. S/RES/713. September 25, 1991.
——— *Resolution 743 (1992)*. S/RES/743. February 21, 1992.
——— *Resolution 758 (1992)*. S/RES/758. June 8, 1992.
——— *Resolution 770 (1992)*. S/RES/770. August 13, 1992.
——— *Resolution 781 (1992)*. S/RES/781. October 9, 1992.
——— *Resolution 795 (1992)*. S/RES/795. December 21, 1992.
——— *Resolution 816 (1993)*. S/RES/816. March 31, 1993.
——— *Resolution 824 (1993)*. S/RES/824. May 6, 1993.
——— *Resolution 827 (1993)*. S/RES/827. May 25, 1993.
——— *Resolution 836 (1993)*. S/RES/836. June 4, 1993.
——— *Resolution 1031 (1995)*. S/RES/1031. December 15, 1995.
——— *Resolution 1088 (1996)*. S/RES/1088. December 12, 1996.
——— *Resolution 1244 (1999)*. S/RES/1244. June 10, 1999.
——— *Resolution 1272 (1999)*. S/RES/1272. October 25, 1999.
——— *Resolution 1386 (2001)*. S/RES/1386. December 20, 2001.
——— *Resolution 1410 (2002)*. S/RES/1410. May 17, 2002.
——— *Resolution 1480 (2003)*. S/RES/1480. May 19, 2003.
——— *Resolution 1423 (2002)*. S/RES/1423. July 12, 2002.
——— *Resolution 1491 (2003)*. S/RES/1491. July 11, 2003.
——— *Resolution 1503 (2003)*. S/RES/1503. (2003). August 28, 2003.
——— *Resolution 1510 (2003)*. S/RES/1510. October 13, 2003.
——— *Resolution 1534 (2004)*. S/RES/1534. (2004). March 26, 2004.
——— *Resolution 1543 (2004)*. S/RES/1543. May 14, 2004.
——— *Resolution 1551 (2004)*. S/RES/1551. July 9, 2004.
——— *Resolution 1573 (2004)*. S/RES/1573. November 16, 2004.
——— *Resolution 1575 (2004)*. S/RES/1575. November 22, 2004.
——— *Resolution 1639 (2005)*. S/RES/1639. November 21, 2005.
——— *Resolution 1704 (2006)*. S/RES/1704. August 25, 2006.
——— *Resolution 1722 (2006)*. S/RES/1722. November 21, 2006.
——— *Resolution 1785 (2007)*. S/RES/1785. November 21, 2007.
——— *Resolution 1802 (2008)*. S/RES/1802. February 25, 2008.
——— *Resolution 1867 (2009)*. S/RES/1867. February 26, 2009.
——— *Resolution 1912 (2010)*. S/RES/1912. February 26, 2010.
——— *Resolution 1845 (2008)*. S/RES/1845. November 20, 2008.
——— *Resolution 1895 (2009)*. S/RES/1895. November 18, 2009.
——— *Resolution 1948 (2010)*. S/RES/1948. November 18, 2010.
——— *Resolution 1969 (2011)*. S/RES/1969. (2011). February 24, 2011.
——— *Resolution 1973 (2011)*. S/RES/1973. March 17, 2011.
——— *Resolution 2019 (2011)*. S/RES/2019. November 16, 2011.

Index

Acquis Communautaire, 222
Afghanistan
   Allegiance to Intervener, risks, 135
   Drone Strikes, 106
   Insurgency, 108, 134, 135
   Intervention, 16, 98, 102–03, 110, 135, 177
      Resistance to, 132, 133, 206
      Soviet Union, 125
   Mc Chrystal, Stanley, 175, 200
   Media Coverage, 58
Ahtisaari, Martti, 31–32, 117–18
al-Assad, Bashar, 129–30, 132
Albania, 123
Algeria, 133, 134, 141
Alkalaj, Sven, 230
Alliance of Independent Social Democrats (SNSD), 18, 34, 70, 78, 146
al-Qaddafi, Muammar, 103, 128
American Civil War, 94
Andrić, Ivo, 85–86, 89
Ashdown, Paddy, 13–15, 19, 80, 166–69, 187–89, 190
Ashton, Catherine, 80, 194
Austria, 115, 183, 229, 230
Avalanche Dynamics and Complex Systems, 171–72

Bahrain, 140
Banja Luka, 26, 30, 33–34, 36, 47, 48, 54, 59, 62, 72, 100
Belgrade, 17, 28, 30, 33, 36, 42, 55, 66, 85, 114, 124, 143, 217, 220, 225
   Control of Yugoslav National Army (JNA), 130, 226
   Kosovo Status, 31–32, 115–19, 203

Belkić, Beriz, 70
Ben Ali, Zine al-Abidine, 131, 132, 140
Benghazi, 103, 106
Berkić, Boško, 37–38
Berlusconi, Silvio, 106
Bildt, Carl, 14
Blair, Tony, 101
Boehner, John, 105
Bolivia, 136
Brčko, 220
Brotherhood and Unity Policy, 10, 116
Brussels, 56, 58, 67, 68, 70, 74, 101, 192, 222
Bulatović, Momir, 55
Bulgaria, 123, 125
Bush, George W., 41, 67, 102

Canada, 2, 23, 100, 103, 128, 204
Chechnya, 128
China, 128, 134, 174
Chirac, Jacques, 101
Churchill, Winston, 94, 95, 106, 107
Clark, Wesley, 100–01
Clausewitz, Carl Von, 2, 90, 91, 92, 93, 94, 107, 108, 130, 210
Clinton, Bill, 12, 40, 98, 101, 180
Clinton, Hillary, 105
Coercive Diplomacy, 107
Cominform, 123–24
Conflict
   Asymmetric Conflict, nature and dynamics, 173–77
   Between Ethnic Groups, nature and dynamics, 112–15
   Centrality of, 148–49, 202–04
   Complexity and Uncertainty, 200–02

Conflict (*cont.*)
  Coordination of Force and Diplomacy, and, 210–11
  Culture Wars, and, 89, 111–12, 115, 120, 198
  Dayton Agreement Lessons for Diplomacy, 212–19
  Disruption of Conflict Systems, 130–33
  Evolution through Intervention in Bosnia, 150–70
  Fluctuation of Resistance in Conflict Systems, Bosnian illustration, 182–94
  Fluidity, 108–09, 119–21, 204
  Focusing on Critical Points, 208–10
  Future Evolution in Bosnia and Herzegovina, 219–23
  Interstate Industrial War, and, 109
  Management War, and, 109–10
  Nonviolent War
    Dynamics, 110–12
    Former Yugoslavia, illustration of, 112–19
  Power, and, 111–12, 120, 142, 157, 198
  Rational Frameworks, inadequacy of, 113–14
  Steering vs. Solving, 204–07
  Strategic Implications of Conflict Resilience in Bosnia and Herzegovina, 195–96
  Tactical Interest in Pushing Conflict into Non Violent Space, 144–45
Constitutional Court of Bosnia and Herzegovina, 46, 48, 154, 163–65, 183–86, 218
Constitutional Reform, 16, 66, 69, 146
Copenhagen Criteria, 220, 222
Council of Europe, 186, 190
Council of Ministers
  Adoption of Police Reform Action Plan, 74
  Amendments to Decision Making Rules, 21, 23, 25, 30, 33, 46, 47, 56, 57, 62, 63, 64, 73, 75, 77
  Blockage, 24, 42, 59, 161
  Budget Approval Authority, 152
  Initial Chair Nomination, 162
  Meeting with Peace Implementation Council, 39
  Nikola Špirić Resignation from, 43, 58, 88
  Outvoting, fear of, 49, 62
  Vetoes, 23

Croat Community of Herzeg-Bosnia, 12
Croatia, 10, 11, 12, 33, 80, 114, 129, 130, 151, 158, 159, 160, 166, 209, 219
Croatian Democratic Union (HDZ), 11, 70, 71, 72, 78, 146, 158, 159, 160
Croatian Democratic Union 1990 (HDZ 1990), 16, 78
Culture Wars, 89, 111–12, 115, 120, 198
Czechoslovakia, 125, 136, 146

Darfur, 128
Dayton Peace Agreement
  Blockage of Institutions, and, 21, 24, 71, 162
  Carl Bildt, and, 14
  Compatibility of Measures of High Representative with, 30, 35, 52, 71, 72
  Complexity, 152
  Constitutional Reform, 17
  Existence of Republika Srpska, and, 79
    Foundation Narrative, 163–64
  Holbrooke, Richard, and, 66
  Izetbegović, Alija, and, 50, 151
  Karadžić, Radovan, 109
  Mandate of the High Representative, 2, 13, 21, 46, 145
  Nationalist Platforms, incompatibility with, 115
  NATO Intervention, and, 129
  Nonviolent War, and, 150, 157
  Obligations to Cooperate with ICTY, 166–69
  Peace Implementation Council, 45, 88
  Power Sharing, 29
  Reversal of Gains in Armed Conflict, 45, 155, 165
  Right to Return, 16, 155–57
  Russian and American Cooperation, 40
  Serbia, compliance with, 36
  Shifting Support, 148, 182
  Silajdžić, Haris, and, 16
  State Building Policy, 13
  Strenghts and Weaknesses of, 212–19
  Transfer of Competencies, 212
  Wright-Patterson Air Force Base Negotiations, 12
    Participation of Croatia and Yugoslavia, 151, 162
    Resistance, 151–54

Index

de Gaulle, Charles, 141
Đilas, Milovan, 28–29
Diplomatic Counterinsurgency
  Application in Bosnia and Herzegovina, 150–70
  Concept, 3, 147, 199
  Liberal Democratic Conundrum, 183
  Limits, 216
  Similarities with Military Counterinsurgency Dynamics, 173–78
Divjak, Jovan, 225–31
Dobrovoljačka Case, 229–31
Dodik, Milorad
  Belgrade Support, 195
  Court of Bosnia and Herzegovina, and, 206
  Divjak, Jovan, 230–31
  EU Integration Process, 221
  Holbrooke, Richard, 66
  ICTY Cooperation, 19–20
  Measures of the High Representative
    Belgrade Support, 36
    Challenge to the Authority of the High Representative, 45–47, 52, 60–61, 88
    Escalation Advantage, 53
    Initial Reaction, 26–27
    International Incapacity to Enforce, 68, 77
    Mount Jahorina Meeting, 55–56
    Peace Implementation Council (PIC) Address, 38
    Popular Fears of Unitary State, 52
    Proposed Solution, 56, 64
    Public Demonstration Address, 36
    Removal from Office Discussions, 52–54, 74
    Republika Srpska National Assembly, 33
    Russian Support, 41
    Threat of Institutional Boycott, 36
    Unconstitutionality Claims, 39, 52
  OHR International Constituency, and, 192–94
  Personal Background, 17–18
  Police Reform, 9, 19, 20, 21, 63
  President of Republika Srpska, 78
  Radicalization, 79, 80
  Referendum, 78–80
  Secession of Republika Srpska, 18, 115
  Špirić, Nikola, and, 24, 39, 40

East Timor, 132, 178, 180, 212
Egypt, 132, 136, 139
ESI. *See* European Stability Initiative (ESI)
EUFOR. *See* European Union: European Union Force (EUFOR)
EULEX. *See* European Union: European Union Rule of Law Mission in Kosovo (EULEX)
EUPM. *See* European Union: European Union Police Mission (EUPM)
European Commission for Democracy through Law (Venice Commission), 186, 190
European Court for Human Rights, 127, 186, 187, 218
European Stability Initiative (ESI), 58, 189
European Union
  Bosnia Integration Process, 15, 19, 67, 189
  Declining Interest in OHR, 45, 70, 192–94, 196
  European Union Force (EUFOR), 53, 179, 197, 220, 228
  European Union Police Mission (EUPM), 179
  European Union Rule of Law Mission in Kosovo (EULEX), 203
  Future Strategic Role in Bosnia and Herzegovina, 219–23
  Incapacity to Effect Outcomes, 81
  Kosovo, 118–19, 219
  Loss of Credibility, 197
  Montenegro Referendum, 15
  Police Reform Conditions, 66
  Rehn, Olli, 76
  Republika Srpska Referendum, 80
  Syria, 129
  Territorial Integrity of Bosnia and Herzegovina, 199
  Visa Bans, 167

Federation of Bosnia and Herzegovina, Entity, 13, 78, 152, 153, 155, 156, 159, 160, 161, 163
Feith, Pieter, 203
Filipović, Ilija, 71
France, 36, 45, 67, 87, 92–93, 100, 101, 106, 127, 128, 134, 141, 192, 226

Galula, David, 133
Ganić, Ejup, 230
Georgia, 136, 193

Germany, 36, 40, 45, 67, 85, 87, 106, 109, 127, 128, 141, 183, 192, 193, 228
Greece, 67, 100, 123

Harper, Stephen, 103, 128
HDZ. *See* Croatian Democratic Union (HDZ)
HDZ 1990. *See* Croatian Democratic Union 1990 (HDZ 1990)
Hercegovačka Banka, 159–61
High Representative, 7, 8
   Ashdown, Paddy, 13–14, 166–69, 187–89
   Bildt, Carl, 14
   Challenge to the Authority of the High Representative
      Administrative Resistance, 187–89
      Bosnian Croat Resistance, 158–62
      Bosnian Serb Resistance, 162–70
      Dodik, Milorad, 26–27, 45–47, 60–61
      Impact on EU Credibility, 69–70
      International Divisions, 67
      Legal Challenges, 183–87, 218
      New Dynamic, 45
      Political and Public Challenges, 189–91
      Protection of Lajčák Authority, 46–47
      Republika Srpska Confrontation Perspective, 88–89
      Republika Srpska National Assembly, 39
      Republika Srpska Realization of International Incapacity to Enforce, 77
      Republika Srpska Referendum, 78–80
      Russia, 41–42
      Self-Reinforcing Resistance, 192–94
      Solution to the Crisis, 73–76
   European Raj Analogy, 58, 189
   Growing Popular Discontent with, 45–46
   Inzko, Valentin, 77, 193
   Lajčák, Miroslav
      Appointment Context, 15–20
      Resignation, 77
   Mandate and Powers, 13, 21, 57
   Peace Implementation Council (PIC)
      Bonn Meeting Consent to More Robust Role, 156
      Political Guidance, 36
      Support Dilemma, 44–45
      Support of High Representative 2007 Measures, 38
   Petritsch, Wolfgang, 14, 159–62, 164
   Power Erosion, 14–16
   Powers Contingent Upon Cooperation, 145
   Reasons and Causes of 2007 Defeat, 194–97
   Rejection of Republika Srpska Proposed Solution, 56–57
   Right to Return Implementation, 155–57
   Schwarz-Schilling, Christian, 15, 186
   Špirić, Nikola
      Effect of Resignation, 44
      Resignation, 43
      UN Security Council Attendance, 59–60
   Westendorp, Carlos, 14
Hitler, Adolf, 94, 95, 173
Holbrooke, Richard, 12, 50, 66, 67, 99, 217
Homs, 97
Horowitz, Donald, 113
Hungary, 64, 125, 136
Hunter, James Davison, 111
Hussein, Saddam, 127

ICJ. *See* International Court of Justice (ICJ)
ICO. *See* International Civilian Office (ICO)
ICTY. *See* International Criminal Tribunal for the Former Yugoslavia (ICTY)
IFOR. *See* North Atlantic Treaty Organization (NATO): Bosnia Implementation Force (IFOR)
International Civilian Office (ICO), 1, 77, 115, 203
International Court of Justice (ICJ), 118–19
International Criminal Tribunal for the Former Yugoslavia (ICTY), 12, 17, 20, 163, 166, 167, 168, 185, 187, 231
International Security Assistance Force (ISAF), 135
Interstate Industrial War, 91–95, 96, 97, 107, 109, 210
Inzko, Valentin, 77, 193
IPTF. *See* United Nations: International Police Task Force (IPTF)
Iran, 129, 136
Iraq, 16, 41, 58, 102, 108, 120, 126, 127, 132, 133, 134, 135, 175, 177
Islamic Declaration, 49–50
Ismić, Admira, 37–38
Italy, 36, 45, 67, 229
Ivanić, Mladen, 71, 169

Index

Izetbegović, Alija, 11, 49, 50, 51, 151, 163, 227, 229, 230
Jelavić, Ante, 159, 162
JNA. *See* Yugoslav National Army (JNA)
Juppé, Alain, 129, 194

Kalinić, Dragan, 167, 185–87
Karadžić, Radovan, 11, 17, 36, 55, 109, 163, 166, 168
KFOR. *See* North Atlantic Treaty Organization (NATO): Kosovo Force (KFOR)
Kilcullen, David, 134
KLA. *See* Kosovo Liberation Army (KLA)
Komšić, Željko, 33, 59, 230
Kosovo
  1981 Demonstrations, 116
  Advisory Opinion of the International Court of Justice (ICJ), 118–19
  Ahtisaari Proposal, 31–32, 118
  Blair, Tony, 101
  Challenge to Foreign Power through Institutions, 143–44
  Clark, Wesley, 101
  Declaration of Independence, 53, 118, 181
  Ethnic Cleansing, 116
  Holbrooke, Richard, 66
  Independent International Commission on Kosovo, 127
  International Civilian Office (ICO), Attack, 1–2, 203
  Kosovo Liberation Army (KLA), 31, 100, 116, 209
  Linkage with Crisis in Bosnia and Herzegovina, 30–33, 36
  Loss of Autonomy, 10, 209
  March 2004 Violence, 117, 207
  Milošević Regime, Withdrawal from, 116
  NATO Intervention, 31, 40, 91, 100–01, 115, 127, 129
  Nonviolent War, 111, 115–19
  OSCE Mission in Kosovo (OMIK), 179
  Petritsch, Wolfgang, 14
  Rambouillet Peace Conference, 116
  United Nations Interim Administration Mission in Kosovo (UNMIK), 117, 118, 129, 143–44, 179, 181, 203, 206

Kosovo Liberation Army (KLA), 31, 100, 116, 209
Koštunica, Vojislav, 30–33
Krajišnik, Momčilo, 162
Kuwait, 126–27
Kuzmanović, Rajko, 34–35

Lagumdžija, Zlatko, 32, 58, 78
Lajčák, Miroslav
  2007 Measures
  Explanatory Note, 29–30
  Fears of Centralization, 209
  Hungarian Embassy Proposal, 63–64
  Inception and Rationale, 20–25, 169
  Legal Expert Discussions, 33–35, 47–51, 56–57, 61–62
  Linkage with Kosovo, 30–33
  Milorad Dodik Initial Reaction, 26–27
  OHR Internal Divisions, 54–55, 65, 67–68
  Parliamentary Assembly Discussions, 68, 70–72
  Peace Implementation Council (PIC) Discussions, 38, 39–42
  Peace Implementation Council (PIC) Support Dilemma, 44–45
  Removal of Milorad Dodik Discussions, 52–54
  Republika Srpska Demonstrations, 36
  Russian Dissent, 40–42
  Appointment Context, 15–20
  Dodik, Milorad
  Challenge to the Authority of the High Representative, 45–47, 52, 60–61, 88–89
  ICTY Cooperation, 19–20
  Initial Reaction to 2007 Measures, 26–27
  Mount Jahorina Meeting, 55–56
  Peace Implementation Council (PIC) Address, 38
  Rejection of Police Reform, 9, 20
  Removal of Office Discussions, 52–54
  Growing Popular Discontent with High Representative Authorities, 45–46
  Involvement in Bosnia through EU External Action Service, 77–80
  Mistakes, 87
  Montenegro Independence, 15
  Police Reform, 18–20, 66
  Resignation, 77

Lajčák, Miroslav (*cont.*)
  Solution to the Crisis, 8, 68–70, 73–76
Špirić, Nikola
  Bratislava Official Visit, 65–66
  Parliamentary Assembly Address, 58
  Peace Implementation Council (PIC) Address, 39–40
  UN Security Council Attendance, 59–60
Laktaši, 17, 18
Lawfare, 176
League of Arab States, 103, 132
Libya, 91, 96, 97, 103–06, 126, 128, 129
Lipovac, Zoran, 34, 62
Lozančić, Niko, 70
Lukić, Radomir, 187–89

Mack, Andrew, 173–74, 176
MacKenzie, Lewis, 229
Management War, 95–98, 106, 107, 109
Martens, Wilfried, 19, 168
Mc Chrystal, Stanley, 175, 200
Medvedev, Dmitry, 39, 180
Mesić, Stjepan, 160
Michnik, Adam, 139–40
Mikerević, Dragan, 169
Military Counterinsurgency, 134–36
Milošević, Slobodan, 10, 12, 30, 31, 32, 33, 55, 99, 100, 116, 119, 129, 136, 151, 162, 209, 226
Mitrović, Slavko, 34–35
Mitsotakis, Konstantin, 55
Mladić, Ratko, 12, 99, 113, 166
Montenegro, 15, 55, 63, 101, 165
Morin, Edgar, 200–01, 224
Mostar, 12, 78, 99, 159, 161
Mount Jahorina, 55–56
Mubarak, Hosni, 132, 139–40

Napoléon, 85, 91–94, 107, 134, 173, 210
NATO. *See* North Atlantic Treaty Organization (NATO)
Netherlands, 103
Nonviolent Insurgency, 122–49
  Concept and Definition, 146–47
  Dynamics, 137–41
  Historical Context, 136–37
  Peace Operations, and, 142–44
  Qualifications, 145–47
  Tactical Advantage, 144–45
Nonviolent War
  Concept, 2, 85–121, 198
  Dayton Agreement as Starting Point, 150
  Defeat of the OHR, 196
  Dynamics, 110–12
  Evolution of Warfare, and, 89–110
  External Connections, 217
  Former Yugoslavia, illustration of, 112–19
  Interverner's Accountability, and, 217
  Kosovo, 115–19
  Limits of Diplomatic Management of, 216
  Nonviolent Confrontation and War, discussion, 119–21
  Peace Spoilers or Actors, 147–49
  Right to Return in Bosnia, 155–57
  State Building in Bosnia, and, 157–65
North Atlantic Treaty Organization (NATO)
  Afghanistan Intervention, 102–03
  Bosnia Implementation Force (IFOR), 179
  Bosnia Intervention, 99–100, 119, 129, 151, 198
  Bosnia Stabilization Force (SFOR), 157, 160–61, 179
  Divjak, Jovan, 228–29
  Dodik, Milorad Resistance, 193
  Kosovo Force (KFOR), 205
  Kosovo Intervention, 31, 40, 100–01, 115–16, 119, 127, 129
  Libya Intervention, 103–06, 128
  Membership Accession Leverage, 195, 216, 220
  Refusal of Bosnia Membership to Partnership for Peace Program, 167
Nye, Joseph, 137

Obama, Barack, 102, 104–05, 128–29, 175
Office of the High Representative (OHR), 1, 4, 7
  Authorities and Powers as Insurance Policy, 219
  Banja Luka Office Legal Expert Discussions, 47–51
  Banja Luka Office Public Statement, 30
  Criticism of Method and Power, 52, 58, 60–61, 67, 88
  Declining Interest in OHR. *See* European Union: Declining Interest in OHR
  Declining Resources and Support, 179, 181

Index

Defeat of 2007
　Impact, 80
　Reasons and Causes, 194–97
Effect of Nikola Špirić Resignation, 44
European Union Special Representative, 70
Growing Popular Discontent with, 45–46, 189–91
Hercegovačka Banka Audit, 161
Internal Divisions, 54
Late Attempts to Recalibrate Power Arrangements, 216, 219
Losing Sight of Conflict, 204
Mandate and Powers, 13, 129
Milorad Bilbija and Dragan Kalinić Case, impact on, 184–86
Non Violent War, destabilizing impact on, 150
Power Erosion, 14–16, 81, 119
Protector of Fragile Central State Institutions, 169
Radomir Lukić Refusal to Step Down, impact on, 187–88
Rejection of Republika Srpska Proposed Solution, 56
Respect of Entity Constitutional Competencies, 79
Sarajevo Office Legal Expert Discussions, 61–62
Self-Reinforcing Resistance Against, 192–94
Serbian Democratic Party (SDS) Financial Reports, 166
State Building Reforms, 212
Tactical Advantage of Nonviolent Insurgency, illustration of, 145
OHR. *See* Office of the High Representative
Organization for Security and Cooperation in Europe (OSCE), 159, 179
OSCE. *See* Organization for Security and Cooperation in Europe (OSCE)
Owen, David, 55

Pale, 33
Pandur, Jozef, 63–64, 73
Parliamentary Assembly
　Amendments to Rules of Procedure, 21, 23, 25, 46, 68, 70
　Blockage, 62, 68, 161
　Budget Approval Authority, 153, 154
　Building, 36
　Nikola Špirić Address, 58
　Olli Rehn Address, 69
　Rejection of Constitutional Reform, 16
　State Building Reform Blockage, 164, 183
Party for Bosnia and Herzegovina (SBIH), 16, 70
Party for Democratic Action (SDA), 11, 32, 50, 71, 72
Party of Democratic Progress (PDP), 71
PDP. *See* Party of Democratic Progress (PDP)
Peace Implementation Council (PIC), 36, 38, 39–42, 44–45, 54, 56, 60, 64, 70, 74, 185
Pecelj, Milovan, 188
Petraeus, David, 134
Petritsch, Wolfgang, 14, 159, 160, 162, 164
PIC. *See* Peace Implementation Council (PIC)
Plavšić, Biljana, 17
Podgorica, 101
Poland, 125, 136, 139
Police Reform, 19, 20, 21, 58, 63, 65, 66, 69, 70, 74, 75, 76, 87, 168, 169, 195
Pristina, 1, 31, 32, 116, 118, 119, 203, 220
Putin, Vladimir, 36, 39, 66

Québec 1995 Referendum, 23

Rambouillet peace conference, 14, 31, 116
Reconstruction and Return Task Force (RRTF), 156
Rehn, Olli, 69, 74, 76
Republika Srpska, 2, 13, 16, 17, 18, 19, 20, 24, 26, 30, 32, 33, 34, 35, 38, 39, 42, 45, 46, 47, 52, 53, 54, 56, 60, 61, 62, 68, 69, 71, 72, 73, 74, 77, 78, 79, 80, 81, 87, 88, 115, 120, 152, 153, 155, 156, 163, 164, 165, 166, 167, 168, 169, 170, 182, 188, 192, 193, 195, 196, 197, 206, 210, 220, 221, 222, 223, 231
Responsibility to Protect, 127–28
Romeo and Juliet in Sarajevo, 37–38
Roosevelt, Franklin Delano, 95
RRTF. *See* Reconstruction and Return Task Force (RRTF)
Rugova, Ibrahim, 116, 209

Russia, 39, 40–42, 45, 53, 60, 66, 118, 128, 129, 180, 193–94, 196
Rwanda, 103, 127, 177

Sarajevo, 7, 18, 22, 27, 35, 36, 37, 39, 41, 47, 49, 51, 54, 55, 57, 59, 60, 61, 63, 70, 74, 76, 99, 100, 155, 162, 163, 217, 225, 226, 227, 228, 229, 230
Saudi Arabia, 129
SBIH. *See* Party for Bosnia and Herzegovina (SBIH)
Schwarz-Schilling, Christian, 14, 19, 186
SDA. *See* Party for Democratic Action (SDA)
SDP. *See* Social Democratic Party (SDP)
SDS. *See* Serbian Democratic Party (SDS)
Selman, Džerard, 56, 59, 62, 77
Serbia, 10, 31, 40, 55, 116, 151, 219, 230
   Republic of Serbia, state, 30, 31, 32, 36, 58, 66, 115, 117, 118, 119, 195, 203, 229, 230, 231
   Republic of the Federal Republic of Yugoslavia, 12, 31, 41, 101
   Republic of the Socialist Federal Republic of Yugoslavia, 10, 116, 209
Serbia and Montenegro, 15, 63, 114, 165, 166
Serbian Democratic Party (SDS), 11, 12, 17, 18, 109, 163, 166, 167, 168, 187
SFOR. *See* North Atlantic Treaty Organization (NATO): Bosnia Stabilization Force (SFOR)
Sharp, Gene, 137–38
Silajdžić, Haris, 16, 17, 18, 19, 115
Slovakia, 15, 65, 77
Slovenia, 10, 114, 209, 226
Smith, Rupert, 91, 210
SNSD. *See* Alliance of Independent Social Democrats (SNSD)
Social Democratic Party (SDP), 32, 58, 78
Solana, Javier, 15, 65, 74, 76, 101
Somalia, 96, 98, 177
South Africa, 136
Soviet Union, 40, 113, 123–25, 136, 191
Spain, 14, 100, 134, 173
Špirić, Nikola
   Bratislava Official Visit, 65–66
   Dodik, Milorad, 24, 39

   Effect of Resignation on OHR, 44
   Parliamentary Assembly Address, 58
   Peace Implementation Council (PIC) Address, 39–40
   Resignation from the Council of Ministers, 43, 58, 88
   UN Security Council Attendance, 59–60
   Willingness to Reconsider Resignation, 45, 56–57
Srebrenica, 12, 99, 103, 113
Stalin, Joseph, 28, 95, 123–25, 129
Stedman, John, 147–49
Sudan, 96, 128
Sweden, 67, 141
Syria, 96, 128–32, 139–40, 149, 204

Tihić, Sulejman, 32, 71, 72
Tito, Josip Broz, 10, 11, 28, 29, 50, 115, 123, 124, 173, 225, 226
Truman, Harry S., 124
Tuđman, Franjo, 12, 151, 158, 159, 160
Tunisia, 131, 136, 140
Turkey, 106, 132

Ukraine, 136
UNHCR. *See* United Nations: United Nations High Commissioner for Refugees (UNHCR)
United Kingdom, 13, 36, 60, 67, 74, 87, 101, 103, 115, 128, 195
United Nations
   Ashdown, Paddy, 14
   East Timor, 180
   General Assembly
      Kosovo
         EU Dialogue, 119
         International Court of Justice (ICJ) Advisory Opinion, 118
      Responsibility to Protect, 128
   International Police Task Force (IPTF), 157, 179
   Kosovo, 118, 143
   Secretary-General
      Kosovo, 143–44
      Reports of the High Representative, 59
   Security Council
      Bosnia State Building, 158
      Condemnation of Croat National Congress Actions, 160
      East Timor, 180

Index

ICTY Cooperation, 166
Kosovo Status, 31, 116–17
Linkage of Civilian Population Protection with Peace and Security, 126
Mandate of Bosnia International Military Presence, 53
Powers of the High Representative, 191
Republika Srpska, 192–94
Špirić, Nikola Attendance, 59–60, 66
Use of Force Authorization, 98, 99, 102, 103, 126, 128, 129, 199
Srebrenica, 12, 99
Syria, 128
United Nations High Commissioner for Refugees (UNHCR), 27, 131, 157
United Nations Integrated Mission in Timor-Leste (UNMIT), 180
United Nations Interim Administration Mission in Kosovo (UNMIK), 117, 118, 129, 143–44, 179, 181, 203, 206
United Nations Mission of Support in East Timor (UNMISET), 180
United Nations Protection Force (UNPROFOR), 91, 99, 151
United Nations Transitional Administration Mission in East Timor (UNTAET), 180
Westendorp, Carlos, 14
United States, 12, 16, 36, 60, 66, 67, 74, 87, 96, 97, 98, 102, 103, 104, 105, 110, 111, 112, 124, 125, 153, 167, 169, 173, 174, 176, 195, 199
UNMIK. *See* United Nations: United Nations Interim Administration Mission in Kosovo (UNMIK)
UNMISET. *See* United Nations: United Nations Mission of Support in East Timor (UNMISET)
UNMIT. *See* United Nations: United Nations Integrated Mission in Timor-Leste (UNMIT)
UNPROFOR. *See* United Nations: United Nations Protection Force (UNPROFOR)
UNTAET. *See* United Nations: United Nations Transitional Administration Mission in East Timor (UNTAET)

Vance, Cyrus, 55
Vance Owen Peace Plan, 55, 130
Venice Commission. *See* European Commission for Democracy through Law (Venice Commission)
Vietnam, 104, 125, 134, 172–74, 175–77
Violent Insurgency, 133–36
Vojvodina, 10

Westendorp, Carlos, 14
Westerwelle, Guido, 194
World Bank, 108, 120–21

Yugoslav National Army (JNA), 11, 130, 226, 229, 230
Yugoslavia
    Federal Republic of Yugoslavia, 10, 11, 14, 31, 50, 116, 151
    Kingdom of Yugoslavia, 85, 134, 173
    Socialist Federal Republic of Yugoslavia, 7, 9, 10, 11, 12, 17, 18, 22, 27, 28, 29, 37, 50, 89, 96, 98, 112, 113, 123, 124, 129, 136, 191, 209, 226

Zagreb, 161, 217
Zedong, Mao, 51, 134, 174
Živković, Milorad, 70

Lightning Source UK Ltd.
Milton Keynes UK
UKOW06f0733300415

250629UK00007B/201/P